Marble Hall, New Orleans Customs House, detail. (*Koch*.)

Greek Revival Architecture in America: BEING AN ACCOUNT OF IMPORTANT TRENDS IN AMERICAN ARCHITECTURE AND AMERICAN LIFE *prior to* THE WAR BETWEEN THE STATES

BY

TALBOT HAMLIN

TOGETHER WITH
A LIST OF ARTICLES ON ARCHITECTURE IN SOME
AMERICAN PERIODICALS PRIOR TO 1850 BY
SARAH HULL JENKINS SIMPSON HAMLIN (1887–1930)
AND
AN INTRODUCTION BY
DEAN LEOPOLD ARNAUD
OF THE SCHOOL OF ARCHITECTURE
COLUMBIA UNIVERSITY

DOVER PUBLICATIONS, INC.
NEW YORK

Published in Canada by General Publishing Company, Ltd., 30 Lesmill Road, Don Mills, Toronto, Ontario.
Published in the United Kingdom by Constable and Company, Ltd., 10 Orange Street, London WC 2.

This Dover edition, first published in 1964, is an unabridged and unaltered republication of the work first published by the Oxford University Press in 1944. This edition is published by special arrangement with the Oxford University Press.

The publisher wishes to express his appreciation of the kind cooperation of the Director and staff of the Avery Library of Columbia University, who made available for reproduction purposes many of the original photographs of the illustrations in this book.

International Standard Book Number: 0-486-21148-7

Manufactured in the United States of America.
Dover Publications, Inc.
180 Varick Street
New York, N. Y. 10014

PREFACE

THIS book is but an introduction to a great subject — the architecture of the entire country in its eager and searching adolescence. For, nation-wide as it was, and created in a day when communication was slower and more difficult than it is in our time, this architecture was necessarily various, changing from region to region, from state to state, as the dictates of climate and material suggested and as the local culture directed.

Thus its roots thrust deeply into local history, and the research which shall make clear its true growth and accomplishment must be local research. It must be based on a study of buildings not as individual spots but as part of their communities and their environment, and on a patient delving into local archives and a persistent search through attics and old trunks to discover pertinent documents; above all, there should be a continuing effort to find, and place in museums or libraries or local historical societies, the original drawings which the early architects prepared.

Nowhere has research of this type been complete; over vast areas of this country it has scarcely begun. If this book can help to stimulate further local study and the production of many local monographs — if, in addition, it may give to some a new vision of the fervent idealisms, social as well as aesthetic, which made an America that was broader than its wide acres and richer than the sum of all its resources — then it will have more than fulfilled its task.

To express my gratitude to all those who have helped in the creation of the book — to the scholars whose works I have so shamelessly used, to those in the Oxford University Press who have aided in giving the volume its physical form, to the myriad people who have assisted me through years in this fascinating study — would be quite impossible, but it is pleasant to set down some of these debts.

First of all, I wish to state my indebtedness to my wife for her sensitive, discriminating, and meticulous assistance in the preparation of the manuscript, for making the index, and for her continuing help and co-operation in the entire project. I wish also to express my gratitude to my Columbia colleagues — especially to Dean Leopold Arnaud, of the School of Architecture, not only for his Introduction but also for his constant encouragement, and to Professor William Bell Dinsmoor, of the Department of Fine Arts and Archaeology, for his careful reading of the manuscript and for advice concerning its publication. I also owe much to the ever willing staff of the Avery Library and to various other departments of the Columbia University Library for skillful assistance in unraveling all sorts of tangled skeins.

To many scholars in the field of the history of American art and architecture I stand deeply indebted. Especially I wish to express my gratitude to Fiske Kimball, whose brilliant pioneering in American architectural history first aroused my interest in it, and on whose works I have leaned heavily. Other scholars in this field to whom I owe much include: Alfred Andrews, for valuable information with regard to Kentucky architecture, and for permission to reproduce illustrations from his master's essay; William Sumner Appleton, for his constant help in matters pertaining to New England, and to Boston in particular, and for his invaluable assistance in opening to me the riches of the Society for the Preservation of New England Antiquities, of which he is the brilliant director; Professor Turpin Bannister, for his co-operation in sharing with me so much of his unique knowledge of New York State architecture, and for permission to reproduce several of his photographs; Lewis Barrington, for permission to reproduce photographs from the *Historic Restorations of the Daughters of the American Revolution;* Dean Wells Bennett, for many valuable suggestions with regard to the architecture of Michigan; Harold S. Brooks, for his guidance around Marshall, Michigan, and for much valuable in-

formation about Marshall history and its buildings; John Albury
Bryan, for much information concerning early St. Louis, and for
permission to reproduce photographs in his collection; Professor
Lee Burns, for assistance with regard to Illinois; John Coolidge,
for constant help in many ways, and for permission to use photographs from his *Mill and Mansion;* Everett Uberto Crosby, for
valuable information concerning Nantucket, and for the identification of many Nantucket houses; Nathaniel Cortlandt Curtis, for
much assistance in the field of New Orleans architecture, and for
permission to reproduce his measured drawings of the St. Louis
Hotel rotunda; Joseph Downs, Curator of the American Wing of
the Metropolitan Museum of Art, for assistance and encouragement of many kinds, and especially for permission to reproduce
illustrations from the Museum collection; President Dixon Ryan
Fox, for his kind help in obtaining reproductions of the Ramée
drawings at Union College; I. Thayer Frary, of the Cleveland
Museum, for invaluable information and assistance in connection
with Ohio architecture, and for permission to reproduce several of
his own brilliant architectural photographs; Mrs. Austin Gallagher, for much information concerning Robert Mills, and for permission to reproduce items from her collection of Millsiana, now
deposited in the Avery Library; Mrs. Agnes Addison Gilchrist, for
valuable aid in matters connected with William Strickland; Professor Henry-Russell Hitchcock, for reading and criticizing the manuscript of the New England chapter, for much assistance arising
out of his unique bibliographical knowledge, and for his help in obtaining Rhode Island illustrations; Dr. Leicester B. Holland, of
the Library of Congress, for constant help in connection with material in the Library of Congress, and for his assistance in obtaining reproductions of drawings and photographs in the Historic
American Buildings Survey; Milton Horn, for calling my attention to many Michigan buildings of the greatest interest; John
Mead Howells, for permission to reproduce photographs from his
unique collection of records of destroyed and altered buildings,
now deposited in the Metropolitan Museum of Art; Richard Koch,

for giving me much valuable information with regard to Louisiana architecture, and for permission to reproduce several of his superb architectural photographs, some of which were taken especially for this work; Professor Emil Lorch, for valuable information with regard to early Michigan buildings, and for permission to reproduce some of his own photographs; Howard Major, a pioneer student of the Greek Revival, for his co-operative attitude in allowing me to reproduce many illustrations from his collection; the Reverend Donald MacDonald Millar, for valuable information concerning Tennessee, and especially with regard to the Hermitage; Dean Rexford Newcomb, for much welcome encouragement, and for permission to use some of his Kentucky photographs; Roger Hale Newton, for many valuable suggestions as to source material and the location and history of important monuments; Lieutenant Charles E. Peterson, for valuable information with regard to the architecture of early Missouri; Italo William Ricciuti, for valuable suggestions in connection with New Orleans architecture, and for permission to reproduce illustrations from his important *New Orleans and Its Environs;* Edward Root, for information concerning Philip Hooker, and for permission to reproduce a photograph of Hyde Hall; Albert Simons, for invaluable help with regard to the buildings and architects of Charleston, for reading and criticizing the manuscript of Chapter 8, and for permission to quote a long letter and to reproduce illustrations from *Charleston, South Carolina,* of which he is co-author with Samuel Lapham; Fletcher Steele, for calling my attention to the Campbell-Whittlesey house in Rochester; Charles M. Stotz, for valuable assistance in connection with Pennsylvania architecture, and for permission to reproduce illustrations from *The Early Architecture of Western Pennsylvania;* Professor Walter H. Taylor, for calling my attention to important buildings in up-state New York, and for permission to reproduce his photographs of them; Professor Everard M. Upjohn and Hobart Upjohn, for permission to examine the papers of Richard Upjohn, and for permission to reproduce a photograph of the Farrar house in Bangor; and A. J. Wall, of the New York

Historical Society, for many valuable suggestions in the New York City field, and for priceless aid in the use of the New York Historical Society collections.

Many co-operative persons have helped me greatly by opening to me their family records. Thus I am indebted to Mrs. Willis Field for much material about her uncle Gideon Shryock; to J. W. Alsop I owe helpful information with regard to the Alsop house in Middletown; to Washington Perine I am most grateful for furnishing me with photographs of the plans made by R. C. Long, Jr., for the Perine family mansion, Homeland; and I am especially grateful to Ferdinand C. Latrobe for his constant helpfulness, and for his gracious permission to me to study and to quote from his digests of the entire corpus of the letters of B. H. Latrobe in his possession.

This book could not have been written without the co-operation and assistance of many museums, historical societies, and similar organizations and their always willing and helpful staffs. I wish especially to express my gratitude to the American Antiquarian Society, Worcester; the California Historical Society, San Francisco; the Dartmouth College Library; the Detroit Public Library; the Essex Institute, Salem; the Federal Hall Museum, New York; the Garden Study Club of Nashville; the Historical Society of Pennsylvania, Philadelphia; the Library of Congress; the Maryland Historical Society, Baltimore; the Metropolitan Museum of Art (especially its American Wing and its photograph department); the Missouri Historical Society, St. Louis; the Museum of the City of New York; the Nantucket Athenaeum; the New Bedford Historical Society; the New York Historical Society; the Providence Athenaeum; the Rhode Island School of Design; the Society for the Preservation of New England Antiquities; Union College; and the Worcester Art Museum.

For the adequate illustration of a subject as broad in scope as this, I have naturally been dependent on the help and the kindness of many individuals and institutions. To all of these I wish to express my sense of gratitude; without their willing and eager assist-

ance I should have been hard put to it. Those who have either furnished illustrations or given me information through which I could
obtain them, in addition to the persons and organizations already
mentioned, include: the American Institute of Architects; the Architects' Emergency Committee, New York; the Architectural
Book Publishing Company; the Avery Library, Columbia University; Roberta Seawell Brandau; the Buhl Foundation; the Car-
negie Library of Pittsburgh; the Columbia University Press; the
Daughters of the American Revolution; Mrs. John V. Donelson;
William Helburn, Inc.; Rudolf Hertzberg; the Historic American
Buildings Survey; Leslie Merrill, Jr.; the Museum of Fine Arts,
Boston; the National Geographic Magazine; Gardner Osborn;
the Pennsylvania Academy of Fine Arts; Charles H. Sawyer; the
State University of Iowa; the Trustees of the State War Memorial,
Little Rock; Tulane University; the Ware Library, Columbia
University; Washington and Lee University; and Mrs. Katherine
A. Wells.

Several chapters of this book have appeared in somewhat dif-
ferent forms in various places. Chapter 2, ' The Birth of American
Architecture,' was published in abbreviated form in *Parnassus*.
Chapter 4, ' The Greek Revival in Philadelphia,' appeared in the
The Pennsylvania Magazine of History and Biography. Part of
Chapter 12, ' Why the Greek Revival Succeeded and Why It
Failed,' was given as a paper in a symposium on the Greek Revival
at the Baltimore Museum of Art, and was published subsequently
as part of *The Greek Tradition*, a collection of the symposium
papers, and later in the *Columbia University Quarterly*. Some
material from several chapters was incorporated in " The Greek
Revival in America and Some of Its Critics," in *The Art Bulletin*.
All of this material has been revised, and some of it rewritten with
extensive additions, since its first publication. I am grateful to the
earlier publishers for permission to use the material here.

My thanks are also due to Professor Mary Ellen Chase and
The Macmillan Company for permission to quote the excerpt from
Silas Crockett which occurs on page 162.

A final word with regard to certain peculiarities of form. The term " Pain(e) influence " signifies influences both from William Pain, a prolific English producer of architectural handbooks in the last decades of the eighteenth century, and from James Paine, a famous English architect of the same period, whose designs, more sophisticated and polished than William Pain's, are nevertheless in the same general style. In the illustration captions, credits are given in the shortest possible terms, for identification only ; complete credits will be found in the list of illustrations.

Avery Library,   TALBOT HAMLIN
Columbia University

6 September 1943

FOREWORD

THE period called 'Greek Revival,' extending roughly from 1820 to 1860, might more fittingly be called ' Middle American,' because at this time the young nation had gained its feet and was striding forward with conscious vigor and confidence. The eclecticism implied by the term ' Greek Revival ' is not the true characteristic of the period. Prodigiously active and intensely dramatic, the history of these years has been given relatively little attention. Especially in the field of architecture, the originality, ingenuity, and refinement of the predominating style has not received the study and appreciation that it merits.

These decades from the twenties to the sixties were vital in every phase of development. Politically, the system of government was crystallizing, and at the same time gaining flexibility to administer to the needs of an increasingly complex society. Economically the expansion was fabulous, for the seemingly limitless natural resources were being developed (and also exploited) ; and the industrial power which has since carried us to national greatness was being established. The population, increasing rapidly, pressed relentlessly to the west, converting successive frontiers into settled territories. Wagons, railroads, steamboats, and clipper ships traversed the land and the seas ; and the activity in production was matched by the activity in transportation.

There was withal a conscious separation from Europe and a fierce will to be American. There was a spirit of confidence, which, if over-youthful, was none the less inspiring. The people had embarked upon a great experiment in government, and had made it work. They had conquered a continent and were beginning to profit from the fruits of their labors. They were witnessing the miracles of science changing the world before their eyes, and they were sure that the change was progress. They looked upon government not as a mere agent for policing and defense, but as an institution for the administration of human welfare; Science and Government should solve the problems of the world. It was a phase of adolescent optimism preceding the confusion, conflict, and disillusion through which the nation passed before reaching maturity.

The widespread enterprise brought a degree of leisure and material well-being which fostered the desire for intellectual advantages, resulting in a remarkable development in education and in the arts. Emerson was expressing the spirit of the people in such words as these:

Our day of dependence, our long apprenticeship to the learning of other lands, draws .to a close. The millions that around us are rushing into life cannot always be fed on the sere remains of foreign harvests. Events and actions arise, that must be sung. . . There are creative manners, there are creative actions and creative words . . . indicative of no custom or authority, but springing spontaneous from the mind's own sense of good and fair.

Thoreau, Webster, Cooper, Irving, Hawthorne, and many others were finding an avid public for their prolific writings. A truly American school of painting developed, fathered by Durand and Cole. These ' Hudson River ' artists and their followers, while not great, showed a perception, technical ability, and capacity to express an original and native spirit which was without precedent in American art.

The existence of this literary and artistic productivity implies a society sufficiently cultivated to foster these works — a society whose way of life required an adequate architectural expression. The problems which confronted the architects were new in many respects, and peculiar to the character and taste prevailing in the young republic. In meeting these demands, the designers produced ingenious plans, gracious conceptions of space treatment, and façades that showed true refinement of proportion and finish.

The fact that decorative detail was based upon classic precedent, and especially upon Greek precedent, was due not merely to an increasing interest in archaeology, but more especially to the enthusiasm which the whole Western World, and particularly the new republic, showed for the struggles of Greece during her wars of independence. The names given to the then new towns, such as Athens, Troy, Ithaca, Ypsilanti, are likewise an American tribute to Greek heroism. But the word 'Revival' is an unfortunate misnomer, for this style was only a revival in that its decorative vocabulary was based upon classic Greek detail. In all other respects it was typically of America. Never before or since has there been less influence from Europe.

This manner called 'Greek Revival' penetrated almost all sections of the country. It moved westward with the advancing frontier and is seen in surprising refinement and beauty in localities which were wilderness but a few years before. The designers of this period seemed to possess an innate talent for adapting the new architectural fashion to the requirements of the region, preserving traditional usages, accepting local building materials, and conforming to climatic exigencies. There is consequently a homogeneous expression with numerous regional variations.

The foresight of these designers also deserves commendation. Today, when we are absorbed in the involved problems of urban redevelopment and town planning, we are apt to forget that our predecessors had sufficient imagination, when laying out town plans, to anticipate growth and to survey and organize not only the center of the town, but also the surrounding area, long before there were sufficient inhabitants to form more than a small village.

In this day of havoc and world conflict, we look to the future with combined confidence, expectancy, and anxiety. Peace will come, and with it a new era and a new architecture. But no matter how great the changes, the new architecture will have its roots in the past and will bear fruit accordingly. It is expedient, then, to examine the past, and in so doing we can take heart, realizing that we are heirs to a fine and strong tradition.

This book will be a welcome record not only for the benefit of Americans, but also for our friends and foes who are looking at us with new attention. The evidence will confound those who have called our culture eclectic and materialistic. The forms of 'Greek Revival' are no longer applicable, but the capacity to solve problems with originality, ingenuity, and taste will endure and inspire the architecture of the post-war world. A book on the peculiarly American style is greatly needed, for no thorough study exists, embracing the United States as a whole, analyzing the general characteristics of the style and the local variations as well.

The writing of a book of this nature required not only a scholarly knowledge of the subject, but also a profound and sympathetic understanding of the culture and thought of the people, their background, their traditions, their aspirations and achievements. The author combines these requirements in the fullest degree. Grandson of a scholarly educator, and son of an eminent architectural historian and teacher, Talbot Hamlin has, since birth, been steeped in the history and tradition of America. As an architect he has had experience in the practical problems of planning and structure; as a lecturer on the theory of architecture he has investigated the difficulties inherent in the art of design; and as a historian he is the author of several books and numerous articles. This volume is the fruit of many years of research and of personal observation. It is a valuable contribution to the American record, and is also a brilliant addition to the many achievements of an esteemed colleague and valued friend.

LEOPOLD ARNAUD

Columbia University
22 March 1943

TABLE OF CONTENTS

ILLUSTRATIONS

TEXT FIGURES

GREEK REVIVAL ARCHITECTURE

IN AMERICA

CHAPTER 1

THE BACKGROUND OF THE CLASSIC REVIVAL: 'LATE COLONIAL' ARCHITECTURE

I. The New Classicism

THE American Revolution brought a cultural as well as a political liberation. Hesitant at first, American leaders turned more and more away from British influence in the arts, though large conservative elements still for many years turned back to the past, and still in matters architectural considered England, if no longer the mother country, at least a benevolent and wise governess. But the cultural leaders of the country — men like Washington and Jefferson — held a different view. If England was now no longer the cultural inspiration, a more vital influence for them came to take its place — that great fecundating inspiration which for three hundred years and more had sent wave after wave of influences across the surface of Western life — the inspiration of the ancient classic world of Greece and Rome. This new cultural direction taken by American leaders — and especially by Thomas Jefferson — was the 'correct' turn; it was a turn in the direction which world sentiment and taste was pursuing, and sooner or later even the most conservative were almost perforce to follow as well. The whole country became at last architecturally free — and architecturally 'classic.' The colonial attitude was dead.

Two factors were present in this process. One was negative — hatred of England. One was positive — idealization of the classic world. Of the first, present knowledge gives a confused picture. The bitternesses aroused by the pre-Revolutionary exactions of the English Government were spasmodically felt, but only by scattered localities. There were radicals, like Jefferson, Patrick Henry, or the intransigent Adamses, whose hatred of English 'tyranny'

made them suspicious of everything English. There were con-
servatives, like Hamilton or Gouverneur Morris, whom the excesses
of the French Revolution and their impact on America through
the unhappy personality of the French minister Genêt drove back
into sympathy with England. There were the great mercantile and
shipping interests, particularly of Boston and Philadelphia, for
whom England and the English colonies were still the best — and
almost the only — customers. Artistic conservatism often necessarily persisted, owing to the fact that many of the skilled craftsmen of the country were either English-trained or but one generation removed from England, and to the fact that, in architecture
at least, all of them depended largely on English books.

Yet the irritation was there, and England, blundering within
twenty-five years into the War of 1812, did little to overcome it.
And a new urge to a national life, a national art, was growing
irresistibly. A paradoxical condition was inevitable, and at least
on land this second English war had its comic sides. Letters from
a great-grandmother of mine, living in Northern Vermont, tell
of a winter when her house was between the British and American
lines; on Thursdays she entertained the American officers, and on
Saturdays the British — it was understood that they should never
interfere with each other. Between whiles she read Byron's latest,
fresh from England — Byron was at heart a rebel too, enamored
of liberty, and died in a war of rebellion.

Little wonder, then, that English forms and English influence
lived on, here and there, particularly in New England. Little wonder, too, that in crossing the ocean they suffered a 'sea change.'
Architectural books might be English, but after the Revolution
the motifs of Adam were altered into the Americanisms of McIntire and Bulfinch, and Pain's 'fancy cornices' into the refined
woodwork of the earlier books of Asher Benjamin.

The second, the positive, factor in the breakdown of colonialism
was not limited to America; idealization of classic antiquity had
been alive all over the world ever since the Renaissance. Addison's
Cato was but one of a long series of heroic dramas on Roman
themes that edified the theatergoers of eighteenth-century Eng-

land; Racine in France had similarly peopled the French stage with his magnificent figures from Greek mythology — Andromaque, Iphigénie, Phèdre. Was it from these that a new popular idealism was slowly forming? In the ' high world ' of fashion, as in the minds of the literati, all of that earlier grandiose Baroque classicism had passed many decades before, in favor of the castles made popular by Walpole and the growing love of medieval panoply; in England fashionable gardens were full of ' dusky grots ' and ' wandering streams.' Yet, underneath the somewhat hysterical swing of fashion, in the minds of the multitude the classic ideal still held sway. And, just at the time when the American and the French Revolutions were coming into troubled gestation, the new discoveries of Pompeii and Herculaneum were giving new life to the Roman ideal, making it at last something almost suddenly reborn, suddenly human and alive.

Perhaps it was these new discoveries, perhaps it was because it had taken decades for the high ideals of Roman and Greek life held up by the essayists and dramatists of France and England to permeate the popular mind and become at home there, perhaps it was merely the fact that eighteenth-century medievalism seemed the rather effete plaything of the wealthy — in any case, the revolutions in France and America brought a quick rush of new life to this enthusiasm for the classic. The Roman citizen became the ideal of the perfect republican, the Roman tribune the great leader, the Roman general the ideal of all generals. Cincinnatus called from his plow to be the leader and the savior of his people — who could be a better image of the patriot? It is no accident that veteran American Revolutionary officers called themselves the Cincinnati, or that the sculptor Horatio Greenough, at a later date, meditating on the idea of Washington — ' Pater Patriae ' — should conceive his monument in an antique mold, a seated Zeus-like figure, nude to the waist, swathed in classic draperies below. What architects of the time thought about this will appear later.

America, then, was born at a time when every writer of letters to the journals — and in those times of excitement and political controversy writing letters to the papers was a flourishing occu-

pation — signed himself ' Brutus ' or ' Civis.' It was a time when
enthusiastic citizens, often harried and perplexed by the throng-
ing problems that surrounded the birth of a new nation, more and
more turned back to ancient Rome (the mother of republics as of
empires) and to ancient Greece (the country whose greatness came
through her democratic city states) for inspiration and for comfort. Those ancient peoples had flowered and prospered; so should
America. The classic world thus became, first, an inspiration; second, a refuge; third, a sort of marvelous vision of a Golden Age.

Of necessity, architecture followed the popular classic trend
rather than the medievalism of the new literary rebellion. Bryant's
verse and the novels of Charles Brockden Brown might follow the
romantics in England, but the architects, in style at least, followed the inspiration of Rome and Greece. Yet their architecture
was not the classicism of the eighteenth century, revamped by
new forms borrowed from Pompeii and Greece. A profound gulf
separates eighteenth-century classicism from that of the nineteenth. A new nation was being born, and Washington and Jefferson realized that the buildings that were to enshrine its activities must also be new; in the country at large the more intelligent
gentlemen-amateur builders as well as the few architects of the
time had come to realize the futility of trying here in the United
States to reconstruct another England.

The ending of the British hegemony was signalized by the first
Federal building in the country — Major Pierre L'Enfant's reconstruction of the New York city hall as Federal Hall. The choice
of L'Enfant as architect showed a distrust of current local tradition as well as of the English as mentors. It was but one evidence
of a widespread cultural movement, a new devotion to French as
opposed to English ideals. The fact that France had aided America
in gaining her independence had helped; L'Enfant himself was
one of the heroes of Lafayette's army. Franklin had received in
Paris a kind of sympathy, as well as admiration, which even the
learned circles of England gave him but grudgingly; the picture
one gathers of his salon in Passy in those feverish years of the de-
clining monarchy, when even the aristocrats and the court were

filled with the twin new ideas of science and liberty, is one which
casts a bright light over the new popularity of French ideals in
American thought. Later Jefferson was similarly thrilled and similarly welcomed, and his letters reveal his delight in this French
environment. Architect at heart as he always was, it was the new
classicism of late Louis XVI work which touched him most — that,
and the excitement of seeing one of the most beautiful and well
preserved of all Roman remains, the Maison Carrée at Nîmes.
After that no more English Palladianism for him, no matter how
pure!

Yet this French world that Franklin and Jefferson knew was
the pre-Revolutionary French world. Its architecture was the refined — perhaps over-refined — classicism of the Louis XVI style,
instinct with the delicacies and gentlenesses of Rousseau's Hôtel
de Salm and Gabriel's Petit Trianon. What set Jefferson apart
was his sudden realization, before the Maison Carrée, that the
classicism he loved and longed to recapture was the dignity and
grandeur of Rome, rather than the mere classic trappings of the
Parisian houses.[1]

In France that revelation was to come only after the French
Revolution, and especially, as a controlling force, with the rise of
Napoleon. Perhaps that is the reason why specifically French
architectural details had such a limited influence in America. Certain planning ideals, such as curve-ended or elliptical rooms and
the ingenious relationship of many varied room shapes and sizes,
were generally accepted.[2] Occasional conceptions monumental in
type can be traced to the same source. That is almost all. Even the
French architects who worked in America in the early years of the
republic, though all of them were trained in Louis XVI France and
some of them — like J. J. Ramée and M. I. Brunel — were political refugees, rapidly modified the strict Louis XVI character of
their designs. L'Enfant's Federal Hall is as far removed from that

[1] Fiske Kimball, *Thomas Jefferson and the First Monument of the Classic Revival in America* (Harrisburg and Washington, 1915), reprinted from the *Journal
of the American Institute of Architects*, Vol. III, Nos. 9–11 (September–November
1915). See especially Jefferson's letter of 13 August 1785, quoted on page 12.

[2] Fiske Kimball, *Domestic Architecture of the American Colonies and of the
Early Republic* (New York: Charles Scribner's Sons, 1922), p. 155.

style as it is from any English precedent, and in his plan for Washington there is probably as much inspiration from the Wren and Evelyn plans of London as from the gardens of Versailles. Already in 1789 the idea of an architecture specifically American was powerful enough to fire the enthusiasm of this young French artillery officer now become architect. Federal Hall, with its first attempt at an ' American order ' in a modified Doric, with the American stars decorating the necking of the capitals and the triglyphs of the frieze, is eloquent of this ideal. In conception too, as in detail, Federal Hall is American rather than French. Its plan is not yet completely understood, despite the descriptions of it we have; obviously it was partly conditioned by the existing structure of the old city hall. Yet the main elements are sufficiently clear. Bulfinch's careful elevation sketch shows a building in which the rustication of the central wall of the loggia and the ironwork in front of the windows indicate French influence, to be sure, but a building in which the proportions, the scale, and the monumentality are of a generalized classic inspiration unlike that current in France or England — that is, American. The cupola has greater monumentality than one finds in a majority of the English or Colonial examples, but its attic section and playful cyma-curved roof are definitely not French.[3] In the interior as well the descriptions tell of simplicity and richness of color and ampleness of space which have the same fresh and original character. In this building the French L'Enfant was already American.

In a somewhat similar way Etienne (or Stephen) Hallet's work on the United States Capitol was American rather than French or English, and a decade later Ramée's Union College designs were equally free and equally American. It must have been a powerful and a congenial atmosphere which so profoundly affected the work of these three French architects when they came to work in the new country.

Another cause for the lack of specifically French details in America, of course, lies in the French Revolution and the growing

[3] The front of Federal Hall is also excellently shown in a careful elevation by A. J. Davis, now in the Metropolitan Museum.

ABOVE, Ramée's elevation for a Union College building. BELOW, Ramée's general plan for Union College. (*Both courtesy President Fox.*)

ABOVE, Dormitory, Union College. J. J. Ramée, architect. (*Courtesy President Fox.*) BELOW, Larkin House, Portsmouth, N.H. (*Howells, Metropolitan Mus. of Art.*)

III

TOP, detail of dining-room door from Oak Hill. (*Mus. of Fine Arts, Boston.*) CENTER, LEFT, mantel by Samuel McIntire from Gardner-White-Pingree House, Salem, Mass. (*Essex.*) CENTER, RIGHT, mantel from the old building of Erasmus Hall High School, Brooklyn. (*Georgian Period.*) BOTTOM, parlor from Oak Hill, Peabody, Mass. Samuel McIntire, architect. (*Mus. of Fine Arts, Boston.*)

ABOVE, Virginia State Capitol, Richmond, prior to its restoration. Thomas Jefferson, architect. (*Howells, Metropolitan Mus. of Art.*) BELOW, Farmington, Charlottesville, Va. The capitals are from another building. (*Frary.*)

American hatred of its excesses and its bloodshed. Had the Revolution developed quietly and peacefully, as its American sympathizers hoped; had Citizen Genêt been a brilliant diplomat instead of a rather stupid enthusiast; had the French revolutionary government been conciliatory instead of overbearing — in other words, had the French-American relations withstood the strains of the French Revolution and the continued French-English hostility — it is possible that French artistic influence would have grown and America might have followed France into the Empire style. But this was not to be, and gradually during the 1790's the French influences waned. Only spasmodically, as in the New York city hall, by Joseph Mangin and John McComb, Jr., did it achieve important architectural results.

At the opening of the nineteenth century there were thus two distinct and often opposed architectural ideals. One was that charterizing especially the mercantile centers, where English commerce kept English memories green — New England, New York, Philadelphia, Newcastle (Delaware), parts of Virginia, and Charleston (South Carolina) — and called ' Late Colonial ' or ' post-Colonial,' based generally on English Adam or Regency forms profoundly modified; it appears at its best perhaps in New England, in the work of McIntire, Bulfinch, Parris, and Benjamin. The other was the Classic Revival movement instigated by Washington and Jefferson; it dominates the work done under Federal auspices, and appears spasmodically at first in Philadelphia and Virginia.

II. Late or Post-Colonial Architecture

Some knowledge of the post-Colonial work in New England and New York is necessary in order to understand the profoundly revolutionary work of the later Greek Revival architects. It was a style of extraordinary richness, rooted alike in the culture of its place and time and in the physical needs of the climate and the building materials it used. It was founded on the work of at least three generations of craftsmen, each improving upon its predecessor in skill, imagination, and resources. Although in the more distant country localities it is in some cases difficult to tell the post-Revolutionary houses from those built before, still, along the coast, where wealthy shipowners and sea captains were more and more often building homes to express their newly gained wealth, and in the cities, where the current fashions held sway, the new style is easily recognizable. It owes much to the Colonial buildings that had preceded it — to their skillful use of timber, their frequent imitation of stone forms in wood, and even their traditional four-room-and-central-hall house plan. In public buildings Colonial simplicity and the ubiquitous cupola still ruled, just as in the majority of churches the old Gibbs formulae remained supreme. Yet differences were creeping in sufficiently to reveal a fundamental change. Designs were more original, experimental, and personal. Delicacy of detail superseded the earlier ruggedness. Ceiling heights were generally greater, and both the windows themselves and the panes of which they were made were much larger. Even in comparatively small houses, pane sizes ten by twelve or even ten by fourteen inches were not uncommon. Wooden detail became more and more complex and was made of more and smaller parts; moldings were often tiny, so that the whole effect became sometimes wiredrawn and thin. Columns and pilasters were much slimmer and entablatures proportionately smaller. More and more pure white in the painted woodwork replaced the grays and blues, greens and yellows, common in Colonial times; interior color was light and clear, punctuated by rich brocaded hangings and oriental rugs.

All of this was of course a distant reflection of the corresponding changes in English taste brought to America in the books of William Pain, James Paine, and the Adam brothers. Yet the differences are enormous. The craftsmen before the Revolution seem to have done their best to reproduce the details of the mother country gleaned from the handbooks of Batty Langley and Swan and Ware; but in those ample houses of Wiscasset and Machias and Salem and Providence, built between 1790 and 1810 (or even later), the craftsman or architect was using his newer books — his Pain and his Adam — as inspiration only. It was as if his new

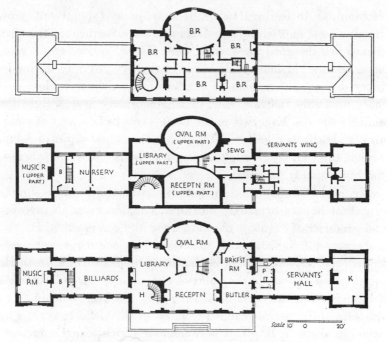

FIGURE 1. GORE HALL, Waltham, Mass. Plans. (*H.A.B.S.*) The curved walls and variety in room shapes characteristic of many post-Revolutionary house plans.

political freedom had carried over almost at once into his designing. He became aware that he was an American, working in America. Wood, which to his father and grandfather had been again and again but a poor substitute for stone, became now itself an inspiration to him. Reedings and flutings brought out its workability, slimness and delicacy its elastic strength. Fluted ovals and paterae burgeoned on doorways and mantels; particularly in rural New York they were used with a profusion at times overlavish and crowded, as though the carver so delighted in his wood and his tools that he could not restrain their use.

In building type, too, the post-Revolutionary world has brought changes. Roofs lose their importance; many of the finest houses are roofed with hipped roofs so gentle in slope as to be invisible. The flat roof surrounded by a balustrade, over a simple rectangular three-story house, is a frequent type. Plans grow freer; closets and secondary stairs are more frequent; rooms are placed and designed for specific uses. Curved stairs become common, and the old elaborately turned balusters give way to simple, tapered shafts, sometimes of extraordinary delicacy. More and more sidelights and fanlights, often elaborately leaded, light the ample hallways. Everywhere the ideal seems to be a sort of clear, airy, and delicate dignity. Yet there are few actual copies of Adam work in this country; though the inspiration has come from abroad, the expression is American.

Samuel McIntire's Salem work is characteristic.[4] It is significant that he was primarily and first a woodcarver, an inventor and producer of exquisite detail in wood and composition. He was a craftsman-designer; and if sometimes his door trims seem overloaded, restless, and lacking in simplicity, and some of his mantels too slim and delicate to the point of effeminacy, it is only because delight in exquisite craftsmanship *per se* has betrayed him. Yet the taste of the time demanded richness of this delicate type. The Adam interiors in England were delicately rich with Pompeiianesque modeled plaster ceilings, and with woodwork and trim often intricately carved with ornament inspired by the late Roman work of the Palace of Diocletian at Spalatro. William Pain and James Paine, the popularizers of the Adam style, adopted its richness of detail and its freedom, but developed it with little reference to its original sources in Pompeii and Spalatro; the details of ' fancy cornices ' and other wood trim with which their books are replete show a character much more English than Roman and are, in fact, a subtle and skillful blend of influences from many sources — Adam, Sheraton, Hepplewhite, and even the Palladianism of Isaac Ware. *Pain's British Palladio* [5] was one of the most popular handbooks used by the post-Revolutionary craftsmen of America (McIntire probably owned it), so that the Adam style reached America largely at second hand and already much modified.

McIntire's interiors show the creative and personal touch that

4 Fiske Kimball, *Mr. Samuel McIntire, Carver, the Architect of Salem* (Portland, Maine: The Southworth-Anthoensen Press, for the Essex Institute, 1940).
5 By William Pain (London: I. and J. Taylor, 1798).

he gave to these English forms. Characteristic are the delicate, low, widely projecting cornices of doors and mantels, the many deeply undercut, exquisitely profiled moldings, the use of delicate rope moldings and rows of little spheres. Especially beautiful is his use of repeated fine reedings continuously crossing the planes of architrave bands, which make such an effective contrast to the long lines of the delicate enframing moldings at right angles to them. Characteristic of his influence, too, are the exquisite New England mantels of this time, with their friezes broken out at ends and center and decorated with delicate composition ornaments of Adam-like urns and garlands — and occasionally more original and personal touches like shocks of wheat and American eagles — and with their slim ' fancy ' colonnettes or delicate pilasters at the sides of the fireplace. One has only to compare these with other American developments of the same English source forms to realize how experimental and creative were the American craftsmen of the period, how eager they were to evolve new and American forms, and how great a part the individual designer played. The craftsman was beginning to develop into the architect.

In the Hudson Valley and parts of Long Island and New Jersey, for instance, these Adam-Pain influences produced a style of lavish wood detail absolutely different in form and spirit from that of New England. Because this is frequently found in gambrel-roofed houses, it has erroneously been called ' Dutch Colonial.' This local style shares only one quality with that of McIntire — intricate delicacy — but, whereas the New England craftsman creatively developed the whole gamut of Pain freedoms, the New York school became obsessed with merely one type of form, the fluted or reeded radiating fan and ellipse. This form was used almost to the exclusion of composition ornament or of the delicate carved urns and garlands found elsewhere ; ellipses and half ellipses, large and small, decorated every flat wooden trim surface, big or little. Superimposed upon each other they became a fantastic geometrical ornament, like that in the frieze of the mantel of the room in the old part of the Erasmus High School, Brooklyn. They became almost a disease ; friezes of doors and mantels were widened to receive the display of fans and ellipses until proportions were lost, and so popular were they that their use persisted in up-state New York until well into the thirties. With them went a similar love of fantastic turned forms — urn shapes used instead of colonnettes for mantels, and tiny columns complicating friezes with, as it were, miniature shrines — and a passion for all sorts of carpenter-made and chip carving such as diamonds, auger holes, and the like.[6]

Individual peculiarities and expressions existed, too, which sometimes gave a distinctive character to a small locality. Thus the rather baroque fantasy of Russell Warren decked the houses of the Bristol, Rhode Island, ' millionaires ' with an extraordinary parade of the classic orders, much attenuated. So too, in Windsor, Vermont, and its neighborhood, some designer of exquisite taste employed delicate Adam-like garlands on exterior details as they were seldom used elsewhere. Many houses in the Finger Lakes district of New York have a monumental order of thin pilasters across their entire façades, used in a way so locally restricted and so similar that some one designer's influence is obvious.

Yet certain common elements are found in all these houses: simple interior wall surfaces, usually of painted plaster, above wainscots of the simplest type, capped by delicately molded chair rails; large windows with the thinnest possible muntins; the most delicate plaster cornices; and a general air of ample clarity, light colors, and, above all, elegance. It was all a fit frame for the delicate Empire costumes of the women, so simple and so fresh, and for the delicate shapes of American-made mahogany furniture of Sheraton and Hepplewhite inspiration.

These interiors were elegant, but they were fragile; at times they seem to us frankly precious, diminutive in decoration, overstudied, sometimes effeminate and lacking in vitality. And more and more into these delicate rooms were coming treasures brought

---

6 William Hindley, who had made an intensive study of Early Republic architecture in the New York neighborhood, saw in this style evidence of the late influence of Major L'Enfant. His theories can be studied in a large number of notebooks and sketchbooks, some in the Avery Library, Columbia University, and some in Federal Hall Museum at the Sub-Treasury building in New York City.

from all over the world by the sea captains and world merchants whose wealth had paid for so many of these houses all along the northern coasts from Portland in Maine to the Chesapeake— treasures in Chinese porcelain and lacquer, and gold-ground *Kasus;* English and Irish glass and silver; French brocades; carved marble mantels from Italy. Cosmopolitanism was becoming fashionable; colonialism was dying. The women of Maine and Massachusetts, accompanying their mariner husbands on long voyages, had seen Vesuvius and perhaps poked around among the newly excavated ruins of Pompeii and the tunnels through the buildings of Herculaneum; they had seen the homes of wealthy merchants in Marseille and the exotic courtyards and patios of New Orleans and Havana. America was becoming conscious of the world, and this lovely, over-wrought, precious style was too unreal and too fragile to endure such a consciousness; something more monumental, more vital, more masculine was demanded, and little by little, between 1810 and 1830, this Late Colonial style was doomed to a lingering but steady decay and eventual disappearance.

Its effect, however, in some sense remained. In plan and exterior design the builders of this period had seemed to seek ideals quite different from those expressed in their attentuated interior trim. Large scale and simplicity of brick surfaces and fenestration characterize most of the larger New England houses, as does the restraint which took the Adam trick of placing rectangular windows within decorated arched recesses and made of it a new and lovely motif. The Larkin house (1817) at Portsmouth, McIntire's John Gardner house (1804–5) — also known as the Gardner-White-Pingree house — at Salem, or even such naïve examples as the Dr. Ambrose Pratt house (1820) in Chester, Connecticut, sometimes attributed to Colonel Belcher, all show this dignity, restraint, and monumentality. With this exterior character went a new and growing freedom of plan conception, founded on a more careful and functional arrangement of rooms and a freer type of room shape — rooms with alcoves, rooms with curved corners, elliptical and circular rooms. The Governor Gore house (1805) in

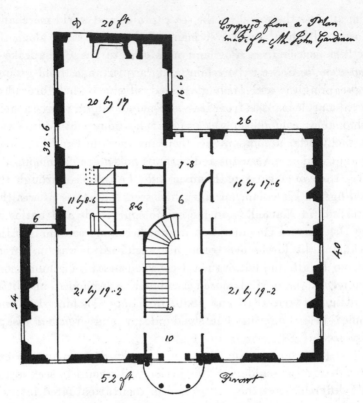

Figure 2. GARDNER–WHITE–PINGREE HOUSE, Salem, Mass. First-floor
plan. (*Essex Institute.*) Samuel McIntire's own drawing, showing variations
from the typical Colonial plan made to increase convenience and efficiency.

Waltham, Massachusetts, and Woodlands (1790) in Philadelphia
are but two of many varied examples which show this widespread
freedom.

These two characteristics — restrained monumentality and
plan freedom — lived on and, at a time when the growing importance of the individual designer was becoming marked, were to
influence profoundly the later Greek Revival work.

III. JEFFERSONIAN CLASSICISM

The contribution to American architecture made by Thomas Jefferson, seconded by Washington, in the plans for the New Federal capital was epoch-making. L'Enfant, undoubtedly a protégé of the first President, had made a beginning in directing Federal architecture along its classic course with his design for Federal Hall in New York, and in the plan of Washington he had created a magnificent formal framework for classical buildings. But in all probability the new Federal structures which were eventually built would have been much less purely classic if Jefferson had not been so constantly interested and eager in giving advice, counsel, and inspiration. To the problem of the Washington architecture he brought all the knowledge he had gained through nearly twenty years of experimentation in his own house, Monticello, and all the inspiration of his years of residence in France, his admiration for the brilliance of French planning, and his almost worshipful veneration of the one important Roman ruin he had seen. But it was not only for his influence in the Federal capital that Jefferson was important. In domestic architecture as well his influence produced a type of large mansion in Maryland and Virginia that undoubtedly made simpler the transition to the later Greek Revival. Bremo is typical. Its free, extended plan and the complete absence from its detail, outside and in, of any of the baroque motifs of the Colonial or any of the dainty fripperies of the Adam-like post-Colonial, bear witness to the quiet and gracious sobriety of his taste. Its bold colonnaded loggia was unique; its simple classic dignity enshrines a new architectural idealism.

It is interesting to note that, precisely at the time when this polished Palladian design was being made, McIntire was building his Gardner-White-Pingree house in Salem, Bulfinch was erecting the famous Park Street houses in Boston, and McComb had recently completed his delicate Grange for Hamilton outside what was then New York.

Of course in Bremo, as in much of Jefferson's work, the inspiration came from Palladio and not from the ancient Roman buildings themselves; yet the templelike wings have the ancient classic feeling, and it is a fact that for Jefferson Palladianism was the simplest path from the baroque Georgian, which he hated, to the pure ancient Roman classic, which he adored. Bremo,[7] built in 1818, is an extremely bold and mature design, more architectonic and assured than the Virginia state capitol — where, as Kimball has shown,[8] the temple form was first used for a public building of importance — and even more assured than Monticello, where earlier beginnings may have cramped him and the complexities of his requirements impeded his free creation.

Monticello, nevertheless, in all probability best represents Jefferson's architecture. The Virginia state capitol as built (1789) was a compromise between what he wanted and what the Commissioners saw fit to permit. Even in Jefferson's design the basic Palladian treatment of the windows and doors in the ' cella,' the building proper, do not seem entirely in harmony with the magnificent classic portico. Here Jefferson is still the amateur. But Monticello, in its final form reached in the last remodeling between 1796 and 1809, in spite of its complexities — for behind each of them there was a reason — is the work of an architect. Fiske Kimball has so authoritatively traced the history of Jefferson's architectural development and the growth of Monticello, so accurately appraised the importance of his position in American architecture, that any further statement is unnecessary.

The character of Monticello depends basically on its designer's search, inside and out, for the simplest, strongest, largest, and most monumental forms. To that everything else is secondary. Its main floor is high, and the exterior cornice is raised well above the windows. The upper floor is concealed behind a parapet and balus-

---

[7] Bremo was built by John Hartwell Cocke. Jefferson was consulted with regard to its construction as early as 1815, but whether or not he was the actual architect is still doubtful. It is possibly Cocke's own design; yet, whoever was the actual designer, Bremo embodies many of Jefferson's ideals. According to Dr. Fiske Kimball, the actual designers were James Dinsmore and John Neilson, who were disciples of Jefferson.

[8] Fiske Kimball, *Thomas Jefferson and the First Monument of the Classic Revival in America* already cited. See also the same author's monumental monograph, *Thomas Jefferson, Architect; Original Designs in the Collection of Thomas Jefferson Coolidge* (Boston: printed for private distribution by the Riverside Press, 1916).

trade. Simple but monumental four-column porticoes in the center of each long side give dignity; the final touch of grandeur is found in the octagonal dome. Simple architraves and cornices of strict classic type decorate the openings. Within there is the same largeness, simplicity, and classic dignity. The high rooms have complete classic entablatures — architrave, frieze, and cornice — of Corinthian or Doric type. The doors are enframed with plain classic architraves, the most important ones crowned with frieze, cornice, and pediment of bold and ample projection; niches occasionally occur, but otherwise the wall surfaces are absolutely plain. The whole effect is as different from the delicacies of McIntire or of Bulfinch as can be imagined, and clearer and simpler than the Adam-inspired classicism of Woodlands, with its almost ostentatious display of columns; it is formal yet gracious dignity incarnate. The same character reposes in the tall airy rooms of Jefferson's remodeled Farmington (1803), near Charlottesville, Virginia.

Exactly how great was Jefferson's influence on the work of Dr. Thornton and Latrobe we may never know, but his association with them was close. He wrote them frequently of his work, particularly of his ideas for the University of Virginia, and they replied with equal fullness. Sometimes he adopted their suggestions; sometimes he improved upon these or substituted other conceptions of his own. Manifestly he learned from them; it is probable that they, too, learned from him. In many cases their work and his own express ideas so similar that no mere accident can explain the fact. Latrobe, of course, as we shall see, was a man of the greatest architectural knowledge, trained in the best schools England could furnish. Yet much of his American work is so different from that of his English preceptors that one wonders what caused the change. Perhaps Jefferson had something to do with it. Dr. Thornton, like Jefferson widely traveled and an amateur, could not but be sensitive to Jefferson's charm and his passionate devotion to his ideals. Robert Mills, who claimed to be the first native-born American to be trained specifically for a career as professional architect, came under Jefferson's influence even more closely while working as a draftsman for him for two years, and during the lifetime of both there remained between them a relationship warm and vivid.[9] Through these three, all of them so important in the future development of American architecture, Jefferson's influence spread more and more widely, and in their work his classicism found eventually even a fuller expression than he himself could have given it. For instance, Thornton's Tudor Place (after 1810) in Washington has a more English appearance superficially than does Jefferson's work; it is not unlike some of those classic houses in England which it is the fashion to lump together under the term ' Regency.' Soane designed at times in a manner not too diferent. Yet in the details there is a classic purity, and in the general composition a monumental feeling, quite different from either the occasional attenuated delicacy of much Regency work or the rather erratic but creative handling of classic forms which Soane exemplified. It is enormously dignified, reposeful, human, satisfactory.

With all its restrained graciousness this new classicism of the Jeffersonian type is never fragile, like the exquisiteness of the Late Colonial. Thomas Hamilton, the Scotch novelist who visited America in 1832, notes that the white houses of New England often were, for him, compromised by the slimness of the columns, which he likens to pipe stems.[10] And that over-attenuation, coupled with the tiny, often over-worked detail, however delightful, was not fitted to express the virility, the restless imagination, the solid achievement of a country that was growing and alive. The McIntire type was doomed by the results of the very exuberance that gave it birth.

The comments of Pavel Petrovich Svinin, a Russian diplomat, author, and artist who was in America from 1811 to 1813, are significant.[11] Of our architecture in general he says, ' Briefly, English architecture prevails here throughout. In New York State,

9 H. M. Pierce Gallagher, *Robert Mills, Architect of the Washington Monument*, 1781–1855 (New York: Columbia University Press, 1935).

10 See page 96.

11 A. Yarmolinsky, *Picturesque United States of America*, 1811, 1812, 1813, *being a Memoir on Paul [Pavel Petrovich] Svinin, Russian Diplomatic Officer, Artist, and Author*, with an Introduction by R. T. H. Halsey (New York: W. E. Rudge, 1930).

settled originally by the Dutch, and in the interior of Pennsylvania, inhabited mostly by the Germans, there are still some old houses built according to the national taste of those peoples; but they are fast disappearing. . . .' And then later he notes the kind of buildings which really aroused his enthusiasm. ' As regards country homes,' he writes, ' the Americans have for some time adopted the Italian style, and I have found here many such homes, of the most modern and very pleasant style of architecture.'

For classicism was the ' modern ' in that period, and it was this classic work, so profoundly influenced by Jefferson, which was to supersede the ' English ' work with surprising rapidity. The day to come was the day of the classicists.

CHAPTER 2

THE BIRTH OF AMERICAN ARCHITECTURE

IT IS peculiarly fitting that for the birth of an architecture distinctly American one must look neither to the seaports of New England with their delicate, rather Adam-style houses, nor to the late Georgian dignity of the South, but rather to Washington itself, that new capital which started to rise so soon after the final adoption of the American Constitution. Planned by the genius of the French officer L'Enfant, its buildings were nevertheless the result of new ideals, and specifically of the new architectural ideals of Washington himself, the polished amateur, and of Jefferson, much more than the polished amateur, almost the professional architect. It was the vision of these two men that set the new buildings for the new republic on a classic rather than an English Renaissance foundation. Jefferson's hatred of what seemed to him the frivolities of English Baroque architecture, as built in the American colonies, is well known and has often been commented upon; to him the dignity of the simple orders which he found in his Palladio and the bigness of conception of the Roman buildings seemed the only fitting inspirations for a new architecture to satisfy the wants of a new republic. It is by no mere chance that the Roman eagle came to roost again in America and, in a new form as the American eagle, became next to the flag itself the universal symbol of the United States.

In another way, too, the founding of Washington and the erecting of its chief buildings were a prophecy of the architectural work which was to come, rather than a mere following of a current tradition. These two leaders, Washington and Jefferson, who despite their political differences so closely collaborated in all matters affecting the new capital city, looked for the fulfillment of their dreams not to the traditional builder, working with his traditional knowledge and taste from a client's sketch, but to the professional architect. The competition for the national Capitol may well be considered the birth of the profession of architecture in this country: for, although its winner, Dr. Thornton, was himself an amateur, the award was made to him as an architect, and all of his chief assistants and followers were architects in the modern sense of the word. The Frenchman, Stephen Hallet, perhaps almost as much responsible as Thornton for the earlier work on the Capitol, was a thoroughly trained designer, a draftsman of both power and delicacy, a refugee from the French Revolution, who had come to Philadelphia from New York in 1797 in connection with an ill-starred attempt to found a great school of arts. George Hadfield, the Englishman, a prize-winning student of the Royal Academy, after winning a brilliant reputation in England came over at the suggestion of Colonel Trumbull, was made superintendent of the Capitol, and became the designer of the first buildings for the executive departments in Washington and later, with Robert Mills, one of the architects of the Washington city hall. The last and greatest of this early group is of course Benjamin Henry Latrobe, to whom we owe so much of the architectural work at the capital, a pupil of Samuel Pepys Cockerell in London and an architect of the greatest imagination, refinement of taste, and engineering ability.

To be sure, all of these men were dogged by misfortune, and their work frequently went unpraised and ill rewarded. L'Enfant, Hallet, Hadfield, and Latrobe all suffered loss rather than gain by their association with the Capitol. Nevertheless, the seed of good architecture was there well sown; the idea of the professional architect, which up to that time had been only the vaguest dream, was now soundly established as an essential feature in all government building.

This emergence of the professional architect, coming at a time of change in popular taste, was ideally fitted to hasten the development of a new and characteristic style. The older eighteenth-century builder-architects worked naturally in the traditions in which they had been brought up, and followed rather than led the fashion. But to the progressive younger architects of this time the English tradition was merely a background of things to examine and, if need be, to reject. The new knowledge of ancient classic buildings, on the other hand, was a continual inspiration, not to copy but to emulate. It was the genius of Latrobe more than of anyone else which made this apparent. For him the inspiration of ancient classic forms offered a spacious pathway out of the dullness of an outworn Baroque tradition, and this idea — that the Classic Revival forms were not new set categories imposing a new slavery of design, but rather a powerful means of breaking off the shackles of the past — became a controlling factor in the American Classic Revival. It was an ideal that a professional architect could understand, but one which the older builder-architects could hardly appreciate. Outside of John McComb, Jr., in New York, and Bulfinch in his earlier work in Boston, there is hardly an architect of the first water in this nineteenth-century America who did not abandon English Renaissance work with extraordinary alacrity and strive to design buildings of a new type — not copies of ancient buildings, but American buildings only the details of which were inspired by the classic.

The existing designs submitted in the Capitol competition form a remarkable group in which the taste of the time can easily be read.[1] Three of them — McIntire's, Hart's, and Diamond's — hark back to eighteenth-century English ideals. Of these, Hart's is manifestly impossible, without scale or monumental quality, a mere enlarged house. James Diamond's design, despite its barbarous drawing, has definite monumental quality; its plan shows real thinking, its architecture a valid quality of simple, almost

---

[1] These competition drawings are preserved in the Maryland Historical Society in Baltimore. Many have been published by Glenn Brown, *History of the United States Capitol*, 2 vols. (Washington: Government Printing Office, 1900, 1903), and by Fiske Kimball and Wells Bennett, 'The Competition for the Federal Buildings, 1792–93,' *Journal of the American Institute of Architects*, Vol. VII, Nos. 1, 3, 5, 7 (January, March, May, December 1919), pp. 8–12, 98–102, 202–10, 335–61, 521–8, and Vol. VIII, No. 3 (March 1920), pp. 117, 124, and ' William Thornton and the Design of the United States Capitol,' *Art Studies Medieval and Modern*, Vol. I (Princeton: Princeton University Press, 1923), an extra number of the *American Journal of Archaeology*, pp. 76–92.

See also I. T. Frary, *They Built the Capitol* (Richmond: Garrett and Massie [c1940]).

V

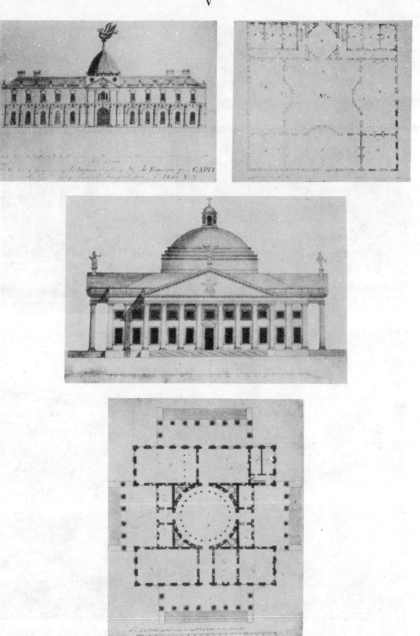

Two competition designs for the United States Capitol: (*Maryland Hist. Soc.*) ABOVE, elevation and plan by James Diamond. BELOW, elevation and plan by Samuel Dobie.

United States Capitol interiors by B. H. Latrobe: ABOVE, LEFT, room beneath the Old Senate. (*Brown.*) ABOVE, RIGHT, Senate entrance, with corn order. BELOW, LEFT, Senate rotunda, with tobacco order. BELOW, RIGHT, Rotunda. (*Last three, Frary.*)

VII

ABOVE, Latrobe's design for the United States Capitol, perspective. (*New York Pub. Lib.*) BELOW, Statuary Hall, the Old House of Representatives. (*Ware Library.*)

Roman Catholic Cathedral, Baltimore, exterior and interior. B. H. Latrobe, architect. (*Schaefer*.)

crude, grandeur. One feels in it the work of a man who was probably a competent builder with a very real understanding of many design problems, who had never learned to draw, and who was completely filled with the ideals of Baroque England. Such a design, if built, might have worked — at first — and it would have had something of the rather grim charm of the brick courts in the Temple in London.

McIntire's drawings are on an entirely different plane and reveal him as much more than a mere maker of delicate doorways and mantels. He evidently realized the opportunity the design of this building offered, and he made the most of it. Aside from the designs of Hallet and Thornton, his design more than any of the others, more even than Dobie's, shows a true grasp of what a capitol should be. It is large in spirit, as it is in size. It is well composed, with end pavilions and a center portico. It is well planned, with stairs well placed and a central hall of real dignity. The proportions of the openings are beautiful and the handling of the basement and terrace unusually accomplished. There are no fripperies; the whole breathes a dignity not unlike that of Sir William Chambers's Somerset House in London. And, still more surprising, all the complications of monumental classic design — the relations of portico and wall, of orders and building — are solved simply, directly, and convincingly. It is almost Michelangelesque, and perhaps owes something, directly or indirectly, to the Palazzo dei Senatori on the Capitoline Hill. This design is undoubtedly McIntire's masterpiece; it is the product of a competent, creative, and disciplined mind.

The design is all the more remarkable because of what McIntire read into the competition program. This had been amazing for its vagueness and understatement; followed literally it might have produced a town hall but never a national capitol. McIntire's imagination was great enough to use it as a framework only, to realize and fill out its inadequacies; he produced a capitol.

Yet this alone was not enough. Anywhere else but in Washington this building might have been built and would have won the plaudits not only of its own time but probably of ours as well; in

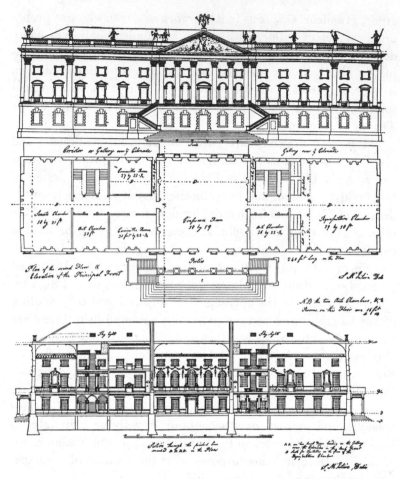

FIGURE 3. McINTIRE'S COMPETITION DRAWINGS FOR THE U. S. CAPITOL. Elevation, plan, section. (*Maryland Hist. Soc.*) Effective, imaginative planning, and impressive exterior and interior design, based on English prototypes.

many ways it was a more accomplished design, more dignified and certainly more integrated, than Bulfinch's Massachusetts capitol, and infinitely more monumental than Bulfinch's Connecticut capitol. It was perhaps the best that the old order of English influence and Pain and Adam inspiration could produce, but it was not good enough. It would have turned back the hands of the clock, whereas for Washington something that looked toward the future and not backward — toward the new America and not toward the old England — was needed. Only a new classicism, a revolutionary classicism as opposed to the old conventions, could do that. Samuel Dobie seems to have realized something of the kind. Stylistically he aimed at something new. The central dome and four great porticoes of his design have definitely monumental scale and grandeur; it is all classic and Palladian. But even that was not sufficient. While it is an advance in style Dobie's design is in every other respect inadequate. Its plan is forced and impractical. Its monumental quality is imposed and not innate, its form derivative — Palladio's Villa Rotunda seen through basically English eyes. It is the Palladianism of the Earl of Burlington, not that of a new and hopeful country. Yet it is among the most ably presented of the designs, so beautifully delineated indeed that one wonders at these accurate and well-rendered drawings coming from an architect otherwise so little known. But, inspired by a villa as it was, it remained a villa though enlarged. It was not yet a capitol.[2]

There remained the two other designers, Thornton and Hallet, and with the large number of existing studies by the one or the other, many unsigned, we come into controversial questions. Hallet, though awarded the second prize and made superintendent of construction and apparently also head draftsman under Thornton, always felt himself wronged. The exact attribution of many of these drawings may never be settled, but three things seem sure: both men submitted designs in accord with a new and basically non-English classicism; both created schemes which had true monumentality, a real sense of what a capitol should be; and in the chief designs of both the basic scheme contained a monumental central area crowned by a dome, with two great wings expressing

2 In 1792, Jefferson, under the pseudonym of Abraham Faws, submitted a design based on Palladio's Villa Rotunda in the competition for the President's house. Was this suggested to his mind by Dobie's design, which he must have known well and studied? Or did Dobie, perhaps, adopt his Capitol scheme because of the influence of Jefferson? A study of Jefferson's, made in 1783, for the Williamsburg Governor's house, shows him already working on a similar idea. See Fiske Kimball's *Domestic Architecture of the American Colonies and of the Early Republic* (New York: Charles Scribner's Sons, 1922), pp. 116, 174.

the two legislative chambers — internal arrangement expressed in external forms.[3]

Thus, at the very beginning of the building of Washington, classicism and monumentality were determined upon and fixed as the ideals of American governmental architecture. Yet even Thornton's conception of monumentality was not deemed sufficient. His Palladianism was still fundamentally British in detail; the parts of the Capitol from his design which still stand are eloquent of that. Behind the endless and unedifying disputes that plagued the early building of the Capitol — disputes between Hallet and Thornton, between the architects and the Commissioners — lies more than human irascibility; the fundamental conflict between a new classicism, as first represented by Hallet, and the older tradition, represented by Thornton, was equally to blame, and the appointment of Latrobe as architect of the Capitol in 1803 was evidence of the victory of the classic ideal. In all the work in Washington and its neighborhood, or where the influence of Thomas Jefferson and Latrobe penetrated most deeply, this ideal with surprising rapidity attained monumental and beautiful expression.

The importance of Latrobe in those early years of a new national American architecture is generally admitted. He came to America at the moment when his talents could be of the greatest use and, despite his frustrations and the endless controversies which surrounded him, left an indelible impression on this country, not only by his own work but also because of his influence on his pupils.[4]

[3] For careful discussions of this whole matter see Glenn Brown, op. cit. Vol. I, pp. 7–30; Wells Bennett, *Stephen Hallet and His Designs for the National Capitol, 1790–94* (Harrisburg and Washington, 1916), reprinted from the *Journal of the American Institute of Architects*, Vol. IV, Nos. 7–10 (July–October 1916). Hallet's temple design, probably made at Jefferson's behest, shows the enthusiasm of the authorities for a classicism based on antique rather than Palladian precedent.

[4] For Latrobe's work see Costen Fitz-Gibbons, 'Latrobe and the Centre Square Pump House,' *The Architectural Record*, Vol. LXII, No. 1 (July 1927), pp. 18–22; Fiske Kimball, 'Latrobe's Designs for the Cathedral of Baltimore,' *The Architectural Record*, Vol. XLII, No. 6 (December 1917), pp. 540–50, and Vol. XLIII, No. 1 (January 1918), pp. 37–45, and 'The Bank of Pennsylvania, an Unknown Masterpiece of American Classicism,' *The Architectural Record*, Vol. XLIV, No. 2 (August 1918), pp. 132–39. See also Chapter 4. Measured drawings of certain Latrobe houses

Latrobe was fundamentally a tragic character. He was thoroughly trained and widely traveled. In London he seems to have won conspicuous position before he had produced any large body of work. It is said that he was offered, though he refused, the post of Surveyor General to the Crown. Then, when the death of his young wife filled him with sudden distaste for the brilliant future his life thus far had promised, he became restless. London became distasteful to him and he set sail for America. Something of this same restlessness stayed with him, carrying him to Baltimore, to Philadelphia, Washington, and Pittsburgh, and finally to New Orleans, where he died. His eager ambition and his overweening self-assurance drove him into many disastrous speculative enterprises. He was constantly irked by American crudities and by the strongly entrenched system of carpenters' companies and builder-architects. In 1812 he wrote to Joseph Delaplaine savagely attacking the Carpenters' Company of Philadelphia:

They have done me the honor to copy and to disgrace by their application almost all my designs from a molding to a plan of a whole building. . . I have changed the taste of a whole city. My very follies and faults and whims have been mimicked, and yet there is not a single instance in which I have been consulted. . .

Disappointed in the small income from his professional life, he wrote in the same year to Godefroy: ' I shall at last make cloth, steam engines or turn tailor for money, for money is honor. . .' Yet all these speculative business ventures — dealing in arms, steam-powered textile factories, steamboats on the Ohio River — ended in failure and loss, and eventually forced him into bankruptcy. Only the magnificent spirit and helpful co-operation of his second wife, Mary Elizabeth Hazlehurst, the daughter of a Philadelphia shipping merchant, saved him from complete nervous collapse after the steamboat debacle at Pittsburgh and brought him back to his second, and immensely creative, period of employment on the United States Capitol after its burning by the British.

are shown in Harry Francis Cunningham, Joseph Arthur Younger, and J. Wilmer Smith's *Measured Drawings of Georgian Architecture in the District of Columbia* (New York: Architectural Book Publishing Company, 1914).

Through all these varied ups and downs, one steady ideal kept alive — a complete and passionate devotion to the highest professional values in the practice of architecture. He may well be called the father of the architectural profession in America. The ideals he instilled, often at great sacrifice, were preserved and strengthened by his pupils, Mills and Strickland, and gradually spread over the entire country to be eventually accepted as the foundation of professional practice.

From England Latrobe brought to America that spirit of growing rebellion against Palladianism and the growing love of simplified versions of ancient classic forms which were current among the younger London architects of the time. In the work of Sir John Soane, only twelve years older than Latrobe, this spirit achieved its most complete English expression. Yet the possibility of direct influence from Soane upon Latrobe seems to be refuted by the dates of Soane's work, for most of his famous and creative novelties were only built after Latrobe had come to America. Fundamentally the two men thought and designed with much the same general outlook; they were both interested in creating a new and living architecture to fit the spirit of the times. Both men, one in England and one in America, directed the architecture of their countries into new ways, and in both men this revolution in taste seems to have been the result of native genius rather than the mere following of the influence of others, for Latrobe's chief teacher — the earlier Cockerell — was in the main a representative of the older and more conservative school.

Nevertheless it is probable that Latrobe, with his wide London acquaintance, moved in the same circles as Soane, and it is possible that through Soane Latrobe was introduced to the remarkable rationalist architectural criticism contained in the works of Marc Antoine Laugier, which Soane so deeply admired that he gave copies of it to all his pupils.[5] Laugier's extraordinarily prophetic functionalism was revolutionary in its entire approach; it swept away the older academicism in architecture with a superbly assured

---

[5] See Arthur Thomas Bolton's *Portrait of Sir John Soane, R.A.* (Frome and London: Butler and Tanner, 1927), pp. 142–3.

logic. The ideal church design it describes is almost the complete opposite of the Rococo churches that were current in France in his day; its vision of the city as an integrated organism was ahead even of the city-planning ideals of the nineteenth century; and it advocated new and creative details — even new and 'modern' orders.

Latrobe's first work in America was the Bank of Pennsylvania in Philadelphia, in 1798. It was not archaeologically conceived, despite its refined Greek Ionic porticoes. It is, on the contrary, a direct and unified conception in which plan, exterior, and interior are all controlled by the needs of the problem. It is unlike any bank built before the Revolution, it is unlike any English prototype, and it is certainly unlike any known classic structure. The enthusiasm with which this design was received shows how ready popular taste was for such a building. The revolutionary importance of Latrobe can be well perceived in the contrast between this refined and spacious design and that of the first Bank of the United States building — usually known as the Girard Bank — in the same city and of almost the same date, designed by Samuel Blodgett. Except for its portico, Blodgett's building is a simple, large, dignified three-story house, barely to be distinguished from many mansions of the period in Salem and Boston. Blodgett had come to Philadelphia from New England, and in this bank he incorporated much of the spirit of the best current work in his native region. The white marble portico which he put on the façade to give it a public character is noble, but it is still in the tradition of English Palladianism. On the other hand, Latrobe's quiet Ionic porticoes, the ample, impressive public space vaulted in masonry, the restrained and classic walls broken only by the necessary windows, the low dome and the graceful lantern with which the whole is crowned — these seem the architecture of a different civilization, and they are. Blodgett's design is of the past; Latrobe's was prophetic of the new American architecture that was still ahead.

Latrobe's Baltimore Cathedral, designed in 1805 and built between 1806 and 1818 (though its portico was not added till 1863), was equally revolutionary. For this Latrobe prepared both classic and Gothic designs. The Gothic design is remarkable in its scale and its broad grasp of basic Gothic principles, yet its detail is naïve; apparently Latrobe was using the Gothic inspiration in the same free and creative manner with which he used his Attic enthusiasm. It was the classic design, however, which the bishop preferred, and this was finally chosen and executed. The Baltimore · Cathedral was, I believe, the first domical church in the eastern United States. It was the first attempt to break completely with the Wren-Gibbs tradition in church design. Its treatment, both outside and in, had the delicacy and freedom of Soane. It is far from being a perfect building; its proportions are probably too wide and low for most tastes, its segmental vaults a little too depressed in effect. But its freedom from traditional precedent and its disdain of any adventitious charm to be obtained through Baroque ornaments are characteristic of their designer and important indications of the popular taste that was developing. The building gains its effect primarily through the use of strong, simple, geometric masses.

Much later, Latrobe actually built two Gothic churches: Christ Church in Washington, and St. Paul's in Alexandria. In both, the exteriors are quaint rather than beautiful, but in both, despite the small cost, he achieved interiors of distinction and beauty perhaps all the more charming because of the occasional naïve character of the Gothic detail.

Latrobe's many houses, although infinitely varied in style, were equally dependent upon simple geometric composition. In them he incorporated the best modern improvements of the day. The Markoe house in Philadelphia, for instance, included a complete bathroom, with bathtub, wash basin, and water closet, as early as 1810. Two of his best houses were in or near Washington — the Van Ness house, and the superb and monumental Brentwood, neither of them now standing. Brentwood was especially significant in its originality of planning. The rooms were wrapped around a great central domed room, which rose to the roof and was skylighted; the smaller rooms projected back to form two wings enclosing a little quiet and protected court with a colon-

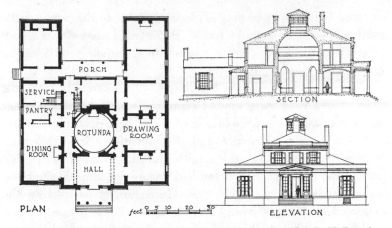

FIGURE 4. BRENTWOOD, near Washington, D.C. Attributed to B. H. Latrobe. (*Cunningham.*) The new freedom in house design; the new restraint in detail typical of much Latrobe work.

naded porch. In both of these houses detail was reduced to a minimum; the effect was gained through exquisite proportion and a kind of elegant restraint.

Despite the charm of some of his minor work, such as the houses for the Pittsburgh arsenal, with their wide proportions, grouped windows, and quiet Regency simplicity, or the Louisiana Bank in New Orleans with its delicate detail and interesting vaulting, it is probably in the Capitol that we get the climax of Latrobe's work. This is not the place for an extended discussion of the controversies which surrounded both the beginning and the end of his employment there; they have been well covered by Fiske Kimball, Glenn Brown, and others.[6] Nor is any more detailed consideration of the history of his works necessary; that, too, has been well discussed in the series of articles by Fiske Kimball mentioned in a foregoing footnote. Until the great store of information that

---

[6] Glenn Brown, op. cit. Wells Bennett, op. cit. 'The First Architect in America, Benjamin Henry Latrobe — Notes and Letters on the Erection of the Capitol at Washington,' *Appleton's Booklovers Magazine,* Vol. vi, No. 3 (September 1905), pp. 345-55. Rexford Newcomb, 'Benjamin Henry Latrobe, Early American Architect,' *The Architect,* Vol. ix, No. 2 (November 1927), pp. 173-7. Benjamin Henry Latrobe, *A Private Letter to the Individual Members of Congress* (Washington: S. H. Smith, 1806). John H. B. Latrobe, *The Capitol and Washington at the Beginning of the Present Century,* an address delivered before the American Institute of Architects, 16 November 1881 (Baltimore: W. K. Boyle [1881]).

exists in the Latrobe papers is made available to the public, little further information can be found. But what is necessary is a consideration of this work in its relation to the whole growth of the Classic Revival ideal in America.

When Latrobe took over the design of the Capitol in 1803, the walls of one wing were almost complete and those of the other well along. The plan of the House wing had been determined. Elsewhere there was a maze of foundations, resulting from the cross-purposes of Thornton and Hallet and the Commissioners. To bring order out of chaos a firm hand was needed, and this Latrobe had. Naturally he made enemies. He began by completing the House of Representatives, with a large oval hall formed of two semicircles connected by a rectangle. It was surrounded by a colonnade of slim Corinthian columns, behind which were the necessary galleries, lobbies, and offices. The plan was based on Thornton's, but the treatment was Latrobe's. In any case this first House of Representatives still had the slim, Adam-like delicacy that characterized the exterior by Thornton. At the same time, Latrobe developed Thornton's plan for the Senate wing, trying to simplify some of its unnecessary complexities, and studied the connection between the wings and the rotunda.

The burning of the Capitol, when Washington was seized by the British in 1814, was architecturally far from an unmixed catastrophe. It gave Latrobe a free hand in the rebuilding of much of the interior, while preserving Thornton's exquisite exterior walls. Latrobe at once changed the awkward oval of the earlier House of Representatives to a semicircle. In the Senate wing much of the lower-floor work, which had been vaulted in masonry, still stood and governed the main disposition; fortunately the lower entrance lobby, with Latrobe's famous corn capitals, could be saved, but the upper floor was largely recast. The result of this rebuilding was the present shape and general design of Statuary Hall and what is now called the Old Supreme Court Room, originally built as the Senate chamber. The essential design of the rotunda which connected the two wings was also largely determined by Latrobe at this time, although it was not completed until later, under Bulfinch.

As the House was first built, its columns were raised on screen walls, with the floor much lower than at present. It proved, in spite of its nobility of proportion, to be most unsatisfactory acoustically, and many years later Latrobe's pupil, Mills, raised the floor to the present height to obviate the worst of this difficulty. Nevertheless, even today Statuary Hall, marred as it is by some of the world's least appealing sculpture, is still a noble and beautiful room.

Studies exist which show that Latrobe had hoped to dome this roof in stone. That he should have so wished is characteristic of the desire for monumental permanence which became a trait of the entire Classic Revival style. Yet with the existing walls and foundations such an attempt would have been, to say the least, foolhardy; one wonders how he even considered this plan to the extent shown in the detailed drawings that he made. It was manifestly impossible, and the idea was abandoned. In the area under the rotunda and in the room beneath the Senate Chamber, however, Latrobe did have an opportunity to use a developed masonry vault; and this room, with its squat columns and its interesting and original vault shapes, is one of the least archaeological and most architecturally significant of any of the Capitol interiors.

This new American Greek Revival, which thus received in Latrobe's work such a distinguished start, is not truly a revival at all. Greek details are used, but imitation of Greek building forms is conspicuously absent. In the United States Capitol both the old Senate Chamber and the old House of Representatives, despite their classic moldings and columns, are new creations, the form of which is felt as the natural result of the demands of the problem, with shapes as different from any eighteenth-century convocation hall as they are from the Senate House in Rome. In them Latrobe was architect first of all, Classic Revivalist second; their classic details were used as certainly more suitable than the eccentricities of any earlier Baroque. Latrobe used these classic details as ways of breaking away from the eighteenth-century manner: as he used them they became new and American.

It is noteworthy also that Latrobe turned to Roman and to Greek inspiration with equal facility, although he preferred, he said, the Greek. The first volume of Stuart and Revett's *The Antiquities of Athens* [7] had been published as early as 1762, and we know that several copies were in this country prior to the Revolution, but up to Latrobe's time the beauty of the forms they showed had gone almost unperceived. It took a Latrobe, perhaps because of his earlier close association with Cockerell and Soane, to understand the exquisiteness of their proportions and the austere richness of their details. Yet, even after his first use of Greek forms in the Bank of Pennsylvania, nearly twenty years elapsed before their use became at all common in American architecture, and then naturally enough it was largely through the work of two of Latrobe's pupils, Mills and Strickland; the Greek Revival phase of the Classic Revival did not become universal in America until the late 1820's. It required the Greek Rebellion, so thoroughly and sympathetically publicized by Byron, to set men's minds aflame with the idea of the beauty and the grandeur that was ancient Greece, just as earlier, immediately after the Revolution, they had been aflame with the idea of the integrity and the grandeur that to them was ancient Rome.

Latrobe, the originator and precursor of this later Greek Revival, expressed in his own work and stated in his own words the principles which later dominated it. ' My principles of good taste,' he writes in a letter to Jefferson, ' are rigid in Grecian architecture. I am a bigoted Greek in the condemnation of the Roman architecture of Baalbec, Palmyra, and Spalatro. . .' But he also says, ' Our religion requires a church wholly different from the [Greek] temples, our legislative assemblies and our courts of justice, buildings of entirely different principles from their basilicas ; and our amusements could not possibly be performed in their theaters and amphitheaters.' [8] This double attitude is well illus-

---

[7] James Stuart and Nicholas Revett, 4 vols. (London: J. Haberkorn, 1762–1816) ; a supplementary volume was issued in 1830.

[8] *The Journal of Latrobe* (New York: D. Appleton and Company, 1905).

trated in his Bank of Pennsylvania (to be treated at greater length in Chapter 4) and his Baltimore Cathedral. In both he uses Greek types of the order, but in both of them the entire basic space conception is fresh, originally conceived, and direct; his admiration for Greek purity of detail never superseded his love for the dignity and the spatial unity of the Roman dome.

Delightful as are his Greek details, he nevertheless did not hesitate at Jefferson's suggestion to create new and American orders, based on the tobacco and the maize, for the United States Capitol. He may have done this the more readily because such an idea had originally been suggested by the French eighteenth-century rationalist architectural critic, Marc Antoine Laugier, who in his *Observations sur l'architecture* [9] hints at such an innovation. Latrobe's new orders made a tremendous stir at the time, and admiration for them was widespread — a sufficient comment on the current desire to develop new and American architectural forms. Even the supercilious and critical Mrs. Trollope was impressed. In her *Domestic Manners of the Americans* [10] she writes:

In a hall leading to some of these rooms, the ceiling is supported by pillars, the capitals of which struck me as peculiarly beautiful. They are composed of the ears and leaves of Indian corn, beautifully arranged, and forming as graceful an outline as the acanthus itself. . . A sense of fitness always enhances the effect of beauty. I will not attempt a long essay on the subject, but if America, in her vastness, her immense natural resources, and her remote grandeur, would be less imitative, she would be infinitely more picturesque and interesting.[11]

Mrs. Trollope was immensely moved by the United States Capitol, in both its interior and exterior.

We were struck [she writes of her first sight of it] with admiration and surprise. None of us, I believe, expected to see so imposing a

9 The Hague and Paris: Desaint, 1765.

10 By Mrs. [Frances Milton] Trollope (London: Whitaker, Trecher & Co., 1832; New York: reprinted 'for the booksellers,' 1832), page 186.

11 An early owner of the copy of this book from which the quotation was taken (who seems to have been one A. V. Zabriskie of Hackensack) has written a marginal note: 'The best idea in the book.'

structure on that side of the Atlantic. . . The beauty and majesty of the American Capitol might defy an abler pen than mine to do it justice.

Later, of the House of Representatives, now Statuary Hall, she says:

The extreme beauty of the chamber was itself a reason for going again and again. [The Senate was] most elegantly fitted up, [the Congressional Library] a very handsome room . . . elegantly furnished . . . the abode of luxury and taste, [and the Rotunda was] indeed a noble hall, a hundred feet in diameter, and of an imposing loftiness, lighted by an ample dome.

Much as Mrs. Trollope hated American manners, American architecture she found almost always surprisingly beautiful, dignified, and gracious. Mills's Washington Monument in Baltimore, which had just been completed when she saw it, delighted her. She is less enthusiastic over Latrobe's Baltimore Cathedral, although she says, ' Its interior, however, has an air of neatness that amounts to elegance.' Nevertheless, she goes on, ' The form is a Greek cross, and a dome in the center; but the proportions are ill-preserved; the dome is too low, and the arches which support it are flattened and too wide for their height.' One wonders if she realized that this very type of low arch was the most English thing in the entire building and a straight legacy from the English work of the Adam brothers and of Soane and their pupils! In Baltimore she was also greatly pleased with the Unitarian Church and the little Gothic chapel that Maximilian Godefroy had built in 1807 for St. Mary's Seminary.[12] She comments on the domes of Baltimore, and contemporary views bring out how strongly the dome of the Cathedral and the greater dome which Latrobe and Godefroy together had designed for the Exchange dominated the city of that time.

Godefroy's career is characteristic of several influences that went into that early melting pot from which a new architecture emerged. A captain in the superbly trained Royal Engineers of Louis XVI, he eventually came to the United States in 1805 and

---

[12] William Sener Rusk, ' Godefroy and Saint Mary's Chapel, Baltimore,' *Liturgical Arts*, Vol. II, Fourth Quarter (June–September 1933), pp. 140–45.

taught ' architecture, drawing and fortification ' in Baltimore; in the chapel for St. Mary's he produced the first church of the Gothic Revival in the United States, and he seems to have been fairly busy as an architect until 1817 or 1818, his best works being the First Presbyterian Church, the Battle Monument, and the Unitarian Church, for which Solomon Willard of Boston modeled the ornament in 1818.[13] He collaborated with Latrobe on the Exchange in 1815; but the collaboration, like all of Latrobe's attempted collaborations, ended in quarrels and mutual dislike. Godefroy left Baltimore in 1819 and exhibited various paintings, many of American scenes, in London during the next few years.[14]

The careers of Joseph François Mangin, McComb's partner on the New York city hall, of Jacques Joseph Ramée, the architect and landscape designer who designed the original plan for Union College at Schenectady, New York, and of Stephen Hallet, the first Superintendent of Construction for the United States Capitol, were surprisingly similar in pattern. All four came to America with great expectations, enjoyed a brief period of tremendous activity and popularity, and later fell into popular disregard or dislike: Mangin merely disappeared from view, Hallet

---

[13] William W. Wheildon, *Memoir of Solomon Willard, Architect and Superintendent of the Bunker Hill Monument* ([Boston:] The Monument Association [c1865]), pp. 39–41. See also Chapter 5.

[14] Godefroy had also been the architect of a courthouse in Richmond, and the original designer of the capitol grounds there — an impressive composition of terraces in the formal French manner. He had married, in Baltimore, a widow, Eliza Spear Anderson, the daughter of Dr. John Crawford, a famous physician who almost anticipated the germ theory in his discussions of yellow fever and other epidemic diseases. Mrs. Godefroy was an accomplished writer and the editor of *The Observer* of Baltimore, in which Latrobe wrote articles on art and architecture and her father articles on medicine.

Between 1819 and 1827 the Godefroys lived in London, where he did a small amount of architectural work; they then moved to France, where after a period of acute poverty he finally obtained a small official position as architect of the Department of Maine, stationed at Laval. Mrs. Godefroy died in Laval on 2 October 1839; Godefroy left there in 1842 and cannot be further traced. Much material concerning them both is included in the Jackson family papers in the possession of the Jackson family in Middletown, Connecticut. Ebenezer Jackson had been one of the Godefroys' most intimate friends in this country, had seen them in France, and apparently had received from them many of the Godefroy papers. These have been published, in part, in the *Maryland Historical Magazine* by Carolina V. Davison, under the title ' Maximilian Godefroy,' Vol. xxix, No. 3 (September 1934), pp. 175–212; and by William D. Hoyt, Jr., under the title ' Eliza Godefroy, Destiny's Footbal,' Vol. xxxvi, No. 1 (March 1941), pp. 10–21.

lived on in obscurity, to die in New Rochelle in 1825, and Ramée and Godefroy left the country.

Joseph Mangin, for instance, first appears in New York in 1794, as an adviser especially recommended by Washington on the fortification of New York. He was soon made a City Surveyor and with his brother Charles established an architectural and engineering practice. In 1802 he appears as co-designer with McComb of the winning design of the New York city hall competition. With the German engineer Goerck he made one of the famous official New York city maps in 1799–1803; this map established the street plan of the entire Corlears Hook area, and the names of two of the easternmost streets, Mangin and Goerck, still preserve the memory of the map makers. As designers of the Park Theater (1795–8), the first St. Patrick's Cathedral (begun in 1809), and the New York state prison (1796–8) at Christopher Street and the Hudson River (where Weehawken Street now runs), the Mangins obviously enjoyed some reputation; yet after the War of 1812 their names appear with less and less frequency. By 1817 they had vanished from the city — perhaps to return to France, now liberated from Napoleon's rule. The work they did was a beautiful, a necessary, a stimulating incident in New York architecture, but it remained an incident only. Probably refugees from the French Revolution, the Mangins evidently remained refugees, at heart aliens, as did their countryman Brunel (later to become the famous English engineer Sir Marc Isambard Brunel), who seems to have worked with them at times. They all vanished quietly out of the American picture, and there was little stir at their departure.

J. J. Ramée had a somewhat similar career, though he made valiant efforts to establish himself in America.[15] An architect and

15 For Ramée, see Codman Hislop and Harold A. Larrabee's ' Joseph Jacques Ramée and the Building of North and South Colleges,' *Union Alumni Monthly,* Vol. xxvii, No. 4 (February 1938), pp. 1–16, and ' The Ramée Plans,' *Union Alumni Monthly,* Vol. xxii, No. 2 (December 1932), pp. 48–53; Harold A Larrabee's ' How Ramée Came to Schenectady,' *Union Alumni Monthly,* Vol. xxvi, No. 4 (February 1937), pp. 111–13, and *Joseph Jacques Ramée and America's First Unified College Plan,* Franco-American Pamphlet Series, No. 1 (New York: American Society of the French Legion of Honor, 1934).

landscape designer, he had fled from the political chaos of the Revolution to Hamburg, where he became a prosperous designer of houses and gardens; he also worked in Denmark. In Hamburg he became acquainted with the famous Anglo-German-American merchant family, the Parishes, and by them was persuaded to come to New York, in 1811, to help open up the vast areas owned by the Ogdens in the northern part of the state. But the work there languished; the grandiose hopes of the developers came to but fragmentary fruition, and Ramée found himself drawn into other work. He designed the beautiful plan for Union College at Schenectady in 1813, following his work for the Fetherstonaugh estate at Duanesburg in 1811–12. Drawings by him for several of the Union College buildings, as well as his general plan, exist at the College and reveal a designer of great ability as well as a draftsman of unusual skill. From 1813 on he seems to have wandered from city to city looking for work. He was in Philadelphia, then in Baltimore. His exquisite triumphal arch design submitted in the competition for the Washington Monument in Baltimore still exists. While there he was in close communication with Latrobe, but he was unsuccessful in establishing the practice he desired, despite such work as the great estate, Calverton, which he designed. At last, failing in his attempt to gain the commission for the design of the Baltimore Exchange — Latrobe and Godefroy were the successful applicants — he returned to France. Much of his Hamburg and Altoona work, and some of his American, he published in Paris under the title of *Parcs et jardins, composés et exécutés dans differens contrées de l'Europe et des états unis d'Amérique*. Of his later French work little is known, but his son Daniel, born in Hamburg, who had been with him in America, became one of the most famous of French architectural historians and an enthusiastic supporter of medievalism in art.[16]

So, like Mangin and Godefroy, Ramée vanished from the

---

[16] Daniel Ramée, the son (1806–87), is best known as the author of the *Histoire générale de l'architecture* (Paris: Amyot, 1860–62) and *Sculptures decoratives, motifs d'ornementation recueillis en France, Italie, et Espagne . . . du douzième au seizième siècle* (Paris: A. Lévy, 1864). He was also the author of the text of many illustrated monographs on medieval building.

American scene, leaving little definite influence except through the Union College work. The remarkable thing in his case is the fact that the work of his we know reveals such an adaptable mind — is in fact so American in spirit. The Union College buildings, like the competition design for the Washington Monument, are neither French nor English in design; but of the two influences it is the English that predominates. Of his northern New York work centered around Ogdensburg and Ogden Island little exists which can be definitely identified. But the Union College work is unique and important; with its central circular building it is the earliest ambitious collegiate group plan in America and may have had an influence on Jefferson's University of Virginia. It is noteworthy that among his existing drawings for the Union buildings those for the central climax, the domed circular building, are conspicuously absent. Had Jefferson seen them? Could they possibly have been borrowed and subsequently lost? The speculation is interesting. . .

Yet despite Ramée's brilliance, despite the adaptable quality of his designs, he never achieved American success. None of his garden designs in the fashionable irregular romantic vein seem to have come to complete realization. Fundamentally his designs looked backward rather than ahead. They were of the Adam-Pain-Stieglitz character. Could this be the reason that in 1817 he returned to Europe a disappointed man, while others less brilliant carved out their own position?

And some of the newer generation of American architects who were growing up, like Mills and Strickland, had equal creative ability though perhaps less technical training, and had in addition a native and thorough knowledge of American materials and American likes and dislikes. Even Latrobe, great architect that he was, seems never to have learned how to get along with American conditions or with the American character. He quarreled with his employers and his associates, and at the end, when he went to New Orleans in 1820 (to die of yellow fever shortly after), it was as an engineer rather than as an architect, and as an embittered and disappointed man. George Hadfield, the Royal Academy gold medal-

ist, was defeated too, though obviously a man of talent who had
come to this country under the best possible auspices. Of him Latrobe writes, somewhat acidly:[17] ' He loiters here, ruined in fortune, temper, and reputation, nor will his irritable pride and
neglected study ever permit him to take the station in the art which
his elegant taste and excellent talent ought to have obtained.' It
may have been that in writing this Latrobe was unconsciously giving voice to his own character. ' Irritable pride ' seems likely to
have been at least in part the reason for his own many troubles.[18]
Could it have been that in both of them there was evidenced something of that same supercilious lack of understanding of the real
spiritual basis of American life which blinded the eyes of Mrs.
Trollope again and again and poisoned her comments? Latrobe's
Journal gives certain indications that this was so. Robert Mills,
Latrobe's student, though he had his ups and downs, never had to
face the history of conflict and bitterness that dogged Hadfield
and Latrobe. William Strickland, another of Latrobe's pupils, like
his master gained fame and considerable fortune from his skill as
an architect and engineer, but unlike him went on from triumph to
triumph, to be buried finally under the rotunda of the Tennessee

17 Op. cit. p. 133.
18 The paramount importance of Latrobe, not only as the initiator of the Greek
Revival but also as the real founder of the architectural profession in the United
States, becomes more and more strong as his career is studied. Brilliant as engineer
and architect, an inventor, a skilled technician in many lines, a man who could wield
a trenchant and powerful pen, Latrobe was a many-sided genius whose career was
hampered so frequently by his own restless ambition, his own confidence in his
talents, and his impetuous and at times petulant temperament. A practically complete body of his letters and many sketchbooks and drawings exist, in the possession
of Mr. Ferdinand C. Latrobe of Baltimore. It is to be hoped that eventually they
may find publication; they are a priceless source of material not only on American
architecture and building but also on American engineering, American speculative
business, and American politics. Toward the end of his life he was considering having Rudolph Ackermann of London publish the body of his work, but the project
was canceled by his premature death. His only publication of architectural interest
in America, outside of controversial pamphlets about the Capitol design, is an extended, correct (as of its time), and extremely well-written article on acoustics,
running to some twenty pages in the first American edition of the Edinburgh Encyclopaedia (Philadelphia: Joseph and Edward Parker, 1832). He also wrote for
this work an article on civil architecture, which apparently was lost. The one published is merely the British article from the original publication. For a more extended consideration of B. H. Latrobe, see my article, ' Benjamin Henry Latrobe:
The Man and the Architect,' in the *Maryland Historical Magazine*, Vol. xxxvii, No.
4 (December 1942), pp. 339–60.

state capitol he had designed. Surely there is more than accident in this. Already, notwithstanding the English heritage of the young country, the Englishman like the Frenchman, whatever his skill, remained culturally an alien. Only the rare exception like John Haviland (1792–1852) became thoroughly Americanized. Haviland's case is particularly instructive (see page 68). He seems to have struck at once into the heart of American architectural life. He realized that American architecture was in a state of flux and that the future was going to be fundamentally different from the past.

The history of the United States Capitol is an excellent example of, as it is the great monument to, this rapid Americanization of architecture. Placed superbly because of the sureness of the imagination of the Frenchman, Pierre L'Enfant, it owed its architectural form successively to the West Indian, Dr. William Thornton, to the Frenchman, Stephen Hallet, and to the Englishmen, Hadfield and Latrobe. The basic defects in its planning, its confusion of circulation, and its much broken up interior are the living evidences of continual misunderstandings, quarrels, and changes in idea. Its essential monumentality is Hallet's; the dignity of the simpler parts of the elevation, Thornton's; the exquisite refinement and perfection of its larger interiors, Latrobe's. Yet none of these men was able to complete the building or to impose his single personality upon it. Its completion remained for the American-born Bulfinch, its architect from 1817 to 1831, who alone seems to have been able to pacify recalcitrant Congresses, to work in harmony with not always sympathetic committees, and somehow to produce a whole which incorporated all the contributions of the other men: this was the building that filled Mrs. Trollope with astonishment and delight. In taste Bulfinch's own contributions are minor, except for the colonnade on the west front, which recalls the Boston state house. Yet architecture is not a matter of details or of refinement alone; it is not merely a matter of superficial form. In large public buildings it is the expression of more than a personal attitude. It is the erection in concrete and tangible form of a people's dream. In the United States Capitol it required the careful and sympathetic administration of Bulfinch to accomplish this. Here one gets the real birth of an American architecture, and here one finds a true expression of the definite character of the American Classic Revival, which out of so many diverse influences — from France and England, from Rome and Greece — but equally out of American conditions, out of American materials and ways of work, out of the very texture of American democracy, created a living architecture.

CHAPTER 3

AMERICAN ARCHITECTURE COMES OF AGE

A STUDY of the work of Latrobe's most famous pupils, Robert Mills (1781–1855) and William Strickland (1787–1854), reveals another of the important elements in the new American Classic Revival — its structural inventiveness and integrity. In their work the Greek Revival movement reached its maturity, based upon soundness of construction and excellence of execution. Robert Mills had as one of his chief interests the development of fireproof building; Strickland called himself sometimes a civil engineer, sometimes an architect — canals, bridges, and breakwaters occupied him almost as much as buildings did, and to both classes of work he applied the same sincerity and the same care.

Mrs. Gallagher's biography of Robert Mills [1] brings out with the greatest clarity the importance which matters of construction and pure engineering had in that architect's work. Her research has demonstrated too that the character of his buildings is an almost perfect expression of the character of the man; that their faults are reflections of his over-seriousness, as their virtues are a reflection of his strength and integrity. In addition, Mills's life shows another element almost as important for the development of a new architecture — the fact that he was deeply interested in all of the political and economic conditions of his day. In his monumental *Statistics of South Carolina*,[2] for instance, he finds opportunities to discuss education, the treatment of the Indians, the penological system of America at the time, and even the position of women. His sense of social responsibility was enormous; necessarily then, through feeling himself a part of the national life

---

[1] H. M. Pierce Gallagher, *Robert Mills, Architect of the Washington Monument, 1781–1855* (New York: Columbia University Press, 1935).

[2] Charleston, S. C.: Hurlbut and Lloyd, 1826.

around him, he could not help but express in his architecture its aspirations, its hesitancies, and its enthusiasms.

The period of the 1820's and 1830's was in many ways unique in the history of America. The balance between a growing industrial system and an expanding agriculture was still held in some sort of equilibrium. The settlement of the new lands west of the Alleghenies, which was progressing with extraordinary rapidity, had outlived the wave of land speculation that succeeded the American Revolution, and had not yet embarked on the new and disastrous era of speculation that was to follow the Civil War. The settlers were mainly men of solid eastern background, many of them with considerable literary culture; and the new settlements which they were building were furnished with academies and even colleges almost as soon as they had their city halls and courthouses. Industrial development in the East was sufficient to keep alive inventiveness and to furnish a sound economic basis for an extraordinary urban development. It had not yet, however, reached that rapidity of growth which destroyed standards almost before it had achieved them; in construction the era of jerry-building was still in the future.

To many it seemed almost as if the promises of the Revolution were being literally fulfilled; as though a new era of peace, quiet prosperity, and cultural progress was at hand, which should be a new thing on the earth, quite different from the fruits of the aristocratic cultures of Europe. Slavery was being seriously questioned, but the terrific sectional differences which later would almost break the country in two were as yet only rumbling prophecies that could, despite the bitterness of the anti-Jackson party, be forgotten by the optimist. And to a great extent people felt that cultural advances were as important and as significant as material prosperity. There is evident throughout the period an element of pride in the achievements of American painters and American writers; this was, to be sure, partly an expression of hope, but nevertheless it may be taken as a sound indication of popular interest and a generally high standard of popular taste. Mrs.

Trollope [3] mentions the significant fact that Americans seemed more hurt when she disparaged American painters than when she disparaged American morals. She comments at various times on the lively interest she met everywhere with regard to the new artists America was producing, as well as on the naïve feeling of many Americans that what they were doing was necessarily better than what was being done abroad at the same time. To her this was one of the most amusing facts in American life; trained as she was in the lush and arrogant gentility of the English portrait painters of her time, she could have but little understanding of the vivid honesty and directness of American painters like Inman and Vanderlyn and Morse, whose merits we are only just beginning to appreciate. We are at last learning that the respect and admiration these artists enjoyed during their lifetime was more than justified and that their popularity speaks well for the taste of their contemporaries.

The impulse to artistic expression was widespread at this time in America. Almost every little country weekly had its column on literature and the fine arts. Everyone was writing verse. The great movement toward literary and artistic expression that blossomed in the Cambridge of Emerson and in the paintings of Morse and Inman was nation-wide and deeply rooted. Mrs. Trollope tells with great amusement of a conversation she had in a hotel at Wheeling, West Virginia, with a young mother ' little like an American female of what they call good standing.' The woman was boasting, naïvely enough, of being the author of a satirical novel directed against the Adams faction and called *Yankee Doodle Court*, as well as of many verses and a comedy called *The Mad Philosopher*. However crude such productions were, their very existence indicates a populace that was eager for native artistic expression and ready to welcome it.

Such a culture will naturally attempt, in architecture, more than it can achieve, yet such a culture will have instinctive regard for permanence, for integrity, and for largeness of conception.

[3] Mrs. [Frances Milton] Trollope, *Domestic Manners of the Americans* (London: Whitaker, Trecher & Co., 1832; New York: reprinted ' for the booksellers,' 1832).

These things the architecture of Robert Mills had. His work is sometimes over-heavy, sometimes crude and almost stodgy in detail, but it is never finicky, it is never merely pretty, and it is all built to last for hundreds of years. Occasionally the simple dignity of his conceptions overrides all his imperfections in detail, and then we have his Washington Monument in Baltimore and the extraordinary conception of the great obelisk to the first President in Washington. The original Mills design adds at the bottom of this simple obelisk a tremendous Greek Doric oval ' Pantheon ' which undoubtedly if built would have damaged its absolute and unified perfection, just as his original conception of the Baltimore monument surrounds the simple shaft with bands of rather meaningless applied ornament; yet in the actual work, which at least in the case of the Baltimore monument was finished under his supervision and directly from his drawings, this superfluous ornament has disappeared and the conception stands in its magnificent simplicity. A somewhat similar change from drawing to building can be seen in the fireproof Record Office in Charleston, South Carolina. The drawing shows a pediment over the colonnade; the executed building replaces this with a cruder but much more powerful sloped parapet. In almost every case Mills's buildings seem to have gone through a similar process toward an increasing power, an increasing austerity, as the conception was executed.

And this same almost dogged austerity is paralleled by the power and simplicity of his structural design. The great Washington office buildings for the Treasury, for the Post Office (now the Land Office), and for the Patent Office as originally built are all masonry-vaulted throughout, and the entire plan conception of each is based on and controlled by the skillful accommodation of the repeated bays (produced by his system of barrel and groined vaults over individual offices) to the functional needs of the building. Seen in this light, the simple plans of the Post Office and Treasury buildings become not merely intelligible but admirable. The large number of buildings designed by Mills which still function — marine hospitals, small local customs houses, the Washington work, and so on — shows the permanence of his construction. The main-

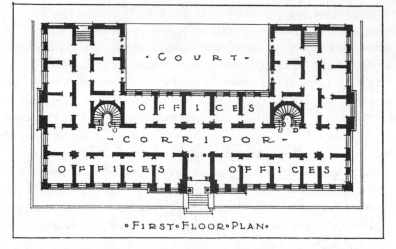

FIGURE 5. POST OFFICE DEPARTMENT, Washington, D.C. Plan. Robert
Mills, architect. (*Gallagher.*) The straightforward rhythmical simplicity typical
of Mills's masonry-vaulted public buildings.

tenance on such buildings is negligible in comparison with the
maintenance on later, more rapid, and more fragile types.

It is characteristic that Mills was never wedded to the copying of Greek forms in his architectural detail. The freedom with
which he treated classic precedent in the Monumental Church at
Richmond is typical of his whole fresh approach. For instance, in
a manuscript which is evidently a foreword to a proposed book
entitled *The Architectural Work of Robert Mills*, printed in the
appendix to Mrs. Gallagher's biography,[4] he writes as follows:

Books are useful to the student, but when he enters upon the practice
of his profession he should lay them aside and only consult them upon
doubtful points or in matters of detail, or as mere studies, not to
copy buildings from.

In the same article he makes his principles of design even more
clear, writing:

Utility and economy will be found to have entered into most of the
studies of the author, and little sacrificed to display; at the same time

4 Op. cit. p. 170.

his endeavors were to produce as much harmony and beauty of arrangement as practicable. The principle assumed and acted upon was that beauty is founded upon order, and that convenience and utility were constituent parts.

And a little bit later:

The subject of domestic economy in the arrangement of private houses has since undergone considerable improvement, particularly in France, and many useful hints are to be gathered from French works on architecture, but the author has made it a rule never to consult books when he had to design a building. His considerations were — first, the object of the building; second, the means appropriated for its construction; third, the situation it was to occupy; these served as guides in forming the outline of his plan.

To be sure, the colonnade of the Treasury building is Ionic and that of the Patent Office the Doric of the Parthenon, but there is no Greek analogy for the Baltimore monument nor any Egyptian obelisk five hundred feet high. Moreover a drawing of a proposed marine hospital shows the classic solecism of two Doric orders, one over the other, supporting the verandas that were integral parts of all the marine hospital schemes, and the lower order is as completely non-archaeological and as free in style as any work of the néo-Grec architects in France. This freedom in detail parallels the structural ingenuity; both became essential factors in the American Greek Revival.

Mills's churches reveal another important feature of the period — the development of new types of building as a result of new building problems. The age was one in which preaching became a major element in American religion; the oncoming era of great popular revivals that was to develop later was already being foreshadowed in the growing crowds that flocked to hear a series of extraordinarily eloquent and popular preachers. To meet this demand the old type of Wren-Gibbs Colonial church was manifestly unsuited, and it is characteristic of the free architectural thinking of the period that Mills had no qualms about developing a series of Protestant churches entirely new in conception, based on the new popularity of eloquent preaching. The auditorium type of church can be said to have been invented by him. One example was the Sansom Street Baptist Church (1808) in Philadelphia, a round church in which four thousand people could comfortably be seated; a circular baptistry was in the center, a pulpit at the end of one diameter, and almost completely around the church was a large stepped gallery supported, as an old print seems to show, on simplified and much modified Corinthian columns. Of architectural ornament there was little or none save the architraves around the arched windows and a cornice between the circular wall and the ceiling. The Octagon Unitarian Church, also in Philadelphia, was opened in 1813; this seems to have been somewhat similar in its interior arrangements. The third of his auditorium churches was the Monumental Church (1812) in Richmond, built as a memorial to the seventy-one who had died in the destruction by fire of the theater that had originally stood on the same site. In his first scheme, which strangely enough was presented as the actual church in the illustrations of John H. Hinton's *History and Topography of the United States*,[5] there is in addition to the octagonal domed structure a monumental portico, forming a sort of loggia, and opposite it a high tower. The executed building is much simpler and in many ways more forceful, and the modified order of the entrance motif is as interesting as it is original, although one may regret that the same kind of slanted parapet wall he had used in the Charleston Record Office in lieu of a pediment replaces the continuous horizontals of the original sketch. The first of a series of monumental rotunda churches was the Circular Church in Charleston, South Carolina, built during 1804–6. This had a great rotunda ninety feet in diameter, with the usual low lantern crowning a dome, and a square projection at the entrance supporting a tower and fronted by a portico of six columns; like the Philadelphia churches, it had an almost continuous gallery around the room, supported on slim posts which aped no existing classic order.

In all of these churches there are many details which might be criticized, but in their basic architectural conception and as space

<hr>

5 Vol. II (Boston: S. Walker, 1844), p. 444.

compositions they reveal a truly architectural mind. They were novel and successful answers to the new demands made upon church design by the age of great American preaching, and their design profoundly affected the general conception of Protestant churches for many decades afterwards.

The houses Robert Mills designed are perhaps less distinguished, less different from the common run, than is his other work. This is understandable; not only was the private house client perhaps more demanding in what he wanted, and possessed of less radical and more conservative ideas, but also Mills's own imagination worked best on a larger scale. Yet his Richmond houses have a large, quiet solidity without, and simple, delicate, and lovely detail within; they have a certain distinction quite different from that of the domestic work of Jefferson or Thornton or Latrobe. It is in some of the earliest houses he designed that his talent shows at its best — for example in the row, part of which still stands, sadly altered, on Ninth Street in Philadelphia. The old photographs show these houses as a group with unusual, gracious dignity, subtly composed with a frankly asymmetric arrangement, and with wide, clear wall spaces. The large recessed segmental arches of the pseudo-Palladian windows are treated with special skill, and the houses reveal a search for simplicity and large scale that is typical of all his designs.

If Mills's work is significant of the architectural thinking of his time, the method he chose of preparing himself for his profession is even more significant. He himself evidently felt this strongly; he claimed that he was the first native-born American regularly trained for the profession of architecture. Of course he was not the first native-born architect; his predecessors were, so far as we know, universally trained as building craftsmen (masons, bricklayers, carpenters, woodcarvers) or else were frankly amateurs — architects, as it were, only by accident. Mills was neither; wishing to become an architect, he began his career by going to college, specializing probably in the classics, which would be of help to him. While in college he wrote an essay on the Tuscan order, the earliest writing of his we have. Later in his course he designed a building for the college. With this cultural background he then worked for a number of years in the best architectural offices he could find — a short time with Hoban, the architect of the White House; two years with Jefferson, where his draftsmanship became assured and exquisite; then with Latrobe, where work on the masonry-vaulted 'Gothic' Bank of Philadelphia gave him a first-hand knowledge of masonry construction and so no doubt deeply affected his later work. This is obviously the education of a professional man, not that of a craftsman, and it shows Mills's feeling of the need for an architectural profession in America. Exactly what made him conscious of this — what made him choose so definitely and wisely the education he received — will probably always remain a speculation. It may have been his admiration for the work of such 'imported' English architects as Latrobe, who were professionally trained; or it may merely be that with unusual prescience he realized that only through professional architects could America receive the creative, independent architecture it needed — that on the contrary the way of the craftsman and amateur architect was necessarily the way to produce bookish detail and reactionary design.

It is difficult to evaluate precisely the entire body of work done by Mills. His taste was far from impeccable; his forms are frequently over-heavy, blocky, even stodgy. His plans (except his church plans) are almost entirely without that play of changing interior space, that combination of curved and rectangular rooms, and that variety which distinguish the best work of his masters, Latrobe and Jefferson. Yet his plans are always eminently practical, common-sense, efficient. In his more important masonry-vaulted public buildings they show a feeling, entirely new in America, for the integration of structure and arrangement and effect. As expressions of this, his buildings had an enormous influence in setting the high governmental standards that were to rule the best public building till 1850; they led inevitably to the solidity, the grandeur, and the permanence of such monuments as the interior of the New York customs house, the state capitols of Ohio and Tennessee, and the third New York Merchants' Exchange.

Even the heavy solidity of his detail was not without its value at the time. In the decade from 1810 to 1820 there was still all too much of the effeminate, attenuated, over-wrought ornament of the Late Colonial; still all too much dependence on the pretty, ' fancy ' forms in the books of Adam and Pain. The woodcarvers had been trained in this ornament and had become so skillful that they were elaborating it for its own sake; reedings and tiny moldings and fans and paterae came from their tools with an all too flowing facility. To such a flood of the merely pretty, the austere restraint and the architectonic quality of the detail Mills designed were needed and effective antidotes.

One more quality of Mills's work must be noted — its dominantly and creatively national character. So far as I know, Robert Mills was the first American designer who realized that the new country demanded a new, an American, architecture. The country's needs were her own, her materials were peculiarly hers, her climate differed essentially from that of Europe. No mere borrowed or derivative architecture could ever fill these needs or use these materials in the best and most appropriate way. But there was a deeper emotional tinge to this desire for an American architecture. The young country was full of pride — pride in her birth, pride in her rapid development economically — and full of confidence in her future. Her separateness from Europe had never been more deeply felt, and even the growing habit of a European journey on the part of those who could afford it only emphasized this conviction. That what would be called today an inferiority complex had something to do with making this pride at times overweening and supercilious cannot be denied; yet surely there was a real foundation of achievement in literature and scholarship and the arts, and some artificial screaming of the eagle is understandable.

Thus America came to want not only art, but an American art; Mills was merely true to his time in feeling that his architecture must be, above all, American. One has only to read his comparison of the Greenough Washington, nude to the waist and draped below, with the Washington of Houdon to realize how deeply he distrusted the 'Greek god' borrowed plumage of the Greenough work. He writes:

Our artists, therefore, should never forget the original models of their country, neither the customs nor manners of their people, when they execute works of art either for their government or for their fellow citizens. Examples of the failure of these artistic works to give satisfaction to the public are unfortunately too numerous; the colossal statue of Washington within the eastern enclosure of the Capitol at Washington — a splendid work — has failed to meet public approval, not only from the costume used but the sitting attitude of the figure . . . but let the American visit the capitol at Richmond and view the statue of Washington [Houdon's], and all other statues fall into the shade before this beautiful and correct representation of the father of his country. This last statue is approved by the million, where but a few admire the others named, and I say to our artists: Study your country's tastes and requirements, and make classic ground *here* for your art. Go not to the old world for your examples. We have entered a new era in the history of the world; it is our destiny to lead, not to be led. Our vast country is before us and our motto Excelsior. The importance of the subject must plead for this digression.[6]

Mills gives evidence here not only of his common sense but of his artistic judgment as well. It was not a Greek Zeus, a European deity, that he wished as a representation of Washington, but a simple, modern, heroic man, an American. And it was the same with his architecture. Robert Mills was ahead of his time, perhaps, in this feeling; but more and more the architects who were his younger contemporaries and his immediate followers came to agree with him. In his and in their work the desire to produce an architecture specifically for America was supreme.

The work of William Strickland reveals many facets. He is characteristic of that pioneer American ingenuity in doing many different things which at its worst produces the jack-of-all-trades, good at none, who whittles useless and intricate toys, sitting on the steps of the country store, but at its best gives rise to an all-round genius of extraordinary productivity. Strickland, the son

6 Gallagher, op. cit. p. 156.

ABOVE, Ramée's competition design for the Washington Monument, Baltimore. (*Gallagher.*)
BELOW, Latrobe's Gothic design for the Baltimore Cathedral, side elevation and section. (*Kimball.*)

ABOVE, LEFT, Mills's original design for the Washington Monument, Washington. ABOVE, RIGHT, Mills's original design for the Washington Monument, Baltimore. (*Both from old engravings, Gallagher.*) BELOW, LEFT, Washington Monument, Baltimore, as built. (*Gallagher.*) BELOW, RIGHT, Sansom Street Church, Philadelphia. Robert Mills, architect. (*Avery Library.*)

Record Office, Charleston, S.C. Robert Mills, architect. (*Gallagher.*) ABOVE, Mills's original elevation study. BELOW, Record Office as built.

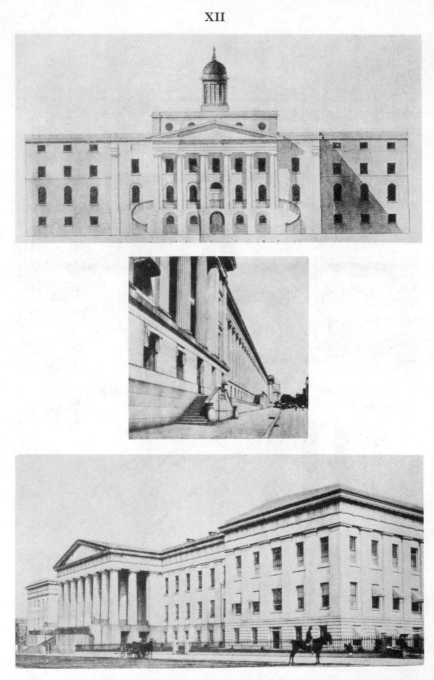

Buildings by Robert Mills: TOP, Insane Asylum, Columbia, S.C., architect's elevation. (*Gallagher.*) CENTER, Treasury Building, Washington, colonnade. (*Avery Library.*) BOTTOM, Patent Office, Washington. (*Ware Library.*)

Buildings by Robert Mills: TOP, LEFT, Ninth Street row houses, Philadelphia. (*Gallagher.*) CENTER, LEFT, Archer House, Richmond. (*Gallagher.*) TOP, RIGHT, New Bedford Customs House. (*Author.*) BOTTOM, Wickham House (*Valentine Museum*), Richmond. (*Gallagher.*)

Tennessee State Capitol, Nashville. William Strickland, architect. (*Wiles-Hood*.) ABOVE, exterior. BELOW, interior, House of Representatives.

Two Strickland churches at Nashville, Tenn. (*Wiles-Hood.*) ABOVE, St. Mary's. BELOW, First Presbyterian Church.

ABOVE, Belmont, near Nashville, Tenn. William Strickland, architect. (*Wiles-Hood.*) BELOW, Athenaeum, Providence, R.I. William Strickland, architect. (*Author.*)

of a carpenter, even as a child became an accomplished draftsman. He worked at scene painting with the best craftsmen of the day during his early teens. By the time he was fifteen, plates drawn and engraved by him were being published in periodicals with as high standards as the *Analectic Magazine*. Finally deciding to become an architect, he entered the office of Latrobe and from the teaching and the example of that great master's combined interest in architecture and engineering, in graceful detail and municipal water supply, he learned to associate and to combine the double careers of engineering and architecture without doing injustice to either. Naturally, like Mills, such a man would develop an attitude toward building design in which largeness of conception and perfection of structure were much more important than any mere questions of ornament.

Strickland's taste was surer than that of Mills, though perhaps in strictly architectural conception he was less experimental. Yet his innovations were many. To Mills's originality and sense of construction he added another quality, a more personal characteristic — grace. His Philadelphia work will be considered in Chapter 4; here it is sufficient merely to call attention to its originality, finesse. The frank delicacy of the wing porches of the Marine Hospital, the broad proportions and the suavity of his Philadelphia Mint, and especially the subtleties of the Philadelphia Exchange with its graceful curved colonnade, its slim lantern, and the quiet, broad proportions of the rectangular portion — all these are eloquent of a designer just as different from his former fellow employee Mills and from his master and teacher Latrobe as his quicker, lighter, more mercurial nature was different from theirs. The contrast in the work of these three men, and the difference between their work as a class and the erratic and creative variety of the early designs of Alexander Jackson Davis on the one hand or the refined elegance of the detail of Minard Lafever on the other, reveal perfectly the enormous variation in personal expression possible within the broad confines of the Greek Revival; it should set at rest forever the notion of the Greek Revival as an inhibiting or regimenting influence.

And a similar freedom is to be found in two other works by Strickland: the Athenaeum at Providence, Rhode Island, and the New Orleans Mint. Strickland was chosen as architect of the Providence building when the preliminary plans made by its Providence architect, Russell Warren, proved too large and too expensive.[7] Warren helped in the execution of the design; apparently he had entertained no hard feelings at having been supplanted by one so distinguished. The building Strickland designed (the contract and drawings for which are still preserved in the Athenaeum files) was a simple, low, wide, rectangular building with a Doric *in antis* porch. It made the best use of the hillside site to provide a large, light basement for meeting rooms, and the main floor was approached by an impressive flight of stone steps with a lovely cast-iron 'Greek' railing. Although the building has been much added to and altered since its construction, its front still remains unchanged; the broad, almost 'unclassic' nature of its proportions and the skillful handling of scale so that in spite of its relatively small size it still has a definite sense of dignity, almost of grandeur, are typical of the free artistic imagination Strickland possessed.

Quite different though equally original is the New Orleans Mint, now used as a city prison. A long, simple, rectangular building, it has a façade that gains importance through its slightly projecting central pavilion crowned with a pediment. In front of this is a portico of Strickland's favorite Ionic columns, spaced rather widely and crowned, not with the typical pediment, but with a flat roof. Delicate acroteria decorate the eaves. The whole is raised on a high basement above the damp New Orleans soil, and it has those graceful, original proportions so characteristic of Strickland's work. Even today, condemned to a use so different from that for which it was designed, it remains one of the most distinguished of the earlier buildings in New Orleans.

[7] See W. D. M.'s 'The Construction of the Athenaeum Building,' *The Athenaeum Bulletin*, Vol. III, Nos. 2, 3 (September, December 1930), and 'The Architect of the Athenaeum Building,' *The Athenaeum Bulletin*, Vol. x, No. 3 (December 1937); Grace F. Leonard and W. Chesley Worthington's *The Providence Athenaeum; a Brief History*, 1753–1939 (Providence: for the Athenaeum, 1940).

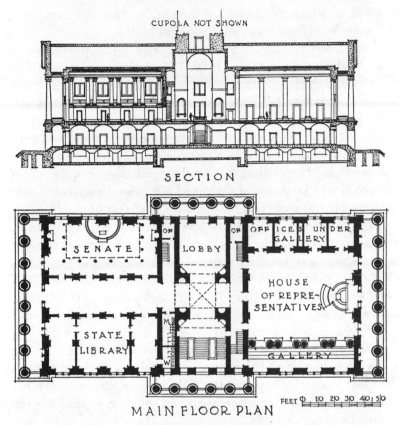

CUPOLA NOT SHOWN

SECTION

MAIN FLOOR PLAN

FEET 0 10 20 30 40 50

FIGURE 6. TENNESSEE STATE CAPITOL, Nashville, Tenn. William Strickland, architect (*H.A.B.S.*) Ingenious and independent planning and large scale in interior design.

Strickland's last years were occupied with the design and superintendence of the Tennessee state capitol at Nashville. Here again he broke with whatever tradition in capitol design there was, deserting entirely the formula of the dome flanked by wings. Instead he built a simple, long, narrow, rectangular structure, with pleasantly spaced, large window areas, and for decoration depended upon four Ionic porticoes at the ends and in the center of either side, with a lantern above similar to the one he had used in the Philadelphia Exchange. The whole crowns most effectively the hill on which it stands, and reveals, as does the Providence Athenaeum, his sensitive feeling for site.

One late house by Strickland deserves mention — Belmont, near Nashville, dating from 1850. It is still recognizably within the Greek Revival tradition, yet in its broadly spreading flat cornice and its rich and delicate cast-iron balconies it shows its architect to have been alert not only to the traditions of the locality, as evidenced by the verandas, but also to the new currents in American style. Its interiors are frankly what we consider today as mid-Victorian, but the building as a whole reveals a general dignity of composition, a largeness of scale, and a graciousness of ornament that are far removed from the ordinary heaviness of their time.

The Tennessee capitol has been adversely criticized for its applied porticoes and its lantern. Still, whatever one may think of these details, it is definitely original, definitely the work of a man thinking in terms of a problem and a site. Its creation proves its designer an architect rather than an archaeologist. It is fitting that within its crypt Strickland should have been buried.

Out of all this artistic effort grew necessarily two things: one a new appreciation of the professional position of the architect; the other a greater and greater realization of the necessity for originality in design — for creation, not copying, as the basis for an American architecture.

As a result of the professional development came the feeling that a professional organization of some kind was necessary. Latrobe had struggled during all his American career against the old system of the builder-designer. Mills had always been strictly professional; Strickland had, as well. Strickland and his pupil Thomas U. Walter were two of the three who issued in 1836 the original invitation to architects for a meeting to found such an association; the third was Alexander Jackson Davis of New York. The outcome of this meeting was the founding of the American Institution of Architects, which, though it enjoyed but a brief life, was an important and probably necessary precursor of the present American Institute of Architects, founded twenty years later.

This first group consisted of Davis, Strickland, Walter, Haviland, Isaiah Rogers, Reichardt, Schmit, and Thomas Thomas. At the second meeting various other important architects were added, including Ithiel Town, Minard Lafever, Asher Benjamin, Alexander Parris, and Ammi B. Young. Walter preserved this professional interest throughout his life. During the later thirties and early forties he was a professor at the Franklin Institute, and many of his lectures are summarized in its *Journal*. Later he was to become and remain for many years president of the American Institute of Architects, a worthy successor to its first president, Richard Upjohn.

The second result, the growing demand for originality, for creation, in American architecture was everywhere evident, in the writings as well as in the work of the best designers. It runs through all the writings of Mills. It is innate in any number of the sketches Davis made, largely for buildings never executed. And it crops up again and again in the lectures and the papers of the Franklin Institute. The layman and the cultured amateur might prefer their Greek forms ' straight ' and admire buildings for correctness rather than for invention, but the attitude of the architect was different. Here are but two examples of their ideals, both from the same year, 1841. Robert Cary Long, Jr., distinguished Greek Revival architect of Baltimore, in an essay called ' The Degeneration of Modern Architecture,' [8] says that for him imitation is the secret of the alleged deterioration of architecture. He goes on:

Must men progress in goodness and in wisdom? Then, must architecture also! Is man so progressive? Then is architecture also, though, we may not know it or see it. Architecture must manifest the changes that are taking place in society, the greater ones, we hope and believe, that are yet to come.

And a little later:

It is as much out of the rule of rationality to think it possible to reinvigorate architecture by forcing it into an antique mould, as to expect that, if disgusted with manhood, we can bring back simplicity

[8] *Journal of The Franklin Institute*, Vol. xxxii, No. 4 (October 1841), p. 246.

and innocence by putting on the garments of youth. Architecture must grow naturally. . . Let us all try and see which of us will first produce something in the art peculiar — characteristic — suited to the age — national.

So spoke the architect. And Thomas U. Walter said in one of his lectures before the Franklin Institute: [9]

The popular idea that to design a building in Grecian taste is nothing more than to copy a Grecian building is altogether erroneous; — even the Greeks themselves never made two buildings alike. . . If architects would oftener *think* as the Greeks thought, than to *do* as the Greeks did, our columnar architecture would possess a higher degree of originality and its character and expression would gradually conform to the local circumstances of the country and the republican spirit of its institutions.

[9] Published in the *Journal of The Franklin Institute,* Vol. xxxi (Third Series Vol. i), No. 1 (January 1841), pp. 11–12.

CHAPTER 4

THE GREEK REVIVAL IN PHILADELPHIA

PHILADELPHIA saw alike the birth and the death of Greek Revival architecture in America: its birth in the Bank of Pennsylvania, which Latrobe designed in the spring of 1798; its death — or should one say its swan song? — in the Ridgeway Branch of the Library Company, designed in the 1870's by Addison Hutton, far out on South Broad Street. And, in the years between, several of the most important Greek Revival architects in the country established their homes in Philadelphia, found there a profitable field for their activity, and designed for it some of the most remarkable of its buildings. Latrobe, Mills, Strickland, Haviland, and Walter all contributed much to the appearance of the rapidly growing city, and in the work of all, whether it was strictly Greek or not, the ideals of the new architectural movement were enshrined and perpetuated.

It is not strange that this should have been the case. Philadelphia was, in the early years of the republic, the undoubted metropolis of the country. It was, in its own characteristic staid way, the center of culture and of art. Boston was still, in architecture, largely under the sway of English late-Georgian inspiration, so beautifully re-created in New England in the domestic work of Bulfinch, the exquisite interiors of McIntire, and the early handbooks of Asher Benjamin. New York, struggling out of the devastation caused by the long British occupation, was still dominated by the transitional work of John McComb, Jr., the Mangins, and such architects as Josiah Brady and the young Martin Thompson; Greek forms were not to become popular there till the later 1820's.

Latrobe's Bank of Pennsylvania was therefore an epoch-making work. Latrobe (1766–1820) brought with him the ferment of the new ideas that were sweeping over English building. And part of this ferment was the new appreciation and understanding of the exquisite refinement of Greek architectural detail, especially as revealed in *The Antiquities of Athens*, by Stuart and Revett.[1] It is interesting that, although there had been several copies of this work in America for years, no attempts by architects or builders to utilize its inspiration in this country were, to my knowledge, made prior to Latrobe's arrival. A movement toward more classic design there certainly had been, as evidenced for instance in Samuel Blodgett's Girard Bank. But not even Jefferson, the great champion of classic form, seems ever to have loved or used the Greek inspiration.

The reasons for this basic conservatism undoubtedly lay in the system of apprentice instruction that controlled the development of builders and architects, and also perhaps in the occasional dominance of such craft organizations as the Carpenters' Company of Philadelphia, which tended to crystallize building forms and details and, through price books and rules of work, to discourage innovations.

Owen Biddle's *The Young Carpenter's Assistant*[2] is characteristic of this conservatism. Its designs, much more restrained and austere than those shown in Asher Benjamin's plates, are all in the dignified Georgian style of the late Philadelphia Colonial. Although occasionally they show some of the delicate attenuation of the New England work, generally they have that kind of quiet correctness so typical of the Philadelphia region. Of the newer classical feeling championed by Jefferson there is scarcely a trace; of even the delicate, creative modifications of the Adam spirit that characterized the work of New England, New Jersey, and New York there is little sign.

Latrobe's Bank of Pennsylvania, with its Greek Ionic porticoes and its graceful low dome in the Soane manner, with its open and monumental plan and its combination of classic dignity and originality, was thus a completely new thing, sapping at the entire

[1] London: J. Haberkorn, 1762–1816. A supplementary volume was issued in 1830.

[2] Philadelphia: Benjamin Johnson, 1805; 2d ed., Johnson and Warner, 1815.

foundation of the older conservative taste.[3] It was the work of a professional architect, of a man trained first of all as a designer and not as a builder. The later conquests of the new Greek movement, in Philadelphia as elsewhere, were very largely the results of the gradual change from the system of builder-architect to that of the professional architect. It is not strange that between the two systems there existed deep-seated incompatibility and a bitter struggle. Nor is it strange that in Philadelphia, then so largely the cultural center of the country, the new system of professional architects as building creators should have won some of its earliest victories.

The Bank of Pennsylvania is important, too, because it shows so definitely the true aim of the new so-called Greek Revival movement. It is in no sense a copy of any ancient building. It does not aim at archaeological correctness, except perhaps in detail. Its plan was developed simply and functionally from the necessities of the building, with a new kind of simplicity and openness. It was a creation and not a copy, although the Ionic order used was taken from the Ionic temple on the Ilissus near Athens.

It is equally characteristic that Latrobe was too much the architect to be limited even to Greek inspiration. He had a large practice in Philadelphia, which included the Burd, Waln, and Markoe houses, the waterworks pumping station, and alterations for the President's House and the University Medical School. The houses were restrained, monumental, refined — quite in the Soane or Regency manner. In them there is scarcely a trace of the Greek forms. Sedgeley was ' Gothic ' — perhaps the first Gothic Revival building in the country — and in the Bank of Philadelphia, built in 1808 from Latrobe's designs under the superintendence of Robert Mills, the Gothic style appeared again, even to the use of masonry ribbed vaults.

The Centre Square pump house, with its Greek porticoes and its high central dome, is also a typical piece of Latrobe design.[4]

---

[3] Fiske Kimball, ' The Bank of Pennsylvania,' *The Architectural Record,* Vol. xliv, No. 2 (August 1918), pp. 132–9.

[4] Costen Fitz-Gibbons, 'Latrobe and the Centre Square Pump House,' *The Architectural Record,* Vol. lxii, No. 1 (July 1927), pp. 18–22.

Like the bank, it combines the Roman dome with Greek details in a structure based on the functional necessities of the building. It is a creation and not a copy, for to Latrobe archaeological forms were always inspirations only.

Latrobe's influence on Philadelphia was not limited to his own work and did not cease upon his removal to Washington, for his two most distinguished pupils and assistants, Robert Mills and William Strickland, both practiced in Philadelphia also, and in their work one can trace with remarkable clarity the gradual shift toward a greater and greater dependence on Greek detail, until the final disappearance of the Soane type of English influence allowed the emergence of a completely new kind of Greek Revival architecture essentially native, such as is best represented in Strickland's Marine Exchange of 1836.

Robert Mills (1781–1855) with Jefferson's advice entered the service of Latrobe, for whom he worked for several years, occasionally also designing buildings on his own. His Burlington County prison at Mount Holly, New Jersey, designed in 1808 and still in use, was built during his Philadelphia residence. It illustrates especially well the basic dignity of composition for which Mills was seeking — bigness of scale and solidity of construction — and, although the actual Greek details upon it are limited to the guttae under the inscription panel, its austere restraint has qualities not unlike those we associate with the Greek inspiration. His other Philadelphia work — such as Washington Hall, in 1809; the row of houses on Ninth and Locust Streets, in the same year; and the two auditorium-type churches, the Sansom Street Baptist Church of 1808 and the Octagon Unitarian Church of 1813 — has only occasional uses of Greek detail. But here again, as in the Burlington County prison, the spirit if not the detail shows the influence of a study of Greek forms and reflects the new movement toward a creative American architecture that was such a marked feature in the best work of the time.

The famous Upper Ferry bridge over the Schuylkill River was another example of this creative independence. Lewis Wernwag was the engineer and Robert Mills the architect. They worked in the closest co-operation; just where the work of one began and that of the other ended is difficult to determine. In any case the bridge was a superb construction with a span of 344 feet; at its time it was said to be the largest single-span bridge in the world. The graceful curve of its timber-trussed approach was sheathed by Mills with the simplest covering, the line of the passageway was indicated by paneling and windows, and at each end there was a simple arched and colonnaded pylon, monumental but not ostentatious. It is typical of the new spirit in American architecture, which so largely conditioned the best work of the Greek Revival period, that here engineering and architecture were integrated so beautifully.[5]

There was one other important work in Philadelphia in which the influence of Mills may perhaps be traced — the waterworks on the Schuylkill River, built between 1811 and 1819. The design is usually attributed to Frederick Graff, who was undoubtedly the engineer in charge, but an examination of the Graff drawings in the Franklin Institute reveals a perhaps significant fact. All of them are extremely detailed so far as the machinery is concerned, but surprisingly sketchy with regard to the buildings themselves. It would seem impossible that the buildings should have been built from them; it is perhaps rather to be surmised that Graff made these drawings for the machinery from another set, now lost, which controlled the architecture. It is also perhaps significant that Mills had been in close touch with the entire project and had in 1810 refused the presidency of the company.[6] It is therefore not beyond the bounds of possibility that Mills designed the buildings, or at least had great influence in their creation. Certainly many of the details of the powerhouse have the closest resemblance to other Mills work of the time, such as the Ninth Street houses; stylis-

---

[5] For Robert Mills, see H. M. Pierce Gallagher's *Robert Mills, Architect of the Washington Monument, 1781–1855* (New York: Columbia University Press, 1935), and Robert Mills's *A Model Jail of the Olden Time: Designs for 'A Debtors Gaol and Work House for Felons,' for Burlington County, State of New Jersey . . .* summarized by Captain George J. Giger (New York: Russell Sage Foundation, 1928).

[6] Ibid., p. 128. See also Harold Donaldson Eberlein's 'The Fairmount Waterworks, Philadelphia,' *The Architectural Record*, Vol. LXII, No. 1 (July 1927), 57–67.

tically the combination of restraint and delicacy would indicate a strong influence from Mills or someone exactly like him.

Mills left Philadelphia in 1814, and the history of his later work, when he had become a complete convert to the Greek Revival, belongs to other localities. It is nevertheless interesting, and important for a correct understanding of the whole Greek Revival movement, that Mills in this early work of his in and around Philadelphia followed so creatively the ideals of Latrobe. With him architecture was creation above everything else, and the spirit was more important than the details; restraint, power, gracious detail in small amounts, structural daring, and engineering ability were all combined. The spirit thus set had not a little to do with the future development of Greek Revival architecture in Philadelphia.

Yet in the large sense the true Greek Revival was only to come later, despite the revolutionary innovations in Latrobe's Bank of Pennsylvania and the waterworks buildings. In its second and more permanent appearance, after the War of 1812, another English-born architect played a great part — John Haviland (1792–1852). Haviland, born at Gundenham Manor, had studied with the accomplished James Elmes in London and had traveled widely on the continent of Europe in his youth and had received as well an excellent technical education. Apparently he came to Philadelphia with Hugh Bridport, in 1816, in connection with the proposed founding of a school of architectural drawing. Not only was Haviland a designer of force, imagination, and originality; he was also gifted with a kind of adaptability that allowed him to adjust himself to his new American environment with amazing rapidity and success. Much more than was the case with Latrobe, he became a thorough American — for Latrobe, like certain other immigrant architects of the time, always preserved a kind of supercilious contempt for American ways and American tastes, and this was continually interfering with his professional career. There is not a trace of this attitude to be found in Haviland, as we may judge from his own works. He threw himself heart and soul into the problems of his new home; he learned American ways and American materials, and launched into his new career with an enthusiasm

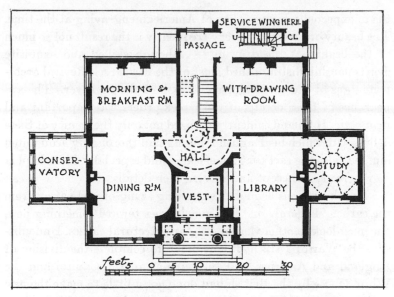

FIGURE 7. MOODY HOUSE, Haverhill, Mass. Plan. John Haviland, architect. (*Haviland.*) Rooms of pleasant and unusual shape combined inventively to produce both ease of service and axial grandeur of effect.

that in itself had something of the true pioneering spirit. He must have been personally attractive, for he speedily gained a wide practice not merely in Philadelphia but all over the northern part of the eastern seaboard. In his first book, *The Builders' Assistant . . . By John Haviland, Architect, and Engraved by Hugh Bridport, Artist,*[7] the designs show among other things the Moody house, which Haviland designed in Haverhill, Massachusetts — a house, by the way, that still stands, though all local record of its design by a Philadelphia architect has long since disappeared.

But *The Builders' Assistant* is noteworthy for many things besides the buildings it shows; in the history of American architecture it is especially significant because in it, for the first time in an American published work, plates of the Greek orders were shown — and well shown — in those delicate line engravings that became so characteristic a feature of the American architectural books published before 1840 and give such eloquent evidence of

[7] Three vols. (Philadelphia: John Bioren and the authors, 1818–21).

the unexpectedly high quality of American engraving at the time. The beauty of these plates very frequently is the result not so much of the beauty of the drawing — although skilled and exquisite draftsmanship distinguished most of the new Greek Revival architects — as of the sensitiveness and skill of the engraver.[8] The appearance of these details of the Greek orders was important and prophetic. Haviland evidently realized not only the beauty of these details with which his English training had thoroughly acquainted him, but also the fact that America — and especially Philadelphia — was ready to accept and receive such details.

For the reasons behind this growing swing of taste away from the earlier ' Federal ' or ' Regency ' types toward something new, one must look to other than purely architectural causes. Undoubtedly the War of 1812 had done much to complete the division of England and America, and the burning of the Capitol and the White House by the British had done not a little to make the new nation conscious of the fact that henceforward it must think as well as act for itself. In Philadelphia, too, there was added the influence of a vivid and consequential personality — that of Nicholas Biddle, traveler, ambassador, dilettante, and banker. As early as 1806 he had visited Greece, fallen victim to its beauty, and in 1814 published in *The Port Folio* George Tucker's paper, ' On Architecture,' which set up Greek forms as the most suitable inspiration for an American architecture. All his life Biddle preserved this interest in architecture and enthusiasm for Greek form. It was he doubtless who was responsible for the competition program for the Bank of the United States (later the customs house) in Philadelphia, in which a Greek temple type was suggested, just as it was he who later, in 1836, caused Walter to add, probably against his own better judgment, the temple-type portico to Andalusia, Biddle's estate. Socially, financially, and culturally Biddle was a

---

8 For example, at the Society for the Preservation of New England Antiquities there is a portfolio of early drawings by Asher Benjamin. They are frequently scratchy, uneven, and rather crude — something like the crude engravings (perhaps engraved by himself?) in his earliest book, in 1797. In all the later books, on the other hand, the plates have an extraordinary definiteness, directness, and clarity. One suspects this quality to have been due to more skillful engravers rather than to any revolutionary change in Benjamin's own drawing.

leader in Philadelphia, and it is probably largely owing to his enthusiasm and example that, once started, the Greek movement in Philadelphia grew by leaps and bounds, in large measure anticipating the taste of the rest of the country by at least a decade.[9] Haviland's book *The Builders' Assistant* is in its detail almost entirely Greek-inspired. But it is seldom archaeological, for Haviland, like Latrobe and the best of the later Greek Revival architects, realized the dangers of pure copying. The details he shows, especially his mantelpieces and doors, are free sometimes almost to the point of eccentricity. In them he attempts to express the Greek feeling for restraint and delicacy, and he makes occasional uses of Greek anthemia and rosettes; yet never does Greek precedent *dictate* design, and he has no fear of combining purely new, creative forms with Greek detail.

In 1837 Haviland issued another work, a revised edition of Owen Biddle's *The Young Carpenter's Assistant*,[10] to which he had added some forty-eight new plates. Here also, though by that period popular taste had become thoroughly Hellenized and demanded a more accurate following of the Greek forms, Haviland retained his early creative approach; although the designs shown are more disciplined and less eccentric than those of the earlier work, they are still definitely personal and creative. The house, the bank, and the church all show the bold invention, the rather heavy-handed composition, and the power accentuated by spots of delicacy, which are the hallmarks Haviland left upon his work. With Haviland, as with all the best of the Greek Revival architects, design came first.

The list of Haviland's work in Philadelphia is a long one. Not all of it by any means is Greek; for, just as Philadelphia was pre-eminent in the adaptation of Greek detail, so, as we have seen, it was one of the earlier places in which Gothic was introduced. It was the Gothic, of course, or rather a sort of simplified ' Castel-

---

9 Thus, whereas the first Greek-Doric-temple-type façade in Philadelphia was planned for the new bank as early as 1818, it was not until 1827-8 that Ithiel Town and Martin Thompson, in the Ascension Church, designed New York's first similar portico.

10 Philadelphia: M'Carty & Davis, 1837.

lated' style that marked Haviland's extraordinary design for the Eastern State Penitentiary, authorized in 1821 though not completed until 1829 — a building that, with Haviland's other prison designs, completely revolutionized prison conceptions in the Western World and had the honor of being perhaps the first American structure to be studied by European building commissions or committees sent across the ocean specifically for that purpose. This is an important fact and typical of Haviland's architectural approach. The problems of penology were troubling many thinkers at the time. Robert Mills came back to these questions periodically after his first experience with them in the design of the Burlington County prison. Individual cell confinement as a means to order and reform was not, naturally, the invention of Haviland alone, nor was the introduction of labor — agricultural or industrial — as part of the prison regimen; but it was Haviland who took these ideas, absorbed them, integrated them, and expressed them in actual structures magnificently planned for their specific purpose. Especially important was his development of the radiating plan to allow simple supervision. The prisons he designed were such an enormous improvement over what had gone before that many of their ideas and arrangements became accepted standards of prison design in the nineteenth century. Like certain other improvements they worked almost too well, for they aided in the unchangeable crystallization of prison forms, so that the new and more creative penological ideas of today have frequently been retarded and hampered in adoption by the very efficiency of developments of the old Haviland type.

Though the penitentiary was Gothic, and of a simple, straightforward kind of Gothic that makes its walls and gates even today things of power and beauty, his favorite style remained Greek. He did houses, churches, theaters, and commercial buildings, and, though perhaps the work is little remembered today, his must have been one of the busiest architectural offices in the town. The colonnade of the First Presbyterian Church of 1820 still shows today his simple good taste, as does the front of St. Andrew's. The old Walnut Street Theater of 1809 revealed the same power

Two buildings by B. H. Latrobe: ABOVE, Bank of Pennsylvania, Philadelphia, architect's perspective. (*Maryland Hist. Soc.*) BELOW, Pumping Station, Philadelphia Waterworks. (*Painting by Krimmel, Pennsylvania Academy of Fine Arts.*)

XVIII

Buildings by John Haviland: TOP, First Presbyterian Church, Philadelphia. (*Wallace.*) CENTER, Moody House, Haverhill, Mass. (*Coolidge.*) Plan, Figure 7. BOTTOM, The Tombs, New York. (*New York Pub. Lib.*)

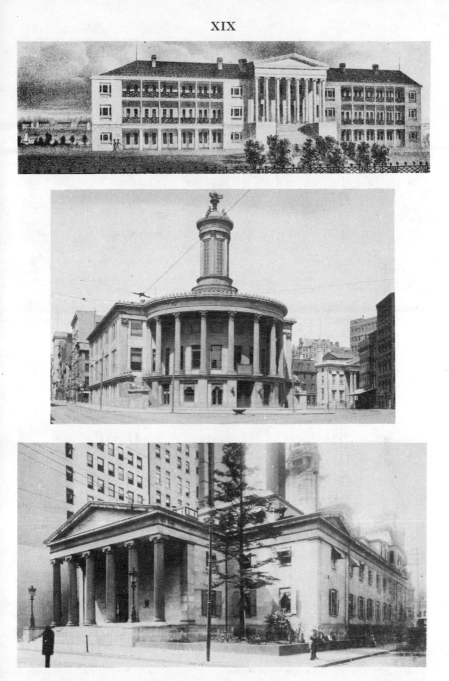

Three Philadelphia buildings by William Strickland: TOP, Naval Hospital. (*Pennsylvania Hist. Soc.*) CENTER, Exchange. (*Wallace.*) BOTTOM, United States Mint. (*Pennsylvania Hist. Soc.*)

Branch Bank of the United States (later Customs House), Philadelphia. William Strickland, architect. (*Avery Library*.) ABOVE, exterior, Davis drawing. BELOW, vaulted banking room. Plan, Figure 8.

as well as the basic monumentality of his conceptions. He was the designer also of the Franklin Institute building of 1826 and of the powerful front of the Deaf and Dumb Asylum on South Broad Street, begun in 1824, which still stands as part of the School of Textiles. It is interesting to note that in this building Haviland, with his customary independence, combines arched recesses in the end pavilions with a Greek Doric portico in the center. He was also the architect of the Philadelphia Arcade, somewhat similar to the famous Providence Arcade by Russell Warren, built about the same time; and several of the ' rows ' and ' squares ' that were being erected in Philadelphia in the 1830's were from his design.

Of his later work less is known. He was the architect of the famous New York Halls of Justice — ' the Tombs ' — of 1836–8, where he experimented with the Egyptian forms as freely and creatively as he had elsewhere used the Greek and the Gothic. A. J. Davis, who won second prize in the competition, claims that his own competition façade had been Egyptian and was the inspiration for the actual work.[11] Even if the idea was Davis's, the touch is unmistakably that of Haviland; after all perhaps the most important quality in this building was its basic monumentality and its closely organized and efficient plan, which remained at least partly workable even when the building had been far outgrown and was housing many times the number of inmates for which it was intended. He was also the architect of the handsome Newark courthouse (1837), likewise an Egyptian design.

Even more important than Haviland in the Greek Revival architecture of Philadelphia was that extraordinary man, William Strickland (1787–1854), engineer and architect, painter and engraver — one of the most interesting personalities, as he was one of the most brilliant and original designers, of the entire Greek Revival movement.[12]

11 See the Davis diary in the print room of the Metropolitan Museum of Art, New York.
12 E. Lester Gilliams, ' A Pioneer American Architect,' *The Architectural Record*, Vol. xxiii, No. 2 (February 1908), pp. 123–35. See also Joseph Jackson's *Early Philadelphia Architects and Engineers* (Philadelphia [n. p.], 1923), which contains an excellent list of Strickland's work. It is good to know that a biography of this significant American is being prepared by Agnes Addison Gilchrist.

Like Mills, Strickland received his chief architectural training from Latrobe, with whom he worked between August 1801 and November 1805 (and possibly later) ; yet the history of his association with Latrobe is quite different. Mills evidently was a plodding, hard worker, absolutely dependable, on whom Latrobe leaned heavily in the carrying out of his ideas. It was he, for instance, who laid out most of the drawings for Latrobe's Baltimore Cathedral (Latrobe himself adding the decorative details), as it was he who superintended the greater part of Latrobe's Philadelphia work — pre-eminently the Bank of Philadelphia. Strickland, on the other hand, appeared to Latrobe as a scatterbrained person, a boy upon whom he wasted much affection, but in whom he saw much potential talent.[13]

Latrobe was a good friend of William Strickland's father, a bricklayer and carpenter-builder of the characteristic old type. The elder Strickland was Latrobe's master mechanic on the ill-fated early construction of the Delaware and Chesapeake Canal, and through that connection young William entered Latrobe's employ. His employment was spasmodic, for he was continually running away, encouraged like a spoiled child by his mother, who probably was responsible for breaking up her husband's association with Latrobe and so preventing him from participating in the Capitol work when Latrobe went to Washington. To my knowledge there is little information with regard to the actual work William did while with Latrobe. He was fired and taken back several times and finally discharged; evidently he was too independent-minded, too light-hearted and curious, to endure patiently the regular draftsman's routine.

William Strickland's first architectural commission, the Philadelphia Masonic Hall (1810), was designed in a strange kind of

---

[13] For these and other details of the relation between Latrobe and his pupils I am indebted to Mr. Ferdinand C. Latrobe, of Baltimore, who was kind enough to furnish me with digests of many of the Latrobe letters of this period. It is to be hoped that this magnificent collection of the letters of one of the most important early American architects, a man so closely associated in so many ways with the development of the young United States, will eventually find publication, and that the originals of the letters may be preserved in a public institution worthy of their possession.

wiredrawn Gothic. From old engravings it appears not to have been a building of especial beauty, and perhaps its burning in 1819 was no great loss; yet it is interesting because it shows the young architect experimenting with and creating new forms by means of the less well known and more questionable of the various architectural manners then accessible. Evidently he was not himself too well satisfied with the building, for on its completion he deserted the profession for almost a decade, becoming a Patent Office draftsman, painter, scene designer, and engraver, and apparently traveling widely through the East. Thus he worked in New York with Hugh Reinagle on scenery for the Park Theater. He painted portraits as well as landscapes; he made aquatint plates. His brother George had made engraving his life work, and for a while William emulated him; but here too the drudgery of engraving must have been uncongenial. Nevertheless he was learning an enormous amount during this period, apparently keeping open eyes for matters structural as well as aesthetic. That he was a draftsman of extraordinary ability is shown by his two large monochrome paintings of New York scenes, now in the New York Historical Society, which are among the very best presentations of the New York of that time in existence. Stokes has dated them as between 1809 and 1814.[14]

Despite his successes in these other fields, Strickland was too deeply imbued with a structural sense to remain permanently satisfied with painting. He was a born architect. As he developed, the structural and engineering sides of architecture became as important to him as the aesthetic, and in his middle life he practiced engineering as gladly and with as great a feeling of satisfaction as he did architecture. He returned to Philadelphia and resumed his architectural practice sometime around 1818. What turned his mind definitely back to architecture was undoubtedly the winning of the competition for the second building of the Bank of the United States, which has already been mentioned. The design of the bank has frequently been attributed to Latrobe on the ground

---

[14] I. N. Phelps Stokes, *The Iconography of Manhattan Island* (New York: R. H. Dodd, 1915–28), Vol. III, Plates 81a and 81b, and description on page 549.

of the resemblance between the completed exterior and certain signed drawings of Latrobe; but the Latrobe drawings show a plan quite different from that of the executed building, and the records are clear.[15] It was the competition program that determined the temple type. Given the size of the lot, the designers of the exterior had only to choose between a six- or an eight-column portico and to determine the order.[16] If two competitors chose an eight-column Parthenon Doric as the basis for their schemes, the exteriors must necessarily have been similar. Strickland was awarded the first prize in the competition, and early records universally attribute it to him. It is shown, for example, in the background of a portrait of him by John Nagle, and in the *Analectic Magazine* for March 1819 he is given as the architect; hence I feel that the entire credit for the design as well as for the construction of the present structure should be his.[17] And there is one additional bit of evidence, perhaps even more convincing: *The Literary Gazette* (successor to the *Analectic Magazine*) on 12 May 1821 (Volume I, No. 19), published an editorial note which, after speaking of current doubts about the identity of the architect of the Bank of the United States, states unreservedly that the credit belongs to Strickland alone and that it was Strickland who had won the first prize in the competition.

The winning of such an important competition was a great feather in the cap of the young architect. It was undoubtedly the greatest possible opportunity, for of all the buildings then being projected this one allowed the most monumental treatment. Its architect was at once raised to a position of fame in the eyes of his contemporaries, and when the building was finally completed it won

---

[15] Fiske Kimball, 'The Bank of the United States,' *The Architectural Record,* Vol. LVIII, No. 6 (December 1925), pp. 581–94.

[16] The program was published in the *Gazette of the United States,* 9 July 1818. The exact wording is, in part:

'The ground plan will include an area of almost ten or eleven thousand square feet in a rectangular figure. . . The building will be faced with marble; and have a portico on each front. . .

'In this edifice the Directors are desirous of exhibiting a chaste imitation of Grecian Architecture, in its simplest and least expensive form.'

[17] The *Analectic Magazine,* Vol. XIII, No. [3] (March 1819), describes the elevation as 'Elevation of "New Bank of the United States" . . . according to the design of Mr. Strickland, which has been adopted by the directors.'

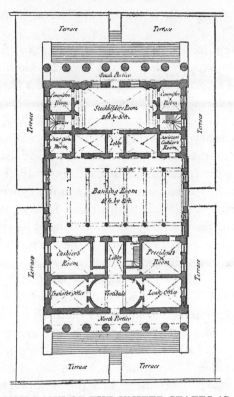

FIGURE 8. BRANCH BANK OF THE UNITED STATES (Customs House),
Philadelphia. Plan. William Strickland, architect. (*Haviland.*) Impressive
vaulted fireproof rooms within the temple outline.

instant popularity and tremendous acclaim. The average person, of
course, saw only the beauty of the Greek colonnade and the lovely
proportions of the pediment; the connoisseur admired it for its
reproduction of Greek grandeur.[18] Architecturally, however, its importance is due to much more than its superficial dress; its plan was
magnificently conceived and its interiors were as efficient as they
were beautiful and well proportioned; in addition it proved conclu-
sively that Greek details could be domesticated in America and that
modern problems could be efficiently answered in buildings based on

[18] It is a matter of great satisfaction to all lovers of American architecture
that the repair and maintenance of this monument have at last been assured, after
years of disgraceful neglect.

Greek inspiration. With it the Greek Revival in America came of age.[19]

In the design for St. Stephen's Church (1823) Strickland returned, not too happily, to his early love, the Gothic, treating it with a kind of original simplicity and heaviness that seems to us today perhaps merely quaint; but in the Swedenborgian Church, later the home of the American Philosophical Society, which Judge Kane in his obituary of Strickland calls that ' cunning little specimen of *bijou* architecture,' [20] detail distinctly Gothic was combined with a dome in the freest and most charming way. The result was a building slightly oriental in flavor, simple, graceful, inviting, and yet dignified in spite of its small size. Like all the best architectural work of the period in America, it owed its special character and its loveliness less to the ' style ' that inspired it than to the innate creativeness of its designer.

But it was in the general frame of the Greek Revival that Strickland found his most congenial and most accomplished expression. His work is all extremely personal, his touch quite unlike the austere grandeur of Mills or the daring experimentalism of A. J. Davis. Gracefulness is in it all, and frequently there is a remarkable freedom of imagination in the way the forms derived from Greek precedent are used. This touch appears markedly in the wide spacing of the colonnade, in the stress on the broad horizontals, and in the quiet wall treatment of the United States Mint at Philadelphia, the cornerstone of which was laid on 4 July 1829. It was an unusually happy example of the application of the Greek orders to a public building, and the existing photographs show

19 In his *Diary* (New York: Dodd, Mead & Co., 1927) under date of 14 February 1838, Philip Hone says of the bank: ' The portico of this glorious edifice, the sight of which always repays me for coming to Philadelphia, appeared more beautiful to me this evening than usual, from the effect of the gas-light. Each of the fluted columns had a jet of light from the inner side so placed as not to be seen from the street, but casting a strong light upon the front of the building, the softness of which, with its flickering from the wind, produced an effect strikingly beautiful. How strange it is that in all the inventions of modern times architecture alone seems to admit of no improvement — every departure from the classical models of antiquity in this science is a departure from grace and beauty.'

20 *Proceedings of the American Philosophical Society*, Vol. VI (Philadelphia: the Society, 1859), p. 28. This obituary is full of valuable information with regard to Strickland's personality as well as his work.

how the interest of its plan as well as the quality of its detail gave it a definite character unlike that of the work of any other designer. Its destruction long since is but one of many similar tragedies which have characterized the history of the growth of Philadelphia as well as that of many other American cities. Architectural excellence has been the last thing considered (if it is considered at all) in judging whether or not an economically obsolete building should be preserved.

The Naval Hospital, or Naval Asylum, of Philadelphia has had a better fate and enjoyed a longer life. Built over a period of years, between 1827 and 1848, it illustrates even better than does the Mint the imaginative freedom with which Strickland attacked his problems. Its central pavilion has an eight-column portico in the Greek Ionic order — an order to which Strickland was especially drawn, using it not only here in Philadelphia on the Mint and the Naval Hospital, but also in New Orleans on the United States Mint there, now a city prison. It is not, however, in this main portico that the chief merit of the Naval Hospital lies, but rather in the bold way in which this powerful central block is combined with the ward wings and in the tall slim porches which line them. Here the problem has controlled. The desire for outside balconies off every ward (a prophetic use of open-air hospital bed space which held true for the naval hospitals both of Mills and Strickland, but was forgotten in much private hospital work until very recently) has been the governing element in the design, and Strickland has succeeded in merging into one integrated whole the monumentality of the central entrance motif and the functional delicacy and openness of the wings.

But it was undoubtedly in the Exchange, opened in 1836, that Strickland achieved his Philadelphia masterpiece. The site was unusual — one of those little uneven spots developed where occasional changes in street direction modify the monotonous rectangular pattern of the old Penn plan of Philadelphia. Built in what was then the financial and business center of the town, the building makes the most of its irregular lot and the interesting vistas opened up at the street intersection on which it stands. Strickland conceived the building as a large rectangle fronted by a circular curve; in every detail of the design the quality of each part is stressed, and yet the whole is brought into the most perfect unity. The windows of the rectangular part are wide, the motion horizontal, the wall surfaces simple; and this, the simpler part of the design, is by itself one of the most charming examples of that true aesthetic functionalism which underlies so much of the best Greek Revival work. But this alone is not enough; in addition horizontal lines lead inevitably to the climax of the building, the superb curved colonnade of the front, with its conical roof and its delicate lantern founded on the Choragic Monument of Lysikrates. Here each part of the composition falls so naturally into place that even the purists can find little to criticize in the derivative nature of the detail. Not only as a building, but also as a piece of city decoration, the Philadelphia Exchange takes its place as one of the great creations of American architecture. Here again the modern state of the building is pathetic; the sprawling sheds that surround the purity of the old forms and fill every vacant square foot of the building lot, like the ruthless wrecking of the interior, seem to bear witness both to a callous disregard of architectural beauty in itself and to a discouraging lack of municipal pride or understanding of the simplest facts of municipal beauty.

Strickland's work in architecture was not limited to these few important structures. Like Mills and Haviland he designed row houses and ' squares,' but only greater and more careful research today could pick out of the lovely red brick blocks that still remain from the city of a century ago those fragments which may rightly be attributed to him. And his fame during his life came almost as much from his engineering skill as from his work as an architect. He was sent to England in 1825 by the Pennsylvania Society for the Promotion of Internal Improvements, to study canals and other public works; his report, published by the society in Philadelphia in 1826, shows the keenness of his observation, his vivid sense of structure, and his enthusiasm for the newest and most modern engineering ways. It is significant, too, that the most important of the published works that bear Strickland's name is *The*

Public Works of the United States of America,[21] of which he was
one of the editors — a sumptuous volume of engravings showing
the advanced accomplishments that the young country had made
in canal, bridge, and factory building and in harbor improvement.
No one can run over these plates in the most cursory fashion without feeling that a century ago there was the closest possible connection between engineering and architecture — that in beauty of
workmanship and sound integrity of design, in grace of detail and
care in appearance, one's aesthetic sense could be satisfied and need
not be expected suddenly to ' black out ' when confronted with a
work of ' mere utility.' If there is one lesson to be learned alike
from the work of Latrobe and of Strickland it is that; and if
America had remained true to this vision the terrific sprawling
ugliness of late nineteenth- and twentieth-century industrial development would never have occurred.[22]

As with Latrobe, Strickland's influence was not limited to the
work which he himself designed, for two of his pupils and employees went on to achieve fame as architects — one, Gideon
Shryock, carrying into the West all the skill and technique he had
learned from his work with Strickland; the other, Thomas Ustick
Walter, practicing largely in Philadelphia but more famous for
having been the final designing architect on the United States
Capitol and for adding the present House and Senate wings and
the great dome which so magnificently crowns it.

Shryock (1802–80) was himself a designer of the greatest
skill; his own work, like that of his master, Strickland, is controlled
by a definite personality. He never parrots his master's work; still
he owes undoubtedly to the work he did with Strickland that great
integrity, that sureness of touch, that feeling for apt and graceful
detail so obvious in his work.[23]

---

[21] London: John Weale, 1841.

[22] It is noteworthy that among the subscribers to the Strickland report for the
Pennsylvania Society were the architects Robert Mills and Alexander Parris.

[23] For Shryock, see *Dictionary of American Biography* (New York: Charles
Scribner's Sons, 1928—); Rexford Newcomb, *Old Kentucky Architecture* (New
York: William Helburn, 1940); and my own ' The A.I.A. Meets in Kentucky,'
Pencil Points, Vol. xxi, No. 5 (May 1940), especially pp. 284–6, as well as photo-
graphs of Gideon Shryock's work in the same number.

Like Strickland, Walter (1804–87) was the son of a builder
and bricklayer. At fifteen he entered Strickland's office, but after
a brief training he left and for seven years studied painting and
the natural sciences. In 1828, however, he returned to Strickland's
office again and in his year there, with the background his own
study had given him, doubtless was able to learn with the greatest
rapidity what Strickland had to offer. He was closely associated
with the Franklin Institute, first as student and later, from 1829
on, as lecturer and ' professor ' in architecture; the *Journal* of the
Institute contains many papers by him. As in the case of Haviland,
a prison was his first important commission; as in the case of
Strickland, he turned to Gothic for his first work and in the Philadelphia county prison (1829) produced a design that, although
lacking the simple power of Haviland's work, has a quaintness and
an imaginative quality, even in its caricatures of Gothic forms,
which are not without beauty. His debtors' prison (1831) was
Egyptian and perhaps the least successful of all his buildings,
though interesting as showing the widening spread of architectural
knowledge — a spread that was eventually to bring with it all the
superficialities of eclecticism.

Walter seems to have been much under the influence of Haviland; the whole character of his executed work has in it with few
exceptions more of the robust power of Haviland than of the exquisite grace that characterized Strickland. Once he had embraced
architecture, he seems to have been extraordinarily busy, building
up a large office and putting out a tremendous amount of work
of all kinds. In 1833 he was appointed architect of Girard College,
and in connection with its design he made a trip to Europe to study
solutions of similar problems there. He was architect of the Wills
Eye Hospital, Preston's Retreat, the First Universalist Church,
and the Crown Street Synagogue. All of this work is powerfully
composed and occasionally, like Haviland's, somewhat ponderous,
but all of it is sound and forthright. It is thus surprising to come
suddenly upon the extreme delicacy of the detail that runs through
parts of Girard College, and upon the rich lightness of the Greek
Corinthian order that is the glory that surrounds its main building.

Girard College was an extraordinary creation in every way. The will of its founder had gone to meticulous lengths in setting dimensions and types for the building, so that in its design Walter was hardly a free agent. The amazing thing is that with such drastic limitations he was able to achieve a building essentially so unified and beautiful. It was perhaps unfortunate that here, as in the Theseum portico he added to Andalusia for Nicholas Biddle, Walter was so obviously carrying out an amateur's wish rather than designing the best solution to the problem, for Mrs. Gilchrist has, by a diligent search through the building committee's reports, discovered that the suggestion for the colonnade and temple form came from Nicholas Biddle. Walter's original design, which won the competition, had been an entirely different scheme.[24]

This building is largely a forgotten masterpiece and its beautiful colonnade, crowning so successfully the slope it dominates, is seldom visited by understanding architects. Its magnificent interiors are deserted and empty. Even when people remember it, it is largely with a half-contemptuous shrug — a gesture they give mistakenly to so many Greek Revival works as being merely reproductions of temples in a land far away. In its own day, in fact, it was often severely criticized. A. J. Davis, who knew it well and claims to have consulted with Walter about its design and to have suggested to him the beautiful delicate staircases of its entrance halls, found it ill proportioned, too short for its length, and ' incorrect and unclassic '; among drawings by Davis in the Avery Library, Columbia University, are several showing his ideas of what the plan should have been. But the length and width of the building and its general arrangement were determined by the will; they could not be changed. And even in its present state there is much more to it than a badly proportioned imitation of a Greek temple. The absolute simplicity of the four dormitory buildings which flank it, two and two; the placing of the five buildings; the gate lodges and entrances — these all reveal no mean imagination, no hesitant sense of design. And when one begins to examine it in

---

[24] I owe this information to Agnes Addison Gilchrist's ' Girard College: The Influence of the Amateur on Greek Architecture,' an article as yet unpublished, the manuscript of which the author most generously put at my disposal.

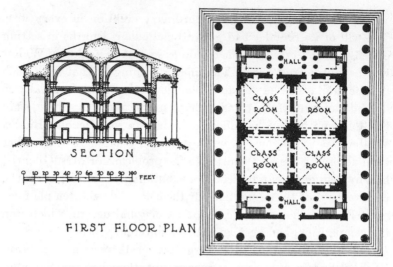

SECTION

FIRST FLOOR PLAN

FIGURE 9. GIRARD COLLEGE, Philadelphia. Thomas U. Walter, architect. (*Author.*) Colossal scale and ingenious vaulted fireproof construction.

more detail one realizes not only the brilliance of Walter's performance, but the kind of conscientious care that could make the nearly two million dollars it cost — an enormous sum for the time — a means for creating a building that would set a new standard in integrity and excellence of construction, in careful study of detail, in structural skill and daring, and in the impressive use of magnificent materials.

The Greek Corinthian order used is certainly impeccable, and carried out in marble the whole building has a reality, a sense of enduring grandeur, that is not always found in Greek Revival work built in less expensive materials. The plan scheme of four great square vaulted rooms to a floor, lighted by wide windows treated in new and independent ways, and entered from the stately stair hall that has already been mentioned, is, given the limitations of the will, a dramatic and beautiful arrangement. The use of low segmental groined vaults in the lower rooms allows the concentration of the weights on square piers in their corners — a scheme structurally sound and economical in itself as well as permitting a great saving in space and cost by allowing the walls between them to be hardly more than screens. The weights and thrust must have been well understood, for there is little sign of settling or cracks. Especially interesting is the way in which Walter made use of the great height enclosed within the pedimented roof and the thickness of the monumental entablature, by placing there rooms crowned with pendentive domes and excellently lighted by skylights in the slope of the roof over the eyes in the domes. Thus Walter was enabled to make sure use of this space behind the entablature; the inevitable darkness of similar spaces was frequently a cause of difficulty or compromise for Classic Revival designers. These rooms, with their low arch springs and their monumental and simple forms, are as handsome as they are useful. The dome thrusts are well abutted by the whole weight of the entablature of the colonnade outside, and this tying together of the building gives great stability to the vertical piers. The whole composition is simple, geometrical, and logical, and built as it is all of cut stone, with the most careful handling of architectural detail, it makes for a series of uniquely effective interiors.

Practically there were disadvantages. The hardness of the materials and the curved shapes of the ceilings made for echo and resonance; the acoustics were bad. Yet instead of attempting to cure this difficulty by the addition of absorbent material where necessary, and so preserving the usefulness of the building, the college has allowed these rooms to be neglected, and the whole interior — save for its small sections used as a museum — is deserted and forlorn. These magnificent upper rooms with their sweeping domes and bold arches were, at least recently, dirty and forgotten, the skylights in some cases broken, the floors covered with pigeon droppings, a dead pigeon or two lying in the corners. What a disgraceful fate for one of the most important *tours de force* of American constructive genius of a century ago! Somehow it seemed typical of the neglect which America has so unexplainably felt for the architectural heritage of the early nineteenth century that this extraordinarily wealthy institution should not have thought it worth while even to keep clean and in repair an expensive building of such magnificent construction and such daring unconventionality in interior design. It is often considered that America has had no tradition of masonry-vault building and that the Greek Revival was a style of unintelligent imitation. Here is a structure that, like many others, proves vividly the contrary — a building full of ingenuity and invention, daringly conceived and owing its final form chiefly to the perfect blend of structural engineering and aesthetic design. Instead of being a forgotten, obsolete structure, slowly disintegrating because of lack of care, it might well become a place of pilgrimage if its virtues could again be understood. Like the vaults in the ground floor of the United States Capitol or those habitually used in the public buildings of Robert Mills — which so frequently make interesting motifs in corridor intersections and the like, now too often concealed by plaster ceilings or intrusive mechanical equipment — and like the magnificent granite vaults of the basement of the Sub-Treasury building in New York by Town and Davis, Ross, and Frazee, these vaults of Girard College show the oneness of structure and design that dominated American architecture a century ago.

Like Strickland, Walter was also an engineer. He spent some time in South America erecting harbor works, but this with him was only an interlude and he returned to the practice of architecture again. The work for which he is best known is not in Philadelphia; it is the Senate and House wings and the dome of the United States Capitol, built in the decade between 1855 and 1865. Of their history it is not necessary to speak; Glenn Brown has treated the subject *in extenso* in his *History of the United States Capitol*.[25] But its quality, its aesthetic design, is interesting as showing the changes that were inexorably taking place in the whole field of American architecture as well as in American life. The very need for this enlargement of the Capitol signified as much, and it is no wonder that in this work Walter made use widely and freely of the iron which American industrialism was rendering more and more available. In many cases one may question this use. It varies from a frank acceptance of the material, as in the imaginative detail of the old Library of Congress room,

25 Two vols. (Washington: Government Printing Office, 1900, 1903).

to such a bold misuse of it as may be seen in the great cast-iron dome. In fact, the detail of all of this Walter work partakes of some of the crudeness and vulgarity of its time. The Greek Revival was dead; the wonder is not that parts of Walter's work in the Capitol are badly detailed, but that they are not infinitely worse. And in larger matters of composition the achievement was extraordinary. Somehow Walter succeeded in wedding his new work to the old in such a way that although the final result was a building completely new, and magnificent in its dimensions and its unity, nevertheless within it the older portions by Thornton, Hallet, Latrobe, and Bulfinch were completely at home and continued to give out their original message. Before such an accomplishment even one's doubt of the great cast-iron dome falters, for it is the outline of that dome and its scale which more than anything else unifies the whole, as it somehow unifies the entire city of Washington — and with the means and skills then available it was only in iron that it could have been built.

Walter helped John McArthur in the design of the Philadelphia city hall. It is difficult to know exactly what his contributions may have been. Certainly the building as completed seems much more the expression of McArthur than of Walter. Yet it may be perhaps due, at least in part, to Walter's criticisms or suggestions that the basic composition of the city hall is dignified and commanding, and that its great tower dominates and unifies its varied parts as much as the Capitol dome does the different portions of that structure.

In his later life Walter was elected president of the American Institute of Architects. No honor could have been more fitting. It was during the period of the Greek Revival that the profession of architecture in America at last came of age and the professional architect became the rule rather than the exception, at least in the case of all the more expensive houses and important public buildings and churches. Walter during his long and busy life must have witnessed much of this development and known personally most of the men whose struggles and achievements, at least in the Philadelphia region, had made it possible. By the time Walter became president of the Institute these days of struggle were over, and it seems particularly appropriate that one who had played such a full part in American architecture should have crowned his life with this office.

There is naturally an immense amount of Greek Revival architecture, in Philadelphia and its environs, that is not by any of these great leaders. Who, for instance, designed the Jefferson Medical College of 1832, with its Ionic colonnade? Much of this Revival work is excellent architecture too, and the names of its designers, their careers, their peculiar styles and achievements, should be rescued from oblivion before it is too late. In Philadelphia, as in all the other cities and towns of the eastern United States, the study of this period in American architecture has hardly more than begun. The surface of the subject has hardly been scratched. There must needs be deep and diligent excavation into local records, searches in attics for old plans, and a sympathetic study of old buildings before an adequate knowledge of the subject can be gained.

But we know enough to make certain definite affirmations about American architecture between, roughly, 1820 and 1850. The first, perhaps, is that it was in this period that the professional architect came to the fore in the United States, and, as in all cases of such an emergence, this was a time of radical experiment and novelty and of sudden and definite change in style. The second is that the term ' Revival' used in connection with ' Greek ' is a misnomer; nowhere were the architects of the time seeking to build copies of Greek buildings, and usually they did so, if at all, only when forced to it by dilettante clients. Instead, to these men, Greek forms were an inspiration to be studied, their beauties a thing to be absorbed and then, in the construction of new buildings, largely forgotten and replaced by invention. A third is that at no time in the history of American architecture have structure and design been so thoroughly integrated, never have engineering and architecture been so thoroughly one, or has construction, in itself beautifully designed and immaculately executed, played so large a part in building effect. (It was, for example, the only period when ma-

ABOVE, LEFT, Haviland's Deaf and Dumb Asylum, Philadelphia. (*New York Pub. Lib.*) ABOVE, RIGHT, stair hall in Girard College, Philadelphia. Thomas U. Walter, architect. (*Pennsylvania Hist. Soc.*) BELOW, Girard College, exterior. (*Wallace.*) Plan, Figure 9.

Boston buildings by Charles Bulfinch: ABOVE, Massachusetts State House before enlargement. (*Art Work of Boston.*) BELOW, LEFT, second Harrison Gray Otis House, Mount Vernon Street. (*Cousins, Essex.*) BELOW, RIGHT, Franklin Terrace, central pavilion. (*Howells, Metropolitan Mus. of Art.*)

TOP, LEFT, hall of the Coleman House, Greenfield, Mass. Asher Benjamin, architect. (*H.A.B.S.*)
TOP, RIGHT, Louisburg Square, Boston. CENTER, Appleton-Parker Houses, Boston. BOTTOM, interior of the Parker House, Boston. (*Last three, Cousins, Essex.*)

Boston buildings by Alexander Parris: TOP and CENTER, end and side of the Quincy Market. (*Author.*) BOTTOM, Sears House, as enlarged for the Somerset Club. (*Ware Library.*) Plan, Figure 10.

sonry vaults in this country were commonly used in important buildings.) And a fourth is that it was the aim of all these designers working in the so-called Greek Revival period to create an architecture that should be new and American — that should express the democracy and all the exuberant hopes that they entertained for a country as cultured as it was busy and rich.

CHAPTER 5

THE GREEK REVIVAL IN BOSTON

IN THE 1820's the differences between Boston and the other
American cities were as marked as they are today. Politically
radical, Boston remained culturally conservative all through the
period of the Revolution and the succeeding three decades. Its
character, set during the prosperous years immediately preceding
the Revolution, was definitely English; even in 1832 Thomas
Hamilton, the Scottish traveler, found that it was ' rather English in appearance and might in truth be easily mistaken for one
of our more populous seaports.' [1] Architecturally the Adam influence was dominant. Charles Bulfinch (1763–1844), whose work
was so important in setting the standard of Boston architecture
prior to 1825, seems to have been much fonder of the delicate
classicism he had seen in England than of the more robust spirit
of the ancient buildings. Did we not know from his correspondence that he had visited the Maison Carrée at Nîmes and even
traveled considerably in Italy itself, we should conclude from his
work that he had never left the British Isles, during his travels. [2]

Samuel McIntire (1757–1811) also seems equally English in
his tastes; in fact, so similar are many of his later designs to some
of the Bulfinch work that it has been difficult — at least in the case
of the Elias Hasket Derby house in Salem — to tell just where
the influence of the one stops and that of the other begins. Sketches
for it by both designers exist; McIntire was the final architect, but
he may have owed much to Bulfinch's suggestions. Neither of these
men copied the English buildings. It is rather that, soaked in the
forms they found in the books of Adam and of William Pain, they

---

[1] *Men and Manners in America* (Edinburgh: W. Blackwood, 1833).

[2] Charles A. Place, *Charles Bulfinch, Architect and Citizen* (Boston and New
York: Houghton Mifflin, 1925); Ellen Susan Bulfinch, *The Life and Letters of
Charles Bulfinch, Architect* (Boston and New York: Houghton Mifflin, 1896).

naturally used these forms in decorating their own buildings. There is a simplicity in the typical Boston house of the first years of the nineteenth century that is quite different from the simplicity of the Regency houses of England; yet the roots of the former underlie the forms of the latter.

The long and valuable life of Bulfinch is the life of the traveled amateur turned gradually and, as it were, almost unconsciously into the professional architect. A member of a distinguished Boston family, his father a great physician, one of his sons the famous author of the *Mythology*, Charles Bulfinch was first and foremost a scholar and a gentleman. He was almost forced into building, first as an expression of natural taste and talent, later as a result of a career checkered with financial misfortune. The family was a typical 'old' Boston family, correct in its taste, conservative, respected. Letters from Charles Bulfinch during his visit to Europe in 1785–7 show how close were the ties that still bound such families to Great Britain. It was there that his architectural taste was formed, his artistic imagination most aroused. It is only natural, then, that his architecture throughout his life remained essentially of the older, more British type, and that he reacted but slowly and with considerable hesitation to the newer winds of the Greek Revival that eddied about him.

Bulfinch was no copyist; even his earlier works, like the old Connecticut state house and the Boston state house, are real creations and entirely ' American '; yet his architecture, like much of that of Benjamin and Parris, is largely a matter of refining and re-refining, of adapting and developing in new and imaginative ways, ideas and motifs that can be traced back to Sir William Chambers and James Gibbs, or to the Adams and William Pain. His exquisite taste and his restrained and almost austere conceptions have a purity that is their own and also New England's; but it is no accident that, with Bulfinch setting the standards and establishing the types, Boston was for years noted for its British appearance.

Thus Bulfinch's life and work, so beautifully and fully covered in Charles Place's biography, need serve only as background in a consideration of the Greek Revival; they were hardly ever an essential part of it. Perhaps it is that very quality which made him the ideal choice to handle the first completion of the United States Capitol. Undeterred by style controversy or discussion, he could accept all that existed — the Thornton simple dignity, the Hallet modifications, the experiments and achievements of Latrobe — and somehow wed them together into one harmonious monument, with a west front designed by him that in some way harmonizes with them all.

Yet some of the Bulfinch buildings were of the first importance in the development of the New England architecture that was to follow. This is especially true of his city houses, the beautifully proportioned fronts of which set the standard followed so faithfully in those lovely streets of Beacon Hill that give Boston so much of its character of elegant and ' genteel ' refinement and charm. Their simplicity itself produced a certain fluidity in style that gave harmony to the work of different periods; for doors could vary and be Adam-like or Greek, the details of the ironwork could be the scrolls of the eighteenth century or the palmettes of the 1830's, and still — with the basic forms of tall slim windows and delicate cornices remaining the same from decade to decade — harmony reigned.

The Boston house, in fact, became as characteristic and unique a type as the houses of New York and Philadelphia. In general the Boston designer had more frontage at his disposal than did the architect of New York, so that Boston houses continued to have central doors to a quite late period, and the plans tended to resemble those of country houses more than was the case in the other two cities. This freedom in size led to great freedom in planning. Typical examples are to be seen in the three Otis houses (the first, 1796–7; the second, 1800; the third, *circa* 1806), in the Perkins house (1804–6) once on the corner of Mount Vernon and Joy streets, and in the Blake-Tuckerman house (before 1815). Banner's Crafts house (1805) at Roxbury and Parris's Sears house (1816) in Boston show a similar love for freely adjusted curves and niches. Boston houses differ from New York houses, too, in

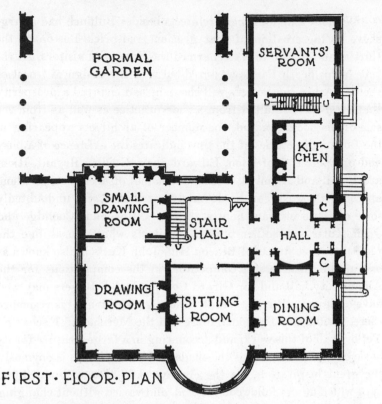

FORMAL GARDEN

SERVANTS' ROOM

KIT~ CHEN

SMALL DRAWING ROOM

STAIR HALL

HALL

DRAWING ROOM

SITTING ROOM

DINING ROOM

FIRST·FLOOR·PLAN

FIGURE 10. SEARS HOUSE (Somerset Club), Boston. Alexander Parris, architect. (*Codman.*) Geometrical ingenuity, large scale, and formal magnificence combined with convenience and livability. (The Somerset Club has added another curved bay, and the interior has been extensively altered.)

having their main entrances close to the ground level, without a 'stoop.' Generally the ground floor was occupied by the smaller reception rooms and service rooms; as in New York, the most important entertainment rooms were on a sort of *piano nobile*. When Town and Davis were practicing in New York in the thirties, they attempted, Davis says, to change the New York tradition of the high stoop and to substitute ground-floor entrances. This innovation may be merely a reflection of the fact that both men knew Boston well, Town through long residence there in his early days and Davis through his study visit in 1827.

Without a doubt other architects besides Bulfinch had a large share in the creation of that gracious red-brick Boston of the thirties and forties that so charmed the European visitors. At the time of his death Parris was credited with the design of 'most of them.'[3] Asher Benjamin's will shows he had enjoyed a prosperity that must have resulted from a wide practice as well as from the sale of his books; indeed, the number of architects appearing in the Boston directories of the time indicates the existence of a busy and prosperous profession. Edward Shaw, Gridley Bryant, Richard Bond, and Ammi B. Young are names of architects to whom all too little work can be definitely attributed, yet undoubtedly some of those pleasant houses are theirs. Cornelius Coolidge and John Kutts were other builder-architects whose works line the pleasant, quiet streets of Beacon Hill. John Kutts is also known as one of the unsuccessful competitors in the competitions for the Albany city hall and for Girard College. Isaiah Rogers may well have designed other important Boston work, during his residence there, besides the Tremont House and the Merchants' Exchange. Yet over all of this work, and accounting in a large measure for its basic conservatism, hangs the shadow of Bulfinch; his is obviously the great inspiration, his the creative skill, that originated the type which others followed, adopted, and varied without changing its controlling spirit.

It was this modified and quiet Americanization of Pain(e) and Adam forms that was broadcast over the eastern United States through the earlier books of Asher Benjamin (1773–1845). He more than any other person is responsible for the character we

---

[3] Obituary in the Boston *Traveller*, 1852. No. 58 Beacon Street (1806) has been attributed to Benjamin; on slighter grounds Nos. 54 and 55 Beacon Street (one the home of the historian Prescott), of about the same date, have also been said to be by him. See Allen Chamberlain's *Beacon Hill: Its Ancient Pastures and Early Mansions* (Boston and New York: Houghton Mifflin Company, 1925). To this writer, an attribution to Peter Banner on purely stylistic grounds seems more plausible. On similar grounds I should hazard an attribution to Benjamin of the row of stone houses on Beacon Street just west of Charles Street. Their dormer windows closely resemble Plate 32 of Benjamin's *The Practical House Carpenter*. According to Chamberlain, other houses on Beacon Hill probably designed by Benjamin include Nos. 92, 94, and 98 Bowdoin Street and No. 9 West Cedar Street.

call roughly Late Colonial; his moldings, his doors and windows, and his mantels and cornices decorate or at least inspire the decoration of numberless houses up and down the New England coast and in the New England river valleys. The widespread distribution of the Benjamin books,[4] which were popular enough to demand frequent reprintings, accomplished a standardization of this style that had a strong influence down to the Civil War.

Yet even Benjamin himself was anything but a mere copyist of English forms. In the prefaces to several of his works he states with great definiteness that his books are for America and that his details have been specifically designed to apply to American conditions and American materials. Thus the proportions of the orders are made more slender, cornices become thinner and more projecting, molding decorations are freer and so designed as to be easily carved in wood. In the preface to *The American Builder's Companion* [5] he writes:

The style of building in this country differs very considerably from that of Great Britain, and other countries, in Europe, which is partly in consequence of the more liberal appropriations made for building in those countries, and of the difference of materials used, particularly in the external decorations. . .

We do not conceive it essentially necessary to adhere exactly to any particular order, provided the proportion and harmony of the parts be carefully preserved. . .

We have ventured to make some alteration in the proportions of the different orders, by lengthening the shafts of the columns two diameters. . .

Being the first who have for a great length of time, published any New System of Architecture, we do not expect to escape some degree of censure. Old fashioned workmen, who have for many years followed the footsteps of Palladio and Langley, will, no doubt, leave their old path with great reluctance. But impressed as we are, with a conviction that reform in some parts of the system of Architecture is loudly demanded, and feeling a confidence from our knowledge of the theory, . . . we have ventured, without the aid of subscription, to exhibit our work to the public view.

4 See page 406.
5 Boston: Etheridge and Bliss, 1806; 5th ed., R. P. and C. Williams, 1826.

Could any declaration of independence be more explicit? And in his actual architectural work Benjamin is frequently still more daring and creative than in his books; the immense variety to be found in his church designs, as shown for instance in the difference between the delicate simplicity and rather sharp richness of the Bennington church [6] and the almost oppressive monumentality of the West Church in Boston, reveals the scope of his imagination. A house (1826–7) in Middlebury, Worcester, Massachusetts, stands to show the nobility of his design at that date; the signed drawings for it are still preserved by the family of the owner.

An English architect also added to this Late Colonial tradition — Peter Banner, who worked in Boston between 1805 and 1822 and in whose work the thinness of Benjamin is carried to an even greater attenuation, almost effeminate, as in the delicate spire of his Park Street Church in Boston or the slim columns of the Crafts house (1805) at Roxbury. It is a fact not without a certain irony that it was precisely this slim and delicate character, founded originally on the work of the Scottish Robert Adam and exemplified so thoroughly in the work of this English Peter Banner, which was architecturally so distressing to the Scotch novelist Thomas Hamilton. He writes in *Men and Manners in America:*

> The country residences of the wealthier citizens are generally adorned with pillars, which often extend from the basement to the very top of the house, (some three or four stories,) supporting, and pretending to support, nothing. The consequence is, that the proportions of these columns are very much those of the stalk of a tobacco-pipe, and it is difficult to conceive anything more unsightly. Even in the public buildings, there is often an obtrusive disregard of every recognized principle of proportion, and clamorous demands are made on the admiration of foreigners, in behalf of buildings which it is impossible to look upon without instant and unhesitating condemnaton.

If this vivid tradition of Adam-inspired and Benjamin-distributed forms was responsible for the conservative appearance of

[6] Now usually attributed to Lavius Fillmore. This church is based, however, on a plate in Benjamin's *The Country Builder's Assistant,* which it closely follows. See also *Concerning the Old First Church of Bennington, a Vermont Shrine,* edited by Dr. Vincent Ravi Booth (New York: Lenz & Riecker, Inc., 1933).

Boston, there were other currents in Boston culture that were as eagerly straining for a different and more classic expression. The change in attitude in cultivated and wealthy circles in Boston society between 1815 and 1825 was revolutionary. Edward Everett and George Ticknor, traveling abroad, discovered a new intellectual ferment in Europe; no longer content with conventional drawing rooms, they sought the philosophers' studies and sipped the learning of the German universities. At the same time their friends and companions at home grew more and more daring in thought, in manners. Unconventionality was no longer virtually a crime; it might almost become, as in the case of Margaret Fuller, a new and fascinating virtue. Even conservative Salem, which had burned witches, was opening its eyes to the new luxury brought by its ships from the Orient and from Europe and was beginning to realize that its past was 'quaint.'

All through New England this new yeast was working — this leaven of individualism, of personal assertion, of freedom inspired by European romanticism and growing cosmopolitan contacts. And the first product of this swift fermentation was classicism — a new and vivid feeling of the reality and beauty of Greece and Rome. It was as though Greek culture and Roman culture had suddenly become symbols of all that was free, refined, thoughtful, and — especially — beautiful in human life.

In Margaret Fuller's fragmentary autobiography published in the *Memoirs of Margaret Fuller Ossoli* [7] she paints a vivid picture of the somewhat extraordinary education she received from her lawyer father in Cambridgeport during the period from about 1816 to 1823. She learned Latin grammar as early as she learned English, and was apparently reading Latin with perfect ease by the time she was eight. Horace, Ovid, Virgil, Cicero, and Caesar were her daily companions and the Roman ideal became part and parcel of her mind. Through Ovid she was introduced to the Greek myths, and more and more the delicacy expressive of the Greeks came to accompany her ideal of Roman dignity and Roman constructive genius. On this foundation she reared a literary culture

[7] Boston: Phillips, Sampson and Company, 1852.

of amazing breadth. Shakespeare, Cervantes, and Molière all were
well known to her before she was fifteen. Granted that she was unusual and her education peculiar, it was nevertheless a symptom
of the intellectual movements of the day. Her autobiographical
passages with regard to this Greek and Latin foundation would
in themselves explain the entire vividness and virility of the Classic
Revival movement in America.

Learned Boston was essentially well versed in the classics, and
it is no accident that several New England towns had libraries or
learned clubs called ' the Athenaeum.' Of these naturally the Boston Athenaeum was the greatest, its library large and well stocked,
its halls filled with sculpture and paintings as well as with books.
' The comparative diffusion of literature in Boston,' writes Hamilton, ' has brought with it a taste for the fine arts. The better
houses are adorned with pictures ; and in the Athenaeum — a public library and reading room — is a collection of casts from the
antique.' Margaret Fuller's letters are full of her enthusiasm for
the Athenaeum gallery, and the pride which Boston took in it was
an expression of honest admiration. Boston indeed during the
1820's shared with Philadelphia the honor of being the art centei
of the United States. The painter Washington Allston and the
sculptor Horatio Greenough were but the two most famous examples of that flowering of Boston in the field of the fine arts which
paralleled its intellectual blossoming.

So Boston at this time became a radical center. Its worship of
Margaret Fuller, its admiration of Dr. Channing, and its eager
if sometimes questioning acceptance of Emerson and the transcen-
dentalists are all expressions of free, skeptical, aesthetically sensitive, and enthusiastic minds. By 1830 cultivated Boston was as
radical as mercantile Boston was conservative.

When Bulfinch was called to Washington to complete the
United States Capitol, in 1817, it was the signal for a new type
of architecture to come to the fore. Even Bulfinch had not been altogether insensitive to the new Classic Revival fervor. The Massachusetts General Hospital, as one example, designed just before

he left, was definitely a step in that direction. Nevertheless his departure threw open the Boston architectural field to new men, and between 1820 and 1840 the revolution in the profession was complete. It centered around three great and very different individuals: Alexander Parris (1780–1852), Solomon Willard (1783–1861), and Isaiah Rogers (1800–1869). Different as they were, they were intimate friends. Willard at one time was a member of the Parris household, and Rogers was a devoted friend of Willard, after whom he named his first son. Moreover the conditions of architectural practice were freer in Boston than in the Philadelphia of Latrobe and Mills. Each recognizing the skill of the others, these architects often called on each other for aid; consequently the problem of attribution of individual buildings is frequently difficult. And through Parris they had a tie with Bulfinch, which prevented any definite schism; Willard even worked for Bulfinch briefly in Washington, carving for him a model of the Capitol as it would be when completed.

Parris was executive for Bulfinch in the building of the Massachusetts General Hospital, and there is in existence a complete set of the plans and elevations signed not by Bulfinch, but by Parris. This system of co-operation had many advantages. It meant that what one knew all of them knew, and there was between them all an eager spirit of joint endeavor admirably fitted to produce rapid and constructive changes. Richard Upjohn, later a famous Gothic Revival architect, worked in Parris's office in Boston between 1834 and 1839, besides doing considerable work of his own. His diary, in the possession of his grandson, Hobart Upjohn, shows that he worked on many buildings sometimes attributed to others besides Parris. A system of piecework payment controlled both architectural and drafting services, and was admirably fitted to stimulate this kind of free association.[8]

It is significant that none of these men — Parris, Willard, Rogers — was trained definitely as an architect. Parris had been

---

[8] I owe this information to the courtesy of Mr. Hobart Upjohn and Professor Everard M. Upjohn of Columbia University. See the latter's *Richard Upjohn, Architect and Churchman* (New York: Columbia University Press, 1939), pp. 35–7.

apprenticed to a carpenter and had been briefly a schoolteacher in the Pembroke schools, but his early interest in architecture led to a rapid development of the professional side of his work. Prior to the War of 1812 his most important building — the dignified three-story Honeywell house, distinguished for its delicate detail, in Portland, Maine — is of the typical Late Colonial type. The David Sears house (1816), now the Somerset Club, Parris's first important Boston work, is however quite different. Here the Bulfinch influence is obvious, but the building has a rather monumental, even heavy, dignity markedly at variance in spirit with the light delicacy that Bulfinch loved. The G. W. Lyman house at the corner of Mount Vernon and Joy Streets, built in 1824, is also attributed to Parris. The American Antiquarian Society owns a sketchbook of beautiful drawings by Alexander Parris from the earlier Portland period; it includes drawings of a Portland church (1807), the Preble house (1807–8), the Portland Bank (1807), and a plan of the Governor's residence (1811–12) at Richmond, Virginia. Does this mean that Parris was the architect of this much attributed building? Or was this careful plan made merely to record a design he had seen and liked?

The Appleton house and its neighbor, the Parker house, Nos. 40 and 42 Beacon Street, completed in 1818, are very likely also by Alexander Parris.[9] They have been attributed to Bulfinch, but their character is manifestly different from that of the greater amount of the Bulfinch work. Besides, Bulfinch had left Boston for Washington in 1817. These two houses have rounded bays not unlike the Sears house, and, also like it, their plans are distinguished by a great use of curve-ended rooms, ingeniously arranged. The detail is unusually rich and full of hints of the Greek Revival that was to follow. Of the architects then practicing in Boston only Benjamin, Banner, and Parris suggest themselves as the possible designers, for these houses are plainly not builders' work. Because of the round bays and the fact that the detail is definitely not of the character Benjamin had thus far used elsewhere, and because none of Banner's characteristic attenuated detail ap-

---

[9] The present top stories of both houses are of later dates.

pears, I feel that the attribution to Parris is a proper one. Moreover, the obituary of Parris that appeared in the Boston *Traveller* in 1852 says of him: ' To no other person do so large a number of the imposing and substantial edifices which characterize our city owe their distinctive merit.' A list of his buildings is then added, concluding with ' many if not most of the edifices built on Beacon, Tremont, and Summer Streets.'

The Appleton and Parker houses are important because in their detail the Late Colonial delicacy has almost completely disappeared and the new, firm, architectonic simplicity of the Classic Revival has taken its place. The imported marble mantels are of the richest sort of ' Piranesi style ' work, but the native-wood trims and doors, the mahogany bookcases, and much of the plastic ornament are now, perhaps for the first time in Boston, all consistent in the clear restraint of the new classic type. Of actual Greek detail there is but little (the Ionic capitals of the porches, a Greek fret here and there, and the acroteria of the bookcases, for instance) ; but of prophetic hints of its spirit — of its concentrated richness contrasted with broad simplicity, of its feeling for large scale, of its love for anthemion ornaments and carefully related curved lines — there is a great deal. These houses can scarcely yet be called Greek Revival but they show the style in gestation ; they express admirably the radical spirit in 1818 Boston that made the Greek Revival inevitable. In them it is obviously struggling to birth.

St. Paul's Church in Tremont Street, designed by Parris and built in 1819, with its great entrance portico and simple pediment, is in the full flower of the Classic Revival. It is perhaps significant that Willard carved the stone Ionic capitals for this building and possibly made some of the drawings, for Willard was the intellectual stimulus as he was the eccentric of this group. Parris's best as well as most radical work is probably the Quincy or Faneuil Hall market (begun 1825) and the row of buildings surrounding it ; the dignity and simplicity of its porticoed central building, together with the straightforward, practical, and yet dignified character of the surrounding structures, give to that part of Boston a kind of aristocratic atmosphere that still remains, clear and strong.

Parris's later work was of an even more utilitarian nature. Like Strickland he was almost better known as an engineer than as an architect. He built the famous drydock in the Boston Navy Yard, and from 1848 till his death he was Civil Engineer in Charge of the Portsmouth Navy Yard. Much of the charm of the older portion of the Portsmouth Navy Yard today comes from the simple and lovely buildings erected during his administration. A characteristic evidence of the originality of his mind is the fact that in certain dredging operations at Portsmouth (as the first instance of the kind in America) he used electric current for detonating blasting charges in underwater work.[10]

Solomon Willard's talents were even more varied. It is fortunate that the Bunker Hill Monument Association published a *Memoir of Solomon Willard*,[11] by his friend William Wheildon, for from it one can gain a vivid picture of his busy life and his somewhat peculiar character. The great-great-grandson of the Reverend Samuel Willard, an early vice-president of Harvard College, Willard was the son of a carpenter and cabinetmaker. He came to Boston at the age of twenty and without any regular apprenticeship whatsoever obtained work at once as a skilled carpenter. His architectural interest was already great and he studied architectural drawing, possibly at the architectural school run by Asher Benjamin. Five years later he suddenly branched out into woodcarving, and carved important architectural detail not only for Banner's Park Street Church but also for some of the work of Bulfinch. From this it was but a short step to sculpture; he later became famous for the figureheads he carved for Boston ships. He seems to have been restless, almost a wanderer by nature, and made at least two trips to the South — one in 1811 and another in 1817–18. It was during this latter trip that he made the model of the national Capitol for Bulfinch. He also made models for Godefroy of the decorative work of the famous Unitarian

---

[10] *Journal of The Franklin Institute*, Vol. xxxi, No. 3 (March 1841), p. 154, letter of 9 November 1840.

[11] Boston: The Monument Association, 1865.

Church of Baltimore. In this decorative detail lies a sufficient indication of Willard's adaptability as well as of his dexterity. The ornament is of an almost Rococo type, evidently carrying out perfectly the wishes of the French architect. It is amazing work to come from a Yankee hand!

During his years in Boston from 1820 on, Willard began to practice as an independent architect and also taught drawing, modeling, physics, and chemistry. He invented an early hot-air heating device so well known that Bulfinch was prompted to consult him with regard to the heating of the White House in Washington. He discovered the Quincy granite quarries, and achieved an efficiency previously unknown in quarrying and in the handling of large pieces of stone by the invention and use of all sorts of ingenious machines. From this Quincy quarry came much of the material for the finest buildings of the period all over the eastern seaboard.

Of his architectural work, the Bunker Hill Monument (1825–42) is undoubtedly the most famous, but he also in partnership with Banner did a church (1820) in Salem that is quite in the older Late Colonial tradition; the Boston branch of the Bank of the United States (1824), a simple piece of Greek Doric in which the columns — with Willard's customary independence — were purposely made without entasis; the Suffolk County and Norfolk County courthouses in Boston and Dedham; and the Quincy school and town hall. He made models of the Parthenon and the Pantheon, which he gave to the Athenaeum, and designed the alterations necessary in its second building; in reward for his many services he was made an honorary member.

All of Willard's later work is simple almost to the point of bareness, but possessed of a strength that is the direct opposite of Late Colonial delicacy. There was on it none of that gewgaw ornament which Thomas Hamilton had so disliked; in a certain stolid dignity it even outdid the quietest and heaviest of the Mills work. Characteristically enough, toward the end of his life Willard suddenly swung from architecture and from quarrying to scientific farming on his place in Quincy, where he died. Carpenter, carver, sculptor, architect, inventor, teacher of the sciences — this strange man, who never married and who passed for an eccentric with many of his acquaintances, was typical of the Boston of the period, with its intellectual curiosity, its experimental vigor, its radicalism; if we can judge from his influence on his friends, he must have had an intellectual power even greater than the vigor that appeared in his many activities. His one published book is a work on the Bunker Hill Monument and the machines used in connection with quarrying its stone.[12]

The simplicity of Willard's architectural work was undoubtedly the result, at least in part, of his feeling for the material, granite, which he loved so much and used so freely. The plain functionalism of his buildings went unappreciated by most of his contemporaries; the Suffolk County courthouse was called a granite barn with an ineffective Greek Doric porch at either end. Yet this very simplicity, at times heavy-handed, was a significant quality in his case, as it was in the case of Robert Mills. It is eloquent of a definite search for the most stripped, the most economical, the most functional architectural forms — a search that lay beneath much of the best work of the American Greek Revival.

In Boston the widespread use of granite helped this search materially. Bulfinch's Boston courthouse (later the city hall) — built in 1810 and demolished in 1862 — shows in its powerful geometric shapes, its octagonal central portion and pedimented wings, and its simple wall surfaces that even with his love of delicacy he was sensitive to the quality of granite. The unbroken walls of his octagonal New South Church (1814) show the same qualities, and it was apropos of this church that the *Boston Spectator* remarked, on 31 December 1814:

The excellent stone from the inexhaustible quarries on the banks of the Merrimack [has added to the] beauty and respectability of the town and neighborhood [through the building of] several banks and publick offices, the Court House, school house, the new University Hall [of Harvard], some private edifices, and the church above de-

---

[12] Solomon Willard, *Plans and Sections of the Obelisk on Bunker's Hill, with Experiments Made in Quarrying the Granite* (Boston: Samuel N. Dickinson, 1843).

Customs House, Boston: ABOVE, competition drawing by Richard Upjohn. (*Avery Library*.)
BELOW, Customs House as built. Ammi B. Young, architect. (*Art Work of Boston*.)

XXVI

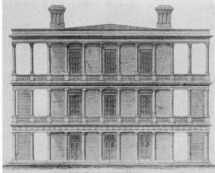

TOP, two Customs Houses by Ammi B. Young. (*Plans of Public Buildings . . .*) LEFT, Galveston, Texas; RIGHT, Bath, Maine. CENTER, Suffolk Bank, State Street, Boston. Isaiah Rogers, architect. (*Ware Library.*) BOTTOM, Brazer's Building, Boston. (*Howells, Metropolitan Mus. of Art.*)

Buildings by Isaiah Rogers: TOP, Tremont House, Boston. (*Old engraving, Hinton.*) CENTER, Merchants' Exchange, Boston. (*Old photograph, Howells, Met. Mus. of Art.*) BOTTOM, LEFT, Charleston Hotel. Isaiah Rogers(?) and Reichardt, architects. (*Tebbs.*) BOTTOM, RIGHT, Burnet House, Cincinnati. (*Cist.*)

New York City Hall. J. Mangin and John McComb, Jr., architects. ABOVE, the Pendleton view. (*Mus. City of New York.*) BELOW, the Rotunda. (*Georgian Period.*)

scribed. . . A purer taste appears to banish superfluous ornament; and the effect is produced by correct proportion and the richness of the material.

The succeeding three decades were to produce a host of Boston buildings, especially business buildings, of which this description would be even more true. The tradition of dignity in commercial structures was established at an early date in Boston. The great India Wharf Stores building — a massive brick structure of six stories, with five-story wings and a magnificently powerful architectural composition — was erected sometime between 1805 and 1807. It has been attributed to Bulfinch, but there is apparently no documentary evidence giving the architect's name and it may well be by another; certainly it has many qualities not found elsewhere in Bulfinch's work. But it was of brick, whereas the peculiar simple effectiveness of the later Boston commercial work came from the use — increasingly direct — of granite.

There is one great difference between this earlier, Bulfinch type of granite architecture and the later type which from 1820 to 1840 made over such large parts of the commercial and industrial areas of Boston. This difference lies in the way the granite was cut and used; the later builders tried to use as few and as large single pieces of granite as possible. Piers, for example, instead of being built of horizontal layers of stone are often of single pieces, perhaps two feet square, extending up from floor to ceiling. These piers carry great plain architrave beams, sometimes with a cornice above, sometimes without; the wall above may be a repetition of this motif, or may be built in a more conventional way with ordinary windows and wall coursing. But ground-floor monolithic piers had by the time of the Greek Revival become almost universal. Sometimes they have delicate Greek Doric antacapital moldings at the top, but the detail is always simplified, delicate, restrained, and austere — as befits the hard, close-grained, gray material — and the total effect of blocks or rows of such buildings is one of functional simplicity and enormous power. The building once at No. 27 State Street, called Brazer's Building,

with its schooled simplicity, its almost modern and yet at the same
time rather Syrian restraint and power, showed the revolutionary
effects a logical use of this dense granite can produce — and it is
significant of the revolutionary, experimental quality of the Greek
Revival that its exponents did not hesitate to produce them.

Alexander Parris, in the rows of buildings around the Quincy
market, treated stone piers in a similar though more delicate way,
with an equally unconventional effect, and it is possible that he
may have been the architect of many of the other refined and dignified warehouses and loft buildings that once made harbor-front
Boston the impressive sight it used to be. In any case, this granite
architecture for these humble, purely utilitarian buildings — an
architecture so restrained in detail, so unconventional in type —
is characteristic of the period's desire to make even these buildings
works of creative architecture and structures of logical and powerful beauty.

To its material, granite, is to be attributed some of the monumental magnificence of the Boston customs house, designed by
Ammi B. Young (1798–1874) and built between 1837 and 1847.
In one sense it is the most highly developed example of the Greek
Revival style in Boston, but its quality is less local than that of
most of the work of Parris and Willard. The admiration it aroused
was quite probably the reason for Young's appointment as Supervising Architect of the Treasury Department, a position he held
through the fifties. Of Young's other work little as yet is definitely known; he is one of many brilliant architects whose careers
cry out for more careful research. He was born in Lebanon, New
Hampshire, and is said to have been a pupil of Alexander Parris.[13] He did some work in Norwich, Vermont. The Congregational
Church there is attributed to him; it is a quiet, refined building of
the Late Colonial, Benjamin type and as lovely as buildings of that
style generally are, but it gives little evidence of the striking originality of the Boston customs house or of his earlier Washington
work. He was also the architect of the Vermont state house at

---

[13] Elie Brault, *Les Architectes par leurs œuvres*, Vol. III (Paris: Laurens
[1893]), p. 421.

Montpelier, built in 1837 though rebuilt (mainly on the old lines) after a fire. In this structure, notwithstanding its somewhat routine general composition, he appears as a thorough master of Greek detail. In 1844 Young added another superb piece of beautifully detailed work to the list of his achievements — the dignified courthouse in Worcester, which still stands, somewhat altered, as the left wing of the present building. It is all of Quincy granite, and its pediment-crowned Corinthian portico *in antis* has that excellence of proportion which gives it an unusual sense of reality, of restrained and commanding power.

The Boston customs house is one of many attempts made by Greek Revival architects to combine a low Roman dome with a pedimented Greek Doric order, and it is probably the most successful of them all. The plan is a simple cross, with one short and one long axis; the monumental order carries through the whole height of the building and is crowned by a simple gabled roof with four pediments. At the intersection of the cross arms there was a large rotunda and over this a low dome, expressed on the outside and lighted by a skylight. The whole is so simple and straightforward, so great in scale, so logical in conception and monumental in plan, and the granite detail is so nobly carried out, that it is no wonder the building gained national fame. Original too, and as effective as it was rare, was the use of columns instead of the more usual antae to decorate the piers between the windows. It was one of the most directly successful attempts ever made to use a pure columnar architecture for a modern building, and it is a great credit to modern Boston that when an enlarged customs house became necessary, instead of razing the old, a great tower was built up through its center, replacing the old dome, so that the greater part of the stern, impressive old building has been preserved.

Young had been engaged as architect for the Treasury Department in 1852, when Mills's influence was rapidly passing. In the following year a separate division called the Construction Branch of the Treasury Department was established, with Captain Alexander H. Bowman of the Engineering Corps of the United States Army as engineer in charge. However, Young was continued as Supervising Architect, a position he held until 1860. These eight years were among the busiest years in the history of the office, especially in its construction of customs houses and post offices, for the rapidly increasing population of the nation, the tremendous growth of trade and commerce, and the westward spread of the country all made necessary an amazing number of new Federal structures. Of practically all of these during this period, Ammi B. Young was the architect; they form a most interesting group of buildings, showing the rapid development of modern types of construction and also the way in which current changes of taste toward more Italianate and baroque forms expressed themselves in the hands of a man trained in the integrity of the earlier manner.

Several standard types of customs houses were developed. All of them used cast-iron columns and a floor construction of brick arches on wrought-iron beams. All of them were classic, with marked ' Italian villa ' character in the detail, and in general the extremely refined profiles of Greek Revival moldings had given place to bolder, cruder, and perhaps more virile forms. One common type has either five or seven bays of arched windows, and a projecting central pavilion three windows wide with five arches beneath on the ground floor. These buildings are usually three stories high, the two upper floors almost identical, and the whole is crowned with a heavy classic cornice and a low-pitched hip roof. Typical examples are the old post office (1855–60) of New Haven, Connecticut, and the almost identical though longer one (1856–60) in Detroit, Michigan.

Another simpler type is of brick, with the arches more closely spaced and usually with only narrow, unpierced wings on either side of the central three-bay pavilion. One of the most attractive of these Federal buildings is the Belfast customs house (1855–7) in Maine, in which the red brick is relieved most charmingly by the painting of the archivolts white and by a rich and delicate white-painted iron balcony over the entrance. Similar in plan to the Belfast building is the Wilmington courthouse (1853–7) in Delaware, but in this case a pediment crowns the central motif and rec-

tangular-headed doors and windows with stone trim replace the
arches of Belfast, just as an Italian balustrade replaces the Belfast iron balcony. The Italian influence comes out more strongly
in the courthouse and post office (1856–61) at Indianapolis and
an almost identical building (1857–60) in Portsmouth, New
Hampshire. Here a rusticated ground floor with segmental arched
openings supports two floors of Italianate windows — the second
floor crowned with pediments, the third merely with cornices. The
different floors are strongly differentiated and a powerful cornice
with a hipped roof tops the whole building.

The best of these Italianate Federal buildings is the still simpler Italian-palace type found in the customs house (1856–7) in
Washington and the somewhat similar Federal building (1856–8)
at Galena, Illinois. In these the classical elements are so generalized
and the proportions so wide and ample that the effect is almost as
Georgian as it is Italian Renaissance, except for the very large
scale of the parts. In these at least, as in some of the simpler examples like that at Belfast, there is evident much of that strong,
simple feeling for wall surface pierced by well-placed openings and
for detail, bold yet discreet, which we associate with the Greek
Revival.

Still another type of larger and more ostentatious classic
structure, almost recalling the Palladianism of eighteenth-century
England, was built occasionally. Characteristic is the Norfolk,
Virginia, customs house (1853–9), with a six-column Roman Corinthian porch of large size crowning a monumental flight of steps;
the whole is rich in detail, impressive in scale, and within the feeling of the times well detailed. Somewhat similar in composition was
the Appraisers' Stores building (1852–9) at St. Louis, before the
addition of an awkward upper story (1887–90). In this example
the colonnade, instead of crowning a flight of steps, is supported
on a heavy rusticated basement with arched doors. There are even
a few examples in which Greek forms are still definitely recalled.
Thus the old customs house and post office (1851–5) at Bangor,
Maine, destroyed in the Bangor fire of 1911, was a small but effective building of granite with a pedimented façade of two Greek

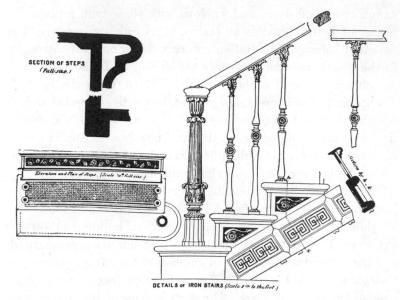

FIGURE 11. CUSTOMS HOUSE, Galveston, Texas. Iron stair detail. Ammi B. Young, architect. (*Young.*) Young's typical good taste and inventiveness in the use of the new material, cast iron.

Corinthian columns *in antis*. Its dignified material and its unforced scale gave it real beauty.

All of these buildings combine to give a solid basis of classic tradition to Federal building in the country, and must have produced a sobering effect on the somewhat effervescent and vulgar taste that was increasingly evident during this period. What sets them apart especially and makes them worthy of study is their radical attack on the problem of fireproof building and their increased use of metal, often detailed — as in the stairs and some of the iron balconies — with great imagination, delicacy, and a true sense of the material. Window sash and frames, doors and door frames were usually of iron and represented a definite step along the road to factory fabrication of building materials. Even the exterior trim, where the building was of brick — the window architraves, and the door archivolts and jambs — were of iron as well. Evidently the government understood the importance of these radical experiments. Plans, elevations, sections, and details of many of these Young-designed buildings were published and distributed widely by the Secretary of the Treasury.[14] The printed letter of gift accompanying these and signed by the Secretary of the Treasury states among other things:

The introduction of wrought-iron beams and girders in these edifices, instead of the groined arches formerly used, is, I believe, wholly new, and this improvement . . . will it is hoped, prove interesting and useful to you, or to those who, through you, may have the opportunity of inspecting them.

For Young, as for most of the creative architects of his period, the Greek Revival was no Procrustean bed into which all buildings had to be forced, but rather a discipline to integrity of construction, simple and powerful composition, restrained and carefully studied detail. These people were looking for the best and most efficient solutions for the building problems of nineteenth-century America.

It was Isaiah Rogers who was undoubtedly the greatest architect of this Boston group; in fact he was one of the most remarkable designers of the entire Greek Revival movement. Like both Willard and Parris he was brought up on a farm near Plymouth. His father, Isaac, had been a shipbuilder, and the constructive urge was so strong in the son that despite the protests of the family he went to Boston when he was sixteen and apprenticed himself to a carpenter. Something of a wanderer, like Willard, the moment his apprenticeship was over he left for the South and spent 1820–21 in Mobile, Alabama, where he had the good fortune to win a competition for the design of the first Mobile theater — a building, to be sure, without great architectural distinction. Yet the winning of this minor competition seems to have settled his future; from that time on he considered himself an architect. Back in Boston again, he apparently spent the next four years in the office of Solomon Willard, whose intimate friend and confidant he became, and in 1826 he opened his own office. Fortune favored him in the

14 *Plans of Public Buildings in Course of Construction, under the Direction of the Secretary of the Treasury, including the Specifications thereof,* Capt. A. H. Bowman, U. S. Corps of Engineers and Engineering, in Charge ([Washington:] Treasury Department, 1855).

matter of his first important commission, which was the Tremont House (1828–9) in Boston.[15] In this work his independent thought and his sure taste helped him to produce an epoch-making work, original (almost revolutionary) in plan and with an exterior so simple as to be almost austere. Moreover, its entire architectural detail was based on Greek forms; there is not a trace of the Late Colonial left.

The Tremont was perhaps the first hotel in America to realize something of the modern ideal; there is nothing here to recall the eighteenth-century inn. Its many rooms — some single, some *en suite* — planted on simple straight corridors with ample stair exits well placed, its rotunda office richly trimmed, its suite of fine public rooms across the main front, and its lavish, formal dining room with a deeply coffered ceiling and a screen of Ionic columns at either end set it apart from the usual run of the hotels of its time almost as much as did its elaborate battery of water closets and the bathrooms with running water in the basement. In this building, for the first time in America if not indeed in the world, mechanical equipment became an important element in architectural design.

Although the building has been long destroyed, engravings of the exterior and careful drawings of its plans and interior details fortunately exist; it was deemed so important that a book on its architecture was published by William Havard Eliot in 1830.[16] Moreover, Rogers's Bangor House, in Bangor, Maine, dating from 1832 and still standing though alterations have destroyed its original beauty, was built on a plan so close to that of the Tremont House that from it one can gain today a good idea of certain portions of the older building. The dignity of the interior trim in some of the Bangor House parlors still remains; its broad simple planes and its large scale are of the best Greek Revival type. In the dining room of the Bangor House the old deeply coffered ceiling also

---

[15] For the contribution of Isaiah Rogers to the development of the American hotel, see Jefferson Williamson's *The American Hotel, an Anecdotal History* (New York: Alfred A. Knopf, 1930).

[16] *A Description of Tremont House, with Architectural Illustrations* (Boston: Gray and Bowen, 1830).

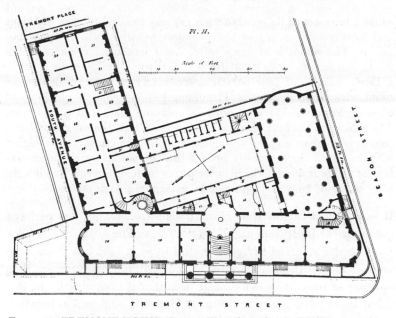

FIGURE 12. TREMONT HOUSE, Boston. First-floor plan. Isaiah Rogers, architect. (*Eliot.*) The first modern hotel in America. On the Tremont Street side, a row of sumptuous reception rooms and parlors (12, 13, 16, 17, 19, 20). The office (14), with colonnaded counter, opened from the rotunda at the right. The magnificent dining room (18) bordered Beacon Street; its services were beneath. The left-hand wing shows typical bedroom arrangement, furnishing both suites and single rooms; similar bedroom arrangements were on the upper floors above parlors and dining room. Notice convenient position of stairs and the beautiful way in which inequalities of the site have been handled. At rear of the court, connected by glazed corridors to bedroom wings, dining room, and rotunda, are the large linen room and famous battery of water closets.

is left, though later alterations have reduced the height of the room and made the ceiling seem over-heavy.

But, however much the Tremont House was admired at its time, Thomas Hamilton could find little good to say of it. His architectural criticisms are based, in this case as in most others, on the single category of some imagined correctness, some agreement with a norm that was not too definite in his own mind. Thus he writes:

I have been too well satisfied with the good living of the Tremont Hotel, not to feel grieved to be compelled to speak disparagingly of its architecture. I beg to say, however, that I allude to it only because I have heard its construction gravely praised by men of talent and intelligence, as one of the proudest achievements of American genius. The edifice is of fine sienite, and I imagine few parts of the world can supply more beautiful material for a building. In front is a Doric portico of four columns, accurately proportioned, but, as usual, without pediment. . . The dining-hall, which is the chief object of admiration, is defective, both in point of taste and proportion. The ceiling, in the first place, is too low; and then the ranges of Ionic columns, which extend the whole length of the apartment, are mingled with Antae of the composite order; thus defacing, by the intermixture of a late Roman barbarism the purer taste of Greece. But it were mere waste of time and patience to enlarge on such matters.

It is only just to note that Hamilton's own learning was perhaps even more at fault than was Rogers's taste. The antae of the composite order referred to by Hamilton were in fact based on those used in the great Ionic temples of Asia Minor; his criticism thus appears as the ostentatious bit of pedantry it undoubtedly is. Besides, Eliot's book on the Tremont House is sufficient refutation of the good Scotsman's remarks. Refinement, careful study, originality in plan as seen in the handling of the corridors and stairs, and exquisite reticence in taste are instinct in every line. Rogers was also the architect of the monumental Ionic Suffolk Bank (1834), one of the buildings which once made Boston's State Street one of the most dignified streets in the country. It was noteworthy for its simple treatment of the granite spandrels between the second- and third-floor windows.

When the first Astor hotel was contemplated in New York, Rogers was the obvious man to design it; accordingly he was invited to New York and lived there from 1834 to 1842. The fame of the old Astor House is so great that little need be said about it except to note that in austerity of exterior treatment and refinement of interior details, as well as in size, it went even further than did the Tremont House in Boston. But a description of this as well as of Rogers's other New York work can more appropriately be left to a later chapter dealing with New York, where with the prestige gained through these hotels Rogers naturally obtained many other commissions.[17] During the New York period he designed the Boston Merchants' Exchange, with its interesting pedimented front supported on four piers crowned by rich anta capitals instead of on the more usual columns.

However, it was primarily as a hotel architect that Rogers was known during his later years, and the list of his work includes almost every one of the largest and most important hotels built in the South and West between 1840 and 1865. The Charleston Hotel, with its lovely Greek Corinthian colonnade,[18] the enormous second St. Charles Hotel in New Orleans, with its lavish colonnaded façade,[19] and the famous Burnet House in Cincinnati most interestingly designed on a hillside site were all by him, as were the later Galt House in Louisville and the six-hundred-room Maxwell House in Nashville, in both of which the change in taste of the Civil War years is, alas, all too plain. But even in this later period, when taste throughout the country had changed so swiftly and, in its search for eclectic novelty, had left so far behind the ideals of integrity and of refinement and appropriateness of detail that had characterized the American Greek Revival, Rogers never completely lost his creative ability or his sense of restraint. Thus the Long View Insane Asylum in Cincinnati, one of his last buildings, has a plan of carefully related separate pavilions that is worked out with great efficiency; the exterior expression as well, in spite of its debased Italianate character, has dignity and power. St. John's Episcopal Church in Cincinnati shows Rogers bringing the same skill to a work in the medieval style; but the simplicity of its wall surfaces, the restraint of its detail, and especially the unusual handling of its twin diagonal towers all reveal more of his innate taste for classic dignity than of his interest in the meretricious

17 See pages 152–4.
18 The attribution of the Charleston Hotel to Rogers has been questioned. Contemporary Charleston accounts of its opening in 1839 say that the architect was 'Reichardt, a German.' Possibly Reichardt supervised its construction from Rogers's drawings. But see page 199, note 18.
19 In the second St. Charles Hotel Rogers followed the general arrangement of the first, which had been designed by James Gallier, but omitted the dome. See page 226.

superficial medievalism that was the usual stock-in-trade of too many architects in the 1860's. During the Civil War, Rogers was Supervising Architect of the Treasury Department in Washington, but the war prevented any great amount of building by the Federal Government. This was perhaps just as well, and it is a pleasant thought that while he was in Washington his one great work was the completion of the old Treasury building along the lines set by its first designer, Robert Mills. Here again, toward the end of his life, he found himself working with the honest masonry structure and the refined Greek detail in which he was so skilled.

To Rogers also, or to someone under his influence, I believe may be attributed the post office and Federal courthouse at Portland, Maine, designed at some period shortly before 1866. Its quiet and restrained white marble exterior, with its arched basement and a monumental Corinthian order above, is so unlike the work of Ammi B. Young, who preceded him in the office, and of A. B. Mullet, who was his successor, that no other authorship seems possible. Mullet, it is only fair to state, had been a pupil and draftsman of Rogers's in Cincinnati; it is possible, of course, that this Portland building, though so entirely different from the superposed orders and complexity of Mullet's later work, may have been designed by him in 1866–70, when Rogers's influence was still strong.

Isaiah Rogers's life was characteristic of the period. It sprang from a growing country, greedy not only for building but, so far as the demand could be met, for good architecture as well. His meteoric rise, from his twenty-sixth year as a beginner in Boston to his thirty-sixth year when he was recognized as one of the two or three most important architects in New York, could probably have happened at no other time in this country's history. Nor would such a career have been likely for anyone with a different background. His friendship for Willard, a restless, eager, and inquiring man, undoubtedly made him the more ready to travel when opportunity offered; from his birth in Marshfield, near Plymouth, of a family directly descended from one of the Mayflower passengers, to his death in Cincinnati, then the ' Queen City of the West,' there was a progress — and, at least during the last fifteen years, a disintegration as well — that was the very pattern of the era.

It was a period when transcendentalism and romanticism went hand in hand, and, though the foundations of it all were classic, medievalism was an inevitable growth. With medievalism came the Gothic. Even Bulfinch essayed a Gothic church in the Federal Street Church (1809) in Boston. Isaiah Rogers designed for the Unitarian Church of Cambridge a building that is, in its combination of interesting basic form and naïve inventive detail, one of the most delightful existing examples of so-called ' Carpenter Gothic.' Sober ' Gothic ' granite churches, with pointed-arched doors and windows and square entrance towers, by Willard and Bryant — for example, the Bowdoin Street Church attributed by Wheildon to Willard — showed in the Gothic vein as early as the twenties much the same simplicity of character these architects had made use of in their classic buildings.

It was all Boston, all of a piece, this later ' Gothic ' work, like the old castellated railroad station in Salem built in the forties; but it was not Greek. And, between the large amount of Colonial work that still remained, the general following of the Bulfinch type in houses, and the incursions of the new Gothic work, Boston never became so much or so fully a Greek Revival city or town as did New York, or Washington, or indeed a host of communities in New England, western New York, Ohio, and Michigan — communities that came either to birth or to maturity when the Greek Revival was at its height.

These four men, Bulfinch, Parris, Willard, and Rogers, were only the leaders of a large and growing group of architects. The Boston of the thirties and forties was the creation of many designers, and their influence spread widely over New England.[20] Ed-

[20] For example, the Boston city directory (1848–9) lists the following architects: Edwin Bailey, Richard Bond, Luther Briggs, J. E. Billings, David Bryant, G. J. F. Bryant, S. C. Bugbee, E. C. Cabot, George M. Dexter, A. Gilman, Harvey Greves, George Gray, James Greenough, J. Le Moulnier, Melvin and Young, C. E. Parker, A. Parris, Charles Roath, William Sparrell, Daniel Sullivan, John Thorndike, J. D. Towle, Theodore Voelckers, M. G. Wheelock, Ammi B. Young.

The list of architects for 1846–7 included also A. Benjamin, C. G. Hall, Isaiah Rogers, Edward Shaw (his last appearance), and Samuel Washburn. C. G. Hall appears as Charles G. Hall in the 1850 list.

ward Shaw, Gridley Bryant (an early co-worker of Willard's in the development of the Quincy quarries), and Thomas Silloway are but three more of many to whom the dignity and charm of the city were due. Though Boston men, they worked also in many places outside of Boston; much of their work will be treated elsewhere when the regional architecture of the time is considered. Even Benjamin was won completely over by the new enthusiasm for Greek detail, and from 1826 on his books distributed to the country carpenters a knowledge of Greek detail, just as earlier they had distributed the refinements of the Late Colonial.

Yet in spite of the current use of Greek detail, Boston architecture retained its native character. Its city house types remained essentially conservative — of red brick, with large ample windows, occasional iron balconies, and delicate cornices and doorways, as we can see them today climbing the streets of Beacon Hill or ranged around the picturesque open space of Louisburg Square — and the simple grandeur of the granite-built stores and offices remained in vogue for decades. In other types of work, however, especially in the churches, the radical nature of Boston intellectualism had fuller play.

CHAPTER 6

THE CLASSIC REVIVAL IN NEW YORK

WHEN the British evacuated New York in 1783 they left a town small in size but already cosmopolitan in make-up and appearance. It was a town dirtied and ruined by fire and by the depredations of the invading army quartered upon it. The stepped gables of Dutch times still lingered here and there; but the predominant flavor was English, and the large houses that lined lower Broadway and parts of Wall Street were perhaps the closest approximation the United States possessed of the dignified eighteenth-century Georgian of English provincial towns. Yet the population had many elements from many sources, and rapidly after the Revolution this mixture of peoples increased. The town was far from being the largest in America; both Philadelphia and Boston surpassed it, and Charleston was close upon its heels.

During the next fifty years the changes in New York were extraordinary but its cosmopolitan character remained. By the end of that time it had outstripped its rivals in population, its magnificent harbor was drawing more and more of the sea trade previously centered in New England, and in extent it had grown north from about Grand Street up to the Twenties, with occasional offshoots still farther north. To its population the refugees from the French Revolution had contributed not a little, and the city's character as a great commercial center was being rapidly established.

But these fifty years had developed characteristics in its life that were much more than mere commercial capacity and an almost triumphant talent for trade, for New York was developing a type of culture among its upper classes that was cosmopolitan in a way shared by no other American center. Boston scholarship was deeper, sounder, and in a sense more separate from European currents, but it was still a culture founded essentially on English precedent with a later admixture of German ' transcendentalism.' Philadelphia was even more conservative. In New York, on the other hand, there was an acute consciousness of what was going on all over the continent of Europe. Even though perhaps superficial according to Boston lights and erratic judged by the quiet and smug progress of Philadelphia, this culture — the result of a collision of influences from all parts of America and from most of the countries of Europe — was essentially vital, interesting, and amusing.

Architecturally such a fifty years' development was ideally fitted for the evolution of new forms and the stimulation of creative minds. To great wealth had been added the necessity for a vast amount of building, and the extremely rapid growth of the city had made it difficult to cling to old ways or old forms.

The great architectural figure of the period immediately after the Revolution was John McComb, Jr., a man excellently trained, who, though his drawings reveal a delight in creative plan forms, was essentially a conservative. The son of an architect of some note, he was apparently bred entirely to the English tradition; throughout his life his aesthetic ideals were developments of either the polished church designs of James Gibbs or the delicate domestic details of Robert Adam and William Pain. An existing house now used as a mission on State Street, the curved and colonnaded front of which forms such a striking incident in the view north from the Battery, has been shown to be probably from his designs; original as it is in conception, however, there is hardly a detail in it that departs markedly from the English pattern. The columns are a little more slim, the detail perhaps a trifle more attenuated, but the basic ideas and ideals might equally well have been there had the Revolution never occurred.

Both the work and the life of John McComb, Jr., are revealing as expressions of the architecture of New York during the first two decades of the nineteenth century. Though a brilliant designer, he nevertheless remained throughout his life primarily the

Architects' elevations of three early New York houses: TOP, LEFT, *circa* 1816–20; TOP, RIGHT, *circa* 1825. Calvin Pollard, architect. (*New York Hist. Soc.*) Plans, Figure 13. BOTTOM, typical elevation made for Columbia College, 1829. Martin Thompson, architect. (*Avery Library.*)

New York houses: TOP, Calvin Pollard's elevation of a house for Dr. Brandreth. (*New York Hist. Soc.*) CENTER, Washington Square North. Martin Thompson(?), architect. (*Abbott, Mus. City of New York.*) BOTTOM, LEFT, Ferris House, the Bronx. (*Howells.*) BOTTOM, RIGHT, Brevoort House, Ninth Street and Fifth Avenue. (*Cousins, Essex.*)

New York house interiors: ABOVE, a Davis drawing. (*New York Hist. Soc.*) BELOW, LEFT, parlor door from the Brevoort House. (*Tebbs.*) BELOW, RIGHT, the parlor in the Forrest House. (*Mus. City of New York.*)

Buildings by Town and Davis: TOP, Rockaway Marine Pavilion. (*New York Hist. Soc.*) CENTER, Lafayette Terrace or Colonnade Row, New York. (*Howells and Metropolitan Mus. of Art.*) BOTTOM, architects' elevation for Lafayette Terrace. (*Avery Library.*)

builder-architect of earlier colonial tradition; though an architect who took meticulous pains with his detail and at the beginning of his career was a daring innovator, he nevertheless remained true to the fundamentally British traditions of Pain, Adam, and Chambers. His father had been a builder-architect in New York before the Revolution, and the designer of such handsome churches as the Brick Church and the North Dutch Church; some of his drawings for them are preserved among the drawings of his son in the New York Historical Society, and show no mean skill in both delineation and design. The father's churches were among the outstanding examples in America of the polished English Palladian Baroque.

Basically the son's churches are examples of the same tradition. St. John's on Varick Street, in which his brother Isaac McComb collaborated, is in essence merely another, lighter, more delicate, more sophisticated version of St. Paul's, built fifty years earlier. His alterations of his father's Brick Church are so harmonious with the older work as to seem to be by the same hand; even the Bleecker Street Church, built in 1822, is still well within the Wren-Gibbs tradition.

Yet the younger McComb was no mere copyist. Particularly in his early studies for Government House he seems eager to break the four-square tradition of the Colonial manor house, and many of his house studies disclose daring innovations in mass as well as in plan. He studied and restudied, evidently *con amore*, the rotunda stairway in the New York city hall, delighted with its new sense of open spaciousness on a geometrical foundation;[1] his free handling of the curved corner and the slim colonnade of No. 7 State Street shows the same freedom in approach that distinguishes the best work of his Boston contemporaries — Bulfinch, Banner, Benjamin, and Parris.

Still, as with these Boston contemporaries, all of McComb's

[1] It is customary with some historians to belittle the contribution of John McComb, Jr., to the New York city hall. This is the unfortunate result of an unfortunate controversy. The McComb drawings are evidence enough of the sensitive skill and artistic conscience he brought to bear on the final result, and he deserves the greatest credit — especially for preserving the delicate French refinement Mangin contributed to the original design.

innovations are within the framework of the British tradition. It is characteristic that in his detailing of the New York city hall his chief *vade mecum* was Sir William Chambers, and he may possibly have used and undoubtedly knew well James Paine's *Plans, Elevations, and Sections of Noblemen and Gentlemen's Houses;* [2] certainly in Queen's College, at Rutgers, he returns to the solid massiveness of an earlier time. Only in one work does a markedly different quality appear — in Washington Hall, at Broadway and Reade Street. Here we have a definite and conscious effort on his part to be completely American. The scheme is a common one, but there is a new and simpler classicism in its pilastered and pedimented front — it is wide and low, unassuming yet monumental, the very opposite of the slimness of No. 7 State Street or Hamilton Grange. Within this classic frame, McComb strives for new and American details, and here the precedent that evidently inspired him was L'Enfant's Federal Hall. The same Doric order is used in both; the same stars decorate the metopes. There is in both a similar search for a new symbolism to express a young nation. And even in the basic elevation concept it is likely that L'Enfant's design was in McComb's mind when he laid out the pediment carried by four pilasters placed above a simply rusticated basement. [3]

McComb's most original work is probably that which is most controlled by utility — the lighthouses and the fortifications, especially the fort that later became Castle Garden and, later still, the Aquarium. Here, where there was the least chance of imposing the Chambers and Paine details, his natural form sense emerged

---

[2] Two vols. (London: the author, 1767-83).

[3] The influence of Pierre L'Enfant on the architecture of America at the end of the eighteenth century was probably far greater than is usually realized. The enthusiasm that greeted his Federal Hall in New York was enormous; surely his great scheme, never completed, for the Robert Morris house in Philadelphia cannot have been his only other important architectural design. We know he worked on St. Paul's in New York, possibly adding the present portico and chancel and preparing designs for the completion of the spire. The late William Hindley, who had studied early ' Federal ' style work for years, considered him one of the chief inventive and liberating influences that formed the taste and the character of the architectural work of the time and freed it from the limitations of its English backgrounds (see page 14).

triumphant, and the lights at Montauk, Cape Henry, and Eton's Neck still exist to show the power of that talent. Elsewhere there is little of the revolutionary in his work. Nothing is there to parallel the Latrobe innovations or the radical simplicity of even the earliest work of Robert Mills. He had entered the building world as a bricklayer; all his life, despite his wide reputation and his brilliance in design, despite the comparative wealth he earned, he remained the builder-architect, seldom the architect as designer alone. And so, with the rapidly changing New York world of the 1830's, his vogue passed and he retired from the architectural picture, which held fresh colors from a new palette he did not know.

For New York was changing; then, as now, it was diligently seeking the novel and the fashionable. Its occasional architectural conservatisms are all the more surprising because they are so exceptional. Who, for instance, designed the Quaker meeting house on Stuyvesant Square, which bears the incongruous date of 1860? How at that late date did its simple brick walls, its beautiful proportions, and its attenuated Doric porches come to preserve and to express so surely the architectural ideals and forms of the early Federal period, which had elsewhere passed away forty years before?

One would like to know what McComb thought of the new men — Town and Thompson and Davis — who were laying out the lines of the new picture. His own later years were devoted to his family and to philanthropy. It is significant that both the John McCombs were pillars of the General Society of Mechanics and Tradesmen, which the father had helped to found, but that the architects chosen to represent the profession as founders of the National Academy of Design were Ithiel Town and Martin Thompson.

The most radical prophecy of what was to follow appeared in the competition for the New York city hall in 1802, and was due largely to the appearance on the scene of a man foreign to the English tradition — Joseph François Mangin, probably a French refugee from the Revolution, a man of imagination (perhaps too much imagination, as his plan for a great dock development on the site of the Collect Pond indicates) and of evident technical ability, an excellent draftsman, engineer, and architect. Mangin and McComb in partnership produced the winning design for the New York city hall, and with this the entire English tradition received its deathblow. None of the English detail that McComb later worked out for it, taken so carefully and modified so skillfully from the well-known English books of Sir William Chambers and others, as McComb's notes prove,[4] could obscure the fact that here for the first time in New York a building was being produced that was not Georgian and not Adam and not Regency. Its use of the orders and their relation to the openings, its sense of scale, and its general placing of detail are if anything more French than English. Yet it is a French style more dainty than that of Louis XIV and more robust than most Louis XVI work. New York's cosmopolitanism was finding its first expression.

Of Mangin's other works in New York, the Park Theater was much admired for its interior and its plan, although the exterior was never decorated with the original pediment and pilasters Mangin had planned for it. His state prison, which stood for many years on the banks of the Hudson just north of what is now Christopher Street, was restrained, beautiful in detail, and excellently planned, though its very nature prevented richness of treatment.[5] It is noteworthy that Mangin was also responsible, in his design for the old St. Patrick's on Prince and Mulberry Streets, begun in 1809, for what was possibly the first attempt at Gothic Revival architecture in New York.[6] He had obviously planned a church with twin towers of the Notre Dame variety fronting an interior of really vast scale; but the towers were completed only a little above the roof and the whole front mishandled by later alterations, so

[4] Preserved in the New York Historical Society.
[5] Drawings for it are among the Schuyler papers in the New York Public Library.
[6] The second Trinity Church, attributed on a Davis sketch to Josiah Brady, may also be called Gothic, but it was of the earlier, eighteenth-century, Batty Langley type of Gothic. St. Patrick's on the other hand, crude as it is, reveals the beginnings of the newer ' Revivalistic ' psychology.

that old engravings show a strange caricature. The church burned in the sixties and has since been rebuilt, but the lower parts of Mangin's walls still stand and show the simple window treatment he had designed and his many strange travesties of Gothic form, which in spite of their queerness have an unusual and impressive effect of great scale. The Mangin-Goerck map of New York is another evidence of Mangin's skill as a draftsman, notwithstanding the criticisms of the time regarding its accuracy; we know too that he was much interested in the problem of the military defenses of the city and that he was consulted with regard to them, first by Washington, who appointed him one of the engineers in charge, and later by Aaron Burr, to whom he also was apparently well known. Beyond this, his work in New York is still a blank page.

Another radical development in these early years was the creation of a special New York type of dwelling. Montgomery Schuyler has covered the history of the New York private house with his customary thoroughness in *The Architectural Record* [7] under the title ' The Small City House in New York.' No detailed treatment therefore is needed here. It is only necessary to point out that the type is a local one, different both from the more ample Boston examples, which often give the impression of being country houses modified for a city location, and from the Philadelphia types, which are usually more crowded and in their treatment more severe. This New York type, usually twenty or twenty-five feet wide and but two rooms deep, with the stairs at the side lighted from the rear windows, and with a colonnaded porch in the back yard leading to the privy, was well established by the 1820's. Two or three stories high, these houses usually had low-pitched roofs with delicate and beautiful dormer windows; in the deeper houses gambrel-roof types were frequent. The main floor was raised considerably above the street level, and the steps leading up to it had delicate iron railings. The door, at one side of the front, was often the only touch of richness to relieve the simplicity of the rest; although the detail of the door treatment changed as fashions

[7] Vol. viii, Nos. 4–6 (April–June 1899), pp. 357–88.

changed, its general composition — consisting of a rich surrounding treatment (if possible, in masonry), leaded sidelights (often very narrow), and a leaded fanlight (either square- or round-headed) — remained constant for a long period. The plane of the door with its fan- and sidelights was usually set well back from the front surface to give an interesting depth of shadow.

Within, well-designed mantels (often of marble), simple plaster cornices, and sometimes richly carved wooden door and window trims gave even to the small houses an effect of luxury. Staircase balusters usually were simply turned and light in scale. One New York characteristic to be found occasionally is the substitution of a scroll in the vertical plane at the bottom of the handrail in place of the horizontal spiral sweep usual in England and elsewhere in America. Sometimes, as in the Seabury-Tredwell (Old Merchant's) house, No. 27 East Fourth Street, this vertical scroll was carved with a long and graceful acanthus leaf, very much in the Duncan Phyfe manner.

On the main floor the two chief rooms were always connected by a wide door; from about 1825 on, this opening was a double sliding door, allowing the two rooms to be thrown together *en suite*. The trim of the sliding door was, next to the mantels, the richest element in the composition. During the 1820's the custom arose of placing pilasters on either side of the door, carrying a lintel with carved square end blocks and a larger rectangular central block of considerable size; often there were cap molds over the blocks as well. The leaves carved in the blocks usually were of acanthus type and projected boldly; they were the last surviving evidences of the older Baroque tradition.[8] This motif, so used, seems a pure localism in New York State; it continued in use well into the thirties, when Greek forms were elsewhere dominant.

The Greek Revival houses of the 1830's are developments of this type. The sliding door between front and back rooms becomes merely part of a large, architectonic, columnar screen. Ionic or Corinthian columns, free-standing, are on either side of the door,

---

[8] In No. 10 Greenwich Street the carving of these blocks is of cornucopias in a definitely French Rococo manner.

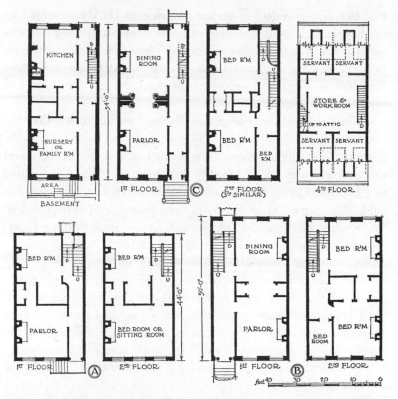

FIGURE 13. DEVELOPMENT OF THE NEW YORK HOUSE PLAN, 1815–
35. A. Typical New York city house before 1820. Calvin Pollard (?), architect.
B. Typical New York house *circa* 1825. Calvin Pollard, architect. Similar to
existing houses on Prince and King Streets. (*A and B, N. Y. Hist. Soc.*) C. Tred-
well (Old Merchant's) House, 27 East Fourth Street, 1832. Has been attributed
to Minard Lafever. (*C, H.A.B.S.*)

and an entablature carries across them from wall to wall. The
other doors in the lower rooms, though often enriched with pilasters, are kept entirely subsidiary in scale, and the fireplace mantels [9] are usually broad and low. Simple, refined moldings, broad
surfaces, and concentrated enrichment in rosettes or bands or
carved capitals or central plaster ceiling roses combined with the
high ceilings (11 to 14 feet high) and the broad areas of plain

[9] It is perhaps significant that post-Revolutionary New York had never liked
the rich overmantels common in Massachusetts, and preferred to keep the simple,
broad, slightly projecting chimney breast as free wall space for the most important
picture or, later, for a large mirror.

wall to create an effect of serene and elegant clarity, accented by the long hangings at the windows, the classic-patterned carpets, and the broad mahogany surfaces of 'American Empire' furniture. These large high rooms made an excellent framework either for quiet family living or, when thrown together, for large and formal entertainments.

The front room was traditionally the 'parlor,' but unlike the 'best parlor' of New England farmhouses it was also used as the general family living room. The room below it in the basement was used as a nursery and family workroom; it might also be used as a breakfast room because of its convenience to the kitchen behind. The rear room on the main floor throughout this period of the twenties, thirties, and forties was the main family dining room; its use as a 'back parlor' only came in later.[10]

On the floor immediately above the main floor were usually three or four bedrooms, two of them large ones with ample dressing rooms and closet space between, and one or two of them small 'hall bedrooms.' Sometimes there were two or even three such floors and at the top of the house an attic floor (often lighted by dormers) containing several small servants' rooms and frequently a large central open space for sewing, 'feminine work' of all kinds, and storage.

The whole made an efficient, gracious, and dignified house for family living. Given the first error in New York land planning — the standardization of the 25-by-100-foot lot, or the 20-by-100-

---

[10] Contemporary evidence on this much disputed point seems overwhelmingly convincing. Thus J[acques Gérard] Milbert, in *Itinéraire pittoresque du fleuve Hudson et des parties latérales de l'Amérique du nord* (Paris: Gauguain & Cie, 1828–9), page 36, in describing a visit to America in 1825 refers to the basement room as 'la nursery.' James Fenimore Cooper, in *Notions of the Americans, Picked up by a Travelling Bachelor*, Vol. I (Philadelphia: Carey, Lea & Carey, 1828), page 145, says of New York houses: 'The basement contains the nursery and the usual offices.' Mrs. Trollope is even more definite. 'In nearly all the houses,' she writes (again in *Domestic Manners of the Americans*, page 161), 'the dining and drawing rooms are on the same floor, with ample folding doors between them; when thrown together they certainly make a very noble apartment, but no doors can be barriers sufficient between dining and drawing rooms.' Finally, Catherine E. Havens, in her *Diary of a Little Girl in Old New York* (New York: Henry Collins Brown [c1919]), under date of 6 August 1849, in recalling a period about five years earlier, refers to the front basement room as 'my nursery.' I owe the Cooper reference to an unpublished paper on 'The New York Row House, 1800–1850,' by Miss N. M. Scott. The list of references given here is not inclusive and might be increased.

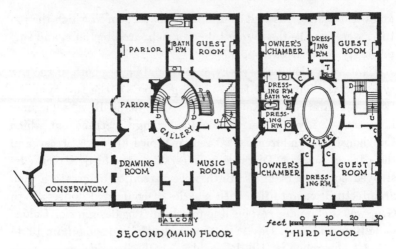

FIGURE 14. PARISH HOUSE, New York. Plans. R. G. Hatfield, architect.
(*N. Y. Pub. Lib.*) Distinguished for the variety of its room shapes, its elaborate
plumbing and highly developed bath and dressing rooms.

foot lot — it is hard to see how the house layout could have been
improved, at least for families moderately well off.

As time went on, numerous changes were made in the details of
this basic scheme. Service stairs behind the main stairs became
common. Oval central main stairs lighted by a skylight at the top
were often used in the earlier period, as for instance in the large
and elegant house at No. 8 Greenwich Street; and skylighting of
a central stair well became nearly universal after 1835. Bathrooms
began to make their appearance in the 1830's, replacing one or
more hall bedrooms, though in the common use of water closets
and plumbing generally New York was more backward than Philadelphia.[11] But, once bathrooms had been adopted, New York rapidly outdistanced other cities in the lavishness and complexity of
the installations. Thus R. G. Hatfield's Parish house (1848) at
Broadway and Seventeenth Street, the plans for which are in the
New York Public Library, had seven water closets and eleven tubs

[11] New York's shortage of water up to the time of the completion of the Croton
aqueduct undoubtedly had much to do with this. Privies at the rear of the back
yard, often connected with the house by attractive wooden colonnades or trellises
or porches, were standard even in large and expensive New York houses until the
1840's.

and wash basins,[12] as well as a master's bathroom in which the fix-
tures were used as the foundation of a rich, architectonic, and surprisingly modern bathroom.[13]

Naturally there were many exceptional houses both of the row
type and the individual free-standing type. Of the row type the
two most interesting examples were Colonnade Row, sometimes
known as Lafayette Terrace or La Grange Terrace (of which
four houses, much altered, still remain), on Lafayette Street, and
the earlier London Terrace on West Twenty-third Street (destroyed some years ago). Both were attempts to create a rich
architectural composition with a series of connected houses; Seth
Geer was the builder responsible for them. The designer of Colonnade Row was A. J. Davis; he also evidently had something to do
— just how much is still debatable — with the other, more modest project as well.

In Colonnade Row (1836) a continuous colonnade of Greek
Corinthian columns, beautifully executed, ran the whole length of
the group above a simple rusticated ground floor. The entrances,
raised but little above the ground level, were decorated with Greek
Doric columns, and on the projecting cheeks of the steps in front
stood slim and elegant cast-iron candelabrum-type lamp posts.[14]
The row is built of Westchester marble, and the detail is well
placed and unusually perfect in conception and elevation. Colonnade Row was New York's most extravagant as well as most original attempt to build dignified, gracious, and elegant houses for
wealthy tenants, and it achieved instantaneous fame. Yet Davis's
wishes for it were even more original; in the Davis collection at the
Avery Library is a drawing, labeled ' Approaching what Lafayette Terrace ought to be,' which shows the houses crowned by interesting vine-grown pergolas and roof gardens.

London Terrace, designed four years earlier (1832), was simpler and more unassuming in every way. Its long low mass of small

12 Miss N. M. Scott's figures.
13 House plans by Calvin Pollard in the New York Historical Society, covering
roughly the period from 1820 to 1850, are an excellent index of the course of development of the more conventional New York home.
14 Some of these lamp posts have been preserved at Ringwood, the Hewitt estate, now a public park in northern New Jersey.

houses was decorated somewhat monotonously with a continuous parade of Greek antae in lieu of pilasters. The scheme may have been borrowed from an earlier pilaster-decorated row that once stood on Charlton Street and antedated the Greek Revival movement. It had Doric pilasters of brick above an arcaded basement, and simple detail of the Late Colonial or Federal type.

Another interesting row or 'terrace' was De Pauw Row on Bleecker Street, probably the work of Samuel Dunbar. This was a group of unusually large houses extending a whole block on the site of the present Mills Hotel. Like some of the rows in London, it obtained its effect by treating the whole as a composition with central and end pavilions. One of the doorways still serves as the entrance to a restaurant in the next block east. Other important rows existed on Bleecker Street; one of these, Le Roy Place (1827), consisted of two rows of stone houses across the street from each other, extending from Mercer to Greene Street.

And there were also the exceptionally large houses, occupying two or more lots. Some of those on Washington Square were of this type, as was the Edwin Forrest house on West Twenty-second Street. There were occasionally free-standing houses in the city too. Two of the finest were the Brevoort (De Rham) house once on the northwest corner of Ninth Street and Fifth Avenue — four-square, dignified, quite different in its paneled front and projecting porch from most New York houses — and the largest of them all, the Stevens 'palace' on Murray Street. Both have been attributed to Davis. The Stevens palace was certainly by him, and many of his drawings for it exist. Its plan, with a great central hall, is monumental to the highest degree and shows that interest in geometrical shape relationships which was such a marked feature of Davis's design. An interior — clear and spacious and refined — preserved for us in a superb colored rendering by Davis in the New York Historical Society, has been thought to represent rooms in the Stevens palace. However, from what we know of the plan of that building, this drawing almost certainly is of a quite different residence.

Occasionally buildings with the characteristics of other localities are found. Such are the bow-fronted houses on the north side of Sixteenth Street and on Union Square, both built about 1836–7. In these the expression has the qualities of Boston work; in scale, in basic form, even in detail they look more like the work of Parris, perhaps, than of the New York builders.

By the late thirties New York had already begun to be the foremost American city in adopting new fashions, in architecture as in other things. A. J. Davis was himself a great innovator, endlessly seeking modifications of characteristic types and current styles. He claimed to be the first designer who rebelled against the ordinary high ' stoop ' and substituted grade entrances, thus developing the typical ' American basement ' type of house. He designed famous Gothic city houses, like the Waddell villa and the ' House of Mansions.' And others too, notably Arnot and Renwick, from 1840 on were doing Gothic variations of the typical New York house.

In the forties as well came the great influx of Italianesque influence; together with the gradually increasing popularity of Connecticut brownstone it revolutionized the appearance of the new streets. Marble also came into increasing use; the ' Marble House,' still standing on the southwest corner of Eighth Street and Fifth Avenue and dating from about 1847, is characteristic. The earliest of these houses carry over some of the simplicity and great scale of the Greek Revival, and the detail is restrained and well executed. The Belmont houses once on lower Fifth Avenue, designed by Frederick Diaper, an English architect, showed the quiet and gracious dignity of which this typically New York type of ' Italian ' was capable.

In 1848 Detlef Lienau, a German-born architect trained in Germany and Paris (where he had worked under Labrouste), arrived in New York and almost at once entered upon a large and wealthy practice. With his work the age of eclecticism in New York house design really began. His Schiff house in 1850 and his Schermerhorn houses on West Twenty-third Street in the following years were superb examples of French nineteenth-century design, rather néo-Grec in their refinement and originality. But in plan as in detail they were no longer examples of the New York tradition. They were beautiful and sumptuous houses, but they were in essence imports.

An interesting element in the later New York houses is the cast-iron balcony or porch, with its lacy and slim supports, its scrolled and open brackets, its curved roof. There are still many examples left, though their number is rapidly diminishing; one of the finest is that of the late Greek Revival Harper house on the west side of Gramercy Park. The history of these balconies is obscure — where they were first used, or who first realized the loveliness of the contrast between their intricate lines and the simple brick surfaces behind them. They are rare before 1840; then they suddenly become common all over the central and southern states. They are to be found in Pennsylvania, New York, and Ohio, though they reached their greatest development in Charleston, Savannah, Mobile, and especially New Orleans. It is perhaps significant that many New Orleans examples were cast there from patterns brought from the North, and that their sudden popularity coincides with a period of great northern commercial penetration of the southern states. Could the New York architects have set the original fashion?

The designers of most of the New York Greek Revival houses are unknown. It is manifest that there was in the city a large number of thoroughly trained and even brilliant designers and craftsmen; but the professional architect, as distinguished from the builder and contractor, had as yet hardly emerged.[15] Even in the early thirties we know that the architects then in New York usually worked with the contractors and builders rather than with the owner, and that contractors bought plans from the architects and

---

[15] The row of houses by John McComb, Jr., on State Street is one of the earliest examples in New York of the type known definitely to have been designed by an architect. In the New York Historical Society there is a collection of drawings by Calvin Pollard (d. 1850), which contains numerous plans and elevations of typical New York houses. One, apparently by a different hand, is on paper dated 1816. It is possibly by the architect-builder to whom Pollard was apprenticed. The Pollard drawings date from about 1825 to 1850; the houses included are of the typical New York variety. Evidently he was one of the designers of many of them. Others were designed by Minard Lafever, Town and Davis, Martin Thompson, and Samuel Dunbar.

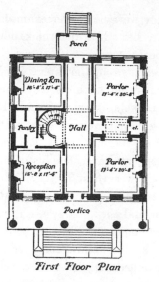

First Floor Plan

Figure 15. MARSHALL HOUSE, formerly in Pelham Bay Park, New York.
(*Great Georgian Houses.*) Magnificent hall and entertainment rooms, and ingenious planning of dining room, pantry, and service stairs, within a formal
temple-type envelope.

draftsmen. Interesting evidence of the skill of these architect-
draftsmen is to be found in a set of drawings, now in the Avery
Library, Columbia University, made for additions to Columbia
College, in 1818, by an architect named James O'Donnell, who was
later the architect of Notre Dame church (1824) in Montreal.
His Columbia drawings for work partly executed are meticulous
and far in advance of those for the original King's College fifty
years earlier, or even of the existing drawings of Asher Benjamin.
Other drawings from an even earlier period now in the McComb
collection at the New York Historical Society, and bearing other
names than McComb's, reveal a similarly advanced technical skill;
it is to men such as these that we evidently owe the polish and ur-
banity of the earlier New York house work.[16]

16 The dating of old New York houses is difficult because of the occasional persistence of earlier forms in later periods; builders' houses are more backward than
architects' houses. A few generalizations, however, may be hazarded:
   1. Steep-roofed houses are *likely* to be early in date; in the period 1830–40 the
visible roof tended more and more to be replaced with a 'flat' roof.
   2. Sliding doors between front and back rooms *generally* indicate a date subse-

Two men stand out from this general mass: Josiah Brady and Martin Thompson. Of Brady's work we know little save the naïve but much admired Gothic of the second Trinity, the later and more ambitious Gothic of St. Thomas's Church, and the dignified Greek Revival of the Anderson house at Throg's Neck; but we do know that he was a master of Alexander Jackson Davis and is referred to by Dunlap [17] as the ' only practicing architect in New York ' at the time. This undoubtedly means that he was the only man who was an architect and not a builder as well. He was also the architect of the Second Congregational Church (1826) at Prince and Mercer Streets, which is interesting for having a porch of heavy, unfluted Greek Doric columns with end piers decorated with round-headed niches. This combination of Greek and Roman forms was undoubtedly a conscious one, expressive of the non-archaeological character so common in American Greek Revival work. The spirit is not unlike that in much work of Haviland's.

Martin Thompson was a man of a different type, artistically advanced and a magnificent designer but professionally conservative — a man who, although like McComb he used the term architect, never entirely released himself from the earlier system of the architect-contractor. His first important work was the building for the Bank of the United States on Wall Street, later the home of the United States Assay Office; its front still stands, re-erected, as the south façade of the American Wing of the Metropolitan Museum

quent to 1825. If in addition the detail is thoroughly Greek, a date after 1830 is probable.

3. The so-called ' American basement ' type of house, entered directly from grade, with inside stairs up to the main floor, was not commonly used so far as I know before 1840. A. J. Davis attempted to eliminate the ' stoop ' as far as possible and he is responsible for this particular innovation.

4. The shape and treatment of window lintels is an indication of period. Windows with brick arches in the Colonial manner indicate a house *probably* built prior to 1820. Stone lintels paneled and with raised central and end blocks are most common between 1820 and 1830. Plain stone lintels are standard for most 1830 houses; however, plain stone lintels with a cap mold alone are sometimes found — they grew more and more common, continuing in use well into the 1860's. Stone lintels rising to a point in the center are especially common in the middle thirties; they were a favorite motif of Martin Thompson, who used them as early as 1829.

5. Brick and brownstone in combination *usually* indicate a date in the 1850's.

[17] William Dunlap, *History of the Rise and Progress of the Arts of Design in the United States*, 2 vols. (New York: G. P. Scott and Co., 1834); new ed. edited by F. W. Bayley and C. F. Goodspeed, 3 vols. (Boston: C. E. Goodspeed & Co., 1918).

of Art. This building, commissioned as early as 1822, is a polished and knowing piece of dignified classic work, well detailed and beautifully executed. In the breadth of its proportions it shows that freedom from rigidly conventional classic proportions — a quality that may have been the result of ignorance but is often the cause of great and characteristic charm — which is frequently typical of American Classic Revival work. His second important work was even more distinguished: the second Merchants' Exchange, burned in the great fire of 1835. This lavish building, with its lovely curve-ended exchange room, its powerful scale combined with delicate detail, was during its brief life one of the most beautiful public buildings in America. Drawings by Thompson for the Columbia Grammar School in 1829 show a monumental building of scholarly Greek Revival type; and an elevation for the houses that were to be erected on Columbia College property on Murray and Chapel streets — all who built on these lots had to agree to follow this elevation in its main lines — is interesting evidence of the advent of Greek detail into New York house design. It is so similar to much of the work built later in Greenwich Village that the conclusion seems probable that Thompson was one of those most often called on by builders for designs. He was probably also the architect of the typical elevation and many of the houses built on the Sailors' Snug Harbor property in Washington Square North. These are so much like the Columbia College drawings as to make that attribution probably correct. In addition, according to family tradition, Martin Thompson was the architect for Sailors' Snug Harbor on Staten Island (the builder of which was Samuel Thomson) and is credited in an obituary in *The American Architect* [18] with the earlier work on Sing Sing prison and with the New York State Arsenal in Central Park, now the Park Department offices. Little is known about his later career. He was evidently a man of some importance, for he was Street Commissioner for a great number of years. Several designs for the proposed enlargement of the city hall in the fifties and

[18] Vol. ii, No. 85 (11 August 1877). I owe this information to Mrs. C. H. Hanscomb, a granddaughter of Martin Thompson.

sixties, for which he was paid by the city, are testimony that he still stood high in public esteem. Later he seems to have retired altogether from the practice of architecture; he died in 1877 in Glen Cove.

Thompson brings us into the new architectural age, for when Ithiel Town established a New York practice in 1826 he took Thompson into partnership.[19] The exact relationship between them is difficult to classify. Such work as the steeple for St. Mark's-in-the-Bouwerie, so unconventional in its simplicity of line, and the famous Canal Street Greek Doric church, which Lafever referred to in 1829 as the finest piece of Greek work in New York, were done under the name of Town and Thompson; yet local New York accounts give all the credit to Thompson. Something similar happens in the case of Town's later partners, Davis and Dakin, but it would be foolish to underestimate the importance of Town's influence and personality. Trained thoroughly in the builder-architect tradition of New England — probably in Asher Benjamin's architectural school in Boston — and responsible for the remarkable early Gothic Trinity Church in New Haven, Town won national fame as the inventor of the Town truss for bridges; and not only fame, for the common use of this type of truss (many of the covered bridges still standing are examples) brought him a large fortune as well. It is his handling of this wealth that reveals the unusual character of the man, for he spent it lavishly on travel, study, and the acquisition of what was undoubtedly by far the largest and finest library of architectural and art books and engravings in the country at the time. One gets echoes of the renown of this collection from many sources over many years. Much of his library at this time was kept in New York and made virtually a public library. *The Picture of New York*,[20] published by Goodrich in 1828, speaks of the ' architectural rooms ' of Town, Thomp-

---

[19] See Roger Hale Newton's *Town and Davis, Architects* (New York: Columbia University Press, 1942). This thorough and detailed study is of immense value, not only for the light it throws on Town and Davis themselves but because it serves as a brilliant introduction to the whole subject of American nineteenth-century architects.

[20] [Edmund M. Blunt,] *The Picture of New York, and Stranger's Guide* . . . (New York: A. T. Goodrich [1828]).

son, and Davis, where anyone who was interested could consult Town's books or pore over his engravings. Later the collection was brought together in New Haven, in Town's house, which had been specifically designed to receive it.[21] The famous Mrs. Lydia Sigourney describes the house and library at great length in an article [22] published in *The Ladies' Companion* in 1839. After Town's death his books and prints were sold in a series of auctions, printed catalogues of which exist; yet the number of books in these catalogues is far below the number we know he owned, and what happened to the rest of them is still a fascinating subject for conjecture.

Town was evidently a man of powerful personality, a great job getter, but also a scholar and an idealist. He was one of the founders of the National Academy of Design. He evidently dreamed of an American architecture and an American art, independent and standing on their own feet, and through his magnificent collection of books wished to open to American architects all of the stores of European knowledge, so that with a real solidity of foundation they might develop an American architecture for American conditions. Just how important he was as a designer it is almost impossible to discover. Certainly both with Thompson and with his more famous partner, Alexander Jackson Davis, the greater amount of the actual drafting and detailed study of the problems was left to his partners. It is probably also true that the design was chiefly theirs too. Town seems to have realized and accepted his real part in the great Classic Revival movement in America — that of being an inspiration, a counselor, a sort of public-relations counsel, and also (because of the wealth that had come to him from his bridges) a magnificent patron as well.

In all the complicated accounts of the partnership of Town and Davis that still exist, although there are many evidences of occasional friction there is never a sign of artistic jealousy on the part of either. The frictions seem entirely financial or personal, and this in spite of the fact that local papers tended everywhere

[21] See page 174.

[22] 'The Residence and Library of Ithiel Town, Esq.,' *The Ladies' Companion,* First Series, Vol. x, No. 1 (January 1839), pp. 123–6.

to give credit to the local member of the firm. Fortunately a tremendous mass of material showing the history of the firm in detail is available and through it one can get a lively picture of the gradual development of a strong architectural profession. In the early years — Davis was taken into partnership in 1829 — the accounts are extremely mixed. Already well known as a draftsman, Davis continued to work for many clients in a sketchy way — apparently selling designs and drawings to builders as well as to individuals — and continued for some time to make those vivid and meticulous sketches of American towns and American buildings which were the basis for so many of the beautiful engravings by which the America of that time is known. At times Davis was even working for other architects, whether as a designer or merely as a delineator it is impossible to say. Thus there is evidence that he made drawings for both Brady and Thompson while at the same time he was a partner of Town.

Notwithstanding this confusion it is typical of these newer professional architects that Alexander Jackson Davis made his approach to architecture first through the medium of sketches of landscapes and buildings. A precocious artist, he was famous for the accurate delineations of buildings he made for lithographers and engravers before he was noted as an architect, and he first appears in the directory as an ' architectural composer.' He served some sort of architectural apprenticeship with Josiah Brady, but his education did not end there, and he made an extended visit to Boston in 1827. In Boston — and this, too, is characteristic of the newer era — he was introduced into the very heart of the intellectual circles. Through his friend Dr. Sargent he was given the run of the Athenaeum. Intellectual Boston was then in the forefront of the new classical movement; at the Athenaeum or in the homes of his Boston acquaintances he must have been immersed in that fruitful and exciting atmosphere which was to stimulate such important literary growth later on. A natural talent for drawing, a year of exposure to the intellectual ferment of Boston classicism — what more stimulating preparation for a young architect could there have been? And a practice of architecture growing from such seeds was of necessity different in kind as well as in expression from one that grew out of any mere practice of the building trades, however diligent and skillful.

Later, in New York, the Town and Davis firm held a similar social position. They were accepted members of the cultural aristocracy; they frequented that society of which Dr. Hosack was perhaps the leading light — a society as cultivated as, and more cosmopolitan than, the more brilliant Boston circles. The 'architectural rooms' of Town, Davis, and Thompson symbolized, as they forwarded, the first acceptance in New York of the architect primarily as an artist and professional man, on a level with the members of the other professions, and not merely as a sort of superior tradesman.

The whole picture one gathers of architecture in the late twenties and early thirties reveals a situation chaotic but violently alive. Outside of the work of John McComb, Jr., which was rapidly diminishing in amount as he withdrew from active practice, New York had — as Boston had at about the same time — a small reservoir of excellent architectural talent: Brady, Thompson, Davis, Lafever, Dunbar, Pollard, and others whose names we do not know. James Gallier has left a vivid impression of the architectural world of New York in his little-known *Autobiography*,[23] where he writes as follows:

On my arrival in New York on the 14th of April, 1832, I considered a large city as the most likely place to expect employment in my profession, but here I found that the majority of people could with difficulty be made to understand what was meant by a professional architect; the builders, that is, the carpenters and bricklayers, all called themselves architects, and were at that time the persons to whom owners of property applied when they required plans for building; the builder hired some poor draftsman, of whom there were some half a dozen in New York at that time, to make the plans, paying him a mere trifle for his services. The drawings so made were, it is true, but of little value, and some proprietors built without having any regular plan. When they wanted a house built, they looked about for one already finished, which they thought suitable for their purpose; and then bargained with a builder to erect for them such another, or

[23] *Autobiography of James Gallier, Architect* (Paris: E. Brière, 1864).

one with such alterations upon the model as they might point out. All this was soon changed, however, and architects began to be employed by proprietors before going to the builders; and in this way, in a short time, the style of buildings public and private showed signs of rapid improvement.

There was at that time, properly speaking, only one architect's office in New York, kept by Town and Davis. Town had been a carpenter, but was no draftsman; he had obtained a patent on a wooden bridge, the *right* to erect which he sold to several parties in the States, and had made some money by it; he had been once or twice to London, and bought there a huge collection of books in various languages upon the arts, and furnished his office with a very respectable library. . . Davis, his partner, was no mechanic, but a good draftsman, and possessed much taste as an artist. . .

Gallier goes on to mention the Dakins — James H., a student and partner of Town, who was later to join Gallier in New Orleans, and Charles, his brother, who accompanied Gallier to the South — and Minard Lafever, with whom he had an ill-fated and disastrous partnership for a year. It is an interesting fact also that the accounts of Town, Davis, and Dakin report the payment of one hundred and seventy-five dollars to Gallier for drawings; it was probably during the making of these that Gallier became acquainted with Dakin.[24]

Trained in the more advanced architectural world of England as Gallier was, this confused professional situation in New York was little to his liking and, disgusted, he left — to found a fortune in New Orleans and become one of its two or three most popular and skillful architects.[25] Yet this New York condition apparently had its advantages. The growth of the city during those years was extraordinarily rapid and the amount of building required was far in excess of what could have been built in a normal architectural way. The builders, however, could call upon this small group of architects, all of them men of talent and skill, for their plans; the builders themselves had standards of execution and a general

24 Gallier states that James H. Dakin was his first employer in New York. He says that he was paid four dollars a day, but the Town, Davis, and Dakin accounts in the Davis collection at the Avery Library give the amount as two and a half dollars per day.
25 See Chapter 9.

knowledge of architectural detail, left over from earlier contractor-architect days, which enabled them to interpret these plans and designs sympathetically. The results are the charming streets of Greenwich Village and parts of the Lower East Side, bordered by houses that are simple and harmonious in exterior proportions, with rooms beautiful in their relationships, with detail — usually in the newly fashionable Greek manner — of refinement and dignity, and with doors as beautiful in detail as they are excellent in general conception. Alone the builders could not have produced this, and working alone the few architects themselves could not have spread over the city such a large amount of satisfactory work.

The ' Old Merchant's [Seabury-Tredwell] House ' (1832) on East Fourth Street is a typical example, fortunately preserved through continuous ownership in one family for over a hundred years ; restored as a museum today, it illustrates how harmoniously the simple mahogany surfaces and the rather heavy carving of so-called American Empire furniture, relieved here and there by the lighter pieces of Duncan Phyfe or his followers, resting on rich French carpets, fitted into those tall and ample rooms. It is characteristic of this house also that many of its details are similar to those shown in the Lafever books.[26] Thus the front door has resemblances to Plate 42 of *The Young Builder's General Instructor*, the colonnaded opening between front and back parlors is like Plate 60 of *The Modern Builders' Guide*, the plaster rose resembles Plate 21 of *The Beauties of Modern Architecture*, and the plaster cornice ornament in the parlor is obviously based on Plate 64 of *The Young Builder's General Instructor*. The house shows too, in the exquisiteness of its carving (the main floor newel with its sweeping acanthus scroll at the bottom of the handrail is characteristic) and in the grace of its iron exterior railings, the high standards of workmanship then current; but it also shows, in a certain naïve quality and occasional confusion of form (such as the extra band of carving over the architrave of the parlor screen), the fact that no one designer who knew his detail as did the architects already mentioned could have been responsible for the execu-

26 See Appendix A.

tion of the work. The larger houses — such as the best of those on the north side of Washington Square, the Rhinelander house at No. 1 Fifth Avenue, the Perry house by James Dakin in Brooklyn, and others — were indubitably the results of the complete architectural services of their respective architects; this was doubtless true also of the churches and public buildings that were erected. But, taken by and large, the greater part of the domestic work of the period was done according to the other system, and we can only wonder that under those conditions its level should have been so extraordinarily high.

As the thirties wore on, this method of constructing buildings gradually disappeared; more and more the architect appears to all intents and purposes to have become the modern professional architect, working on a fee basis for individual clients, not only designing but also overseeing contracts and detail and superintending the construction. As this development proceeded, the method of payment necessarily began to change. In the earlier system, payment seems to have been largely arranged at so much a drawing, and Davis at least continued this practice in billing individual clients for whom he was furnishing full services. Typical prices quoted are:

In 1848: —

Designs without superintendence or working drawings —

Cottage or villa of $1,000	$50.00
of $2,500	$60.00
of $5,000	$75.00
of $10,000	$100.00
of $20,000	$150.00

Designs already done, selected from the artist's portfolio $25.00

Design for simple farmhouse	$30.00
for lodge, garden building, etc. . .	$25.00
for entrance gate with adjoining fence	$15.00
for front elevation only of house . .	$15.00
for church of moderate size	$100.00

In 1850: —

For full professional services . . . . 5 per cent

Set of drawings and specifications . . . 1 per cent

Drawings separately (medium class of buildings) —

Principal floor plan $15.00

Upper floor plans $5.00

Elevation of principal front $15.00

Specifications $15.00

Section showing interior $10.00

These prices should be multiplied by from three to five, to give their counterparts today.

The same development toward professional autonomy also brought two more modern elements into the picture: the student draftsman and the large architectural office. In an era when architectural schools as we know them today did not yet exist,[27] the only method of entry into the profession was through the office of either an architect or a builder. Town and Davis made a special point of having student draftsmen who paid them various amounts in order to learn the profession; some of the existing drawings coming from the Davis office (drawings of Greek temple plans, or orders, or the like) are undoubtedly the work of such students. But an office doing the work they did required much more than student draftsmen, and the trained draftsman working on a salary became an essential element in the scheme. Unfortunately no complete list of the Town-Davis draftsmen exists, although occasional names can be picked out. Such for instance was James H. Dakin, who was first a draftsman, for a time a partner, and later left to join Gallier in New Orleans; also there were John Stirewalt of North Carolina, Robert Seaton of New Orleans, Richard Lathers of Georgetown (Washington), J. A. Suydam, William Harrison, and J. C. Cady, later a partner in the once well-known firm of Cady, Berg & See.

[27] Schools of architectural drawing, however, were not uncommon. Asher Benjamin conducted one in Boston; John Haviland and Hugh Bridport taught architecture in Philadelphia, and Robert T. Elliott in Detroit. Undoubtedly there were many other similar schools elsewhere.

The pay of these men was sometimes quite high. Gallier mentions wages up to seven dollars a day, which would be the equivalent today of approximately one hundred and fifty to two hundred dollars a week. By the middle forties, through the power and prestige of other architects like Upjohn and Renwick, who were chiefly associated with the Gothic Revival, the launching of the architectural profession was well-nigh complete; as far as its functions went, the architectural office of those days was doing almost the same work as the architectural office of today. Payment was usually on a percentage basis, most frequently five or six per cent; but in connection with this it must be remembered that the difficulties and complications of modern structural systems and modern mechanical equipment scarcely existed as yet.

The decade of the thirties was essentially the era of the triumph of the Greek Revival in New York. Greek detail began to appear spasmodically in the late twenties, although it had been influencing work in Washington and Baltimore almost from the break of the century, and although even in staid Boston — in occasional work as early as 1818 — the Greek inspiration is apparent. The reason for this late date for the New York Greek Revival is possibly to be sought in the enduring influence of such powerful personalities as that of John McComb, Jr. The work of Mangin and the fact that New York had a strong body of French settlers also played a part. The birth of the Greek Revival in New York corresponds surprisingly closely with the time of Town's arrival here; in fact Davis credits Town with building the first Greek doorway in New York. Here the influence of Town's magnificent library can be read. The architectural rooms of Town, Davis, and Thompson at the Exchange became a center for the artistic élite of New York. Town and Thompson, both founders of the National Academy of Design (Town in the 'First Fifteen' and Thompson in the 'Second Fifteen'), together with Davis, who was influential in that other great institution, the American Institute of Arts, had the closest possible contact with many of the important artists of the America of their day, and furthermore all three had wide acquaintance throughout New York society. This combination of magnificent library, three men of great originality and talent, and an influence that permeated the entire intellectual life of New York could not but have a great effect; though New York was one of the last of the cities to take up the Greek Revival, it rapidly became the city in which Greek forms enjoyed the widest repute and were most brilliantly and lavishly used.

Minard Lafever (1797–1854) belonged to a different world from that frequented by Town and Davis, but his influence also was deep and wide. Trained as a carpenter in the Finger Lakes region of New York, to which his family had moved in his early childhood from his birthplace near Morristown, he was entirely self-taught architecturally. He preserved all his life something of the common-sense practicality of his early training, and during at least the early part of his practice in New York (where he arrived in 1828) he worked as a draftsman for builders. It was hard and not particularly rewarding work, as the Gallier quotation [28] shows, and apparently it prevented Lafever from emerging as a full-fledged professional architect until the forties. Davis never mentions him, yet undoubtedly his designs and his books exerted a tremendous influence in the New York of that time. It is by his first three books that his Greek Revival work must be judged: *The Young Builder's General Instructor* (1829), *The Modern Builders' Guide* (1833), and *The Beauties of Modern Architecture* (1835). His artistic progress from the crudity of the first to the polished restraint of the last is amazing in so brief a period; it shows Lafever to have been not only an omnivorous reader but a designer of unusual and continually growing aesthetic sensitiveness. All the books are simple and unassuming. All bear witness to their author's carpenter training and his eagerness to help those who like himself entered architecture through the building trades. Yet all the books show a driving, imaginative, creative force that expresses itself with clear and lovely restraint. The second and third contain probably the most exquisite and the least archaeo-

[28] See page 140.

logical of all American Greek Revival detail — personal, inventive, restrained.[29]

As a pure creator of beautiful form — the pure artist in architecture — Lafever was at his time unrivaled. The exquisite character of the plates in his book, their bold modifications of Greek precedent, their controlling sense of artistic restraint and propriety, their sure spotting of ornament — especially the rosettes he loved so much — not only go to show what freedom is included in the term 'Greek Revival' but also reveal Lafever as perhaps the greatest designer of architectural decoration of his time in America. The broad acceptance of his leadership over large parts of America bears witness as well to the general high level of popular taste. To him more than to any other one man is due the clear, inviting quality of the interiors of Greek Revival houses and the crisp, imaginative character of the wood and plaster detail that so frequently accents and beautifies them.

Nevertheless, of Lafever's Greek work in New York almost nothing is known. The old St. James's Church on James Street near Chatham Square is probably by him; its gallery front design appears in *The Beauties of Modern Architecture*, and the granite door with its delicately scrolled lintel cornice is purely in his style. But, although we know little definite Greek Revival work by him, his touch can be read in door and mantel and interior details in many houses all over the city, and his influence spread far beyond.

Lafever was to earn a great fame in Brooklyn later with a series of superb Gothic Revival churches, of which Holy Trinity (1844–7) is the largest and most famous, the Church of the Saviour near by (1844) the most refined and exquisite. Packer Collegiate Institute with its rather prim, simple English Gothic is his too, as are the stone tunnel and steps at the river end of Montague Street — a monument of true Greek simplicity. The Reformed Church of the Heights (1851) and the old Brooklyn Savings Bank (1847), both recently destroyed, showed his brilliant use of the later eclectic classic forms that began to come in in the

[29] See Appendix A.

forties; much of this work he included in his last great book, *The
Complete Architectural Instructor,* published posthumously in
New York by G. P. Putnam in 1857.

His Brooklyn fame was chiefly as a Gothicist, but his influence
outside the city was almost entirely Greek and came from the wide
distribution of his books, particularly in the West and the South.
So to the man of Brooklyn 'Lafever' meant Gothic, but at the
very same moment to the man of Ohio or New Orleans 'Lafever'
meant Greek.

In New York houses the general plan and proportions were so
fixed by the satisfactory traditional norm that the Greek inspiration could only be used in details — how exquisitely may be seen
in the beautiful and restrained plates of the Lafever books. It is
the free application of the Greek inspiration to forms and materials essentially new and different that gives this style in New York
houses its peculiar vitality. To men like Dunbar and Lafever, and
to Davis in his earlier house work, the Greek forms were not divine
revelations to be copied unthinkingly; they were, rather, a new
alphabet of grace, restraint, and beauty with which a new and
vital language could be formed. Simple surfaces replaced the
fussy small-scale moldings of the earlier wooden door and window
trim; anthemia, Greek volutes, and especially rosettes were used
in new and lovely ways of which the Greeks had never dreamed.
Some of the Davis houses for Ravenswood in Astoria show the
same freedom in basic design that Lafever showed in detail; they
reveal, too, that Davis was already experimenting with the vivid
and imaginative spatial areas which in plan set off so many of his
houses from the usual works of the time.

In business buildings, as in residences, the Greek Revival
brought with it new forms, to give harmony and a new kind of graciousness to large areas of lower New York. The tremendous
growth of New York commerce created an overwhelming need for
warehouses, factories, offices, and banks; in the decade of the thirties Water, Front, Pearl, and Gold streets were rapidly filling with
dignified buildings to take care of the increased trade, just as
Wall Street was changing as its earlier bank buildings — essen-

tially domestic in exterior character — were one by one replaced by new buildings with monumental, official-looking, colonnaded fronts. The first of these was Martin Thompson's Phenix Bank (1825) ; a decade later others by Isaiah Rogers added to the new monumentality of Wall Street.

To this movement that little by little was making over the appearance of lower Manhattan the great fire of 1835 gave an enormous impetus. It destroyed practically every structure between Broad Street, Wall Street, and the East River. In the burned regions whole streets of new buildings rose with surprising rapidity, and it is in these — and in similar structures contemporary with them elsewhere — that the new type of building can best be seen. Its essentials were : a ground floor supported on monolithic granite piers, often with Greek anta capitals and carrying a simply molded granite architrave ; above this three or four stories of brick or granite wall, pierced with well-proportioned windows, regularly spaced and often furnished with iron shutters ; then, as a crown to the whole, a restrained, simple cornice of moderate projection, with moldings of Greek profile. Occasionally an attic story is found under the cornice, with oval windows surrounded by wreaths to form a frieze or rectangular windows with decorative iron grilles. A surprising number of such buildings are still standing, still being used for their original purpose ; the uniformity of their cornice lines, the monumental repetition of their granite piers, and the rhythmical regularity of their openings give a pleasant harmony and unity to the streets they border. The best of these buildings are simple, useful, unostentatious, human in scale, and restrained and delicate in detail.

This type of building was not originated after the great fire ; it had begun to come into use at the very beginning of the decade. As with so many other innovations of the time, Davis in his notes claims that Town created the first such structure — the first store with granite piers — in the Tappan Store on Wall Street in 1831. In Boston, as we have seen, granite had been in common use much earlier, and it is possible that Davis's extended visits to Boston in 1827–8 as well as Town's earlier residence there may have had an influence in their introducing the new, powerful Massachusetts material to New York.

A drawing of the elevation of the Tappan Store still exists; in proportion and treatment it is obviously the prototype of an enormous amount of early New York work as well as of many similar buildings in the Ohio River towns. There still stand at the east end of Fulton Street a large block of such warehouses and, near by in Water Street, a granite-fronted building, which, though larger in size and more richly detailed, is so similar in spirit and proportion to the Tappan Store — so sure in its design and with such exquisite refinement in its moldings and restrained ornament — that an attribution to Town and Davis themselves seems to be indicated.

This general type was susceptible of many variations without having its essential dignity and usefulness destroyed. In the work executed after the fire, brick instead of stone was usually used for the upper floors. Window widths and spacings were varied. In the latter part of the decade cast iron was substituted for granite for the lintels and in exceptional cases for the piers as well. The large building or group of uniform buildings that Pierre Lorillard erected on Gold Street at the head of Webb Street in 1837 is typical; its tall entrance motif crowned by a pediment that looks down Webb Street is a pleasant accent in the street picture, and its window widths, its slim, decorated lintels, and its tall proportions are those which cast iron alone made possible. Over the two-story cast-iron piers are the three sardonic, impish faces put there to celebrate Lorillard's victory over those who felt that Webb Street should have been continued on west, over the Lorillard property. Farther down on Gold Street, at the northeast corner of its intersection with Ferry Street, Lorillard put up another large building, and his unknown architect used there the same details he had in the other structure, varying them in this case by giving the building a rounded corner. It is characteristic of the spirit of the New York Greek Revival architects that within the general frame of a single building scheme, and with the use of detail of generally Greek type, two such important innovations as these could have been made; for these buildings show what must be one of the very

earliest large-scale uses of cast iron as a structural material, and
one of the first uses of the rounded corner at a street intersection.
Yet the full sweep of Greek Revival taste could only reveal
itself effectively in churches and public buildings. Before the great
fire in 1835 Martin Thompson's Bank of the United States, later
the Assay Office, and his second Merchants' Exchange, one of
the most distinguished buildings of the period (in which he succeeded in blending the new classicism with a cupola of the earlier
tradition in a remarkably successful way), had already joined with
the city hall of Mangin and McComb in giving New York great
distinction in its public buildings. Josiah Brady's St. Thomas's
Church was an early and rather crude attempt at Gothic, but it
showed how the Colonial tradition in church design had passed.
Town and Thompson's Ascension Church (1827–9) on Canal
Street was already in the full vein of the Greek Revival, with its
six-column Theseum-type portico; Davis's smaller but more delicate church (1831) on Bleecker Street was in the same Greek
spirit. The Greenwich Presbyterian Church on West Thirteenth
Street, probably by Samuel Dunbar, is the only example of this
full temple type still standing in New York.

Especially important in their broad influence were two churches
by Town and Davis: the Carmine Street Church with its recessed
porch and two Greek Doric columns *in antis* (a front much copied, so that it became almost a standard church façade, with recessed porch between two solid enclosed areas for stairs and storage and with coupled antae on each side, thus creating a five-part
composition); and the exquisite Eglise du Saint Esprit (1832–4),
the French Protestant church, with an Ionic portico of great
beauty and a high dome. The Reformed Dutch Church was by
Calvin Pollard; the Amity Street Baptist Church, a six-column
Greek temple, by Samuel Dunbar. A number of Greek Revival
churches, for the most part greatly altered, remain scattered
through the older parts of the city.

Several new and monumental theaters also showed the growing popularity of the Greek forms. One of Ithiel Town's first New
York jobs was the Bowery Theater (1825), with a large Greek

Doric portico later preserved in the second Bowery Theater built by J. Sera on the same site after the fire. The National Theater (1833), with an interesting façade of Greek antae, a well-handled sloping blocking course, and well-proportioned openings, was possibly by Calvin Pollard; he was at least the architect for its reconstruction after a fire in 1840.[30] Hone remarks in his *Diary* [31] on the lavish beauty of the new interior.

After the great fire New York architects could no longer fill the need for new buildings. Isaiah Rogers (1800–1869), who had made his fame as the architect of the Tremont House in Boston, was invited to New York to design the new and magnificent Astor House (1832–6), where the ideas of mechanical equipment, luxurious interior design, architectural skill in planning, and dignified and monumental exterior design that had characterized the earlier Boston hotel were carried to an even greater extreme. Plumbing, which had been confined to the first floor and basement in the Tremont House, was at last carried here through all the stories, each having its own bath and toilet rooms fed from a roof tank to which water was raised by a steam pump. All of this caused a sensation in its day; the Astor House was a great advance over even the luxuries of the famous City Hotel designed by McComb. The whole conception was as different from that as its severe and magnificent granite façade differed from the delicate Adam detail of the earlier structure. A new type of building almost twentieth-century in conception was being born, and the Greek Revival was one of the chief liberating forces which made these new ideas possible.

Rogers spent fifteen profitable years in New York. His next great work, the third Merchants' Exchange, on the site of the second building, but much larger, set again a new standard in taste and accomplishment. Nowhere in the country save possibly in Mills's Treasury building in Washington had such a monumental structure been so grandly conceived, so simply and directly planned, and so beautifully detailed. Its great Ionic colonnade —

---

[30] The contract drawings are preserved in the New York Historical Society.

[31] *The Diary of Philip Hone,* edited with an Introduction by Allan Nevins, Vol. I (New York: Dodd, Mead & Company, 1927), p. 503.

TOP, section, Church of Saint Esprit, New York, by A. J. Davis. (*Metropolitan Mus. of Art.*) CENTER, elevation of parlor doors by Calvin Pollard. (*New York Hist. Soc.*) BELOW, a Greek Revival bathroom, from a plumber's advertisement. (*Mus. City of New York.*)

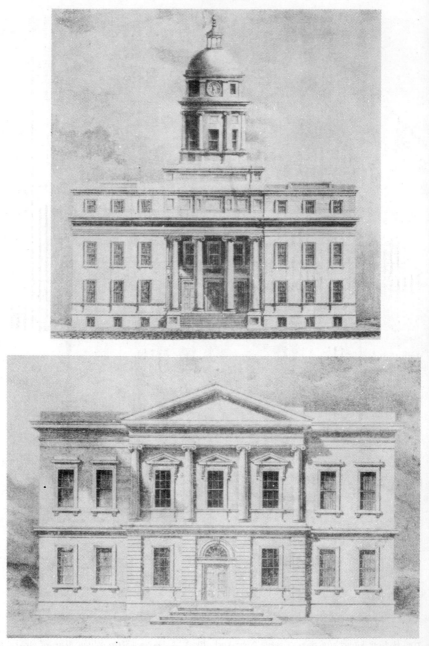

Two New York buildings by Martin Thompson: (*Lithographs after A. J. Davis, New York Pub. Lib.*) ABOVE, the second Merchants' Exchange. BELOW, Branch Bank of the United States.

ABOVE, LEFT, typical warehouse, Water Street, *circa* 1835. ABOVE, RIGHT, detail of granite warehouse, Water Street. Town and Davis(?), architects. BELOW, LEFT, St. James's Church, James Street. Minard Lafever, architect. BELOW, RIGHT, typical warehouses, Fulton Street (*All, author.*)

Third Merchants' Exchange (later Customs House), New York. Isaiah Rogers, architect. (*American Architect.*) ABOVE, exterior. BELOW, rotunda.

superb in scale, with granite columns from the Quincy quarries of his friend Solomon Willard — and its impressive recessed porch still exist as the lower portion of the National City Bank, and have a power expressed in but few buildings in the neighborhood. Built with an exterior of granite throughout and made fireproof by the use of vaulting for its floor construction, the Merchants' Exchange had as its interior climax a great rotunda, eighty feet in diameter, with a caissoned brick dome. This rotunda was as grand and simple in design as it was great in dimensions. Four recesses opened from it, each with two Corinthian columns *in antis*. The walls between were quietly paneled in single big rectangles, and interesting delicate bronze and iron balconies gave passage behind the columns at each floor level. Such a conception as this shows what a small part the copying of Greek work played in the great architectural triumphs of that period. The Greek Ionic order was used on the exterior, but the Corinthian within was a freshly designed Corinthian, neither Greek nor Roman. In scale, monumentality, and direct simplicity of plan the inspiration was more Roman than Greek, yet the whole was welded inextricably into one powerful organic conception that shows Rogers as a great architect in the fullest sense of the word.

Of his other New York work the Middle Dutch Church on Lafayette Place was perhaps the best. Again the power of the large scale he loved and his skill in combining traditional conceptions with a fresh point of view were both present. Particularly impressive was the bold and buttresslike projection of the antae along the sides in contrast with the delicate acroteria. St. Peter's Roman Catholic Church on Barclay Street has also been attributed to Rogers by Montgomery Schuyler [32] on the grounds of its great scale and beautiful detail; if it is not by Rogers, at least it shows the same urge toward large conceptions that was his most marked attribute. His design for the Astor Place Opera House was less dis-

[32] 'The Old "Greek Revival," ' *The American Architect and Building News,* Part I: Vol. xcviii, No. 1816 (12 October 1910), pp. 121–6; Part II: Vol. xcviii, No. 1826 (21 December 1910), pp. 201–4; Part III: Vol. xcix, No. 1836 (1 March 1911), pp. 81–4, 86–7; Part IV: Vol. xcix, No. 1845 (3 May 1911), pp. 161–6, 168. This is the pioneer study of the period, valuable in many ways although later research has changed or invalidated many of its attributions.

tinguished, for he was hampered by smallness both of site and of appropriation, yet even here he succeeded in giving to the design a simple and powerful composition that had not only classic dignity but also an imaginative handling of mass not often associated with Greek Revival work.

Almost across the street from Rogers's Merchants' Exchange stood the New York customs house, completed in the year Rogers's building was begun. This interesting structure, now the Sub-Treasury, is obviously the result of several minds. A competition for it was won by Town and Davis with a design basically similar in plan conception and identical in exterior treatment with the executed building, except for the fact that above the Greek temple roof Town and Davis had planned a low exposed dome over the central rotunda. The colonnade, the high steps, the membering of the flank — in fact, all the exterior aspects of the present building — are definitely theirs. The interior treatment just as definitely is not. The Commissioners in charge of the work were perhaps rightly frightened at the lightness of the construction indicated on the Town and Davis plan, and they employed William Ross, an English architect visiting in New York, to restudy the interior. According to Ross's own story, published in a letter to [Loudon's] *The Architectural Magazine*,[33] and from the plans he published in this article, the basic ideas of the executed design seem to be his. But before construction was started one of America's early and brilliant sculptors, who had been from time to time also an architect, stone-cutter, and contractor — John Frazee — was employed by the Commissioners as architect for the building, and all the detailing and probably the working drawings were his.[34]

The result was bound to be a conception lacking in unity. The exterior is one thing and the interior another, yet both in their way are superb. The most interesting thing about the whole design is its massive and daring construction and Frazee's beautiful exe-

---

[33] Vol. ii, No. [12] (December 1835), pp. 526–32.

[34] *Nichols' Illustrated New York: A Series of Views of the Empire City and Its Environs* (New York: C. B. and F. B. Nichols, 1847). Only seven views were published. The text is unusually complete and authoritative for books of this kind. It gives an extended account of the customs house and its architects and apportions the credit due to each designer.

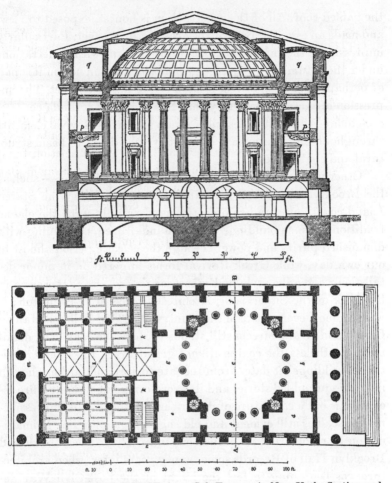

FIGURE 16. CUSTOMS HOUSE (now Sub-Treasury), New York. Section and plan. Town & Davis, Ross, and Frazee, architects. (*Loudon.*) Daringly monumental, fireproof, vaulted construction, developing interiors of dignified beauty.

cution of it.[35] Like the greater number of the public buildings erected at the time, it was fireproof and vaulted in masonry — the office portions largely in simple groins supported at their intersections by strong columns, the central area by a dome concealed under

[35] One of Frazee's full-size details for an anthemion band for the customs house is in the Avery Library, Columbia University. It is unfortunate that none of the beautiful metal furniture Frazee designed for this building has been preserved.

the gabled roof. All of the construction is honest, exposed to view, and made an essential part of the architectural effect. Particularly impressive is the shallow cut-granite ring vault with penetrations under the rotunda supported on squat Doric columns; on its span of perhaps fifty or sixty feet it has a rise of about ten feet. The impression of power and dignity that this basement rotunda conveys even today is difficult to describe. Again the Greek Revival elements throughout this interior are completely subsidiary to basic structural and spatial ideals.

Other public buildings in New York and its environs — such as the Brooklyn city hall, by an architect named King, the Staten Island courthouse, and so on — followed rapidly until the classic tradition for such buildings became standardized, continuing with diminished purity and power through the eclectic period almost to our own day, while Greek Revival forms lingered on in minor details long after the style had otherwise passed away. It was so in the work of the Supervising Architect's office in Washington; it was so almost everywhere in the country. The Odd Fellows' Hall on Center and Grand streets still stands to show the coarsened detail but nevertheless the compositional grandeur of the later transitional buildings; it dates from the late forties and, although with its grotesque added stories and its excrescences of signs and fire escapes it is but a caricature of its former self, some of its impressiveness of scale is still evident and old engravings allow one in imagination to reconstruct its earlier monumentality. Even the domed Brooklyn Hall of Records some twenty years later, when architecture was beginning to feel the blight of the post-Civil War debauch, still preserves in many elements of its interior detail lingering hints of the delicacy and the imagination of the then almost forgotten Greek Revival.

Two very important results followed upon the development of the architect as a professional man, primarily a designer and no longer a builder as well. The first was artistic liberation; the second was place liberation. Once an architect was recognized as a creative individuality there was an instant challenge to his inventiveness quite different from the traditional pressure of the earlier system; the architect had much greater opportunity for experiment when designing for an individual client who trusted him than when working for a builder and an anonymous owner. Thus, as professional architecture advanced, style freedom increased and eclecticism began to appear, though as yet only tentatively. In general the best works of the period, like many of the Davis houses and much of Lafever's work, are freely creative rather than eclectic in spirit and full of plastic experiments. Hence we get such unusual developments as Lafever's Bartow house in the Bronx — with its simple stone façade, its ample scale, and its rich interior detail — and all of the vital though sometimes erratic experiments that distinguished the Davis work of the 1840's and are so obvious in his sketches, which reveal a most eager, creative, and inventive mind. Where mere copying or archaeological correctness has dominated, this seems in most cases to have resulted through the influence of some dilettante owner rather than through the taste of the architect.

The second effect of this rise of professionalism, a liberation from working in one place, was as important in its effect on the country as a whole. When the architect is a builder his work necessarily is restricted to an area close to his office, but once he is accepted as a designer working through other contractors there is no limit to the area in which his designs can be built save that of time and practicability. We have already seen how the works of Isaiah Rogers dot almost the entire country east of the Mississippi, and this was even more the case with the firm of Town and Davis. Town was much away from the office, in the South and in the Middle West, partly no doubt in connection with his bridges and also frankly as a sort of contact man for the partnership. State capitols for North Carolina, Indiana, and Illinois came from the firm's office, and Davis was called in as consultant in connection with the Ohio capitol. Educational buildings by the firm included Alumni Hall at Yale, the Virginia Military Institute, an elaborate series of designs for the University of Michigan, and Davidson College in North Carolina. Town and Davis were also the architects for the North Carolina Hospital for the Insane, and their long list of domestic work includes examples in Maryland, Michigan, Virginia, and New England.

Thus, powerful influences spread out widely from this New York center and helped set the standards that made even the local vernacular architecture unusually successful. Moreover, men trained in the New York offices themselves settled and worked in other places often far removed. For example, the second Robert Cary Long of Baltimore was at one time a draftsman for Martin Thompson and signed some of the Columbia Grammar School drawings; James Gallier was a partner of Lafever for a year before he left for New Orleans; and James Dakin, who with Gallier obtained most of the important architectural commissions in New Orleans during the forties and fifties, was a student and later a partner of Town and Davis. How many other similar examples there were it would be impossible to state without more accurate information than we now possess concerning the make-up of these New York offices, but the slight indications we do have seem to show a much greater number than one would get, say in Boston, where the influence was chiefly local. Throughout the southern half of the country at the time and in some of the more northern parts of the West the high standard of this architecture, achieved so soon after the forests had been cut down to allow settlement, again and again stems from two great sources: first, the pupils of Strickland, tracing as it were their artistic heritage through him back to Mills and Latrobe; and, second, the influence of the New York offices. For that reason the importance of the Greek Revival in New York can hardly be overstressed.

CHAPTER 7

THE PROVINCIAL GREEK REVIVAL:
THE NEW ENGLAND STATES

IT HAS become the custom to accept the greater amount of early American architecture outside the large cities as the work of a sort of folk culture, the spontaneous creation of unknown craftsmen who, by virtue of some forgotten magic, produced out of their inner consciousness, with few or no drawings, the buildings we love and admire. It is of course true that popular taste was high in the early nineteenth century and demanded design of beautiful clarity; to that extent, at least, we may call this country Greek Revival a people's art. Yet the more we examine it, the more we search all the records, and the more we know of the conditions under which it was produced, the more we must realize that behind these buildings were individual designers, that plans were made and elevations drawn before the structures arose, and that the forms the buildings took were consciously created.

Much the same change in judgment has been necessary here as that which has during the last half century revolutionized our conception of the Gothic cathedral builders. Our increased knowledge, our growing care in archaeology, and our enlarged acquaintance with the original source material have forced the abandonment of the old romantic theory of the cathedrals as spontaneous creations of a people's soul; we know now that great buildings have had great designers, and out of the mists of the past the architects are gradually emerging. So, here in America, little by little research is proving that our Late Colonial and Classic Revival architecture was *designed*. The designers may have called themselves builders, but in actual fact they were architects as well; one is constantly amazed at discovering the number of those who chose the professional rather than the craft title, and many of them were actual

professional men in work as well as in name. Thus in the Boston
city directory in 1846–7 there were twenty architects, in 1848–9
twenty-five; in the Detroit directory of 1837 at least six men so
called themselves. New Orleans, during the period of its great
prosperity from 1835 to 1855, had among others the Galliers,
father and son, the two Dakins, De Pouilly, and several members
of the Freret family; Louisville had Shryock, who worked in many
localities in the Ohio and Mississippi valleys; and Providence had
J. H. Greene, J. C. Bucklin, and Russell Warren. Mr. Frary [1] has
discovered the names and works of many architects and builders
of this period in Ohio, and Professor Burns [2] has done the same
for Indiana.

Everywhere that intensive research in the history of these
lovely towns and villages has been carried on, the same story has
been true; the beautiful churches, the handsome courthouses, the
welcoming and dignified houses did not just happen — they were
planned, and they were beautiful because someone had so conceived
them and seen that they were built according to his conception.

To list all these architects is as yet impossible; an immense
amount of research is still to be done. The picture of the New York
architectural world in those decades, from 1820 to 1850, is fairly
clear; we know much about the Boston, Philadelphia, Washington,
New Orleans, and St. Louis architects. But outside the great cities
the picture grows confused, and only future local study can clarify
it. Yet the indications are that material still exists, at least in many
places, and, properly sifted, would help us to learn who the men
were who built these structures spread so widely over the eastern
half of the country, who so rapidly in the West changed wilderness
and forest into lovely towns and designed the dignified columned
mansions of Kennebunk or Nantucket or Ann Arbor.

We find the work of Asher Benjamin and Elias Carter dotted
over western and central Massachusetts. Benjamin's refined and
simplified American versions of Adam and Pain(e) detail decorate

[1] See page 282.
[2] See page 300.

his Coleman house at Greenfield, some of the houses in Windsor, Vermont, and the West Church in Boston, now a public library. To Carter we owe the best of the Greek Revival work of Worcester — those great square houses with dignified continuous two-story colonnades that constitute the unique type he created; his churches are less known and less unusual. We have a long list of the work of Isaac Damon, especially his beautiful churches in Northampton, Massachusetts. We have the names of Henry and Robert Sikes and Chauncey Shepard, architects who worked in the Connecticut Valley. Our picture of their work and their personalities, however, is still for the most part vague and perplexing.

Around New Haven it was Colonel Belcher with his characteristic naïve variations of Pain detail — witness his Old Lyme Congregational Church — who set the character; later it was Hoadley (1774–1839), who designed among many other houses the Noah Webster house in New Haven, and became in the late twenties and thirties the local representative of Town and Davis. Town started his practice with the Center and Trinity churches in New Haven — the one a characteristic example of the Late Colonial Gibbs-type meeting house, the other the earliest Gothic Revival church in New England — and went on with ever increasing power and variety, without doubt introducing Greek forms into Connecticut in the Doric porches of various New Haven houses built before his departure for New York.[3] He was followed by his pupil and protégé, Henry Austin, who was the fashionable architect of all central Connecticut throughout the late thirties, forties, and fifties, working first in the Greek Revival manner and later in the 'Bracketed' style, producing villas with broad spreading cornices, flat roofs, and large window and wall spaces that sometimes show more vivid imagination than restraint. His work reached its zenith in the extraordinary New Haven railroad station, with its ingenious,

---

[3] The Burr house in Fairfield has a Greek Doric porch across the front that is popularly ascribed to 1790. However, according to Hurd's *History of Fairfield County* (1881), the house originally was a duplicate of the famous Hancock house in Boston and was built in 1779. Its present form and the Greek columns date from an alteration *c.* 1831. I owe this information to Mrs. Angeline Scott Donley, South Branch Librarian, Bridgeport, Conn.

prophetically modern, two-level plan (the waiting room and offices above, extending over the tracks, and the platforms below) and its fantastic 'Moorish' detail.

In Maine the early houses of Alexander Parris in Portland are but one example of how the work of an accomplished architect gives character and sets the tone of a locality. Farther east the quiet solid beauty of the houses that prosperous shipowners and captains built along the harbors of Ellsworth and Bluehill, Columbia Falls and Machias, during the twenties and thirties, is famous and was long taken for granted as an example of a folk art. Now we have learned better; we know that the proportions of these buildings were consciously planned, their spare and delicate detail consciously applied. That exquisite string of lavish churches in Bluehill,[4] East Bluehill, and the neighborhood, climaxed by the magnificent colonnade and tower of the Ellsworth church,[5] are the work of Thomas Lord of Bluehill. He was proud of them; some of his drawings still exist, and in his old age he set down with obvious pride a list of the buildings he had designed.[6]

---

[4] Rufus G. F. Candage, *Historical Sketches of Bluehill, Maine* (Ellsworth: Hancock County Publishing Co., 1905). The Congregational Church was built in 1842–3.

[5] Albert H. Davis, *History of Ellsworth, Maine* (Lewiston: Lewiston Journal Printshop, 1927). The Congregational Church here was completed in 1847.

[6] Thomas Lord was the original of Thomas Winship in Mary Ellen Chase's superb novelized social history of eastern coastal Maine, *Silas Crockett* (New York: The Macmillan Company, 1935), and the statistics quoted there are taken verbatim from Lord's papers, now in the possession of Miss Florence Morse. Quoting, with changed names, the Lord papers, Miss Chase writes (pp. 95, 96): 'Thomas Winship began his joiner work in May of the year 1807 in the counties of Hancock and Washington in the then State of Massachusetts. He has designed and built in all fourteen meeting-houses without assistance in planning by any save himself and what he has read and seen with his own eyes. Of these he has made a separate record for whoever may follow him. In addition he has worked as superintendent and labourer alike on

84 dwelling-houses	18 barns and sheds
83 vessels of various	12 vessel heads
builds	5 stores
12 school-houses	14 taverns

. . . besides 197 coffins. . . This work has been done in fourteen different towns and villages.' Quoted by permission of The Macmillan Company, publishers.

It is interesting to note this combination of house, church, and boat building. There are many characteristic details in some of these Down East houses — a certain flatness and delicacy of moldings, a sort of austere 'tightness' and simplicity of design, a use of pilasters as hardly more than covering-strips — which definitely suggest the careful work and the restraint of ship cabins and ship design generally.

So it is wherever the history of Greek Revival buildings has been carefully studied. These sea captains were traveled men of culture and taste; they demanded, and received, the best for the buildings they needed. The settlers who built so many of the towns of Ohio and Michigan and Illinois and Tennessee were, many of them, not the picturesque pioneers of fiction; they were solid citizens with the polished background of New England or Maryland or Virginia behind them, men who read widely and much, and whose libraries were an important part of their baggage; men brought up on the Bible and Shakespeare and Milton. They were eager readers of Byron. They were men who started academies and colleges in the town they created almost as soon as the forests had been cut down.

The conservatism of the older parts of New England is evidenced by the persistence of the Late Colonial traditions and forms until almost the middle of the nineteenth century, through large parts of Massachusetts, Rhode Island, Connecticut, and up the Connecticut Valley into Vermont and New Hampshire. In many villages the influence of the Greek Revival is hardly apparent at all; only in details here and there do Greek forms appear. Occasionally a Greek Doric porch was added to an older house; more frequently the entire house was built at one time according to the older traditions, and observed the new fashion only in its entrance and porch and perhaps in the heavier proportions and Greek profiles of its mantels and interior trim.

From 1800 on, the country work obviously is deeply indebted to the books of Asher Benjamin; some of it was undoubtedly designed by builder-architects who had studied at his architectural school in Boston. And just as he is slightly grudging in his attitude toward the Greek detail after 1826, when he first shows the Greek orders in the fifth edition of *The American Builder's Companion*,[7] so it is with this country work in large parts of New England. The other Benjamin books — *The Practical House Car-*

---

[7] *Or, A New System of Architecture.* . . (Boston: Etheridge and Bliss, 1806); 5th ed. (Boston: R. P. and C. Williams, 1826).

penter (called *The Architect; or, Practical House Carpenter* in the 1841 and subsequent editions),[8] the *Practice of Architecture*,[9] and *The Builder's Guide* [10] — show ' Greek ' doorways and ' frontispieces ' and give profiles of the new, broader trims, but that is all except in the last, in which the designs are more lavish and more Greek.[11] And what he does with the Greek detail used is equally characteristic : he makes it all rather heavy, almost stodgy, trying unconsciously to bring it within the earlier, more Roman, classic tradition ; there is in it little of the delicate invention and the contrast of simple planes with the most refined rosettes and anthemions which characterize the Greek Revival books of Minard Lafever.

Later the books of Edward Shaw [12] became almost equally influential. Shaw's *Civil Architecture* [13] must have been exceedingly popular. First published complete in 1831, it had reached its fourth edition by 1835 ; it continued being published for forty years and more, its last edition being the eleventh, of which several printings were issued in Philadelphia until as late as 1876. It is more of a complete builder's and architect's handbook than are the Benjamin items ; it has fewer designs and details, though more material on geometry, mensuration, and construction. But Shaw's *Rural*

---

8 Boston: R. P. and C. Williams, and Annin and Smith, 1830. Fourteen issues to [1857].

9 Boston: the author, and Carter, Hendie & Co.; New York: Collins & Co.; 1833. Seven other editions to 1851.

10 *Or, Complete System of Architecture* (Boston: Perkins and Marvin; Philadelphia: Henry Perkins; 1839). Third and subsequent editions called *The Architect; or, Complete Builder's Guide*. Four reissues to 1854.

11 *Practice of Architecture* and *The Builder's Guide* both also contain designs for Greek Revival churches. The influence of Lafever's ornament is obvious in the later Benjamin books.

12 Harriette F. Farwell's *Shaw Records: A Memorial of Roger Shaw, 1594–1661* (Bethel, Maine: E. C. Bowler, 1904) gives Edward Shaw the architect as of the fourth generation descended from Roger Shaw. He was born 2 August 1784, in Hampton, New Hampshire, but later moved to Chester, now Hill, New Hampshire, and later still, about 1822, to Boston. The family was evidently structural-minded, for his brother Benjamin, ten years younger, was a carpenter and an early settler of Jackson, Michigan; another brother, David, was a lumber merchant and built his own house at Sanbornton, New Hampshire; still another, John, was a mason on the Merrimack River.

13 Parts I and II (Boston: Shaw and Stratton, 1830) ; the whole work (Boston: Lincoln and Edwards, 1831) ; 2nd ed., enlarged (Boston: Marsh, Capen & Lyon, 1832) ; 4th ed. (Boston: Marsh, Capen & Lyon, 1835) ; 11th ed. (Philadelphia: Henry Carey Baird & Co., 1876).

Architecture [14] has many designs of houses and churches that exerted a wide influence. The popularity of these books perhaps evidences the growing complexity of the building trades and the greater thoroughness that was required of builders and architects in this period.

The plates included are thoroughly in the Boston tradition. Shaw's Greek Revival design has the same forthright heaviness as Benjamin's, and something of the same kind of robust beauty. For both men, the Greek fret took the place of the rosettes and anthemions of Lafever. Thus throughout New England one finds a wide use of the fret, usually of simple type and large in size, employed for panel decorations, for lintels, and even for pilasters. This use is often crude and is absolutely without Greek precedent; in the later years of the movement (in the late forties and fifties) these New England frets became formless and diffuse.

Shaw's influence was not limited to his books, but came also from the actual buildings he designed. His practice was widespread and, like the plates in his books, not limited to Greek Revival forms; it shows him an early and eager supporter of the Gothic styles that were beginning to come into use. Thus, although much of his work is Greek, the wooden churches of Machias and East Machias, Maine, are in a charmingly original type of Carpenter Gothic. The design for East Machias was published, almost ten years after its construction, in Shaw's *Rural Architecture*, which also shows another Gothic church design much like that at Machias. In Addison, Maine, there is a story-and-a-half house with a Greek Doric porch which much resembles plates in Shaw's *Rural Architecture*. The simplest ' Ionic house ' shown has also many Maine descendants. In Manchester, New Hampshire, too, there is a handsome Gothic city hall from his design.

Another important handbook for New England builders was Chester Hills's *The Builder's Guide*.[15] This work has completeness as its chief merit, together with the fact that its lithographed

14 Boston: James B. Dow, 1843.
15 New York: D. Appleton and Co., 1836 [c1834]; republished in Hartford by Case, Tiffany, and Burnham, in 1846, with additions of villa plans by Henry Austin and a chapter on School Architecture by Henry Barnard.

plates of the orders are on a larger scale than those of Benjamin and Lafever. Several of its designs are taken line for line from Peter Nicholson; its doorways and porches are modifications of designs published earlier by Minard Lafever or Edward Shaw. Hills, the complete eclectic in his book, was an architect of some note in Hartford, Connecticut, where he had a large practice. It is possible that much of the simpler and more conventional work in the Connecticut Valley may be of his design. *The Carpenter's Assistant*, by William Brown,[16] is an interesting handbook of the later period when ' Gothic ' and ' Italian ' designs were becoming as popular as ' Greek.'

But in all this New England work so largely based on earlier Colonial ideas, in its detail frequently so superficial and at times so crude, there is a basic faithfulness to climate and materials which inevitably produces minor regionalisms within the larger pattern. The stone buildings that grew up around the quarries of New Hampshire and Cape Ann are characteristic examples; the use of this relatively intractable material forced in them the simplicity and power that the granite buildings of Boston possess. Similar regional expressions are to be found in the relatively low roof slopes and compactness of plan, together with the somewhat smaller window openings, typical of many Maine houses of the time, as well as in the common New England country practice of combining house, sheds, wood shed, outhouse, and barn into one long composition, frequently L-shaped, as a protection against savage winter gales and heavy snows.

The tremendous popularity of the so-called story-and-a-half house with all the chief living rooms and bedrooms on the ground floor is another example of the results of a more realistic acceptance of climate and living ways. This of course is not limited to New England but is found in New Jersey, New York, and the North generally — wherever, in fact, the discovery has been made that many of the old, typically Colonial two-story houses with through halls and much waste space are likely to be cold and

16 Worcester, Mass.: Edward Livermore, 1848.

drafty.[17] But the whole period was notable for a new attack on the problems of house planning, wherever the old traditions did not interfere.

The new attitudes that governed the Greek Revival period thus had their greatest opportunity in the rapidly growing towns (especially those without too long a history) and in the newly settled parts of the country, like eastern Maine. Bangor, for instance, was increasing rapidly in size as the lumber trade poured wealth into its coffers, and thus grew up as an essentially Greek Revival community, with impressive brick houses richly finished, freely designed, magnificently furnished. It called chiefly on Boston architects — on Rogers for its grand hotel, on Upjohn for several houses and its epoch-making Gothic Episcopal church.[18] But the local designers must have been apt pupils, and the great houses that line Broadway in Bangor are eloquent of the beauty of their work.

Similarly Belfast, with its prosperous shipping and shipbuilding trade, became a town of handsome square Greek houses of a definitely recognizable type, a fact which seems to argue the existence of some brilliant though occasionally erratic local architect.[19] Farther east, Bluehill, Ellsworth, Harrison, Columbia Falls, Machias, and other towns were booming, and lovely house after lovely house, white church after white church, shows an extraordinarily high standard of Greek Revival design. Some of them we know

[17] Minard Lafever, for instance, in his description of a plate (LXIII) in *The Young Builder's General Instructor* (Newark: W. Tuttle & Co., 1829) showing his ideal farmhouse, says:

'In designing a cottage for domestic conveniences, the designer should have in view frugality, convenience, and neatness, in a plain style. He should also be aware of the inconvenience of apartments being too large, as well as too contracted; for it is well known that in common, the Farm House is too large . . . therefore it is a duty as well as an interest devolving upon a builder never to advise a farmer to build his house more than one full story besides the basement . . . He must likewise be aware, and impress it upon the mind of the occupant, that a wide hall running through the house in any direction is room lost, and an opening for the reception of cold in the winter. . .'

[18] Everard M. Upjohn, *Richard Upjohn, Architect and Churchman* (New York: Columbia University Press, 1939), pp. 32–5, Figs. 1–4.

[19] There is a definite resemblance between the Wilson house (*circa* 1840) in Belfast and the Isaac Farrar (Symphony) house (1833–6) in Bangor, by Richard Upjohn.

were the work of Captain Lord[20] of Bluehill, but adequate research would undoubtedly rescue the names of other capable and well-trained designers.

The general picture in Massachusetts is more confused. Here local traditions were strong, and it was in the newer towns that the new Greek style found its chief strength — in Nantucket and New Bedford, which the whale fisheries were rocketing into prominence; in Worcester, then so rapidly growing; in Northampton and Amherst, where the existence of a definite group of the intelligentsia fostered the new movement; and up and down the Connecticut River valley. Of course the newer churches everywhere were chiefly in the Greek vein, although Massachusetts was already well supplied with churches. The Parish Church at Concord, with its Greek Doric portico and an excellent tower and spire, is characteristic of these newer structures. Nantucket as we see it today owes much of its quality to the period between 1820 and 1850. New Bedford owed its greatest Greek Revival monument — the late lamented John Avery Parker (Bennett) house (1834), built all of stone — to Russell Warren of Providence, who also designed the charming little New Bedford railroad station done in a free Egyptian manner, as well as the great granite city hall of 1837-8 (now part of the public library), built in a severe and well-composed Greek vein, monumental in mass and material, refined and original in detail. The famous granite customs house of New Bedford is from the designs of Robert Mills.[21] But there must have been local architects too. Richard Upjohn, shortly after his arrival from England, found there his first profitable employment, in 1830, as draftsman for a builder and lumber dealer, one Samuel Leonard. Later, in 1833, it was there he first began to practice as an independent architect.[22]

Nantucket[23] is especially interesting as showing the ideal the

20 See page 162.

21 H. M. Pierce Gallagher, *Robert Mills, Architect of the Washington Monument, 1781-1855* (New York: Columbia University Press, 1935).

22 Upjohn, op. cit. pp. 30-35.

23 For Nantucket, see Everett U[berto] Crosby's *95% Perfect, The Older Residences of Nantucket* (Nantucket: The Inquirer & Mirror Press [c1937]), and Julius A. Schweinfurth's *An Architectural Monograph on the Early Dwellings of Nan-*

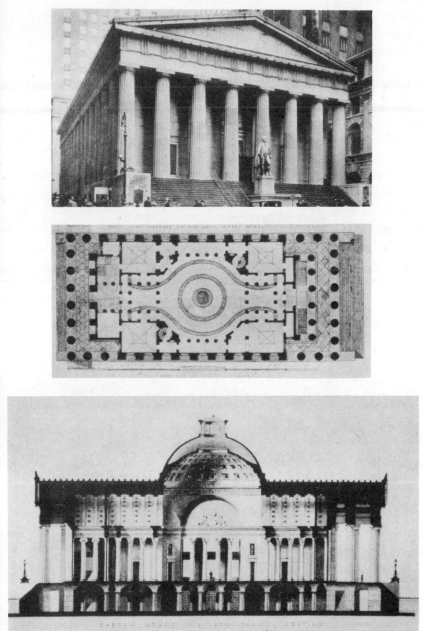

Customs House (Sub-Treasury), New York. Town & Davis, Ross, and Frazee, architects. TOP, photograph. (*Federal Hall Mus.*) Plan, Figure 16. CENTER, plan. (*Metropolitan Mus. of Art.*) BOTTOM, section. (*Avery Library.*)

TOP, houses from Shaw's *Rural Architecture:* LEFT, Doric; RIGHT, Ionic. CENTER, farmhouse elevation from Lafever's *Young Builder's General Instructor.* BOTTOM, Isaac Farrar House, Bangor, Me. Richard Upjohn, architect. (*Old photograph, Upjohn.*)

TOP, house at Provincetown, Mass. (*Author*.) CENTER, house at Richmond, Maine. (*Wells*.) BOTTOM, office and store building, Main Street, Nantucket, 1847. (*Author*.)

Nantucket houses. (*Author*.) ABOVE, Gadd House, Orange Street. BELOW, Griscom House, Main Street.

Nantucket houses. (*Author.*) ABOVE, Hadwen-Salter House, Main Street. Attributed to Russell Warren. BELOW, early functionalism, No. 4 Beach Street.

Worcester houses by Elias Carter. (*Worcester Art Mus.*) TOP, Levi Lincoln House. CENTER, Simeon Burt House. BOTTOM, stair hall, Salisbury House.

Greek Revival in the Connecticut Valley. (*Old engravings of Davis drawings, Hinton.*) ABOVE, Bowers House, Northampton, Mass. Ithiel Town, architect. BELOW, Amherst College, Amherst, Mass.

ABOVE, LEFT, Skinner House, New Haven. Town and Davis, architects. (*Old photograph, Newton.*) ABOVE, RIGHT, 1thiel Town's House and Library, New Haven. (*Metropolitan Mus. of Art.*) BELOW, LEFT, Alsop House, Middletown. (*H.A.B.S.*) BELOW, RIGHT, Greek Revival house in Providence, New Haven.

town builders of these prosperous towns were seeking to realize. A great fire in 1846 wiped out much of the older part of town and almost all of its business area. The town was then at the peak of its whaling prosperity, and it set about rebuilding at once; the lovely brick business buildings which line the north side of Main Street show perfectly the restraint, the large scale, the power of mass composition, and the simplicity of classic detail which were all part of this ideal. It is characteristic, too, that shortly after the fire elms were planted along both sides of Main Street and along some of the other important streets. Evidently it was important to these practical-minded merchants and sea captains not only to have buildings beautiful in proportion and adequate in dignity, but also to add to them the green of foliage and the gracious shadow of trees. The Methodist Church at Nantucket, with a large, well-detailed Ionic portico, dates from ten years before the fire; but the Athenaeum, with a much more richly detailed Ionic order, was built in 1847. Its recessed *in antis* porch has marked individuality, and the whole building is said to resemble closely the Universalist Church which had stood on the same site before the fire.

Yet with all this Greek Revival fashion the houses remain generally conservative in type. The three brick Starbuck houses on Main Street are usually called Colonial and resemble in many ways the Salem work of 1810, but they were not built until 1835–7; only a minor detail here and there reveals the Greek influence. The great house Moor's End dates from almost the same period; it is even more conservative in its taste, for the columnar porches of the Starbuck houses are here replaced by a brick, arched, recessed porch of complete simplicity, and there is hardly a detail on the house by which it could be dated accurately. The smaller houses as well continued the standard Nantucket forms; they preserved the old roof slopes and the four-bay scheme almost untouched, and detail of Greek inspiration or Late Colonial type seems to have been used at the same time. Perhaps the influence of conservative shipbuilder-carpenter-contractor-architects is to be read in this

tucket, Vol. III, No. 6, in the White Pine Series of Architectural Monographs (New York: Russell F. Whitehead, December 1917). For the best illustrations, see Samuel Chamberlain's *Yantucket* (New York: Hastings House, 1941).

continuity. After the fire a change did creep in, and Greek forms — at least for the larger houses — became usual. Thus the Griscom house on Main Street, although it resembles the Starbuck houses in general composition, has a Greek order for its porch and Greek detail on the cupola, and in the houses that grew up north of Main Street after the fire Greek Doric porches became almost standard.

From the same period, 1845–7, date the two great Greek Revival houses on Main Street which lift their neighboring four-column porticoes so pleasantly under the elms. One is in a simple Greek Corinthian, the other in a Greek Ionic; the detail of both is unusually rich, sophisticated, and elegant. They were built for the two daughters in the Starbuck family — the left-hand house, now called the Chambliss house, for Eliza, who married Nathaniel Banery; the right-hand, the Ionic, known as the Salter house, for Eunice, who married William Hadwen. Both of these houses, like the Athenaeum, have a quality so advanced that off-island architects have been suggested as their designers. Thus it has been suggested that possibly Russell Warren may have been the architect of the Hadwen-Salter house.

The more typical local variation of the Greek Revival can best be seen in the later houses of Beach Street, Center Street, Liberty Street, Fair Street, and Orange Street. Characteristic is the Gadd house on Orange Street, with a pedimented end toward the street, decorated with rich anta-type pilasters, and a side entrance under a porch with stumpy Ionic columns. Typical too of the occasional erratic but imaginative experiments which the period frequently produced is the house at No. 4 Beach Street, where fluted columns without capitals or bases serve as the constructional posts of the house and carry a pedimented roof of somewhat steep slope. The exterior house wall is set close behind the posts in precisely the same manner in which the Perret Brothers treated the posts and wall of the theater at the Paris Exposition of 1925. In the pedimented end is an odd double window with short columns carrying a heavy, steeply sloped, triangular cap.

Little has been built in the central part of Nantucket since the Civil War. The effect of the town as one strolls through it to-day is exactly that intended by its builders of nearly a century ago. One cannot help feeling that behind its beauty is much more than the charm of the antique; there is a definite sense of com-position, of balance of greenery and building, of harmony in de-sign, of careful choice of materials, of intelligent street layout and humane land usage which, taken together, combine to form one of the most harmonious and attractive of American seaport towns. One cannot help feeling, also, that these qualities are not accidental; they are the living expression of community life as the people of the Greek Revival desired it to be.

Worcester is especially rich in the work of Elias Carter (1781–1864),[24] a typical example of the New England builder-architect who changed over from an earlier devotion to the refined Late Colonial of Benjamin (with whom at one time he had worked) to a full understanding of the Greek Revival. He was in complete control of it, evidently having with a sure taste picked up its de-tails from books, and he became a master in making the style flex-ible to his own creations. His early work, like that in Brimfield, is imaginative and refined, but it was not till he settled in Worcester in 1828 that his full talent was revealed. He did an enormous amount of work there — churches, business blocks, and houses; it is by the last that he is best known. His houses are large in scale, dignified and simple in mass, and wherever he could he used a two-story colonnade of Greek Doric or Ionic columns extending the full width of the house. Some people, because of these colonnades, have sought to find in them a southern influence. In reality these Worcester examples frequently pre-date many of the southern mansions. It is thus more probable that their use by Carter was a completely independent invention. Characteristic examples are the Daniel Waldo house (1830) with its interesting and unusual attic treatment, somewhat like that in some of Russell Warren's early Bristol, Rhode Island, houses; the Colonel Levi Lincoln house (1836) with its ' fasces '-type flutes and its great simplicity;

[24] Mrs. Harriette M. Forbes, ' Elias Carter, Architect, of Worcester, Mass.,' *Old-Time New England,* the bulletin of the Society for the Preservation of New England Antiquities, Vol. xi, No. 2 (October 1920), pp. 58–71.

and especially the Colonel Simeon Burt house (1834) with its rich and delicate coping and its central cupola. The Stephen Salisbury house (1836–8), now the Worcester Red Cross center, shows a remarkable originality. It has rusticated piers, circular top-floor windows with wreathes, Gothic hood molds over the second-floor windows, and a one-story Greek Doric piazza, all combined into a composition of great unity, simplicity, and charm. Within, its staircase is noteworthy. The first floor has a through hall, of the old Colonial type; the circular stair swings daringly across this, and on the second floor rises into a rotunda with delicate Corinthian columns which support a shallow coffered dome with a central skylight. The effect is graceful, gracious, and original. The trim details of the Salisbury house are firm and simple, quite in the Benjamin manner; Carter seems to have retained his admiration for his earlier colleague, and may have been in close touch with him. Carter is said to have spent some time in Georgia. Could he have designed some of the lovely houses of Macon which are not unlike his Burt house? Captain Lewis Bigelow was another Worcester architect of skill; an elevation by him for a large six-columned Ionic house is preserved in the American Antiquarian Society collection.

Farther west, Springfield and Northampton and Amherst were the sites of an important Greek Revival development. Northampton and Amherst were in the closest touch with the intelligentsia of Boston in those decades; the founding of Round Hill School in Northampton was watched as excitedly by Boston as by its own town.[25] In the great Bowers house, by Ithiel Town, with its superb scale and magnificent Ionic colonnade, Northampton had a monument to be compared with the Parker (Bennett) house in New Bedford. But the smaller work was almost equally distinguished. The Dewey house — now on the Smith College campus — and, at Amherst, the old Boltwood house (1828), now destroyed, which was of the same general type, both had four-columned Ionic porticoes with pediments. Both have been attributed

[25] See Van Wyck Brooks's *The Flowering of New England* (New York: E. P. Dutton & Co., 1936).

to George Cutler of Amherst, who may also have been the architect of much other similar work near by.[26]

But in some ways the most striking and original creation of the locality is the oldest group of Amherst College — North and South colleges and the chapel, built between 1821 and 1827. The designer seems to have been Colonel Isaac Damon; at least he was paid for drawings as well as for other expenses [27] and did a tremendous amount of other work, especially bridges, up and down the valley.

The conception of Amherst College, with its two almost starkly simple dormitories of 1821 and 1822 flanking the bold Greek Doric portico of the chapel, built in 1827 and crowned with a simple, square, flat-topped tower in three stages, was as new as it was superbly effective and economical. Earlier general plans, like those of Ramée for Union and of Jefferson for the University of Virginia, had been for groups larger and more diffuse. The earlier New England colleges had all been, like Dartmouth, of the Colonial or Late Colonial type. Harvard, with its first buildings on three sides of a quadrangle, and Yale, with its long rows of simple structures, represented the most that had been achieved in collegiate group structures in New England. But the Amherst buildings had a firmness of design and a monumentality of composition which were, for New England, new. Superbly set on the summit of a hill, these buildings had a great effect. One sees them perfectly in the famous engraving after an A. J. Davis drawing made probably in 1828, shortly after their completion.

In Connecticut too the picture varies — from the basic conservatism of many farmhouses to the almost cosmopolitan modernity of New Haven, Hartford, and Middletown. Connecticut in striving especially for richly delicate exterior effects had developed some of the loveliest and most refined of Late Colonial expressions, and we find here a lavish use of Palladian windows, rich thin

---

[26] The attribution of these houses can be questioned. Cutler would have been scarcely more than a boy when they were built. It is possible that Isaac Damon may have been the architect of both houses as well as of the Amherst chapel.

[27] This information I owe to Mr. Newton F. McKeon, Librarian of Amherst College.

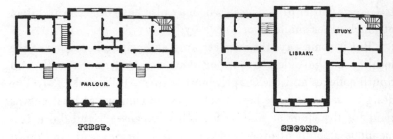

FIRST.   SECOND.

FIGURE 17. HOUSE AND LIBRARY OF ITHIEL TOWN, New Haven, Conn.
Plans. Ithiel Town, architect. (*Met. Mus. of Art.*) An unusual house plan, developed around the great library room and study on the second floor.

cornices less erratic and inventive than Benjamin's, and occasionally slim two-story pilasters or, as in Farmington and Litchfield,
two-story free-standing columns. Connecticut emigrants carried
this delicacy of touch with them westward into western New York,
the Western Reserve of Ohio (as in the exquisite church of Tallmadge, so like that at Lyme, Connecticut, or as in the house on
the grounds of the academy at Hudson, Ohio), and even into
Michigan, where it bloomed again to rival the more up-to-date
Greek structures. The touch is particularly apparent in some of
the houses of Ann Arbor. It is not strange that a style of such
peculiar and delicate loveliness as that of Essex, of Litchfield, or of
Newton should linger long in the work of the older builders like
Isaac Damon and Colonel Belcher.[28]

Yet the influence that radiated from New Haven, Hartford,
and Middletown was essentially that of the new Greek fashion. The
importance of New Haven as a radical, cultural center in the period
between the War of 1812 and, say, 1835 was enormous. It was no
accident that Timothy Dwight's famous letters [29] are full of an
acute aesthetic sensitiveness, as evidenced in remarkable pleas for

[28] This work is best illustrated in the White Pine Series of Architectural Monographs (New York: Russell F. Whitehead). See especially, for Connecticut: Vol.
v, No. 1 (February 1919) ; Vol. vi, No. 6 (December 1920) ; Vol. vii, No. 6 (December 1921) ; Vol. ix, No. 6 (December 1923) ; Vol. x, No. 1 (February 1924). For
Massachusetts: Vol. ii, No. 2 (April 1916) ; Vol. vi, No. 5 (October 1920) ; Vol. x,
No. 5 (October 1924) ; Vol. xi, No. 4 (August 1925).

[29] *Travels in New-England and New-York* (London: William Baynes and Son,
and Ogle, Duncan & Co., 1823). See especially Vol. iii, pp. 403, 404, with regard to
Albany, and Vol. iv, p. 73, for a remarkable correlation of architectural dignity
and moral worth,

city beauty and architectural magnificence. It was no accident that
Colonel Trumbull gave to Yale his famous collection of paintings
in return for an annuity, and designed the gallery that the college
built to house them. Ithiel Town, though born in Thompson, Connecticut, trained in Boston, and working for many years in New
York, seemed to consider New Haven his real home, and built there
the famous house and library for his superb collection of books and
engravings so admired by Mrs. Sigourney.[30] Town's importance
in spreading the gospel of the Greek Revival cannot be forgotten;
although one of his two New Haven churches is in the Late Colonial vein and the other in the Gothic, it seems likely that it was he
who, in the years before he went to New York in 1826, designed
many of the staid New Haven houses with Greek Doric porches.[31]
It was also Town who, in the state capitol (1827–31) he built on
the green in New Haven, produced the first Greek Doric temple
in New England — a structure that gave the green an unusually
classic appearance.

In 1828 Abram Hillhouse invited Town and his new partner,
Davis, to design the famous Hillhouse place, Sachem's Wood,
with its graceful Ionic portico and its handsome mass and original
plan. Leading up to it was Hillhouse Avenue, designed by the
owner; the houses that soon rose along it (chiefly for his friends)
were Greek also, some designed by Town and Davis (including
Town's own home) and some by a young protégé and pupil of
Town's, Henry Austin (1804–91). The Austin houses are generally of the so-called 'Italian villa' type. Similar Greek houses

30 Lydia Sigourney, 'The Residence and Library of Ithiel Town, Esq.,' *The
Ladies' Companion, a Monthly Magazine,* 1st Series, Vol. x, No. 1 (January 1839),
pp. 123–6. See also George Dudley Seymour's *The Residence and Library of Ithiel
Town* (1784–1844), *the Home of the Greek Revivalist* (New Haven [n.p.], April
1930), and the Hoadley papers in the Connecticut Historical Society. Ithiel Town's
house on Hillhouse Avenue was later altered by Henry Austin for Joseph Earl
Sheffield. It still stands, and some of the original interior trim is preserved on the
upper floor. Sales catalogues of the Town library, sold after his death, exist.

31 It is noteworthy that the Darling house in New Haven, built by Town, built in
1815 and torn down in 1932, had a simple urban classic dignity that looks forward
more to the New York houses of the 1830's than it looks back to the Bulfinch Boston types. In it Town used a bold Greek fret to decorate the trim of the outside
front door. See J. Frederick Kelly's 'A Forgotten Incident in the Life of Ithiel
Town,' *Old-Time New England,* Vol. xxxi, No. 3 (January 1941), pp. 62–9.

began to blossom all over the city and in other towns near by. The Russell house (1828–30) at Middletown, by Town and Davis, which now belongs to Wesleyan University, was superintended by Hoadley, one of the older builder-architects; but its design is in the richest Greek vein and its Corinthian columns and open plan are urban and magnificent rather than in the simple old tradition.[32] The columns were those intended originally for Town's Eagle Bank in New Haven; the bank failed and the building was never carried to completion. There is much other good Greek work in Middletown.

The Alsop house (1838), also in Middletown, has been attributed to Austin and to Town and to a Connecticut architect, Henry A. Sikes, of Suffield;[33] but its unique plan and its quite different character suggest the possibility of still other designers. Large in scale, with an impressive suite of living and drawing rooms across the front, it is set apart by its delicate iron porch and its light bracketed cornice as well as by the grisaille statues in niches and the decorative painted frieze which enhance its otherwise severely simple walls. Its interior color decoration is famous; it has been attributed to Brumidi (who later worked under Thomas U. Walter on the United States Capitol) and has been dated as late as 1849 or 1850.[34] I am inclined to believe, however, that this decoration is by some other wandering French or Italian painter, and dates from the time of the completion of the house.[35] Such rich polychrome interiors were less rare than we think. The Forrest house in New York as well as some of those on Washington

[32] Thus its suite of front and back parlors, with sliding doors between, is of a definitely New York type; its use here probably results from the New York practice of its architects.

[33] The attribution to Sikes seems scarcely tenable in view of the fact that he was still a student draftsman in the office of Town and Davis as late as 1840.

[34] Edward B. Allen, *Early American Wall Paintings*, 1710–1850 (New Haven: Yale University Press, 1926).

[35] Since writing this I have been informed by Mrs. Robert H. Fife, who has known the Alsops well, that the Alsop family tradition has it that the builder of the house took his bride for their wedding journey on an extended trip through France and Italy and, returning, brought back with him a group of skilled Italian craftsmen. The general plan of the house he devised himself and then had the help of a local architect in seeing it into final form, the actual construction and the entire decoration being the work of the Italian craftsmen he had brought with him for that purpose.

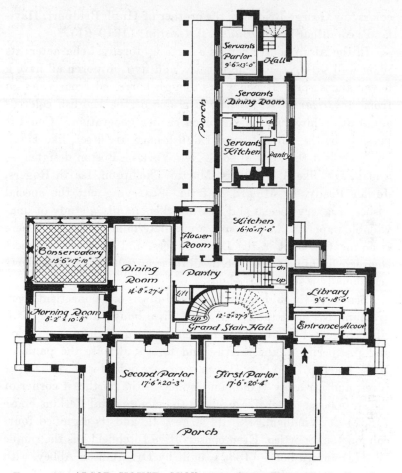

FIGURE 18. ALSOP HOUSE, Middletown, Conn. Plan. (*Great Georgian Houses.*) One of the most original and highly developed Greek Revival house plans, conveniently arranged for living and entertaining on the grand scale.

Square North had rich wall decorations done in a manner not too unlike those of the Alsop house, and from a letter of Latrobe we know that as early as 1808 Latrobe's William Waln house in Philadelphia was frescoed [36] with scenes based on Flaxman's illustrations for the *Iliad* or *Odyssey* and painted ' in flat Etruscan

[36] I owe this information to the courtesy of Mr. Ferdinand C. Latrobe of Baltimore.

colors ' by George Bridport, the brother of Hugh Bridport, Haviland's co-author in *The Builders' Assistant* (1819–21).[37]

In the Alsop house there is a certain ' foreign ' character; its plain wall surfaces, its thin cornice, and its iron porch all have a flavor almost pure Regency, as though borrowed from a design from *Ackermann's Repository* [38] or one of the English colored-aquatint architectural books of an earlier generation.[39] Could it possibly be the work of some English-born architect, like Haviland? Or is it the work of some New York or Boston designer — a man, say, like A. J. Davis, Martin Thompson, Isaiah Rogers, Josiah Brady, or Minard Lafever — carrying out the special wishes of a very special and wealthy client? Only a study of unavailable papers and documents would determine this point. There is no mention of it in the Davis papers, and we have an almost complete list of his work; yet, of all the group, his work alone shows occasionally a similar freedom.

Scattered through the villages and towns of Connecticut there are hundreds of attractive Greek Revival houses and many beautiful churches; this would indicate a great growth in population and prosperity in the thirties and forties, despite the panic of 1837. Hartford and New Haven were once dotted with such structures, and far-away Windham County in the northeast corner of the state boasts several, especially the monumental Perkins house (1832) at Windham, with its large scale and its dignified four-column Ionic portico. Even conservative Litchfield has the simple W. H. Sanford house (1832), built by Dr. Alanson Abbey, with its severe Greek Doric colonnade on three sides and its simple hipped roof.

But it is the Greek Revival churches of Connecticut which best show the architecture of the period, perhaps only because they have suffered less from time than have the houses. In the churches

---

37 See Appendix A.

38 *Ackermann's Repository of Arts, Literature, Commerce, Manufactures, Fashions and Politics* (London: R. Ackermann, 1809–28).

39 Professor Henry-Russell Hitchcock, Jr., considers the Alsop house ' pure Potsdam ' in type, like some of the work of Schinkel. He thinks it ' too good for Austin ' and probably the work of someone in the Town and Davis circle or of Minard Lafever.

the extraordinary thing is the way the same qualities of firm design, appropriate detail, and a basic grasp of architectonic consistency hold sway in the simplest ones — mere small gabled rectangles, perhaps with paneled pilasters at the corners and a
square belfry — as well as in the richest and most complex, like
the church at Suffield, which combines a six-column Ionic portico with one of the most exquisite spires in New England, rising
from an octagon of Greek Corinthian columns, urn-crowned. The
church at Milford is a typical example of the dignity and the
beauty of these Connecticut Greek Revival churches; its tower is
especially successful in proportion, and it is strong yet delicate in
detail. Connecticut had always been distinguished for its churches
— the old church by Belcher at Lyme and the beautiful church
(1818) by Elias Carter at Killingly are but two examples — and
the gradual adaptation of Greek forms to church design merely
gave this tradition a new impetus. The lovely church at East Hartford, with its hexastyle portico, built by Chauncey Shepard as late
as 1853, and the earlier West Hartford church with Ionic columns *in antis*, perhaps by the same designer, are characteristic.

And, in the southeast corner of the state, Stonington was growing rapidly from the fruits of its shipping and its boatbuilding in
these years; naturally, like Nantucket or New Bedford, its buildings are largely Greek. Especially interesting are the customs
house (possibly another Robert Mills design) ; the First National
Bank, a simple Greek Doric four-column temple; the Arcade market; and the Second Congregational Church, with its four-column
Doric portico and its square Ionic tower crowned with a cubical
attic for the clock.

However, it was in the smallest of the New England states,
Rhode Island, that the Greek Revival was perhaps most successful and its monuments most notable. Many things contributed to
this. Not only did Narragansett Bay furnish perfect harbors for
a growing trade in those days, but at the same time industry —
especially the textile industry — was, in Rhode Island, enjoying
an unexampled prosperity and growth. Moreover the great Rhode
Island industrial masters were principally men of high ideals and

a social point of view remarkably broad. In addition, toward the end of the Greek Revival period, the attractions of the Rhode Island coast, especially at Newport — the delicious softness and fragrance of the air, the beauty of rocky shores and magnificent surf, the beaches and quiet harbors — were bringing to Rhode Island the élite of Boston and New York, who were discovering there a summer dwelling place admirably fitted for that new closeness to nature the Romantic movement had made fashionable.[40]

Rhode Island, founded in revolt against the religious intolerance of Massachusetts, had always retained something of its early independence of thought. The new riches from shipping and industry, coupled with contact with the best thought of Boston and New York through the earlier summer residents, prevented provincial stagnation without diminishing local pride. The intellectual atmosphere, like the economic condition, was thus admirably fitted for a vital and independent architectural flowering.

The first results of the new prosperity can be seen especially well in the extraordinarily vivid and original houses that Russell Warren (1783–1860) built for the shipmasters of Bristol in the decade from 1808 on. They are lavish fantasies on the theme of Late Colonial design, original at times to the point of eccentricity. Especially noteworthy are the De Wolf-Middleton house (1808) and the De Wolf-Colt house (1810) with the interesting loggia-like attic treatment over a two-story Corinthian order. Thirty years later, in 1840, the same architect, Russell Warren, built in Poppersquash, near Bristol, a third De Wolf house, that for Mark Anthony De Wolf, with a great six-column Greek Corinthian portico crowned by a pediment.

Providence, of course, was growing during the same period. There John Holden Greene (1777–1850) was designing a superb series of houses and churches in a style as rich as Warren's, though less arbitrarily original — houses that still make the hill around

<hr />

[40] The history of Newport can be paralleled by that of almost all the earlier American summer resorts. Discovered first by the artists and advanced thinkers of the day, these spots achieved a vogue and a popularity that soon brought in the wealthy and the fashionable. The newcomers, setting an artificial standard of conspicuous expenditure, soon displaced the earlier, simpler summer folk.

Brown University one of the loveliest sections of any American city, for Providence is possessed of the almost unique good fortune of having its best residential section today in the same area that held it a century and more ago.

Greene's houses, with their ample size, their beautifully proportioned red brick walls, their white cornices and entrance porches, and their rich interior woodwork (not too unlike that of McIntire), are all variations of well-known earlier types. Of his Providence churches, the First Congregational Church is in the lavish Late Colonial manner; it is especially known for its fine rectangular, oval-domed interior with slim Corinthian columns at the corners. He almost duplicated this design in the square, domed Independent Presbyterian Church in Savannah, Georgia. His St. John's Episcopal Church (1810) is on the other hand Gothic, as is the Dorr house of about the same time. The church is said to have been influenced by Bulfinch's Gothic Federal Street Church of the year before, but Greene's interpretation of the style is quite personal. In plan not unlike the First Congregational Church, it is a large square with corner columns within, but it has an additional transept and chancel element east of the square domed vault, and is quite picturesque. The entrance end, with its plaster groined vault, its choir gallery and organ, is also imaginative, but the Gothic detail throughout is almost incredibly naïve, apparently based on Batty Langley's *Gothic Architecture*,[41] which Greene may have owned. Yet notwithstanding these two excursions into the Gothic field, with their intricate and charming Chippendale or Langley Gothic detail, Greene remained an essentially conservative designer all his life, and seldom — to my knowledge, never — used Greek forms.

The Greek Revival in Rhode Island is basically the work of two men: James Bucklin, who had been apprenticed to Greene; and Russell Warren, who, unlike Greene, welcomed the new style eagerly. In their hands it became fluid and expressive, and the Greek work of Rhode Island rapidly came to equal that done anywhere in America. One of the earliest of its monuments, the Provi-

41 *Improved by Rules and Proportions.* . . (London: J. Millan, 1747).

dence Arcade of 1828, is also one of the best. It was designed by both Warren and Bucklin, and has been in constant use as a shopping center since its completion. Of great exterior dignity in its granite Ionic order, it has a light and open interior, skylighted, with balconies of rich and elegant cast iron.[42] With the customary freedom of the best Greek Revival designers, its architects have not hesitated to use arched openings where they wished. Providence was enormously proud of it and rightly so, and engravings of it were widely published. Nevertheless it could not please the critical Thomas Hamilton, who wrote of Providence in *Men and Manners in America:* [43]

The only building which makes any pretension to architectural display is the Arcade, fashioned at either extremity with an Ionic portico. Judging by the eye, the shaft of the columns is in the proportion of the Grecian Doric, an order beautiful in itself, but which, of course, is utterly barbarized by an Ionic entablature. By the way, I know not anything in which the absence of taste in America is more signally displayed than in their architecture.

Providence was as fortunate in its more commercial buildings of those times as in its lavish hillside houses. Greene's Bristol Hotel (1824) on Market Square had used granite in large pieces superbly, much as Parris had used it in the Quincy Market buildings in Boston; the Washington Buildings (1843) in Providence, by Bucklin, showed what truly urbane yet reticent grandeur the Greek Revival could produce with simple means. Covering a whole block front, this quiet brick row with its granite base and its granite pedimented central pavilion was appropriate and beautiful; it gave promise of a development of urban character and harmony, and of cities that should be architectural throughout instead of merely in spots, which, alas, the future was soon totally to belie.[44] Other noteworthy Greek buildings in Providence were Mann-

---

[42] The Weybosset Street façade is Warren's, the rest of the building probably Bucklin's.

[43] Edinburgh: W. Blackwood, 1833.

[44] A somewhat similar atmosphere of quiet dignity and harmony may still be seen here and there in lower New York, in some of the harborside streets of Boston, and in the older commercial buildings of New Bedford, all from about the same period (1825–45).

ing Hall (1833), formerly the library of Brown University, by Bucklin, and the same architect's ' Cabinet ' of the Rhode Island Historical Society; Strickland's Athenaeum; Warren's Shepard house; and the superb Westminster Street Church, with its rich eight-column portico, by Warren and Bucklin. Bucklin's odd dome, added with a portico in 1836 to the Weybosset Street Congregational Church (1809), is one of many attempts to combine a dome with a Greek Doric portico, and hardly more successful than the others. Outside of Providence Warren designed the Smithville Seminary (the old Lapham Institute, later the Washington Academy) at North Scituate, a splendid composition of pedimented center and end pavilions with interesting connecting wings. He is sometimes credited with the design of the Nathaniel Russell house in Charleston, South Carolina, built as early as the period prior to 1811, when he was active in Bristol. Nathaniel Russell had gone to Charleston from Providence.[45]

Warren was evidently a much appreciated and widely sought architect. We know he practiced extensively in New Bedford, and the Minutes of the Athenaeum — for which he had made a preliminary design much too large and expensive — mention that when it came time to build Warren was away in Halifax superintending work there. Warren also was possibly the architect of Elmhyrst, at One Mile Corner in Newport, which in its originality and its attic treatment recalls his earlier Bristol work, though its date (*circa* 1840) is evidenced by its Greek Ionic order and Greek detail.

Much of the most delightful and interesting Greek Revival work in Rhode Island is anonymous country work and, especially, work in the mill towns. Such is the Chestnut Hill Baptist Church at Exeter, with its simple paneled pilasters, its austerely graceful square belfry, and its fret in a panel over the door; or the four-column Greek Doric church (1836) at Slatersville. Such, too, are the industrial housing rows and groups built around the mills at the time, and some of the mills themselves. In these mill towns

---

[45] See M. A. DeWolfe Howe's *A Venture in Remembrance* (Boston: Little, Brown & Company, 1941).

was established a sense of community — a pleasantness of simple architectural forms, an ampleness of planning, a free use of trees planted along the streets — which set a standard of decency and amenity that in Rhode Island persisted long; as late as 1873, in Hope, rows of quiet mansarded cottages were built which were a pleasing contrast to the hosts of crowded slums rising in other mill towns elsewhere in the country in those years. The names of some of the towns themselves ('Hope,' 'Peacedale') express the ideals the Rhode Island industrialists chiefly held. It is one of the trage- dies of American architecture that community ideals so high, so decent, and so humane, already realized and expressed in these Rhode Island towns of the twenties, thirties, and forties, were later to be so ruthlessly overthrown, so carelessly forgotten, that the words 'industrial town' and 'slum' became by 1900 almost synon- ymous. . . Examples of those early industrial housing groups are Quidnick (1847), White Rock (1849), Riverpoint (1850), Lons- dale and Berkeley (in the early 1870's).

But this humane industrial housing was by no means limited to Rhode Island. Everywhere in New England the earlier indus- trialists seem to have felt their responsibility to their employees, and to have had a definite pride in both the appearance and the ample accommodations of the housing furnished to them. This can be seen especially in the towns on the Merrimack River — Manchester, Nashua, and Lowell. In them were built, at the same time with the mills, blocks of ample and dignified boardinghouses and rows of single-family or semi-detached houses for overseers and the like. These buildings were distinguished by gracious de- tail and pleasant proportion all through the thirties and forties, and they were placed with a definite sense of community beauty and efficient relationship to the mills. Trees were planted, and fre- quently advantage was taken of the power canals to bring the beauty of water into the town picture. The result bid fair to de- velop a completely new kind of community in America — a com- munity of pleasant residences forming a band between the mills on the river front and the shopping center and public buildings along the main highway some distance back from the shore. Be-

Rhode Island architecture: TOP, LEFT, Washington Buildings, Providence. (*Old photograph, Rhode Island School of Design.*) TOP, RIGHT, Arcade, Providence. (*Author*). CENTER, church at Wickford. (*Author*.) BOTTOM, Elmhyrst, Newport. (*Rhode Island School of Design.*)

New England industrial communities: TOP, employees' boardinghouse, Quidnick, R.I., 1847. CENTER, church at Slatersville, R.I. (*Both, Fed. Art Project.*) BOTTOM, LEFT, housing for the Amoskeag Company, Manchester, N.H. BOTTOM, RIGHT, boardinghouses at Somersworth, N.H. (*Both, Coolidge.*)

Unitarian Church, Baltimore. M. Godefroy, architect. ABOVE, exterior. (*Essex.*) BELOW, interior. (*Old engraving, Maryland Hist. Soc.*)

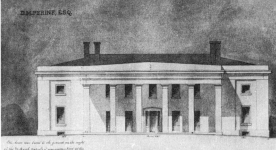

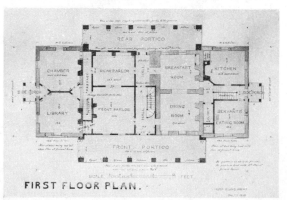

Baltimore buildings: TOP, LEFT, Battle Monument. M. Godefroy, architect. (*Avery Library*.) TOP, RIGHT, house at No. 515 Park Avenue. (*Major*.) CENTER and BOTTOM, R. C. Long's drawings for Homeland. (*Perine*.)

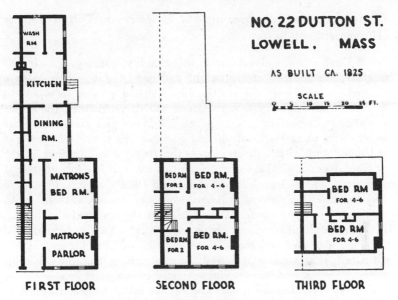

NO. 22 DUTTON ST.
LOWELL . MASS

AS BUILT CA. 1825

SCALE

FIRST FLOOR   SECOND FLOOR   THIRD FLOOR

FIGURE 19. EMPLOYEES' BOARDINGHOUSE, Lowell, Mass. Plans. (*Coolidge.*) The matron's parlor and the dining room were also used as sitting rooms for the boarders.

yond the highway on higher ground stood the mansions of the owners and managers.

Increasingly from 1850 on, tremendous changes in business practice, leading to the formation of great corporations of absentee owners who controlled the mills, a growing search for profits at any cost, exaggerated competition, and a new and tremendous flood of foreign immigration put an end to this hope. By the seventies little was left of the older paternalistic idealism, and the slums and jerry-building reigned supreme.[46]

Travelers bring back varying accounts of New England in the thirties and forties. Much of it, like much of America then, was still somewhat raw and crude; much of it was brand new. But underneath it all there seemed to be some kind of feeling of exhilaration, of hope, of beauty sought and appreciated. Dickens, for example, though he found in America plenty to complain of, liked

[46] For a brilliant analysis of this development in Lowell, see John Coolidge's *Mill and Mansion: A Study of Architecture and Society in Lowell, Massachusetts, 1820–1865* (New York: Columbia University Press, 1942).

at least the looks of America in 1842. In *American Notes* (Chapter III) he writes of Boston:

When I got into the streets upon this Sunday morning, the air was so clear, the houses were so bright and gay; the sign boards were painted in such gaudy colors; the gilded letters were so very golden, the bricks were so very red, the stone was so very white, the blinds and area railings were so very green, the knobs and plates upon the street doors so marvellously bright and twinkling; and all so slight and unsubstantial in appearance — that every thoroughfare in the city looked exactly like a scene in a pantomime. . . The suburbs are, if possible, even more unsubstantial looking than the city. The white wooden houses (so white that it makes one wink to look at them), with their green jalousie blinds, are so sprinkled and dropped about in all directions, without seeming to have any root at all in the ground; and the small churches and chapels are so prim, and bright, and highly varnished; that I almost believed the whole affair could be taken up piecemeal like a child's toy, and crammed into a little box.

The city is a beautiful one, and cannot fail, I should imagine, to impress all strangers very favorably. The private dwelling houses are, for the most part, large and elegant; the shops extremely good; and the public buildings handsome.

Later (Chapter V) in describing the trip from Boston to Hartford he says:

Every little colony of houses has its church and schoolhouse peeping from among the white roofs and shady trees; every house is the whitest of the white; every Venetian blind the greenest of the green; every fine day's sky the bluest of the blue. . . All the buildings looked as if they had been built and painted that morning, and could be taken down on Monday with very little trouble. In the keen evening air, every sharp outline looked a hundred times sharper than ever.

Such was the brilliant impression made upon many travelers by the New England of a century ago. There was in it all a certain exuberance, a certain gaiety, which we tend to forget in thinking of those early days; above all there was the harmony of the new growth, the harmony which the Greek Revival had brought with it.

CHAPTER 8

THE PROVINCIAL GREEK REVIVAL:
IN THE OLD SOUTH

BALTIMORE was in an unusually fortunate position, from 1820 on, for the development of the new architecture. Close to the national capital, it could not help being deeply affected by the building of the great new government structures there; yet it was in close touch with Philadelphia also. It was a sort of crossroads station between the North and the South; possessed of an excellent harbor, it was rapidly growing in population and in wealth and becoming an important cultural center — like Boston, Philadelphia, and, later, New York — as the influence of the older centers like Annapolis waned. It boasted of its more recent nickname, the 'Monumental City,' and sought architecturally to be worthy of it. Latrobe, Mills, Godefroy, and Ramée all did important work there, and Baltimore had her own consequential local architects as well — especially Robert Cary Long, Sr. (1770–1833), and his son Robert Cary Long, Jr. (1810–49), who designed many buildings there and in the neighborhood; the son was the author of some of the most thoughtful and farsighted of the architectural papers contributed to the Franklin Institute in Philadelphia.

The name 'Monumental City' came from Godefroy's impressive Battle Monument, a dignified classic memorial more Roman than Greek, and from Mills's great Doric column erected between 1815 and 1829 as a memorial to Washington;[1] but it was a monumental city in more ways than that. The square containing the Battle Monument and the development of Charles Street, with the hilltop park where the Washington Monument rises, gave the city layout a formal and monumental quality, and this was increased by the large number of domes over important structures in

[1] H. M. Pierce Gallagher, *Robert Mills, Architect of the Washington Monument, 1781–1855* (New York: Columbia University Press, 1935).

the city and by the dignified reserve and great scale of some of its earlier public buildings.

Such was the Peale Museum (1813; altered in 1830), designed by the elder Long; such too, pre-eminently, was the great cathedral Latrobe designed in a sort of Soane-like classic, with low, broad proportions and Greek details; [2] and such was Godefroy's interesting and original, square, domed Unitarian Church, with its arcaded loggia and unusual Rococo details (modeled by Solomon Willard of Boston) and its wide and ample interior — now, alas, hidden and destroyed by late-nineteenth-century alterations. [3] To Godefroy and Latrobe in association also goes the credit for the complex Exchange building, the dome of which was a distinctive feature in the Baltimore of a century ago. Its wall treatment was simple and not especially successful, but its intricate plan and basic mass composition had a new prophetic quality in their integration of many parts into one composition beneath the crowning dome.

To the elder Long must be attributed the Union Bank of Maryland, with its unusually rich sculptural decoration by Andrei and Franzoni, and the old building of the University of Maryland, with its impressive Doric colonnade. [4] The younger Long probably was the architect of many of those impressive and refined houses that rose along Charles Street, Monument Street, and around Mount Vernon Square during the 1830's and 1840's — houses which still give a remarkable air of ample comfort and refinement, of quiet, assured taste, to that part of the Baltimore of today. He also was the architect of the second Homeland (on Charles Street), built in 1839 as an alteration of an older house that had partly burned; his drawing is preserved and shows a dignified seven-bay house with a wide porch of two-story square Doric anta-type piers. This house also burned in 1843, and a third was built in 1846, ob-

---

[2] See page 32.

[3] See page 38. The original coffered dome and much of the original finish of the four great arches and pendentives which supported it still remain intact above the present plaster ceiling. One wishes that it might be restored to its original airy grandeur; the change would be a simple matter.

[4] Clayton C. Hall (editor), *Baltimore, Its History and Its People*, Vol. 1 (Chicago: Lewis Historical Publishing Co., 1912), p. 89.

viously on the same foundations and also designed by him. The difference between these last two houses is significant of the growing freedom of design at the time, a freedom Long himself expressed so well in a paper for the Franklin Institute.[5] The third house has a recessed loggia between two projecting end wings, above which rises the five-bay second story with a simple hipped roof and a central gabled cupola. It lacks the superb monumental breadth of its predecessor, but it is more intimate and more human in scale.[6]

Besides the Washington Monument, Robert Mills did other work in Baltimore. A row of simple brick houses with pleasant arched doors attributed to him still stands, though much altered, and it is possible that he was also the designer of some of the larger and more impressive houses — many of which had their main entrances at the side, somewhat set back from the street — as well as of others even more elaborate, including a large mansion for Dr. Dedian, with a colonnade of six Greek Corinthian columns across the front.[7] He was also the architect of the domed First Baptist Church there, opened in 1818, with its characteristic round interior [8] and an exterior modeled somewhat on that of the Pantheon, and of St. John's Episcopal Church, both burned in the great Baltimore fire.

The urban houses of Baltimore, like those on Mount Vernon Square, are typical of its culture and its position. They combine something of the quiet dignity of Boston's Beacon Hill, something of the restraint of design common in Philadelphia, and somethir ˙ of the richness of Greek Revival detail which New York lr Yet there is in them a special kind of breadth and great sc

[5] Quoted on page 61. Long's drawing of the second house is reproducea Swepson Earle's *The Chesapeake Bay Country* (Baltimore: Thompson-Ellis & C\ 1924).

[6] Robert Cary Long, Jr., also designed the Baltimore jail (1832). He died of cholera on 9 May 1849 at Morristown, New Jersey, while superintending the construction of a church he had designed. See Joseph Jackson's *Development of American Architecture, 1783–1830* (Philadelphia: David McKay [1926]), pp. 120–22.

[7] Gallagher, op. cit. pp. 79, 80, 96; ills. opp. pp. 86, 98.

[8] The relation of this design to Jefferson's later design for the rotunda of the University of Virginia and to Ramée's central building at Union deserves more study.

spacious feeling given by the high ceilings and tall windows, and an occasional use of free-standing columnar porticoes, all of which set them apart. In interior detail the influence of the Lafever books is often apparent, as it is so frequently in houses in other parts of the country. Almost nowhere else is the complete break with the richness of Federal-style detail, such as one gets in Homewood, so apparent as in Baltimore.

The breadth, the restraint, the sense of concentrated detail, and the large sizes so dear to Greek Revival Baltimore lasted on well into the 1840's; they reached almost their climax in the Bishop's Palace of Baltimore erected toward the end of the decade, the simple stuccoed front of which occupies an entire block front.

Richmond, like Baltimore, was a swiftly growing town in the Greek Revival period, and bears a deep impress of the new style. Jefferson had set there a dominant classic feeling in the superbly placed Virginia state capitol, and Mills carried on the tradition in a series of important houses and in his famous ' Monumental Church.' His Wickham house, now the Valentine Museum, is one of the country's most formally simple yet elegant houses of the general ' Regency ' type; Greek influence was limited to the mural decoration, which originally included scenes from the *Iliad* and the *Odyssey* and a head of Homer, but the restraint of the whole was eloquent of the new classic ideals. The Archer house was more conventional, in its end chimneys, its roof balustrade, and its entrance; but in the White House of the Confederacy, built originally for Dr. John Brockenborough, Mills uses a bold two-story Greek Doric portico. The Greek influences are obvious also in the interior Ionic order of the Monumental Church. All this work was designed between 1811 and 1814; it is thus as prophetic of the Greek Revival still to come as it is expressive of the freedom of design which characterizes Mills's early work.[9]

Of later and more typical Greek Revival buildings erected between 1825 and 1850 Richmond has magnificent examples, most

[9] See pages 50, 55; Gallagher, op. cit. pp. 78–80, 88–93, and illustrations opposite pp. 80, 82, 90, 92, 94; Mary Wingfield Scott, *Houses of Old Richmond* (Richmond: The Valentine Museum, 1941); Frances Archer Christian and [Mrs.] Susanne Williams Massie, *Homes and Gardens of Old Virginia* (Richmond: Garrett and Massie [c1931]).

of them as yet little studied and many of them in a deplorable state of blight and disrepair. Churches — especially St. Paul's Episcopal Church (1845), with a magnificent eight-column Greek Corinthian porch and an original and effective tower — and houses tell the story of the universality of the Greek taste; they show the restraint, the elegance and power of detail, and the harmony of the style. The Planters' Hotel by Isaiah Rogers was characteristic, in its red brick, its white trim, its portico, and its freedom of planning; the occasional experimentalism of the time is well shown in the famous Egyptian building of the Medical School.

But, aside from Richmond and a few individual buildings in other cities like Alexandria and Norfolk and Petersburg, the great houses of country Virginia, like those of Maryland, remained largely untouched by the new fashion until late in the period. There were exceptions, of course. George Hadfield, in the superb simplified Greek Doric portico of Arlington, as early as 1826 hit upon the one type of design powerful enough to make the house count when seen from Washington across the Potomac. Berry Hill,[10] built between 1835 and 1840 in Halifax County for James Coles Bruce, has a great 'Parthenon' colonnade across the front and two small four-column Greek Doric offices flanking its forecourt.

Elsewhere in Virginia the Greek Revival is chiefly to be sought in the public buildings and the churches of the growing towns in the hill country. There is, for example, a fine Greek Revival church, probably of the 1840's, in Fredericksburg, and there are several towns with beautiful Greek courthouses in handsome squares.[11] That at Goochland is especially good, and the ' Acropolis ' of Palmyra [12] — with its monumental Greek Revival civic

[10] Fiske Kimball, *Domestic Architecture of the American Colonies and of the Early Republic* (New York: Charles Scribner's Sons, 1922), pp. 180, 182.

[11] In the Avery Library, Columbia University, there is a handsome colored elevation of a Greek Revival church for Petersburg, Virginia, designed by Calvin Pollard of New York. It is possible that much of this local Virginia Greek Revival work was designed by architects from outside the state.

[12] These were called to my attention by Professor Carl Feiss, who in association with Frederic R. Stevenson is the author of a much needed book on the development of American city planning, *Our Heritage of Planned Communities*, to be published shortly by the Columbia University Press.

buildings so attractively placed on a bluff — is an impressive example of that sense of civic design which so frequently accompanied the Greek Revival alike in Ohio and in the new towns growing up still farther west.

Generally, however, the history of Greek Revival architecture in the southern states is a confused story of local influences, of conservatism in taste, and of a sudden and late flowering. Local pride was great; cities and towns in those critical decades of the twenties and thirties seem culturally to have been almost self-supporting, with little reciprocal exchange, so that even cities as similar in location and as close together as Charleston and Savannah show marked differences in their architecture. Away from such trading centers as these, the great plantation owners were rooted in a tradition of conservative pride in family, and in wealth, which made them, it would seem, singularly averse to changes in taste except in the most superficial ways; many houses of the 1820's in Virginia as well as in Georgia and the Carolinas are still essentially of eighteenth-century design. Moreover the natural conservatism of this plantation society made the plantation owners reluctant to destroy the fine old family mansions and replace them until absolute necessity compelled.

Yet in certain areas the power of strong local architectural personalities who were upholders of the Classic Revival was enormous; one is confronted with the paradox of a few scattered and extremely advanced Greek Revival designs existing, a decade or two before the Greek Revival gained ascendancy in the North, in places where the great mass of building remained incurably conservative.

The first of these revolutionary influences was the two-story porch Washington added to Mount Vernon in 1786-7, which was the precedent for the two-story porches so often added to earlier houses in the South or made part of the original design in later houses — particularly during the 1840's. The second influence lay in the work of Thomas Jefferson, which naturally was dominant in western and northern Virginia and found its most characteristic expression in the pedimented two-story classic entrance porch.

Neither of these influences was Greek in any way, and neither — despite Jefferson's own originality in house planning — affected the fundamentals of architecture. The one gave rise to the custom of two-story porches extending the whole width of the house, the other to a common custom of using classic Palladian detail in ornament and of having a pediment over the entrance door. It was not the revolutionary designs for Bremo [13] and Monticello which were copied by the greater number of the southern planters, but rather the Roman Doric portico Jefferson added to Montpelier, the old home of President Madison.

The architecture of North Carolina [14] is typical of the varied local influences in much southern work. In the districts settled first along the coast, occasional works like the Cupola House in Edenton show the same Jacobean characteristics that are found in the earliest houses of Virginia and South Carolina; but by the middle of the eighteenth century the special conditions of dampness and heat, together perhaps with influences from Virginia, had produced a definite local type in which the porch or piazza plays a dominant part. These piazzas were not monumental porticoes but simple rows of turned posts, sometimes treated like Doric columns supporting a continuation of the main roof. In almost all the houses the chimneys were built outside the end walls, with offsets where fireplaces occur. When the houses were two stories high, the two-story porch gave them a much more 'classical' appearance than that of houses of similar date in other localities, and contribute to such coast towns as New Bern or Beaufort a feeling of elegant grandeur quite independent of the size of the houses.

13 Bremo's design is very possibly not Jefferson's, although he was consulted with regard to it. See note on page 18.

14 For the architecture of North Carolina, see Frances Benjamin Johnston and Thomas Tileston Waterman's *The Early Architecture of North Carolina* (Chapel Hill: University of North Carolina Press, 1941), and [Mrs.] Bayard (Morgan) Wootten and Archibald Henderson's *Old Homes and Gardens of North Carolina*, with photographs by Bayard Wootten, historical text by Archibald Henderson (Chapel Hill: University of North Carolina Press, for the Garden Club of North Carolina [c1939]). The corpus of work included in the photographs of these two volumes will give an excellent picture of the general types of North Carolina work. In addition, the plans and the most enlightening analytical text by T. T. Waterman do much to explain its development in detail. I owe to these two books the greater amount of the North Carolina material I am using here.

Farther west in Piedmont, however, where the settlers came largely from Pennsylvania, and some from Virginia, the development was quite different; both the Moravians and the Quakers, in turn, contributed definite types of house plan and detail to the North Carolina tradition. The Moravian buildings in Winston-Salem — churches, communal dwellings, and houses alike — in their austere simplicity have a beauty unique in the South; their hooded doors and brick-arched windows, like their interesting railings of cut-out planks set vertically, are full of reminiscences of their builders' original German homeland. As time went on and communications improved, of course these differences tended to lessen; yet almost to the middle of the nineteenth century one finds more quiet, formal dignity in the west, great exuberance and elegance in the east.

In general the work was extremely conservative, and Greek forms crept in only gradually. Prospect Hill (1825–7), for instance, near Airlie, suggests eighteenth-century Connecticut in its tall corner porch supported by slim Doric columns; the trim both outside and in shows an amazingly intricate and richly delicate local development of Adamesque modifications. Nowhere is there a trace of the classical restraint that was governing architecture elsewhere. In the Coleman-White-Jones house (1825–30), at Warrenton, the same motifs occur on the exterior, though here combined with a hint of the classic fashion in an almost brutally heavy one-story porch of four Roman Doric columns.

Yet, paradoxically enough, in a few individual buildings there are touches of Greek feeling at an unusually early date. Such, for example, are the slim Doric columns with rather Greek capitals in the superb plantation house of Hayes, built as early as 1801. Its designer must have seen somewhere a copy of Stuart and Revett and dared to take the suggestions for its capitals from that unconventional source; otherwise the house is quite normal in its English curved wings and its rich Adam-like interior trim. The Mordecai house in Raleigh, built originally in the mid-eighteenth century, had a new front and porch added in 1824, and here we find Greek detail of a sophistication and original grace which makes one wonder about its designer. The porch is in two floors. The lower story with columns of generally Greek type, fluted only at the top, has a simple, wide, three-band architrave without frieze or cornice; the upper floor has graceful Greek Ionic columns carrying an entablature of simple frieze and cornice. The whole combination is unusually well handled, original, strong, gracious; nevertheless the Greek influence in much of the detail is obvious. Is it possible that Robert Mills may have had a hand in it? The treatment of the lower columns especially reminds one of some of his work, as does the brilliant modification of the standard entablature.

Greek details appear also at an early date in some of the work of John and Jacob Stigerwalt.[15] John, the father, was working in the Piedmont area in the early years of the nineteenth century. His work is largely in the earlier and more conservative manner, but the work of the son, Jacob, shows the Greek influences dominant. In his own house, Mill Hill (1821), near Concord, he carries a simple Greek Doric porch of five columns across the entire length of the house in the simplest and most direct way. Later, in the large houses Swan Ponds (1835–40) and Creekside (1836), the interior trim as well as the exterior is Greek, and mantels are used which are interesting naïve variations of the Greek-fret mantel Benjamin showed in Plate 51 of *The Practical House Carpenter* (1830). Yet all of this Stigerwalt Greek detail is modified delightfully either through ignorance or intention. Characteristic, for instance, is the effective entablature of the pedimented porch of Creekside. The columns are more Roman than Greek; the entablature consists of a simple flat band carrying the cornice; and on the flat band, as though to suggest triglyphs, are applied a series of regularly spaced projecting rectangular wood blocks. Other simpler and perhaps more normal Greek Revival houses are also found, such as Clover Hill (1830) near Lenoir, with its continuous high Ionic porch, typically more Roman than Greek, or the Poteat house (1835) at Yanceyville, with an excellent two-story portico

---

[15] A 'John Stirewalt' of North Carolina was a draftsman for Town and Davis during the 1830's. Could he possibly have been a son of Jacob and a grandson of the original John, and may some of their knowledge of Greek detail have developed from this connection? (See page 144.)

three bays wide, perhaps by the same architect. In 1830 a beautiful oval ballroom was added to the Halliday-Williams house at Fayetteville, in which the delicate Ionic pilasters, with their lovely wreathed entablature, and the exquisite trim of the entrance door have a sophisticated ' Greek ' character one would expect to find in New York rather than in North Carolina.

But the most polished of the Greek Revival domestic work dates from the 1840's. Such is the superb Greek Doric façade added in 1840 to Orton (originally built in 1725) at Cape Fear. The climax was reached in the Belo house (1849) at Winston-Salem, which has a front as original in conception as it is skillful in execution. A monumental two-story Corinthian portico serves as a central feature and is flanked by two-story porches at the sides — the lower with Corinthian columns, the upper entirely of the most delicate cast iron; the combination of the two materials (wood and iron) is handled with the greatest imagination and sensitiveness, and makes the house one of the loveliest as it is one of the most original in the South.

In public buildings the state was more advanced. The handsome First Presbyterian Church (1819) at New Bern is characteristic in its dignity and elegance. It looks very much like many Connecticut churches of a slightly earlier date, and is attributed traditionally to one Uriah Sandy, who may have come from Connecticut and been the designer as well of several of the houses in this neighborhood, with gambrel roofs of marked Connecticut type. In the county courthouse and sheriff's office (1831) at Jackson, there may be seen in one group both the advanced Greek type, in the simple portico of the courthouse, and a most original local design, in the sheriff's office, which has stepped brick gables with little pyramids on the end of each step. Otherwise the building has the true Greek Revival simplicity in its few well-proportioned openings, and strangely enough the combination is winning rather than incoherent. The old market house (1838) at Fayetteville is another example of North Carolina inventiveness used with conspicuous success. A square building carrying a handsome cupola, it has rather stumpy Ionic pilasters around its

enclosed second floor, and the market below shows the most interesting combinations of round and pointed arches. The later courthouses are more polished. That at Dallas (1846), now the town
hall, gets a surprising effect from the simplest means: masonry
walls with the most direct openings, a simple Greek cornice and
pediment, and a fine double flight of stone steps over an arch to
lead to the upper arched doorway. The courthouse (1845) at Hillsboro is one of the best of its type anywhere in the country. Its four-
column, widely spaced Greek Doric portico, its unusually forceful and well-designed cupola, and its quiet brick walls are almost
perfect of their kind.

The climax of the Greek Revival work in North Carolina is
undoubtedly the state capitol, built between 1833 and 1840. Town
and Davis of New York were the designing architects; associated
with them as superintendent was David Paton. It is a capitol of
modest size but monumental quality achieved through the simple,
direct handling of every part. Especially interesting are the side
elevation, with its row of antae, and, within, the austere rotunda
and rich detail of the Greek Corinthian assembly chamber. Paton
is said to have been the son of an Edinburgh builder [16] and to
have been trained in the office of Soane in London. How much he
contributed to the final result cannot be determined with certainty.
It is possible that some of the detail may have been from his pencil.
One thing at least is sure — the beautiful execution which guaran-
teed the effectiveness of the building. It would be interesting to
trace other work by him. Surely this cannot be his only American
monument.

There were other personal influences elsewhere in the South
which gave rise to local developments the very excellence of which
was a bar to further development. Such for example was the influence of Gabriel Manigault in Charleston. Manigault's exquisite
taste and his delicate, sensitive invention are apparent in the
Joseph Manigault house (1790) with its charming circular gate
lodge, in South Carolina Hall (1804), and especially in the United

---

16 Montgomery Schuyler, 'The Old Greek Revival' [Third Part], *The American Architect*, Vol. xcix, No. 1836 (1 March 1911), pp. 81–4, 86–7.

States Bank and City Hall (1801). In his work there are traces of the influence of Adam and Paine, and of Louis XVI detail; but he made of these a new synthesis quite personal in its restraint and unlike the work of his contemporaries elsewhere. It set a standard so high that Charleston builders who followed it found little temptation to seek new forms; aside from a few exceptional buildings by Robert Mills, true Greek Revival work became common in Charleston only in the forties.

Perhaps, too, the excellence of the typical Charleston house had something to do with this conservatism.[17] The demands of the warmth and dampness of the Charleston climate were severe, and a kind of house as well as a type of house placing and orientation had been developed which answered these demands perfectly. Not only the looks of the individual buildings but even the entire appearance of the city was affected, and a great deal of the beauty and character of the town — a character that is unique in American cities — comes from the frank acceptance of these natural conditions. The greater number of the houses had galleries or piazzas of two or three stories along the entire south or west sides of the building, to shade the windows and give space for outdoor living. The houses were usually set with their narrow ends toward the street and close to it, on lots wide enough to give space for a sizable side garden, usually walled. This rhythmical repetition of house, piazza, and garden creates both harmony and variety, and offers an almost boundless opportunity for beautiful and varied details in the handling of wall and gate, fence and piazza. The twin hipped-roof houses at No. 21 Charles Street are characteristic.

To this type the Greek Revival brought few changes. Greek orders, sometimes much attenuated, served as piazza posts; 'Greek' detail, often eccentric, replaced the earlier Federal or Adam ornament, but even then traces of the preceding styles were frequently retained. In the Charles Allston house built c. 1820 but altered in 1838, the roof balustrade is of the earlier type, but

---

[17] See Albert Simons and Samuel Lapham, Jr., *Charleston, South Carolina* (New York: Press of the American Institute of Architects, 1927).

the piazza orders are Greek and a delicate iron porch decorates the front. Here the basement porch columns are heavy, unfluted Doric, those on the main floor Greek Doric also but much attenuated, and the top-floor posts are Greek Corinthian; the interior trim, however, is a personal interpretation of rich Pain or Benjamin precedent. In the newer parts of town the colonnade, in one or two stories, became more and more important. A typical example is Aiken Row, in Wragg Square, where the alternation of the colonnaded porches and rich foliage creates a street picture of great beauty.

Another element that came into greater and greater use was the cast-iron porch or balcony, like that on the Allston house; in the more crowded parts of town these lavish laces of iron contrast delightfully with the brick or stucco behind. Where these iron porches originated is still a debatable question; they were common in the forties alike in the North and the South, in the East and the West.

Generally speaking, the Greek Revival came slowly to Charleston; even the Charleston market hall (1841) and Bennett's rice mill (1844) used detail of Roman and Renaissance inspiration, and the portico added to the College of Charleston in 1850 by E. Blake White was more Roman than Greek. By 1838, however, Charleston possessed in the magnificent Greek Corinthian portico of the Charleston Hotel, designed by Reichardt,[18] one of the most superb street façades the movement produced. The more conventional Greek Revival houses became fashionable in Charleston later still; the Roper and Aiken houses, both of the late forties, are characteristic of this later work. Another lavish example is Milford (1852–3) near Pinewood, distinguished by its unusually ample scale and its great Corinthian portico across the front.

In public buildings the Greek influence appears hesitantly in the attenuated Greek Doric columns of the lower stage of the

18 I owe this attribution to Mr. Albert Simons and Mr. S. G. Stoney of Charleston. The Charleston *Courier* of 28 October 1839, in a story dealing with the opening of the hotel, gives credit to ' Reichardt, a German,' as the architect. Jefferson Williamson, on page 14 of *The American Hotel, an Anecdotal History* (New York: Alfred A. Knopf, 1930), attributes it to Isaiah Rogers.

portico Frederick Wesner added in 1825 to the South Carolina Hall of 1804, but the portico was in all its main features — its wide spacings, its oval pediment window, its slim proportions — typical of the earlier town. It was not until the later thirties that the example of the superb Mills buildings was commonly followed. Then a series of Greek Doric temple churches were built, like the Hazel Street Synagogue (1838), with a correct six-column Theseum portico designed by a New York architect named Warner or Warren,[19] and the very similar Wentworth Street Baptist Church. The same type was used as late as 1853 in the Bethel Methodist Church. In 1840 Thomas U. Walter's beautiful Hibernian Hall — won by the architect in a competition — signalized the final victory of the Greek movement.

Robert Mills and William Jay may share the honor of having been the first to introduce the Greek Revival movement into the Southeast — the former in Camden, Columbia, and Charleston, in a few important works built during his ten years' residence in Columbia between 1820 and 1830; the latter in a group of masterpieces in Savannah built between 1816 and 1825. It is significant that their work, admired as it was, seems totally to have failed to change the dominant conservatism or to have started a new style.[20]

[19] This architect was probably Russell Warren of Providence, who was responsible for other work in Charleston. See Beatrice Ravenel's *The Architects of Charleston* (Charleston: Carolina Art Association. 1946).

[20] Mr. Albert Simons, our greatest authority on the architecture of this region, suggests that economic conditions may have had much to do with this apparent conservatism. He writes in a letter to me:

'Can this be explained on the grounds of conservatism alone? Or does not a glance at the curve of commercial prosperity of the country disclose a deep trough falling from 1820 down to a low point in 1830 and climbing up again in 1840? That there were no more fine buildings in Savannah for Jay to design after 1825, and that in 1830 Mills left what had been an active practice in South Carolina to take a government job in Washington, indicates not so much a lack of appreciative clientele as it does a general lack of prosperity. About the only building of any architectural distinction erected in Charleston in the thirties is St. Philip's Church, rebuilt after it was destroyed in 1835. The Presbyterian Church on Edisto Island, built in 1831, is also exceptional in this depression period. It has a fully developed tetrastyle Greek Doric portico as the dominant element of its façade.

'There was a destructive fire in Charleston in 1838 and with the revival of prosperity in the forties there was a veritable building boom which continued up to the firing on Fort Sumter. There are still in Charleston whole blocks of commercial buildings and also of residences which are completely Greek Revival in their broad expanses of stuccoed wall surfaces and refined crisp moldings. Perhaps the most interesting building of this period is the Hibernian Hall, erected in 1840. Mills took

FRONT ELEVATION

ABOVE, LEFT, Calvin Pollard's elevation for a church at Petersburg, Va. (*Avery Library.*) ABOVE, RIGHT, and BELOW, exterior and interior of St. Paul's Church, Richmond, Va. (*Cook.*)

TOP, Berry Hill, in Virginia. (*Cook.*) CENTER, Hillsboro Courthouse, N.C. (*Johnston.*) BOTTOM, Arlington House, Arlington, Va. George Hadfield, architect. (*Tebbs.*)

North Carolina State Capitol, Raleigh. Town & Davis and David Paton, architects. (*Johnston.*)
ABOVE, exterior. BELOW, House of Representatives.

North Carolina houses. (*Johnston.*) LEFT, Belo, Winston-Salem. RIGHT, portico added to Orton Plantation.

Charleston houses: ABOVE, LEFT, No. 21 Charles Street. ABOVE, RIGHT, Charles Allston House. BELOW, LEFT, Mikell (John Ficken) House. (*These three, A.I.A. and Metropolitan Mus. of Art.*) BELOW, RIGHT, Roper House. (*Tebbs.*)

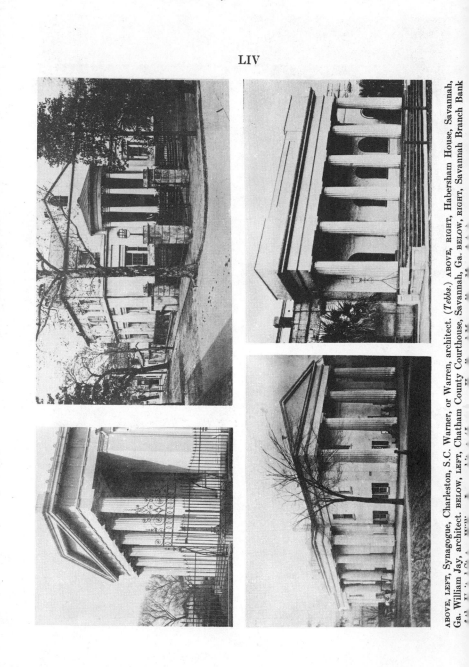

ABOVE, LEFT, Synagogue, Charleston, S.C. Warner, or Warren, architect. (*Tebbs*.) ABOVE, RIGHT, Habersham House, Savannah, Ga. William Jay, architect. BELOW, LEFT, Chatham County Courthouse, Savannah, Ga. BELOW, RIGHT, Savannah Branch Bank

Greek Revival houses in Georgia: ABOVE, Ralph Small House, Macon. (*Tebbs, Major.*) BELOW, Deering House, Athens. (*Bannister.*)

ABOVE, Gaineswood, Demopolis, Ala. (*Tebbs*.) BELOW, house at Athens, Ga. (*Tebbs, Major.*)

Even Mills's own work in South Carolina remained, for him, unusually conservative in style, except for two important examples: the Record Office in Charleston and the revolutionary state insane asylum at Columbia. The De Bruhl house and the Hampton-Preston house (Chicora College), both (1818) at Columbia, like his Wickham house (1812) in Richmond, are ' Federal ' rather than Greek Revival in detail. The Baptist Church in Charleston uses a Greek Doric order, and Mills himself called it ' pure Greek in style '; but its doors are arched and its scheme is essentially conservative. The state insane asylum, however, in its boldness of conception, its inventive quality, simplicity, and power, is typical of Robert Mills at his best; it is one of those masterpieces by which the movement we call Greek Revival most clearly vindicated its own ideals. It is owing, I believe, only to the conservatism of the South at that time that the functional excellence of this design and its complete consistency of detail and composition did not have a wider influence.

The work of William Jay in Savannah was similarly creative and restrained, similarly isolated and without wide influence on what came after. Jay was one of the most original architects of the period, inventive and with almost perfect taste, a man who has remained — as his city of Savannah, with its remarkable early parks and avenues, has remained — too little known and studied. In addition to possessing the customary restraint noticeable behind the Regency work of England, he was gifted with a remarkable fertility of mind and added a new kind of detail in which Greek motifs were used delicately and freely, but with no archaeological flavor whatsoever. The Habersham house (1820) is typical in its exquisite proportions, its simple use of refined classic detail (which reminds one of the best of Latrobe or Thornton), and its rich and original semicircular Greek Corinthian porch. Jay was the architect also of the Scarborough house and probably of Telfair Academy, about the same date, both of which reveal a similar freedom

part in the competition for this building, but the design of Thomas U. Walter was selected. This would seem to indicate that by the forties public taste preferred the more archaeological interpretation of Greek forms to the freer and more original style of Mills.'

and refinement; he also designed the Savannah branch of the United States Bank, which in its bold combination of Doric portico and simple massive stone wall with great arched windows had a power that was in the best sense monumental. Time has dealt harshly with Jay's buildings; many of the best have perished in the last twenty years, victims alike of 'progress,' blight, and an almost total lack of local appreciation and pride in them. The McAlpin house (1835) and Christ Church (1838), designed by James Hamilton Couper, both in the later, developed Greek Revival vein, show how different were the aims of this work from the quiet restraint of Jay.

The old Chatham County courthouse has also been attributed to Jay, but it has a different character, with its pedimented end porches and its flat-roofed porches at the sides. Robert Mills's diary contains a sketch of a courthouse for Savannah, the drawings for which were mailed from Washington on 24 May 1830. It is larger than the courthouse built, but it has basically the same long, narrow plan, with pedimented end porches; it is possible that Mills may have designed the executed structure, reducing in the final drawings the dimensions of his first sketch. Certainly the building looks more like the work of Mills than that of Jay.

Other interesting examples which show the inventiveness that existed in the South in the early nineteenth century, and yet at the same time the isolated — as it were, childless — quality of the work, are not uncommon among the Georgia and Carolina plantation houses. Such is the amazingly original, classic, and powerfully composed South End House (now owned by Howard Coffin), built between 1810 and 1812 on Sapelo Island. But until almost the middle of the thirties the eastern part of the South, save in these rare instances, remained essentially as it had been at the beginning of the century.

In the hill towns of central and northern Georgia the history is different. Here we have a series of new towns, or towns achieving rather suddenly a new prosperity, and a great influx of new and rather wealthy settlers. Here, in Athens, in Macon, in Milledgeville, as in northern Alabama at Tuscaloosa and farther west in

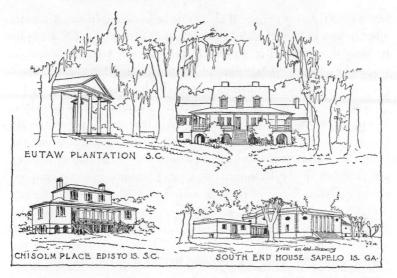

EUTAW PLANTATION S.C.

CHISOLM PLACE EDISTO IS. S.C.

SOUTH END HOUSE SAPELO IS. GA.

FIGURE 20. THREE CHARACTERISTIC PLANTATION HOUSES OF THE
COASTAL SOUTH. (*Author.*) Some of the types developed prior to the Greek
Revival.

Mississippi, an enormous amount of new building went on, in
which the newer ideas — or perhaps, rather, the relative lack of
any inhibiting conservative tradition — gave rise to a new fresh
type of residence in which at last the Greek Revival movement
controlled.

To understand the development of these novel types one must
appreciate the differences in climate and in ways of life between
the southern plantations and the more northern towns and villages. A warmer climate at once suggested plans more open and
spreading than those of the North, as well as the general use of a
piazza or veranda for under-cover outdoor living and to shade the
important windows from the hot noonday sun. Both of these developments, of course, had taken place before the time of the Greek
Revival; low spreading houses, with the first floor raised well above
the ground and occasionally a second floor under a hipped roof
with dormers, with a portico on two sides or all around, had become almost standard in South Carolina and coastal Georgia.
Typical examples are Otranto (1790), on Goose Creek, and Eu-

taw (1808). Is the origin of this type to be found in the still more open houses of the British West Indies? Or is it possibly an independent development in answer to special conditions? A study of tropical and subtropical colonial architecture — English, French, Spanish — might reveal unexpected similarities.[21]

But there are many plantation houses, even of fairly late date, in which the influence of the simple old Georgian types continues dominant with little modification due to climate, and in which the Greek Revival if evident at all is present only in details of door or porch. Such is the Calhoun house at Clemson, South Carolina, where a Greek Doric portico is added to a T-shaped farmhouse which might be found almost anywhere in the eastern states; or the Chisholm place (1840) on Edisto Island, South Carolina, with its definite Regency flavor and a porch between low wings on the garden side only. This persistence of Georgian and English types is especially noteworthy west of the Alleghenies in Tennessee and Kentucky.

The difference between the social life of the plantation and that of the North was enormous. Still largely ' feudal ' in type, the plantations were widely scattered and social life was to be obtained only by constant and large-scale visiting. Southern hospitality was a necessity if there were to be social contacts at all; entertaining was on a vast, almost princely basis seldom approximated in the North. Large houses were inevitable, and plans were more and more altered from the older types by the requirements of large social functions. Halls were increased in size and rooms thrown *en suite* with large doors between; often a ballroom was added. Thus in the Napier house (typically Greek Revival) in Macon, Georgia, a normal plan — a central hall with two rooms on either side — is enlarged by having a great ballroom across the back as long as the entire width of the house. In Cragfont (1802), in Sumner County, Tennessee, the dining room is cen-

---

[21] It is perhaps significant that the Spanish commander's house at Baton Rouge, Louisiana, shown by Diego Angulo Iñiguez in *Planos de Monumentos arquitectonicos de América y Filipinas existentes en el Archivo de Indias* (Seville: Universitad de Seville, 1933), Plate 144, is a simple rectangular gabled building surrounded by a hipped-roof porch on all four sides.

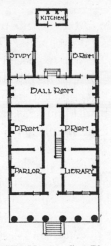

FIGURE 21. NAPIER HOUSE, Macon, Ga. Plan. (*Horton*.) Characteristic Greek Revival town house, showing the large ballroom often found in southern mansions.

tral at the rear, with the kitchen behind in the vertical bar of an inverted T; above these, on the second floor, is the ballroom, connected with the dining room by a spiral stair; verandas in two stories flank both sides. In the Jackson house, Forks of Cyprus, Lauderdale County, Alabama, built in 1820 (with a two-story portico completely around it, perhaps added later), the stair hall itself in the center of the rear is enlarged to ballroom size.

During the period between 1830 and 1855 the planning of southern houses, especially in upper Georgia, Alabama, Mississippi, and west of the mountains generally, underwent endless changes. Outside of Louisiana, where special influences and special conditions were present, experimentation in planning was the rule rather than the exception. Just as in New England and the North all sorts of new house forms came into being in this exuberantly creative period, so in the South new kinds of house plan rapidly developed. Especially common was the T-shaped plan, with the vertical bar directed forward and the entrance at its end. Frequently this was made into a single rectangle, as broad as the projection of the arms of the T, by a great colonnade at the front and sides of the vertical bar. This type is found especially in Ma-

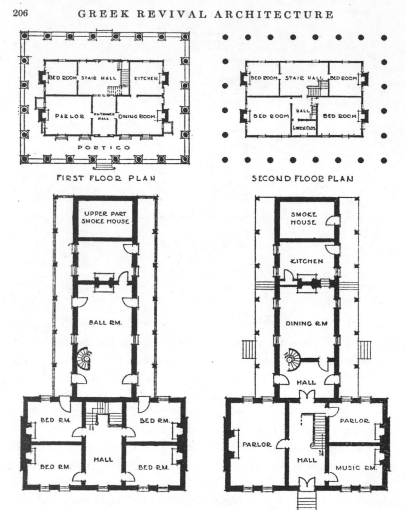

FIGURE 22. TWO TYPICAL SOUTHERN PLANTATION HOUSE PLANS.
(*Frazer Smith.*) Above, Jackson House at Forks of Cyprus, Ala. Type with
portico all around and highly developed stair hall. Below, Cragfont, Tenn.
T-shaped plan, with two-story galleries on each side of the rear wing. Note the
communicating dining room and ballroom.

con and Columbus, Georgia, and in Alabama; but it is often to be
seen elsewhere and its effect is monumental to the highest degree.

Another common plan type had a large projecting rear wing
forming an L. Often this wing was devoted to guest rooms, and

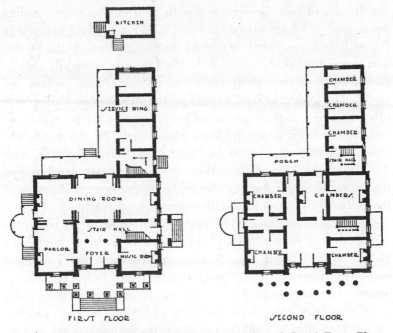

FIGURE 23. GEORGE POLK MANSION, 'Rattle and Snap,' Tenn. Plans.
(*Frazer Smith.*) L-shaped plan, with wing containing bedchambers, like the
New Orleans garçonnière. A monumental first-floor arrangement, superbly
planned for large-scale formal entertainment. Many porches for outdoor living.

frequently it had a two-story porch along its inner side instead of
a hall. This wing is found even in the city houses of New Orleans,
where it is called a ' garçonnière,' but it is used on country houses
as well.

Many of these country places were magnificent in scale — the
most lavish and pretentious usually dating from the forties and
fifties. A characteristic example is George Polk's mansion, Rattle and Snap, in Maury County, Tennessee, built about 1845, with
its garçonnière, its rear porch, its recessed entrance porch, its ten
magnificent façade columns, and its four great first-floor rooms
en suite. Other interesting examples are Rosemount at Forkland,
Alabama, built in 1832 (unusually early for its type), with its
superb hall; and Waverly, in Lowndes County, Mississippi, built
in 1858, with a great two-story hall filling the entire area between

the front and back porches and with twin curved stairs leading up to a second-floor balcony around it. This gradual increase in the scale and monumentality of house design through the forties, and almost to the very brink of the Civil War, is especially notable in the more western plantations and in commercial centers and ports. The great cotton fortunes of the Mississippi Valley were often creations of the years after 1835, whereas the prosperity of the more eastern southern states was already on the wane. The great Mikell house (1853) in Charleston, South Carolina, with its T-shaped plan and Corinthian portico, reveals something of this later, more ostentatious classic. So do the two great houses of the early fifties, Belmont and Bellemeade, near Nashville, Tennessee, both probably designed by Strickland and revealing the growing break with earlier ' Greek ' types; it is true also of Manning's Folly, Milford Plantation, Sumter, South Carolina. The great houses of Natchez, Mississippi, tell the same story. These later houses are enormous in scale, ceiling height, and room size; lavish in interior trim, at times to the point of lush decadence; palatial rather than domestic, and accurately disclosing a kind of economic unbalance that could not last.

In exterior appearance it was the two-story colonnade, usually with Greek detail, which set the earlier, more modest, more attractive type; nowhere did the Greek Revival produce a more perfect blending of the dignified and the gracious, the impressive and the domestic, than in the lovely houses of the thirties and forties in upstate Georgia and Alabama. In Athens, in Macon, in Columbus — in Tecumseh, Tuscaloosa, and Tuskegee — these porticoes give a character unique in America. There is great variety of detail in them; it was not taken literally, line for line, from handbook plates. All the orders are found, with entablatures frequently varying from the norm. Above the entablatures there is sometimes the simple sweep of low-pitched roof, sometimes a coping rising gently to the center and decorated with acroteria, sometimes (but rarely) a full pediment. Occasionally the colonnades are but one story high, especially on the smaller houses and cottages, and sometimes plain square or octagonal posts replace the columns. The old Governor's Mansion at Milledgeville is a splendid example of the conventional type more usual elsewhere in the country, but perhaps the most refined of the characteristic Georgia examples is the exquisite Ralph Small house at Macon.

The designers of these houses are largely unknown. Confronted by the often novel and magnificent plans and beautiful exteriors, it is difficult to believe the usual legend of mere client design carried out by the local carpenter. Mrs. Thaddeus Horton [22] has rescued from oblivion the name of one architect — a gentleman, to be sure, for whom architecture was an avocation — James Hamilton Couper of Hopeton, near Darien, Georgia. He is said to have designed many of the great houses in the neighborhood between 1820 and 1850, and he was the architect of the handsome Greek Ionic Christ Church at Savannah. J. Frazer Smith [23] has recorded the contract, with the plan and elevation accompanying it, of a typical Louisiana plantation house built in 1831 in St. Landry Parish. The owner was Hypolite Chrétien, the builders were Samuel Young and Jonathan Harris, and the drawing shows not only a careful plan and elevation but an entrance door detail besides. He believes that the clients largely dictated the plans of the houses and that the excellence of detail came from the fact that the trim was usually ordered ahead of time, all made and ready to install, from steam planing mills.[24]

Yet there were probably more trained architects of skill working in this area than we realize. The great cotton prosperity from the thirties on brought into the South a great number of settlers from the North; among them we know some were architects, like James Gallier and the Dakin brothers. Isaiah Rogers worked briefly in Mobile, and Smith [25] notes the names of Thomas James and Baron von Steinwelm as architects there in 1828. Elias Carter

---

[22] 'Amateur Architects of the South,' *Architecture*, Vol. xxxvii, No. 5 (May 1918), pp. 127–32.

[23] *White Pillars, Early Life and Architecture of the Lower Mississippi Valley Country* (New York: William Helburn, 1941), p. 217.

[24] This might account for the widespread use of forms showing the influence of Lafever. In designing trim, the mills would undoubtedly make use of the best handbook sources available, and among Greek Revival handbooks Lafever's were pre-eminent. Ibid. pp. 228–9.

[25] Ibid. p. 219.

worked for some time in the early thirties ' in the South '; could he have designed the Ralph Small house at Macon which so resembles his Simeon Burt house in Worcester? Mills worked extensively in South Carolina during the early part of the period, Strickland in Nashville toward the end. Without doubt the architectural handbooks,[26] especially those of Nicholson and Lafever, were widely used and helped to spread the Greek gospel and to determine endless details of trim section and mantel and door design. But behind such excellence of design as is apparent in the best of these houses one is forced to infer a designer — a true architect in work if not in name. Only much wider and more intensive local research can discover these architects and restore to them their rightful reputation.

Besides the houses, a few churches, the state capitols, and the courthouses, it is the colleges which chiefly distinguish the Greek Revival in the South, for the tremendous development in higher education which characterized early America was not limited to the North. Many academies grew into colleges, and many colleges of earlier foundation grew enormously in size during the twenties, thirties, and forties, requiring frequently either brand-new buildings or extensive rebuilding of old ones. The University of South Carolina at Columbia is typical. Its simple, almost stark, gray stucco buildings are grouped pleasantly. Many of them, from Rutledge Hall (1805) to the library (1840), were the work of Robert Mills or at least built definitely under his influence. Only in the last one, the library, is a change made from a simple rhythm of wall and window, through the introduction of a white-columned Greek Doric portico carrying a characteristic Mills coping, and through the omission of the stucco from the brick wall. Inside, the library room is a superbly designed and richly finished interior; Roger Hale Newton has recently shown,[27] on the basis of drawings by A. J. Davis in the Avery Library, that this is an almost line-for-line copy of the Congressional Library in the United States Capitol, probably designed by Bulfinch.

[26] See Appendix A.
[27] 'Bulfinch's Design for the Library of Congress,' *The Art Bulletin*, Vol. xxiii, No. 3 (September 1941), pp. 221–2.

One of the most impressive of these early Southern colleges is the main group of Washington and Lee University, at Lexington, Virginia. Here, in 1842, a simple existing single building was made the central motif in a long and imposing composition by adding to it connecting wings with large end buildings. The front of the older building was altered to fit the new design, and a cupola was added. The three-story central building is pedimented, with a portico of six slim Roman Doric columns; the two-story wings have Doric pilasters; the end pavilions, hipped-roofed and three stories high like the central mass, are fronted with porticoes of square paneled antae. The order is Roman rather than Greek, but the simple lines, battered base, and rectangular openings of the cupola are full of true ' Greek ' simplicity. The whole group, with its strong white accents of pier, pilaster, and column against the red brick walls, forms a dignified monument. A statue of Washington, added in 1844, crowns the cupola. No more impressive expression of the educational ideals of the time could be imagined than this classic group, its pediment and orders seen through embowering trees, over swelling American lawns, its cupola crowned with the image of the *Pater Patriae*.

Still more Greek were Ivy Hall and the chapel, with its six-column Doric portico and belfry tower, built in 1831 for the University of Georgia at Athens. The old Medical College building of 1834 at Augusta is also a striking example of the purest and most direct Greek design, unusual in the rich acroteria that crown its pediment. The buildings of the University of North Carolina, at Chapel Hill, are from many periods; A. J. Davis of New York restudied several of them, altered them, and built a new library building in an effort to weld the whole group into an impressive and monumental scheme. Thus a portico was added to Gerrard Hall, and the end elevations of Old West and Old East halls were revised in 1856–8 [28] with a stunning long vertical window quite modern in feeling and characteristic of Davis's search for new and original forms. The library, which dates from 1850–52 [29] and is

[28] Dates from Davis diary in the Metropolitan Museum of Art.
[29] Ibid.

also by Davis, shows the same search. The column capitals of its portico are generally Corinthian in type, but native corn and tobacco replace the Roman acanthus leaves with even more skill than that with which Latrobe had made a similar experiment in the United States Capitol nearly forty years before. Not far away in North Carolina is Davidson College. Again A. J. Davis was the architect, and here he used his vertical combined windows with recessed spandrels between in the boldest possible way on the two long buildings flanking the central chapel, which has a truly colossal Tuscan portico. The whole forms a composition of power and scale that is almost unrivaled in the country. He used a somewhat similar motif in the state insane asylum (1850), at Raleigh, which he designed.

In all of these buildings the effort to produce adequately grouped and beautifully designed college buildings in the then most recent current style is obvious. Collegiate education then sought architectural expression in the most ' modern ' vein, as it stood (or tried to stand) in intellectual matters for the most advanced thinking of the time. It seems, therefore, all the more pity now that so frequently present-day colleges in the South, even some of those founded in this old and still-living tradition, should have discovered nothing better than a debased Gothic style in which to carry out their recent buildings.[30]

The Greek Revival architecture of the South appears upon analysis to have been a much more profound and significant movement than would seem evident at first from the false and sentimental glamor with which an equally shallow and sentimental modern view of the ante-bellum South has enshrined it. Like Greek Revival architecture elsewhere, the Greek Revival of the South stood for the direct solution of practical problems, the frank acceptance of climates and ways of life, the breakdown of the older traditions dating back to colonial times, and the attempt to create a new and American architecture.

[30] See Montgomery Schuyler's ' The Southern Colleges,' No. 8 in a series on The Architecture of American Colleges in *The Architectural Record*, Vol. xxx, No. 1 (July 1911), pp. 57–84.

CHAPTER 9

THE PROVINCIAL GREEK REVIVAL:
THE GULF COAST, NEW ORLEANS, AND TEXAS

FOUNDED by Bienville in 1718, New Orleans was a French colony until the treaties of Fontainebleau (1762) and Paris (1763) transferred it to Spain. Spanish till 1801, it then became, through the Treaty of Ildefonso, French again. In 1803, through the Louisiana Purchase, it was at last made a part of the United States. Such a checkered career could not but leave its architectural mark, and although the older French and Spanish buildings have largely perished — in the great fire of 1788, which wiped out four-fifths of the city, and that of 1794, when perhaps a third was destroyed — nevertheless the French and the Spanish impress is still to be found. The final style that grew up in New Orleans and its neighborhood was the result of all of these confused influences modified by the insistent demands of a damp and warm climate, where there is an eight-month summer but a wet and chilly winter which prevents the use of pure tropic forms.

The population too, like the architecture, shows the effect of this variegated history. The first French settlers, with the wave of Spanish families who came later, became known under the generic name of 'Creoles.' To them was added an influx of American settlers after the American purchase, and, as soon as the magnificent commercial opportunities offered by the site of New Orleans as the great port of the Mississippi Valley were realized, the population of the new American type increased by leaps and bounds.

When the completion of the Erie Canal drew most of the produce of the northern Mississippi Valley to more convenient Atlantic ports, the new prosperity that resulted from vastly increased cotton growing took the place of the earlier commercial attractions and gave rise to a prosperity even more flamboyant than that which had preceded; so that from 1830 on to the Civil War there was another great influx of new settlers from the North and the East. Even the geography of the town shows the evidences of this development. The rectangle of closely spaced little streets at right angles known as the Vieux Carré was the outgrowth of Bienville's original colony, and it remained for long years as the special home of the Creole families, who stuck tenaciously to the general house-plan types they had developed, however much the styles of decoration upon them might change. Beyond Canal Street the Faubourg Ste. Marie was the place chosen for the residence of the prosperous earlier American settlers, while the ' Garden District ' still farther out became the favored seat for the homes of the wealthy American population from 1835 up to the Civil War.

The early permanent French buildings were generally simple in the extreme — little rectangular houses, one story high, built in a sort of half-timber construction stuccoed over, a type known locally as *briqueté entre poteaux* (' brickwork between posts '). The roofs were generally hipped, with broadly projecting eaves to shade the fronts as the only evidence of the effort to build to meet the southern climate. Sometimes to the two or three rooms of the main rectangle a service ell was added in the back at one side of the lot, leaving the largest possible interior court in the angle. Tiled roofs were required by law after 1794, and a few of these — made locally — still remain; but slate was imported and became almost the universal roofing material after 1800. These essentially simple houses have a definitely French provincial character, especially in their hipped roofs and in the placing of the houses near together and close to the street line. It is interesting to find that the same type of simple one-story structures, basically similar in plan although with different roofs and vastly different details, continued to be built in the Vieux Carré until well past the middle of the nineteenth century.

French, too, was the general rectangularity and simplicity of the layout centered on a large open square, the *Place d'Armes* (' parade ground '), now Jackson Square, with markets bordering its sides and important buildings at its head. It is a type of city

plan unique in the early United States, and it gave the town —
even when still small — a remarkably urban appearance. Urban
also was the Ursuline Convent built in 1734, which later became
the Archbishop's Palace and with its hipped roofs and tall windows
seems almost a bit from some French city transplanted to America.[1]
The Spanish influence was less perhaps that of old Spain than
it was an influence from other Spanish-American and insular colonies, for Spain had had long experience in colonial building and
understood well the special requirements of such warm and damp
climates. In the important buildings — the Cabildo (city hall)
built in 1795, the parish church (1794), and the Presbytère, not
built till 1815 but almost duplicating in its exterior design the
Cabildo — the Spanish colonial authorities were as firmly and
broadly monumental as they could be. And it is interesting to note
that the exterior of the Cabildo, in the general proportion of its
arcades, is in many respects almost a linear duplicate of a similar
building erected at Antequera in Mexico — the Casas Reales, dated
1781, the plans of which are preserved in the Archives of the Indies
in Seville.[2] Something of the early love of wrought iron in New
Orleans buildings may also be due to an original Spanish impetus,
and much of the earlier wrought iron is said to have been imported,
already fabricated, perhaps from Spain but more probably, I believe, from Mexico.

In house design the Spanish influence was quite different.
In the same Archives of the Indies in Seville is preserved the drawing of the Spanish governor's house at Baton Rouge. This, significantly enough, shows a simple rectangular house of considerable
size surrounded by a continuous veranda on all four sides; slim
wooden posts hold up a simple hipped roof. In the old Spanish customs house in the Bayou St. John district, built about 1784 in
New Orleans, there still stands a building that is merely an enlarged version of this original theme. The Spanish customs house
is in two stories, the posts of the lower story being of stuccoed

[1] See Nathaniel Cortlandt Curtis's *New Orleans: Its Old Houses, Shops, and
Public Buildings* (Philadelphia and London: J. B. Lippincott Company, 1933).

[2] Diego Angulo Iñiguez, *Planos de Monumentos arquitectonicos de América y
Filipinas existentes en el Archivo de Indias* (Seville: Universitad de Seville, 1933).

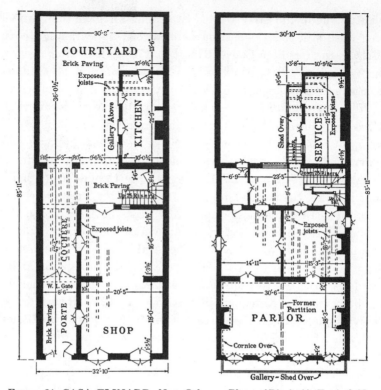

FIGURE 24. CASA FLINARD, New Orleans. Plans. (*Ricciuti.*) Typical New Orleans town house plan, with *corps de logis,* porte-cochere, courtyard, and garçonnière.

brick and those of the upper floor of slim turned columns. There is in the detail a certain obvious ' Americanization,' perhaps partially resulting from later alterations, but in all essential elements this scheme is in its basic ideas similar to that of the drawing in Seville raised to a two-story height. The type was copied in other early dwellings near by, such as the Ducayet house, and this in turn embodies the foundation idea of the typical Louisiana plantation.

Within the early city itself two- or three-story types came largely to supersede the still earlier one-story type soon after the great fire of 1794, and in these houses of the early nineteenth century one sees the final New Orleans city type already fully devel-

TOP, LEFT, house on Prince Street, Athens, Ga. TOP, RIGHT, Governor's Mansion, Milledgeville, Ga. (*These two, Tebbs, Major.*) CENTER, Washington and Lee University, Lexington, Va. (*Washington and Lee Univ.*) BOTTOM, A. J. Davis's study for Insane Asylum, Raleigh, N.C. (*Avery Library.*)

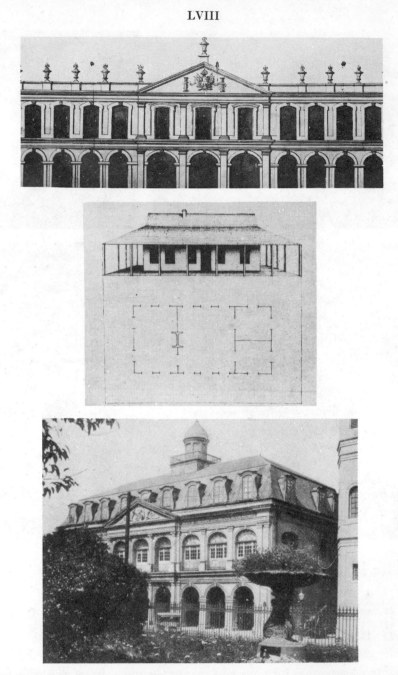

TOP, Spanish drawing, Casas Reales, Antequera, Mexico. CENTER, Spanish drawing, Governor's Residence, Baton Rouge. (*Both, Iñiguez.*) BOTTOM, The Cabildo, New Orleans. (*Avery Library.*)

New Orleans buildings: ABOVE, LEFT, early house, Kerlerec Street. (*Hertzberg*.) ABOVE, RIGHT, Julia Row, Julia Street. James Dakin, architect. (*Koch*.) BELOW, LEFT, Girod House. (*Hertzberg*.) BELOW, RIGHT, Louisiana Bank. B. H. Latrobe, architect. (*Hertzberg*.)

Greek Revival detail in New Orleans: ABOVE, LEFT, Boston Club. James Gallier, Sr., architect. (*Koch.*) ABOVE, RIGHT, houses on Esplanade Avenue. BELOW, LEFT, door, Bienvenue House, 1836. BELOW, RIGHT, door in the Vieux Carré. (*Last three, Hertzberg.*)

oped. Fundamentally it consists of a *corps de logis*, or main residential portion, stretching across the street front of the lot and usually two rooms deep. On the ground floor, at one side, is a passage large enough for carriages to drive through, leading under the *corps de logis* and into the courtyard at the rear; at its side and filling the rest of the ground floor is usually a shop and storage room. The stair hall leads off the passage at the rear of the main block in one corner, and behind the stair hall stretches a wing originally intended to contain the service elements of the house. Later, as the house sizes increased, the wing too was lengthened and its courtyard side would often be bordered by an open veranda on each floor. The service portion would occupy perhaps only the ground floor of this wing; the rooms above would be used for the younger members of the family and their guests — hence the universal New Orleans name of ' garçonnière.' Within this general pattern there was enormous variation. The simple, dignified exterior of stuccoed brick such as one sees in the Girod house of 1821 or in many others in the older parts of the Vieux Carré, where the floor heights and the tall windows often present a curiously Continental expression, gave way from 1830 on to unstuccoed brick; the delicate wrought-iron balconies supported on graceful brackets to be found on such houses as the Marchand house (1806) and the Absinthe House (1806), or on the Louisiana State Bank (1822) built by Benjamin Fox from designs by B. H. Latrobe, effloresced into the ' lace ' of the extraordinary cast-iron porches, climbing frequently from curb to roof, which became common in the forties and fifties and gave to so much of the Vieux Carré its characteristic appearance. A house on Toulouse Street, built about 1822 by Benjamin F. Fox, shows a transitional state in which there are covered balconies on both of the upper floors of a three-story building, but the railings are still of quiet wrought iron and only the balcony supports, the slimmest possible colonnettes, are cast. In the newer portion of the Vieux Carré, on the side toward Canal Street, the later builders of the Greek Revival period built during the 1830's blocks of houses which in their street façades are almost perfect duplications of New York types and strangely similar to those in some of the older streets of Greenwich Village; yet, once within, one discovers that the plan is basically still the old New Orleans plan of *corps de logis*, garçonnière, and court. Even in the very center of the Vieux Carré, the new movement resulting from the influx of Greek Revival ideas exerted its sway in the Pontalba apartment houses that line the two flanks of Jackson Square (the old Place d'Armes). These buildings, with their unified façades, were erected between 1848 and 1851 from the design of James Gallier, Jr. They reveal the growing sense of the monumental in civic design which the Greek Revival inevitably brought with it, and yet combine with this much of the free use of iron that is associated with the more normal Vieux Carré buildings. In fact, wherever new buildings were erected within the Vieux Carré during this period, the new formal dignity combined with the exquisite refinement of Greek detail makes its appearance — as for instance in the Petit Salon (now a woman's club), which flanks the Cabildo, and in the magnificent simplicity and perfect scale of the Greek-detailed Arsenal across the street from it. In mere details, of course, the influence of the Greek Revival in the Vieux Carré buildings is much more evident on careful study after one's eyes have become used to piercing under the lace of ironwork and realizing what lies beneath. There are perfect Greek Revival houses on Bourbon Street and exquisite doors of the purest Greek type scattered all through the district. Many are illustrated in Italo William Ricciuti's *New Orleans and Its Environs*.[3] In the Garden District also, as late as the 1870's, one finds in the opulent Bradish Johnson house (now the McGehee School), designed by James Freret, a garçonnière, or rather a servants' wing of garçonnière type, which seems almost like that of a building forty years earlier.

In the American districts outside the Vieux Carré naturally one finds frequent changes. The Julia Row, for instance, thirteen houses built on Julia Street for the cream of American society in the city in 1840 and designed by James H. Dakin,[4] is more north-

---

[3] New York: William Helburn, 1938; especially Plates 20, 21, 22, 74, 75, and 76.
[4] See a letter from Charles J. Dakin in the *Daily Picayune*, 17 July 1900. For the text of this letter see footnote on pages 226–7.

ern, more almost New York, in type, as though the American settlers were trying definitely to break with the typical tradition; and
the famous Boston Club, designed by James Gallier, Sr., as a
house for W. N. Mercer, is an accomplished piece of the most
polished Greek Revival city design.

Yet in the Garden District houses, built chiefly between 1835
and the Civil War, the insistent demands of the New Orleans climate again asserted themselves; though the houses are usually individual dwellings built on large lots, the need for outdoor living
and for shadowed windows makes almost universal either the continuous porches of the 'Spanish' plantation type or the storied
galleries that furnish pleasant outdoor sitting spaces on every
floor. The Garden District houses thus fall into three general
classes: those like the Maginnis house or the Thomas Toby house
(originally an overseer's house on a plantation), in which the
plantation type is approximated; those like the Forsyth residence
or the Lonsdale-McStea house, in which a more usual Colonial
tradition dictates the two-story composition and the large gables
with end chimneys, while the New Orleans climate adds front
porches of superposed orders and sometimes iron balconies on the
ends as well; and a third type consisting of those which fall under
neither of the first two, where the somewhat exceptional character
is the result of skillful and conscious original architectural design.
The Gauche house of 1856, with a Greek Doric porch and an exquisite cast-iron railed balcony and cornice cresting extending
around its square form, is characteristic of this last type, as is the
beautiful Logan-Henderson house, probably designed by James
Gallier, Sr., which has a lovely Greek Corinthian entrance porch
and a beautiful circular vestibule hall within.

Still another type is found both in the Vieux Carré and the
Garden District: the so-called raised cottage, a one-story building
on a high basement, usually with a pedimented entrance portico
reached by symmetrical stairs at one or both of the sides. The
Beauregard house of 1826, designed by the Spanish architect
Francisco Correjolles, is the best known and most highly developed example.

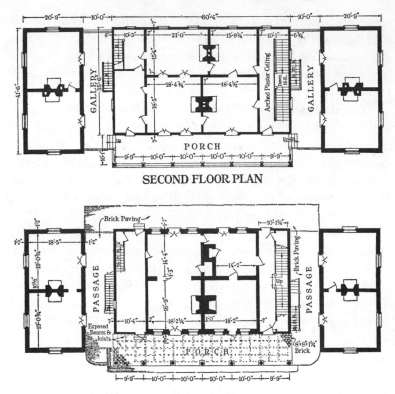

SECOND FLOOR PLAN

FIRST FLOOR PLAN

FIGURE 25. ORMOND PLANTATION, near New Orleans. (*Ricciuti.*) Formally designed rooms, so arranged as to give the greatest possible amount of through-ventilation; large, open porch areas.

The typical Louisiana plantation type is more renowned. Its square mass is surrounded by a colonnade of round columns extending the full height from ground to roof and supporting the second-floor veranda at their mid-point; usually there is a simple hipped roof, sometimes with dormer windows to light the attic. Such are Three Oaks in St. Bernard Parish; the earlier Hermitage (1812) at Geismar; Oak Alley (1837) at Donaldsonville; and the René Beauregard plantation (1840) at St. Bernard, designed by James Gallier, Sr. In plan there is frequently a large central hall with magnificent rooms on either side, but occasionally end halls with separate stairs exist at both ends of the house — as at Ormond — and often vertical circulation is furnished by exterior stairs in the colonnades as well. The effort seems to be always to get large rooms arranged *en suite* to allow the fullest possible through ventilation and the handsomest possible interior effects.

But there were many plantations in which the Greek Revival influence is more obvious than in these purely traditional types. Classicism everywhere during this period was working for greater regularity in design, greater monumentality of conception; the block plans show that in the relation between the main house and the many minor buildings — guest houses, offices, servants' quarters — which make up the whole plantation there is often an extraordinarily sure sense of studied, symmetrical, and pleasant arrangement. Even the main houses themselves frequently show the more classically monumental forms that were fashionable. A characteristic example is The Shadows at New Iberia, built about 1830, in red brick, with its two-story porch on one side only and with a more formalized plan. Here the influence seems definitely somehow northern, and the aspect of the whole — in color as well as in the formality of its design — reminds one of Maryland or Delaware, although the plan is of the plantation type. The same northern influence is apparent in the red brick Grima house in the Vieux Carré itself. It is of approximately the same date as The Shadows; could the same architect have been at work in both? [5] The Brame house at Clinton, Louisiana, boasts a great six-column Greek Doric colonnade with a pediment enclosing a semicircular window; Marston's Bank, also at Clinton, has a six-column Ionic colonnaded porch, also with a pediment, and the somewhat similar Maidwood is equally classic. In these one may suspect the hand of some accomplished Greek Revival architect, trained probably elsewhere, like Gallier and Dakin.

5 But the interior detail of the two houses is quite different in character, that of the Grima house being almost over-lush and extremely sophisticated in its use of classic details — as for instance in the screen between the front and back parlors, with Greek Corinthian columns, folding doors, and an elaborate carved frieze — whereas the same motif in The Shadows is almost naïve in its fluted pilasters and its molding profiles. The Grima house has occasionally been attributed to James Gallier, Sr., but seems to have been built four or five years before he arrived in New Orleans.

Over the interior detail of all of these houses of so many dif-
fering types the fashions of the period played wth surprising
unanimity. The great ceiling height prevalent gave all of the
rooms an atmosphere of dignity, of scale, quite different from
that generally found in the rest of the country, but the details
themselves — of doors and mantels and cornices — from the Late
Colonial period down through the Victorian era follow similar
elements found not only in buildings of the same date almost
everywhere in America but in the building handbooks. One special New Orleans characteristic — the high, narrow chimney
breast above a normal-sized mantel, such as is found in the Casa
Flinard or the Girod house — tended to die out as the Greek Revival forms, with their additional insistence on horizontal dignity
and big scale, became stronger. Similarly, occasional evidences of
the French Empire style, like the drawing-room mantel of the
Girod house — pale reflections of Percier and Fontaine — also
enjoyed a brief vogue. From 1830 the molded trims and corner
blocks, the Greek profiles, and the mantel types shown in northern
books become almost universal. Thus a mantel from The Shadows
is almost identically like one found in the earliest Lafever book,
and the marble mantels of the Grima house and the Casa Flinard
strongly resemble Lafever designs.

After the arrival of James Gallier with Charles B. Dakin and
later the coming of James H. Dakin, Charles's brother, in 1835,
this so-called northern influence becomes more and more strong.
Gallier had worked for two years in New York and for one of those
years had been Lafever's partner. Either the influence of Gallier
upon Lafever was tremendous and partly responsible for the exquisite Greek Revival character of Lafever's later books, or else
Gallier himself fell strongly under the influence of the New York
man. In any case a marked similarity may be found in New Orleans, as in so many other parts of the country, between much of
the existing interior detail and the characteristic detail shown by
Lafever.[6] It is hard to deny the Lafever influence in much other

6 The Lafever influence is obviously earlier than the coming of Gallier and
wider than the spread of Gallier's own work. For example, the plaster cornice of
one of the parlors at The Shadows (1830) seems clearly to recall Plate LXIV of

New Orleans detail, especially that in the Forsyth house in the Garden District, much of the detail in the Logan-Henderson house, and the exquisite library trim of the Albert Schwartz house at No. 730 Esplanade Avenue, where the rich door heads and the rosettes of the cornice have that particular blend of richness and restraint that was the hallmark of Lafever's best design.

The extraordinary thing seems to be that, with all the variations of background which characterized mid-nineteenth-century New Orleans — English, American, French, Spanish — and with all the claims for social supremacy which the French and Spanish Creole families asserted and maintained, in the buildings that all of them erected — in Vieux Carré or Garden District or plantation country beyond — the current American type (the Greek Revival) declared itself with ever growing power.

And this same tendency toward some kind of generalized 'American' type controlled the works of the best-known New Orleans architects of the time, whatever their background. One of the two most famous and productive was Jacques Nicolas Bussière de Pouilly. He was born in Burgundy in 1805, was educated at the Ecole des Beaux Arts, and came to New Orleans about 1830, working there until his death in 1875. An existing notebook of his is most revealing. It contains many sketch plans and elevations for houses and other work in New Orleans and also outside. Greek Revival or néo-Grec influence is dominant, but in the sketches it is the neo-classicism of the French books of Normand and Krafft [7] that is the inspiration, rather than the books of Lafever or his American co-workers. The architecture as shown in the drawings is liney and much of it over-detailed. The interesting thing is that, in such executed buildings as one sees on Esplanade Avenue and the more outlying parts of the Vieux Carré, most of this European character little by little seems to evaporate. As interpreted

'stucco cornices and centre flowers' in Lafever's *The Young Builder's Instructor.* The front parlor cornice of the Old Merchant's House in New York, built two years later, uses an almost identical detail. See also Appendix A.

[7] For instance, J. Ch. [K.] Krafft and N. Ransonnette's *Plans, coupes, élévations des plus beaux maisons . . . construites à Paris. . .* (Paris: the authors, 1801–3), or J. Ch. [K.] Krafft's *Portes cochères, portes d'entrée, croisées, balcons. . .* (Paris: Scherff, 1810), or Charles Normand's *Recueil varié de plans et de façades. . .* (Paris: the author, 1831).

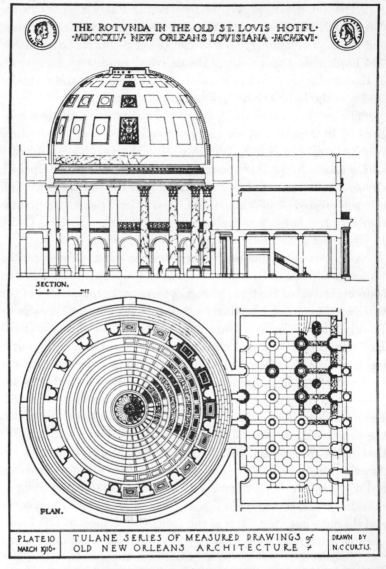

FIGURE 26. ST. LOUIS HOTEL, New Orleans. The rotunda. Jacques Bussière de Pouilly, architect. (*Curtis.*) Elegance, magnificence, and great scale, to express the lavish formality of New Orleans life.

by the carpenters and masons and stucco-workers of actual New Orleans, these Krafft and Normand designs become quite American and at home. De Pouilly's masterpiece was the great St. Louis Hotel built between 1836 and 1840, a building distinguished by true urban monumentality of plan, with a magnificent domed rotunda as its central motif. The whole, with its richly detailed polychromed interiors, must have been one of the most superb hotels in America at its time and its destruction within living memory one of those architectural tragedies too numerous in American cities. The hotel was not Greek Revival in feeling; its classicism was of a more generalized type, yet its quietly composed exterior seemed quite harmonious in spirit, if not in detail, with the more usual current Greek vernacular.

James Gallier, whose privately printed *Autobiography* [8] gives priceless details on the conditions of architectural practice in America as well as on the history of the development of New Orleans, went through a similar kind of Americanization. He was born in Ireland in 1798 and studied in the art schools of Dublin and later in various architectural and building offices in England. Realizing the great opportunities to be had in America, he came to New York in 1832 and worked there for approximately two years. Apparently dissatisfied with possibilities for advancement which the then current system offered, and not too well pleased with his partner Lafever, he left for the Gulf Coast in 1834. He began his southern career by winning the competition for the Mobile city hall, which however was never built; then he went on to New Orleans, where he fell almost at once into a wide and important practice. He brought with him as a partner Charles Dakin. Charles's brother, James H. Dakin, a pupil and later a partner of Town and Davis in New York, joined them a year later, in 1835, and the firm of Dakin and Gallier became the architects of the first St. Charles Hotel, built between 1834 and 1836. Soon after this Charles left for Mobile, and Gallier and James H. Dakin separated, each to found a firm which had tremendous influence on the architecture of the neighborhood.

---

[8] *Autobiography of James Gallier, Architect* (Paris: E. Brière, 1864).

The St. Charles Hotel was even grander, if less refined, than the St. Louis, with a superb and monumental granite colonnade at the entrance and a central rotunda within that was even more magnificent than the rotunda of the St. Louis Hotel. Its exterior was of granite from Quincy, Massachusetts, and Gallier in his *Autobiography* notes the difficulty of working in New Orleans where so much of the material and so many of the details of which a building was made had to be manufactured elsewhere and shipped in. The St. Charles Hotel was burned in 1850; the second St. Charles, which replaced it in 1851, was designed by Isaiah Rogers, but photographs seem to show that its basic exterior scheme largely followed the Gallier original. James Gallier designed much domestic as well as important public work in New Orleans. Especially interesting is the Dr. W. N. Mercer house, now the Boston Club, on Canal Street, which illustrates perfectly the strong New York influence obvious in much of Gallier's work.

His most significant public works were probably Christ Church (1835–7), which he did in partnership with James H. Dakin, and the New Orleans city hall (1845–50). Christ Church boasted a six-column Ionic portico, exquisitely detailed. This now forms the front of the Knights of Columbus building on Carondelet Street. The city hall, one of the handsomest of its time in the country, also used an Ionic order but one of far larger scale and more impressively handled. Like the St. Charles Hotel the city hall was built of Quincy granite and Westchester marble; although its interior has been too widely and too carelessly altered to allow of any true judgment of its interior effect, its exterior is still one of the most beautiful examples of the smaller Greek Revival public buildings to be found anywhere.[9]

[9] There has been considerable controversy with regard to which New Orleans buildings should be credited to Gallier and which to Dakin. The following letter printed in the New Orleans *Daily Picayune*, 17 July 1900, from a son of James H. Dakin, communicated to me by a grandson, Hyatt Lemoine, now of New York, clarifies many of these questions:

HONOR TO WHOM HONOR IS DUE.

New Orleans, July 15, 1900.

Editor Picayune: In your valuable Journal of this date appears an article about the late James Gallier, which I desire, in justice to my father, the late Colonel James H. Dakin, to correct.

In the later 1840's James Gallier's eyes became too weak for him to continue practice and he retired to a life of leisure and foreign travel, which is chronicled in his *Autobiography*. He died in the famous shipwreck of the steamer *Evening Star* off Cape Hatteras in 1868. His practice was taken over by his son, James Gal-

First — James Gallier was not the architect of the St. Patrick's church. The architects were Dakin & Dakin, a firm composed of James H. and Charles B. Dakin. In this connection allow me to quote as follows from documents in my possession: " The plan will be 93 feet by 164 feet on the ground, and from the sidewalk to the summit of the tower 190 feet. The style of architecture has been taken from the famed York Minster cathedral. It will by far surpass every attempt at Gothic architecture on this side of the Atlantic, and may proudly challenge comparison with any parochial edifice in Europe. The cost will be about $100,000."

Second — James Gallier had nothing whatever to do with the statehouse at Baton Rouge. It was designed and erected under the personal supervision of James H. Dakin, who died in Baton Rouge on the 10th of May, 1852.

At the breaking out of the war between the United States and Mexico Colonel Dakin commanded the Second Regiment of Louisiana Volunteers. Returning to New Orleans in 1847, he received the appointment of architect of the custom-house. Lieutenant Beauregard, of the corps of engineers (afterwards the celebrated Confederate general) being in charge. Plans and specifications for the erection of the statehouse were advertised for by the commissioners — Colonel Maunsel White, Dudley D. Avery and Walter Brashear — on the part of the state. The plans of Colonel Dakin were accepted, and for a while he superintended both custom-house and statehouse. Affairs not progressing favorably at Baton Rouge, he made a proposition to the commissioners to resign as architect of the custom-house and remove to Baton Rouge and give his entire time and personal supervision to the erection of the statehouse. Proposition being accepted, he tendered his resignation to the government and removed to Baton Rouge and personally superintended the building, and had the pleasure of seeing the same completed and accepted by the state.

Colonel Dakin was also the architect of the M. E. church, which was located at the corner of Poydras and Carondelet streets, costing $50,000. It was destroyed by fire, if I mistake not, on the same date as was the old St. Charles Hotel.

There was a partnership existing under the firm name of Dakin, Gallier & Dakin in 1835, during which time Christ church, on Canal street, was begun in the autumn of 1835, completed in the summer of 1837 and consecrated during the same year, the Rev. Mr. Wheaton being pastor. Its cost was about $48,000.

The Merchants' Exchange, fronting on Royal street and Exchange place, was also constructed by Messrs. Dakin & Dakin in 1835–36, costing $100,000.

The " Union Terrace," the present site of the Grand Opera House on Canal street, was also constructed in 1836–37, under the immediate direction of Messrs. Dakin & Dakin, costing $100,000. The " Thirteen Buildings," on Julia street, were also the production of Colonel Jas. H. Dakin. Colonel Dakin was but 27 years of age when he came to New Orleans in 1834, and immediately assumed the leading architectural rank of the country. His brother, Charles B. Dakin, was admitted to partnership in 1835; the latter died in Iberville parish in 1839, aged 28 years; James H. Dakin died in Baton Rouge, 1852, aged 45 years.

Jas. Gallier, Sr., was, if I mistake not, lost at sea, together with General Palfrey and many other prominent Orleanians, when the Evening Star went down.

Excuse length, and if of enough interest, please publish, but do make corrections. Very respectfully,

CHAS. J. DAKIN,
1411 Baronne street.

lier, Jr. (1829–70), who had been trained in his father's office. The son's best-known works were the Pontalba Apartments on Jackson Square and the famous French Opera House. The Pontalba Apartments must have been done when he was scarcely over twenty years old, but in their design he undoubtedly enjoyed the closest possible co-operation with his father. The French Opera House (1859) was built complete within a year, an extraordinary record for the time. Although it was no longer Greek Revival save in occasional refinements of molding profile, there is in it despite its late date almost nothing of that heavy-handed vulgarity to be seen in some of the early Victorian work that was little by little creeping inevitably into the city buildings. Its plan was clear, simple, and ingenious, based more on French than on English or American precedent; yet, as in the case of De Pouilly's St. Louis Hotel, the exterior showed that kind of simple directness of form and refinement of detail unlikely to have resulted without the discipline and training in Greek Revival design.

The later work of James H. Dakin was more varied and more erratic than that of the Galliers. He was evidently deeply indebted to his New York training with Town and Davis, and the experimentalism of Davis and his refusal to be bound by styles or conventions either in plan or appearance had developed in Dakin a desire to be similarly ' different.' Like Davis he was evidently more the designer than the constructor, and Gallier tells of coming to his rescue when the tower of St. Patrick's Church started to settle and fall. St. Patrick's (1835–6) was said to have been ' modeled after York Minster,' but in its roughly stuccoed brick exterior and the inventive, rather liney richness of its interior plaster detail there is almost nothing that is historical. The chancel, covered by a plaster vault of extraordinary richness in its Gothic ribbing, and lighted by glass ceiling lights set between the ribs, is instead an original creation of considerable charm and quaintness.

The same originality of conception and the same rather naïve inventiveness in Gothic detail controlled Dakin's design for the old Louisiana state capitol at Baton Rouge, now a museum. This piled-up, picturesque, castellated mass with its corner turrets and rich traceried windows is perhaps not good as abstract architecture, but it is definitely creative and original. It shares with the old Georgia capitol at Milledgeville the honor of being the only Gothic state capitol dating from before the Civil War. Many of its interior details — of open circular stairs and the like — are quite charming in their free originality and in the way the Gothic detail is applied to them, and the big window of the Senate front has definite effectiveness of composition.

Other Louisiana public buildings were more in the Greek Revival vein, yet frequently quite unlike similar buildings in other parts of the country. A characteristic type was the country courthouse, which like the plantation house often had a colonnade running around all four sides, as at Homer. Especially interesting is the courthouse at Clinton, where the nearly square colonnaded building has a domed cupola rising somewhat incongruously, though with a certain quaintness, over its center. The courthouse is in the middle of the town square. Around the square runs a 'Lawyers' Row' of law offices, each one a little Doric temple. The whole forms a charming and unusual town composition.[10]

New Orleans also was rich in buildings of a public or semi-public nature. Latrobe had made the designs for the Louisiana Bank just before his untimely death in 1820; it is a restrained, simple building, beautifully detailed, with a graceful wrought-iron balcony and a most interesting vaulted interior. The Louisiana State Bank, some five years later, is at once more ostentatious and more banal, with a large free-standing pedimented portico of Corinthian columns.

In New Orleans as well is William Strickland's beautiful United States Mint, now used as a prison, which has been mentioned earlier.[11] Mills too worked in New Orleans; he probably designed the old Marine Hospital, long since destroyed, built in a kind of much modified Gothic. But perhaps the most extraordinary of all the New Orleans public buildings of the period is the great

10 I owe this information to Mr. Richard Koch of New Orleans.
11 Page 79.

customs house on Canal Street, begun in 1849 from the designs of a local architect, A. T. Wood. It is a huge, rather gaunt, granite mass, with exterior detail unlike any ancient work whatsoever, although it probably represents a rather uneducated person's idea of Egyptian. Its greatest merit lies in its interior marble hall; 128 feet long, 84 feet wide, and 58 feet high, with columns of the Greek Corinthian order, it is impressive in its size and effective in its proportions. The entire vast building was not completed until after the Civil War; its history from the beginning was clouded with scandal and incompetence, its designer an architect only by courtesy. Yet somehow the whole, even in its awkwardness, perhaps even in its occasional downright ugliness, has a kind of power, a sort of forthright arrogance, that is impressive if only as an expression of the bold pride of New Orleans in cotton-boom days.[12]

Just outside New Orleans are the Jackson barracks (1834–7), built from the designs, it is said, of one Lieutenant Wilkinson. The group is a sort of vastly enlarged Louisiana plantation, with the simplest and most naïve details, yet effective because of its unusually well-organized and formal plan. The barracks buildings are fronted with the usual Louisiana ' galleries,' which in the main buildings run around all four sides; the general grouping of the buildings around a large central parade ground is excellent in scale and proportion.

The influence of New Orleans spread far and wide — up the Mississippi, eastward along the Gulf Coast, west and south into Texas. Thus as far north as Memphis there is to be found the old Frazier house dating from the early 1840's, which essentially is merely one of the New Orleans raised cottages somewhat formalized, with a four-column Greek Doric portico. It achieves remarkable dignity — one might almost say monumentality — for a house of its size. The legend is that it was built from the plans of a French architect, name unknown, who was traveling in this country and is said to have been responsible for a number of homes in the South. Could this be merely a romanticized tradition of an

12 For its history in detail, see Stanley C. Arthur's *A History of the United States Custom House, New Orleans* (New Orleans: Survey of Federal Archives in Louisiana, 1940).

architect of French origin from New Orleans — perhaps J. N. B.
de Pouilly or one of the Freret family (who were New Orleans
architects for four generations)? Certainly the type is a New
Orleans type.

The history of Mobile, Alabama, reveals many parallelisms to
that of New Orleans. Like New Orleans it was French first, then
Spanish; it was not taken over formally by the United States
until 1813. It is characteristic that Iñiguez [13] publishes from the
Seville archives some *pabellones* from Mobile, dated 1752, which
are typical Louisiana *briqueté entre poteaux* (half-timber) construction, with steeply pitched French-type roofs. The notes let-
tered on these drawings are in French and the plans are exquisitely
drawn. Under American government Mobile boomed as a port
before the Civil War and seems to have had several architects who
were extremely busy. It was there, for instance, that James Gallier
and Charles Dakin on their arrival from the North had their first
architectural success, Dakin winning the competition for a proposed city hall; it was probably this success that was responsible
for their appointment as architects for the St. Charles Hotel in
New Orleans. Later Charles Dakin returned to Mobile to practice
and died there shortly after. Naturally in building types the influence of near-by New Orleans was supreme. There are streets of red
brick houses with elaborate cast-iron porches and Greek Revival
detail which are almost identically like the houses on Esplanade
Avenue in the larger city. Interesting also are the United States
Marine Hospital, probably by Robert Mills; James and Charles
Dakin's sophisticated Ionic Government Street Presbyterian
Church (1837), of a type originated by A. J. Davis; the Barton
Academy (1836), with a Greek Ionic porch and an odd colonnade-
surrounded little dome, also by the Dakins; and the colonnaded
City Hospital, naïve yet impressive. [14]

In Texas, too, the influence of New Orleans is to be found.
Even as far away as San Antonio there are numerous buildings
of the 1840's of definite Greek Revival inspiration. In some there

13 Op. cit. Plate 140.
14 *Art Work of Mobile and Vicinity*, with a historical study by Peter Joseph
Hamilton (Chicago: W. H. Parish, 1894).

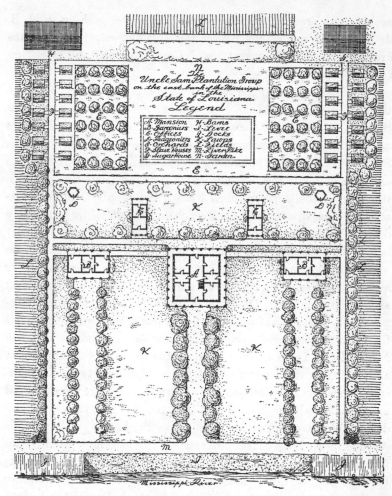

FIGURE 27. UNCLE SAM PLANTATION, La. Block plan. (*Frazer Smith.*)
Formal layout of the entire plantation, and symmetrical placing of minor buildings, to give the maximum architectural effect.

is evident a distant Mexican influence in the handling of masonry,
and a kind of charming blend of the almost Mediterranean solidity seen in the South with the basic fenestration and the porches
of the American North. In others, as in the old Governor's house,
the New Orleans touch is much clearer; its two-story porch across
the entire front in Louisiana plantation style has rich railings of

Greek Revival detail in New Orleans. (*Hertzberg.*) ABOVE, LEFT, Forsyth Residence, Garden District, interior. ABOVE, RIGHT, Girod House, Vieux Carré, mantel. BELOW, Logan-Henderson House, Garden District. James Gallier, Sr., architect. Door detail, and front.

LXII

Louisiana mansions: ABOVE, LEFT, Ducayet House, Bayou St. John, New Orleans. (*Hertzberg.*) ABOVE, RIGHT, Maidwood Plantation. (*Tebbs.*) BELOW, LEFT, Forsyth House, Garden District, New Orleans. (*Hertzberg.*) BELOW, RIGHT, Oak Alley, Donaldsonville. (*Hertzberg.*)

New Orleans public buildings: ABOVE, Marble Hall, United States Customs House. (*Koch*) See Frontispiece. BELOW, City Hall. James Gallier, Sr., architect. (*Avery Library*.)

TOP, Government Street Presbyterian Church, Mobile, Ala. James and Charles Dakin, architects. (*Art Work of Mobile*.) CENTER, old house in San Antonio, Texas. (*Author*.) BOTTOM, Old Louisiana State Capitol, Baton Rouge. James Dakin, architect. (*Barrington and D.A.R.*)

Tennessee mansions: ABOVE, Cleveland Hall, Donelson. (*Donelson.*) BELOW, The Hermitage, Nashville. (*Tebbs.*)

Tennessee grandeur. (*Anderson.*) ABOVE, Rattle and Snap (Oakwood Hall), porch. BELOW, Pillow-Halliday House, Columbia, entrance.

Kentucky houses. (*Newcomb.*) ABOVE, LEFT, The Grange, near Paris, 1818. ABOVE, RIGHT, Castlewood, near Richmond. Interior detail of typical Kentucky type. BELOW, LEFT, Diamond Point, Harrodsburg. Exterior of front door. BELOW, RIGHT, Mansfield, Lexington.

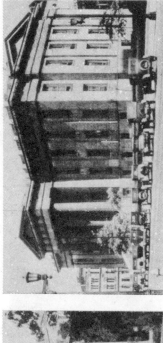

Kentucky buildings: ABOVE, LEFT, Old Capitol, Frankfort. Gideon Shryock, architect. ABOVE, RIGHT, Louisville Courthouse. Gideon Shryock, architect. (*Both, Newcomb.*) BELOW, LEFT, Junius Ward House, Georgetown. (*Andrews.*) BELOW, RIGHT, Louisville Bank. Gideon Shryock, architect. (*Caufield & Shook.*)

cast iron brought to San Antonio, tradition says, from New Orleans itself.

The Greek Revival in the New Orleans region thus was modified by, as it modified in turn, building types developed from a variety of sources, under the influence of definite and difficult climate conditions and characteristic living ways. French, Spanish, and American influences all contributed to the final result; yet despite this variety in historical background, despite the many political overturns and changes of allegiance, the climate and the ways of life unified all, and the Greek Revival proved its vitality and its adaptability by furnishing congenial forms into which this combined inheritance could flow. As in other parts of America, the best of the Greek Revival architects of this region were interested not in creating Greek temples, but merely in finding out the best answers for the pressing building problems of the growing communities in terms of the styles and taste then current. The Vieux Carré is a unique and a particularly American monument, because it enshrines so thoroughly this fascinating history of the building of a single community from many sources. It is good to know that New Orleans has recognized the peculiar value of this heritage and by means of the Vieux Carré Commission has set up legal means by which it may be preserved for the America of the future as well as for the America of today.

CHAPTER 10

WESTWARD WAYS:
THROUGH THE SOUTH TO THE MISSISSIPPI

EVEN before the Revolution, intrepid settlers — trappers, hunters, and a few farmers — were following the adventurous Daniel Boone through the Cumberland Gap at the western end of Virginia into the mountainous valleys of eastern Tennessee and pressing northward into eastern Kentucky. They were chiefly upcountry small farmers from the highlands of Virginia or from the Carolinas. Not slave holders, and comparatively poor, they built their log cabins, cleared their little farms, and established a type of mountain community, primitive yet self-assured, which has existed almost unbroken in the hill country down to the present day. After the Revolution and the confused period of the Indian wars, after the cession to the United States of the claims on this new territory held by the older coastal states, and especially after the War of 1812 was over, the flood of settlement became wide and irresistible; only fifty years bridge the gap between relatively primitive log-cabin settlements and the cultured and highly developed civilization of Nashville or Lexington.

As the country became safer, the character of the immigration also changed. Great landowners were attracted by the fertile valleys and the bluegrass of the plateaus. Plantation owners saw the possibilities latent in this rich new land and brought with them the aristocratic culture as well as the slavery of the southern states. Other settlers from Maryland, Pennsylvania, and the North, following the westward route through Pittsburgh and down the Ohio River, brought their own contribution of energy, imagination, and commerce. The architecture that grew up as these states developed shows this history. Almost nowhere else save perhaps in the Western Reserve of Ohio can the background of the settlers be so easily seen in their buildings, and nowhere else is there a clearer expression of the colonial cultural lag that results from the attempts of settlers in a new country to build for themselves the kind of buildings to which they were accustomed in the places whence they came.

Tennessee was admitted as a state in 1796, and already certain features that were to remain constant in Tennessee architecture were evident. Both the Blount mansion (1792) in Knoxville — said to have been the first frame house west of the Alleghenies in the state — and the even less pretentious Chisholm house are simple clapboard mansions, bare of ornament and with details of trim and mantel characteristic of the more modest houses of the Revolutionary period in western Virginia. The Netherland house (the so-called Old Tavern) at Kingsport, as late as 1811, is quite as simple as these in trim and finish and clapboarded walls, but it shows in addition a quality — which became a definite regional characteristic through Tennessee for almost forty years — of long, narrow, high proportions, with a roof of medium slope. Typical of this same proportion are the large narrow Kennedy-Hunter house at Knoxville; the Lockett house Longueval at Knoxville; the John Netherland house Rosemont (1810), a characteristic Colonial five-bay building at Rogersville; and Elmwood (1819) at Athens. The last shows also another representative Tennessee feature: a narrow porch two stories high with superposed posts or columns, four columns wide and crowned with a pediment. From 1800 on, the usual material for the houses is brick, which gives occasionally a strangely Philadelphia or Pennsylvania look to some of them, as in the Park-Temple house (about 1800) at Knoxville, with its arched door and a Palladian window above.

The same general proportions continue in use almost unchanged throughout the Greek Revival period, with only minor changes in detail to indicate the coming of new fashions. Characteristic, for instance, is Brazelton Place (1832) at New Market, where the porch is but one story high, with crude Greek Doric columns; yet the whole has the same long, narrow, high Tennessee proportions. In Cleveland Hall, at Donelson, the same type ap-

pears in 1841 — a house that might almost be called the typical
Tennessee mansion, with its dignified brick end chimneys, its
great length, its unbroken roof, and its beautiful if naïve Greek
Doric portico. Even as late as 1846 the same type persists in the
Stickley house at Madisonville, which has the characteristic Tennessee two-story porch. Here the details are of excellent character,
refined, delicate, sure; the house is said to have been designed by
' an English architect named Blanchard,' [1] who came to Tennessee from Pennsylvania.

As the great plantation owners began more and more to dominate the fertile lands, other ideas from other sources inevitably
appeared. There is a prophetic individuality, for example, in the
Carter house, The Mansion, at Elizabethton, built sometime toward the close of the eighteenth century, with its extraordinary
great hall, its lavish Baroque fireplace, and its small panels. This
interior finish is said to have been made originally in 1749–50.[2]
Both the independence of the plan and the re-use of the old
Baroque eighteenth-century material are characteristic. Thus the
Ramsey house at Knoxville, about 1800, built of roughly cut Tennessee marble, has extraordinary carved wood cornices with deep
rich brackets unique, so far as I know, at its date. Its design is
attributed to one Thomas Hope, an English architect brought to
Charleston by Ralph Izard to build his house there as early as
1757.[3] Hope, if this tradition was true, must have been an extremely old man when he designed the Ramsey house. Could there
be some possible confusion here with the fact that the Ramsey
family may have owned one of the books issued in the early nineteenth century by the English dilettante decorator Thomas Hope?
The detail of this unusual house is not of the later Hope's characteristic type, however, and its definitely Baroque quality might
give support to the legend. If so, it would be most interesting to
try to identify other work by the same man. Could he possibly have

---

[1] The Garden Study Club of Nashville and Mrs. John Trotwood Moore, *History of Homes and Gardens of Tennessee,* edited by Roberta Seawell Brandau
(Nashville: Parthenon Press, 1936).
[2] Ibid.
[3] Ibid.

been the designer of the Baroque detail in the Carter house in Elizabethton? And could it have been detail built for the new house in an old style by an old designer, instead of detail brought from across the mountains?

In the thirties the great Tennessee families, under the combined influence of their wish to be up to date in their buildings and the knowledge they had of the new kinds of plantation house being built in the newer portions of Alabama, Mississippi, and Louisiana, became extremely imaginative and inventive in their development of building types. Obviously these later builders of great houses enjoyed the services of skilled designers and workmen who knew their trade, were well acquainted with the Greek orders, and were men of definite originality. They brought polish as well as invention to these great Tennessee houses of the thirties and forties. Many of them deserve undoubtedly to be ranked among the real architects of the period, though their names are lost; just as in the early fifties families around Nashville called upon Strickland (who was then building the Nashville capitol) for the design of their houses, so these men of the decades previous must have called upon the best architects they could find.

By the 1830's Tennessee had ceased to be an isolated frontier region. It was a flourishing sovereign state with wide cultural and commercial interests, in close touch — through Memphis — with all the vivid influences coming from the North and the South along the Mississippi River. This new cultural breadth and vitality shows in the houses; although the old high, narrow types, as we have seen, persisted here and there until the fifties and although in places a certain naïveté is evident — as for instance in the church at Jonesboro,[4] where a belfry with a spire of definitely eighteenth-century Baroque character crowns a Greek Doric portico — the more advanced people were building themselves houses of great originality, polish, and sophistication. Such, for example, is the one-and-a-half-story hip-roofed Hazen-Webb house, Middlebrook (1845), at Knoxville, with its recessed Greek Doric porch, one of the many American attempts at wide, spreading, one-story plans;

4 Ibid.

or the Pillow-Halliday house (1845) at Columbia, with its beautifully detailed recessed porch of four Greek Ionic columns. Such too is the dignified — one might say almost perfectly characteristic — Greek Revival house Tulip Grove (1832–4), at Donelson, which has a remarkably sophisticated balance between its red brick and its white detail, with a continuous Greek Doric entablature and a two-story Greek Doric porch. Typical also of the same search for dignity and originality of detail in the Greek vein was Polk Place in Nashville, probably built soon after 1840, with its recessed side porch and its projecting entrance porch. In the grounds was the Greek Doric tomb of James K. Polk, built soon after his death in 1849.

This recessed porch, with the second-floor balcony carried midpoint of the columns, and with railings either of a sort of Chinese Chippendale pattern in wood or later of exquisite cast or wrought iron, is found again and again in the large Tennessee houses. Another characteristic that runs through them all is the unusual story heights (ceiling heights between twelve and fifteen feet are not uncommon), so that windows tend more and more to tall, slim proportions and the buildings themselves, even when but two stories high, achieve by virtue of their height a classic dignity which has in it something almost Italian. It is this unusual height that is at least partly responsible for the characteristic high, narrow proportions of so many of the Tennessee houses. The three Pillow houses at Columbia, probably by the same architect, all show this typical combination of height with rich recessed porches. In the Pillow-Halliday house, Clifton Place, the porch is further emphasized by having the recessed walls in white to contrast with the brick on either side. The S. D. Williams house, Fairview (1850), at Jefferson City, a handsome five-bay house with hipped roof and one-story end wings, has the three central bays forming a recessed porch with a pediment above; but instead of the usual Greek Ionic or Doric columns it has porch posts that are octagonal, with caps and an entablature which may be a naïve interpretation of Batty Langley's eighteenth-century Gothic.

The influence of the more characteristic southern plantation mansions is shown especially in Rattle and Snap, begun in 1845 by George Polk, the plan of which has already been referred to.[5] Here the magnificence of the ten-column Greek Corinthian portico is echoed on the ends by porches of some of the loveliest and most delicate ironwork in the South. President Andrew Jackson's home, The Hermitage, near Nashville, is another example of the more characteristic southern plantation type, with its porticoes across both long sides. The house was an older one built in 1819, but its present condition dates from a reconstruction completed in 1835 after a fire.[6] From the older building it preserves its simple five-bay scheme, but the six columns across the front — of the simpler Greek Corinthian type developed from the capitals of the Temple of the Winds in Athens — are all of the new time. The reconstruction was in the hands of Joseph Reiff and William Hume, who were the builders of Tulip Grove in Donelson, but it is hard to believe that the design for the reconstruction is theirs. Miss Agnes Addison (Mrs. John M. Gilchrist) has discovered documents which seem to show that the architect was D. Morrison. But perhaps the basic idea came from Washington. Jackson, in Washington, took the greatest interest in the rebuilding of his home, as we know from his correspondence. Could it be that Robert Mills, the friend and appointee of Jackson, furnished the original idea for the design? It seems natural that the President might have turned to his government architect for suggestions in such an emergency, and this possibility is rendered still more conceivable by the fact that there exists a drawing by Robert Mills for a house for Dr. Dedian in Baltimore,[7] which is in scheme, as in detail, much like the rebuilt Hermitage. The exquisite proportions of the domed tomb for Andrew Jackson in the Hermitage grounds also seem to show, in their balance of light delicacy and dignity, an architecturally creative mind of the first water.

As in Louisiana, the climax of size and luxury in these Ten-

[5] See page 207.

[6] Stanley F. Horn, *The Hermitage, Home of Old Hickory* (Richmond: Garrett and Massie, 1938). The fact that a broken original wooden leaf was once replaced with cast iron gave rise to the frequent statement that the Hermitage acanthus leaves are of iron. Iron, however, was often used for Corinthian leaves, especially in country districts.

[7] See page 189.

nessee houses came only in the fifties. The greatest monuments are three estates near Nashville: Riverwood, Belmont, and Belle Meade. In Riverwood a colonnade and an exquisite iron balcony were added at this time to an older house. The alteration is attributed to Strickland. The other two houses are almost certainly by him — Belle Meade, rebuilt in 1853 after a fire, with a portico of six square antae and an interesting parapet with acroteria, all in the most exquisitely detailed stone; Belmont (1850), superb in size and scale and lavish decoration, already showing some marks of that Italianization and that freedom which characterized the coming of the Victorian era. Here in Belmont the traditional recessed porch is used again, but the whole scale and scope of the design are so broad, so dignified, so rich, and so large that the effect is truly palatial.

Of Strickland's other work in the neighborhood it is here unnecessary to speak.[8] The state capitol has already been described, but there is an interesting Presbyterian church in Nashville that is probably also Strickland's — one of the few daringly original attempts to domesticate Egyptian influence for American use. It is a large structure with twin towers and a great portico recessed between them, and the use of Egyptian detail in molding profile and capital does not vitiate the strength and power of its basic conception and its great scale.

Kentucky was admitted as a state in 1792, even earlier than Tennessee; but, as in Tennessee and many other parts of the then western frontier, no serious large-scale settlement could occur until after the solution of the Indian problem through the campaigns of Anthony Wayne and the resulting sale of the Cherokee lands. Its position between the Alleghenies and the Mississippi, east and west, and between the Ohio River and Tennessee, north and south, made it always a border country, attached much more closely to the commercial civilization of the North than was its neighbor state to the south. It is significant that in the Civil War Kentucky

---

[8] 'The Architecture of Nashville,' *Journal of the American Institute of Architects,* Vol. VII, No. 4 (April 1919), pp. 159–70.

never seceded, but it is equally significant that this decision to stand by the Union was violently contested by large parts of its population and that the plantations that grew up in the fertile bluegrass country were entirely southern in their make-up and economy. Yet the Ohio River was a natural commercial and migration route which had its eastern end in the northern state of Pennsylvania, and many of the Kentucky settlers came from the North via Pittsburgh rather than through the Cumberland Gap from the South.

Thus Kentucky had from the beginning a culture of double parentage. Its towns were more urban, more like those of the North; its plantations, on the other hand, in architecture as in development, were almost more of the South and more conservative than those of Tennessee. Many of the earlier houses have an almost New England character — such as the DuPuy stone farmhouse in Woodward County, which would seem almost at home in western Pennsylvania or in Vermont.[9] This northern character runs through even the more pretentious houses, and the details of mantels and of doors in the houses built in the 1790's and the first decade of the nineteenth century are again and again fantastic or folk examples of that rich ' carpenter ' detail popularized by the early books of Asher Benjamin and modified by a great use of oval paterae and fan shapes that recall the Late Colonial of New York. Even in general mass the houses seem to be more like the great houses of Pennsylvania, for instance, than like those of Virginia or Tennessee. Although as in all the southern houses the ceiling heights are usually great, there is a corresponding amplitude in the horizontal dimensions, so that seldom does that high, thin proportion typical of Tennessee occur. The Dr. McDowell house at Danville, built before 1795, is characteristic of the simple clapboarded type sometimes found; but Federal Hill (about 1795) at Bardstown and the much more monumental Liberty Hall

9 See Rexford Newcomb's *Old Kentucky Architecture* (New York: William Helburn, 1940), which contains excellent photographs and measured drawings of the greater number of the Kentucky buildings referred to in this chapter. Professor Newcomb's book is a valuable presentation of the architectural development of a region. In its clear illustrations as in its simple and definite text it is a model which should be followed for every state east of the Mississippi.

(1796) at Frankfort, with its pedimented central motif and its rich Palladian window, might both be found with little change either in Pennsylvania, Delaware, or Maryland.

The same general type persisted for a long period; it is found in the Benjamin Gratz house (1806) at Lexington — where the door with its oval fanlight and sidelights has amusing ' Gothic ' clustered colonnettes — and in Wickland (1813) at Bardstown, a house superb in its scale and its restrained richness; it strongly influenced many houses of later, more definitely Classic Revival types, such as Castlewood (1825) and even the Alexander Johnstone house at Danville as late as 1845. Wickland is said to have been designed by John Marshall Brown and John Rogers, who are reputed to have designed many other great Kentucky houses. They were obviously architects with a nice sense of proportion and a feeling for scale and detail, but their taste remained essentially conservative; they were still designing advanced examples of eighteenth-century architecture, and their detail reveals a dependence upon the early handbooks. John Rogers was also the architect of St. Joseph's Proto-Cathedral at Bardstown in 1816. In the handling of the arched windows of the flank and the rectangular panels above them there is genuine feeling, and the large Roman Ionic portico at the front indicates a search for monumentality; but the tower and spire, however charming in their simple details, have little architectonic relationship to the spirit of the work below; there is a definite awkwardness in the relation of the spire itself to the cyma roof out of which it grows, just as there is an equal awkwardness in the engaged columns and the long entablature over them which enframe the clock.

Another type that came in during the early years of the nineteenth century was the spreading one-story house, perhaps distantly related to Homewood in Baltimore. An excellent example is Rose Hill (1818) in Lexington, with its low pedimented wings and higher central block. The Grange (of the same year), near Paris, shows the same form detailed with naïve polygonal piers in a porch that is manifestly trying to be Greek. The finest example of the type is undoubtedly Ridgeway (1804–5) at St. Matthews.

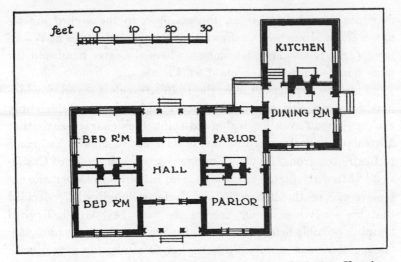

FIGURE 28. STEELE PLACE, Harrodsburg Pike, near Lexington, Ky. *circa* 1820. Plan. (*Andrews.*) Characteristic Kentucky one-story plan; formal elegance on a small scale.

in which the polish of the detail equals the sophistication of the composition.

Yet in almost all of these houses one feels a new breath, coming from the very wideness of the lands being settled, coming from a new feeling for space and a new desire for size and airiness. It is this quality that sets off the earlier Kentucky houses from their more eastern prototypes. Again and again the designer used the details to which he had become accustomed in the East, but he used them with a new exuberance which gradually tended to create its own expressive forms, and he used them nearly always in rooms that were wider and higher than those of the more crowded East. It was almost as if these families, seldom perhaps wealthy except in land, delighted to bring indoors something of the sweep and the sense of space of the swelling bluegrass pastures outside the door.

As the East became more and more forgotten and local craftsmen began to develop, the rich detail of the eastern Late Colonial suffered a great change, producing the most interesting types of fan and oval decoration and contrasting wide simple surfaces with intricate carved detail — as, for example, in the arched lunette of the china cabinets at Castlewood or the similar details at Wood-lawn (1827), also near Richmond, where the same hand and the same mind seem to have been at work.

This new type of detail in the 1820's reveals a search for big-ness, for simplicity, for restraint accented by richness, which only the developed Greek Revival could fulfil. It is characteristic that Matthias Shryock, a prosperous builder-architect who had come to Lexington from Maryland, was perhaps the designer of Castle-wood (often attributed to his son), and is known to have made ex-tensive use of the Benjamin and Lafever handbooks,[10] decided that his son Gideon must receive the very best Greek Revival training possible before he entered the building business himself.[11] Gideon thus was sent to Philadelphia to study for a year with Strickland, and from this year he brought back an enthusiasm for Greek detail and a creative proficiency in using it that made him one of the most skillful of all the earlier Greek Revival architects of the country. His first big work was the state capitol at Frank-fort, won by him in competition in 1827 and built during the next two years. This structure is extraordinary in many ways. Here in Frankfort — what was then the Far West — a building was erected which in its delicate Greek Ionic order, as in its basic monumentality of planning, was almost a decade ahead of its time even when judged by sophisticated eastern standards; for Ithiel Town had just created a furor with his Greek-Doric-temple capitol of Connecticut in New Haven, and Strickland's own Phila-delphia Exchange was still at the time of this competition a decade away. There are many things in the Kentucky capitol that are perhaps naïve. The profiles are occasionally crude, and the orna-ment — like the wave in the frieze of the Senate chamber — coarse and hardly understood; yet there was in the design not only vital-

10 For lists of the books of Benjamin and Lafever see Bibliography, Section VIII, A.

11 I am deeply indebted to Mrs. Willis Field of Lexington, a niece of Gideon Shryock, for the greater part of my information concerning him. See also my arti-cle, 'The A. I. A. Meets in Kentucky,' *Pencil Points*, Vol. XXI, No. 5 (May 1940), pp. 279–94. The same number carries many excellent illustrations of Shryock's work.

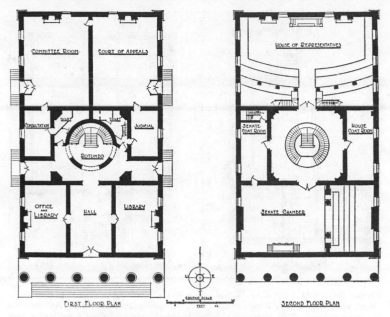

FIGURE 29. KENTUCKY STATE CAPITOL, Frankfort, Ky. Gideon Shryock, architect. (*Newcomb.*) Excellent arrangement of parts, producing formal grandeur at a modest scale.

ity and'aesthetic creation but also a definite sense of architecture as combining use and construction and beauty first of all. The plan is sensible, and the central double circular star of marble, built as a curved arch, rising gracefully under the overarching dome, is beautifully conceived and exquisitely executed.

Gideon Shryock's work achieved, as it deserved, almost instantaneous fame. Even the other competitors in the competition are said to have agreed unanimously that his design was the best. The impetus it gave to the use of Greek forms was irresistible, and more and more in houses as in public buildings Greek details began to creep in. Shryock himself was no rigid Revivalist. The freedom of the capitol design itself shows that, and in the Orlando Brown house at Frankfort, which he designed in 1835, he built what at first sight seems merely a traditional, rather old-fashioned, brick Kentucky house, only allowing his classic training to count in a meticulous clarification of all the elements and in such a careful

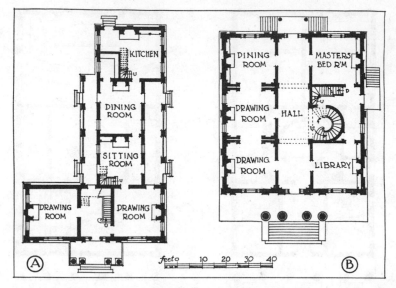

Figure 30. TWO TYPICAL KENTUCKY HOUSE PLANS. (*Andrews.*) A.
Waveland, Higby Mill Road, near Lexington, *circa* 1835. Cited by Andrews as
the most characteristic Kentucky Greek Revival house. Formal façade and long
wing with two-story galleries. B. Junius Ward House, near Georgetown, 1859.
The palatial formality and magnificence of the immediately pre-war years.

study of proportions that the simple front itself attains a definite
if modest classic grandeur.

Elsewhere the Greek Revival in house design came in more
obviously, in the more usual ways, by the addition of Greek porticoes to older houses or, as the style became better understood, by
the design of new kinds of houses in which the choice of Greek
detail seems almost the controlling element. The architects and
builders seem to have been as avid in their use of the eastern Greek
Revival handbooks as the earlier generation had been in its use of
the Benjamin books. Characteristic, for instance, is Diamond
Point (1840) at Harrodsburg, where beneath the great Greek
Doric portico is an entrance door in which the cap and frieze are
taken line for line from a Lafever plate [12] but are combined with
Greek Doric columns flanking the door. More polished uses of the
Greek orders are found in the widely spaced Ionic colonnade added

[12] Plate 19 in *The Beauties of Modern Architecture*. Plate 25 shows a somewhat
similar detail, combined with Ionic columns, used for a sliding door.

to the Chestnut house in Danville, or in the Doric four-column portico of the Adams house at the same place. Mansfield (1845) at Lexington, possibly by Thomas Lewinski, one of the many variations of the old one-story Homewood type, is crowded and finicky in its effect; but the essential dignity of the style is beautifully shown in Scotland (1840–45) near Frankfort, and in the simple, dignified, and beautifully proportioned recessed porch of the McClure house at Danville as late as 1852. Thomas Lewinski designed many of these handsome Greek Revival houses. He is said to have been born in London of a Polish family, and to have trained as an architect there. He was at one time a major in the Royal Engineers. Apparently he was brought to Kentucky by Cassius Clay, to work on Clay's place, White Hall; he also designed a great deal of other work for the Clay family during the middle forties. His professional diary, covering the period from early 1845 to mid-1847, still exists. His wife was a sister of Thomas Watkins, who married a daughter of John McMurtry (1912–90), and the association between Lewinski and McMurtry was evidently close, though much of McMurtry's later work was of a confused Victorian eclectic type.

Yet the style had its greatest triumphs in its public buildings. Morrison College (1833) at Transylvania, in Lexington, by Gideon Shryock, achieves tremendous dignity in its six-column Doric pedimented portico; the same dignity in a quieter and perhaps more charming manner is found in the Old Daughters' College (1845), now the Beaumont Inn, at Harrodsburg, or in the Old Centre College at Danville.

It was Gideon Shryock who seems to have handled the style best and with the greatest freedom. The Jefferson County courthouse at Louisville (1835–50) is large, simple, almost bleak perhaps, with that uncompromising definiteness of form, that straightforward use of detail, which we are inclined to associate more with Robert Mills than with William Strickland. In the Louisville Board of Education building Shryock expresses a quite different kind of feeling. The recessed Ionic porch is exquisite in proportion and delicacy. Perhaps the climax of Shryock's work is to be found in the Bank of Louisville (1837), where he has combined Greek columns in a recessed porch with delicately battered end piers, instead of the more usual antae, in a way that is as successful as it is original. Equally original is the development of the central ornament — perhaps borrowed distantly from a Lafever plate [13] — carved on the face of the cornice corona and replacing its cymatium. The whole building is interesting in plan and again shows the Greek Revival designer not as a copier of past forms but as a creator using the utmost originality within a basic and living tradition.

The classic forms the use of which had been stimulated by the Greek Revival lived on long in Kentucky, although the Gothic had begun to appear, as in the lavish house, Ingleside (1852), at Lexington, by John McMurtry, or the great house, Loudoun (1849–50), by A. J. Davis, New York. Both are immensely creative in the handling of the Gothic forms, which were still understood but superficially. The Gothic houses in Kentucky reveal much influence from Davis and from the works of A. J. Downing; Ingleside and Loudoun resemble also many plates of English noblemen's Gothic halls in the last years of the eighteenth century. There is other charming work of Gothic type scattered through the state, based largely on Davis and Downing — such as the exquisite Mound Cottage at Danville or McMurtry's sexton's cottage in the Episcopal cemetery in Lexington.[14] But perhaps the most extraordinary of the Gothic buildings of early Kentucky was the Abbey of Gethsemani, built between 1851 and 1866, a structure as remarkable for its cloister garden and the length of its church — which had a true chevet of ambulatory and apsidal chapels — as it was for the remarkably effective, simple, and somewhat heavy-handed detail.

Yet the classic tradition lived on also. Francis Costigan [15] (1810–65) in the Kentucky School for the Blind at Louisville, as late as 1855, designed an extraordinary building with a most interesting plan of stepped pavilions, in which the effect of the

---

13 Such, for instance, as Plate 26 in *The Beauties of Modern Architecture.*

14 Mr. Clay Lancaster, of Kentucky, is now making a careful study of John McMurtry and his work. I am grateful to him for much Kentucky information.

15 Francis Costigan worked chiefly in Indiana. It was probably on account of his success in the design of the Institution for the Blind in Indianapolis that he was engaged to design the similar building at Louisville. See page 300.

Old St. Louis Cathedral. Morton and Laveille, architects. (*Dorrill.*) ABOVE, exterior. BELOW, interior.

The Greek Revival in Missouri: ABOVE, LEFT, Bartholomew Berthold House, St. Louis, 1829. (*Missouri Hist. Soc.*) ABOVE, RIGHT, first building, University of Missouri, Columbia. Stephen Hills, architect. (*Bryan.*) BELOW, LEFT, Chouteau House, St. Louis, 1830. (*Missouri Hist. Soc.*) BELOW, RIGHT, Old Capitol, Jefferson City. Stephen Hills, architect. (*Missouri Hist. Soc.*)

The Greek Revival in the Mississippi Valley: TOP, LEFT, Courthouse, St. Louis. (*Bryan*.) TOP, RIGHT, Stanton Hall, Natchez, Miss. (*Tebbs*.) CENTER, Governor's Mansion, Jackson, Miss. (*H.A.B.S.*) BOTTOM, Arkansas State Capitol, Little Rock. Shryock and Weigert, architects. (*State War Memorial*.)

Mississippi Valley capitols: ABOVE, Old Iowa Capitol, Iowa City. John Francis Rague, architect. (*Univ. of Iowa.*) BELOW, Old Mississippi Capitol, Jackson. Morrison, Lawrence, and Nichols, architects. (*H.A.B.S.*)

simplicity of Greek detail is still apparent although the actual inspiration has changed back to Roman or Renaissance. Shryock himself seems to have been the designer of the old Louisville waterworks, with their unusual metal Doric-columned water tower and the handsome, almost Palladian building behind. This dates from 1861 to 1867.[16]

Thus in Kentucky, as elsewhere, the Greek Revival appears as the great unifying American style of its time. It liberated the designer from the trammels of traditions that were dying or dead; it stood for the unity of construction and design; in its successes in courthouse and in college building, as in the state house itself, it became the authentic voice of the new country west of the Alleghenies as it was the expression of the best thought of the older regions farther east.[17]

At the western borders the new settlers of Tennessee and Kentucky found themselves confronted not only by the great Mississippi River but also by a culture predominantly French and Spanish, which had already established trading posts up and down the banks of the river. Until the time of the Louisiana Purchase the white traders with the Mississippi Valley Indians, who had stationed their fur companies at important points, were mainly French, despite the fact that for the greater part of the time the government was officially Spanish; this French background is evident in much of the early architecture of the region, as it is in that of New Orleans.

The largest community was of course St. Louis, two hundred miles up the river from the mouth of the Ohio. It had been founded as a trading post as early as 1764 and was destined to become one of the great trade centers of the central United States, strategi-

16 The attribution of this group to Shryock has been questioned, since his name does not appear upon the tablet attached to the water tower. However, Mrs. Willis Field, Shryock's niece, owns a signed elevation of the waterworks office, which seems to make the attribution of the works themselves to him probable.

17 I am much indebted to Mr. Alfred Andrews, who is making a careful study of Greek Revival architecture in Kentucky, for many suggestions of value in my own work and in my conclusions. As part of this study he has prepared a master's essay, 'Greek Revival Houses in Kentucky,' in the Department of Art and Archaeology, Columbia University, 1942.

cally situated on the river valley route, as well as a place where all sorts of trade activity from west and southwest found their natural focus. Naturally to its small nucleus of French business people there was added after the Louisiana Purchase a rapidly growing settlement of Americans, lured as the French had been by the prospects of a profitable trade in furs. Many of them came from Kentucky, but many others from the northern states and from New England. Later, after the War of 1812, foreign immigrants — especially of Irish and German origin — began to come to the rapidly growing town in greater and greater numbers. The result was a city with an amazingly cosmopolitan attitude even at a time when it was scarcely more than an overgrown village. It was a city vividly alive culturally, as it was commercially, and it attracted accomplished architects and designers both French and American.

The earliest buildings were much like the early buildings of New Orleans, built of that simple half-timber construction known as *briqueté entre poteaux*. Of this early Missouri work little remains — none in St. Louis — but in Ste. Genevieve, founded in 1735, some thirty years earlier than St. Louis, there are a few priceless examples.[18] The work naturally is cruder than that in New Orleans, and this earlier French development seems to have had but little lasting effect. However, in occasional churches something of a Continental feeling seems to be present. Such, for example, is the church of the Vincentian Order at Perryville, built between 1827 and 1837. With its grandiose cross-shaped plan and its façade with a projecting pedimented pavilion flanked by twin towers, it all retains a touch of the true Baroque — perhaps partly French, partly Spanish. Yet generally the future, even in the case of Roman Catholic churches, lay largely in the

---

18 For the early architecture of Missouri, see Charles E. Peterson's 'French Houses of the Illinois Country,' *Missouriana,* Vol. x, No. 10 (August–September 1938), pp. 4–7, and his *Early Ste. Genevieve and Its Architecture,* reprinted from the *Missouri Historical Review,* Vol. xxxv, No. 2 (January 1941), pp. 207–32. See also for the entire subject of Mississippi Valley architecture the same author's *A List of Published Writings of Specific Interest in the Study of the Historic Architecture of the Mississippi Valley,* 2nd ed. (St. Louis: National Park Service, Historic American Buildings Survey, 1940).

direction of quieter, more classic designs — definitely, shall we say, American.

Characteristic of the architects to whom the Classic Revival architecture of St. Louis, and of Missouri generally, may be credited was Gabriel Paul, born in San Domingo and educated in France, who came to Baltimore with his mother in 1802 and went on to St. Louis in 1816. He was the architect of the first Roman Catholic cathedral in St. Louis, and also of the Bartholomew Berthold house, built in 1829 and destroyed in 1866, where significantly enough the style was a combination of the brick dignity of Baltimore with the two-story porches so loved in Tennessee and Kentucky. Even earlier than the Berthold house was the Carr house (1820), a dignified brick building with end chimneys and a rich railing at the break in its gambrel roof and with a sophisticated handling of the façade, which has a slightly projecting center bay and a delicately detailed pedimented porch.

Two other early architects formed the firm of Morton and Laveille. George Morton was born in Edinburgh in 1790 and had come to the United States in 1815, settled in Pittsburgh, and then moved on to St. Louis in 1823. Laveille had been a Harrisburg man and had probably known Morton in Pennsylvania earlier. Their first large work in St. Louis was the Episcopal Church (1825). A year later they designed the Jefferson Barracks and the first St. Louis courthouse, the plans of which still exist though the building was torn down in 1854 to make way for the last (the east) wing of the new courthouse. They seem to have had a busy and prosperous practice. Perhaps their best-known work is the beautiful St. Louis Cathedral (the ' Old Cathedral '), completed in 1834, which replaced Paul's earlier and cruder edifice. The St. Louis Cathedral is a work that combines in a surprisingly polished and yet original way a Doric porch with a pediment, many details of rather austere Soane or Latrobe types, and a well-designed tower and spire of generally Baroque character. The marriage of these diverse forms is so subtly and sensitively arranged that one is aware of the multiplicity of influences only after a detailed analysis; the first impression is one of quiet dignity, large scale, restraint, and good taste. Behind this gracious and dignified front is an interior equally compelling and distinguished, and the whole takes its place among the most successful of all the churches in America at this period.

The extraordinary growth of the city, coupled with the prosperity that its strategic position entailed, made excellent soil for rapid architectural development. In 1821, when Missouri was admitted as a state, the population of St. Louis was about 5,600; in 1840 the population was 16,500, and in 1850 nearly 78,000. When one considers the disastrous architectural results that have frequently accompanied such astounding city growth in the nineteenth century, the astonishing thing about the St. Louis work is the high quality the best of the work showed. There is little in it of boom-town ostentation, and some of it both in design and in execution shows standards as high as those in any other part of the country. That again and again is the amazing thing about this architecture of the Middle West, true alike in Tennessee, in Kentucky, in Ohio. The shacks and the cabins gave way almost immediately to work of graciousness, permanence, soundness of construction, and real beauty. The builders seem to have realized that it was no temporary bonanza that brought them to their new homes, but rather the desire to found and develop permanent and dignified places for human living.

In St. Louis this sense of permanence, this demand for excellence of design, is shown in almost all the older churches as well as in other buildings of an educational or public service type. Such for instance are the churches — e.g. the Second Baptist Church (1847) — designed by Oliver Hart, who came to St. Louis from Norwich, Connecticut, in 1837. Such was the Second Presbyterian Church (1839) designed by Lucas Bradley, with its Greek Doric entrance; or what is perhaps the last of the Greek Revival churches, the handsome Trinitarian Congregational Church (1859), with its six-column Corinthian portico and its rich Corinthian pilasters along the flank, designed by George I. Barnett, who had come to St. Louis from England in 1839 and brought with him a talent schooled in all the sophistication of the English fashions as well as a keen and realistic sense of what the new country demanded. Such too was the St. Louis Hospital, the center (1831) of which was designed by Hugh O'Neil, the wings built six years later from the designs of Stuart Matthews. In this a central recessed porch of square Greek Doric antae is used with excellent effect and gives marked effectiveness and monumentality to a building otherwise severely simple and economical. The St. Louis courthouse is another example of this wish for dignified public buildings. A competition for it was held in 1839 and was won by Henry Singleton, who alone is responsible for the dignified design of the lower portions.[19] The courthouse was built with a cross-shaped plan and the simplest possible classic detail of Greek inspiration. It was built over a long period of years, and the present central dome — which departs entirely from the Singleton scheme — was not completed until the sixties, from the design of William Rumbold. Rumbold was undoubtedly influenced by the use of cast iron for the dome of the United States Capitol, then under construction; although his high drum fits but oddly on the long horizontals of the building below, it is significant to find St. Louis, so far in the West, pioneering in the use of the new building material.[20]

Even more important perhaps, as illustrations of the dignity sought for and achieved in Missouri public buildings, were the first building of the University of Missouri (1840–41), at Columbia, and the first permanent Missouri state capitol (1838–45). Both were designed by a Stephen Hills, who like Laveille came from Harrisburg, where he had been the architect for the Pennsylvania state capitol in 1820.[21] In the Missouri state capitol

19 George Barnett's first St. Louis work was as a draftsman under Singleton.

20 Much of the earlier commercial architecture of St. Louis in the late forties and early fifties, built along the river front, also made creative and independent use of cast iron. Many of these buildings have been destroyed in connection with the development of the Jefferson Memorial in St. Louis. Fortunately, however, through the care of Mr. Charles E. Peterson, architect in charge of the National Park Service, these buildings were all carefully recorded before their destruction. They have been noted at some length by Sigfried Giedion in *Space, Time, and Architecture* (Cambridge: Harvard University Press, 1941), pp. 134–8 and Fig. 126.

21 Mr. John A. Bryan writes me that the Commissioners of the Missouri capitol, liking the Pennsylvania capitol, invited Hills to Missouri to build them a replica. Later he returned to his early home in England. He is said to have come back

he reproduced the basic scheme of the Harrisburg building, but modified and improved its proportions, retaining however the recessed circular porch with its projecting semicircular portico and the dome with the surrounding free-standing colonnade to carry up the circular feeling. It was a most interesting spatial conception; in its combination of something of the Baroque imaginative freedom in uniting geometrical forms with the restraint and discipline of detail inherent in the Greek Revival movement, it was significant of the ideals which the advanced architects of the time were trying to further. The first building of the University of Missouri is less monumental, more gracious and inviting; the proportions of the six-column Ionic portico are excellent, and the relation of these to the octagonal drum with its elliptical windows and low dome above is an unusually successful solution of an extremely difficult problem.

In houses, too, St. Louis was abreast if not ahead of the times. The Chouteau house (1830), with its quiet, formal four-column Greek Ionic portico, would have been a distinguished creation in any town in the country at its period. The Russell house (1842), with its quiet stone walls and its one-story Greek Doric porch, has an excellent domestic and yet dignified quality. As one would expect from the close touch between St. Louis and New Orleans, cast-iron porches were found in many of the St. Louis houses from 1840 on. They are not, however, the two- or three-story verandas so common in New Orleans, but usually cast-iron variations of the northern one-story piazza, although the lavish detail of the individual posts and arches and railings has many traces of the New Orleans type. The continual influx of new blood into the town in those days of rapid growth and the continual coming to St. Louis of architects from England and Ireland and from other parts of the United States prevented that development of purely local characteristics which was so strongly in evidence farther south, and brought into the growing city at a very early date those tendencies toward more Italianate forms that were soon to dominate the coun-

to America after some years and to have stayed in this country till his death. He is also said to have worked in Chicago.

try. Thus a lovely house (1841) on Allen Street and the General Thomas Price house (1842) at Jefferson City both show the combination of cast iron with the new Italianate forms handled with unusual command.[22]

Outside of St. Louis the newer settlers frequently built large and expensive houses which in many ways recalled similar work east of the Mississippi. A characteristic example is Prairie Park, near Arrow Rock, which was built by Dr. John Sappington in 1844. Its tall, narrow proportions and its end chimneys as well as its two-story porch suggest many of the Tennessee great houses. Like them it is built of brick. The Greek Revival influence appears in the pedimented porch of superposed orders. The house is unusual in possessing a ' captain's walk ' and a central cupola.[23]

But this vivid effort to bring to the newly opened lands bordering the Mississippi the most developed fruits of American architectural progress was not limited to Missouri. Up the river, farther north, even Iowa had its Greek Revival capitol (1840–42) at Iowa City, by John Francis Rague. It is a simple but excellently designed building which still stands as part of the University of Iowa.[24]

To the south, Arkansas was not to be outdone and, despite the primitiveness of large portions of the state, in its first state capitol produced one of the most exquisite and original of the smaller state houses of the time. The state government invited Gideon Shryock to come from Kentucky to design its new edifice, and the exterior was constructed between 1833 and 1836. Shryock's superintendent and pupil, George Weigert, reduced the size of the contemplated building when Shryock's original plans were found to be somewhat too ambitious, but carefully preserved Shryock's general scheme and the refinement of his detail. The structure was built originally as three buildings, each three bays wide and pedi-

22 The chief source for the early architecture of Missouri is John A. Bryan's *Missouri's Contribution to American Architecture* (St. Louis: The St. Louis Architectural Club, 1928).
23 *Life*, Vol. xii, No. 9 (2 March 1942).
24 Federal Writers' Project, Works Progress Administration, *Iowa, A Guide to the Hawkeye State*, in the American Guide Series (New York: Viking Press, 1938); *The Western Architect*, Vol. ii, No. 1 (January 1903), p. 6.

ment-crowned. The end buildings had simple antae; the central structure had a full free-standing Greek Doric porch and was capped by a little cupola. The relation of heights and widths in the three buildings was beautifully balanced to preserve the domination of the central motif, and when the three were connected in 1840 by low wings fronted with delicate cast-iron porches the final result was not only a building of exquisite proportion and great dignity for its size, but also one of the most individual and original creations of its type. Fortunately it has been preserved and is now the State War Memorial of Arkansas.[25]

Less original but even more imposing was the lavish old capitol of Mississippi at Jackson. The building was contemplated in 1833 and David Morrison of Nashville offered a preliminary design, but John Lawrence of Nashville was appointed architect. When some of the construction done under him was found defective in 1835, William Nichols, who had been the architect of the earlier Alabama state capitol at Tuscaloosa, replaced Lawrence and carried the building to completion in 1839. Just how much of the credit for the final result is due to each of these three designers is not known, but the result was impressive, well planned, and particularly in its interior detail exquisitely carried out. The building was of the ' normal ' capitol type, with a domed central section containing a rotunda, an extraordinary vestibule with two spiral stairs, and a rich semicircular reception room, the whole approached by a six-column portico. The two wings were much simpler and gave definition through their slightly projecting end pavilions. One contained the Assembly, with a colonnaded segmental end of great interest; the other a circular Senate chamber. It was in one respect merely a smaller interpretation of the United States Capitol as completed by Bulfinch; yet in every way its plan was more direct and simple, its circulation more clear and logical. Nevertheless it preserved much of the geometrical interest of the earlier building in the variety of its rooms. The whole was richly detailed with care and imagination; it is a tragedy that a

---

[25] See Theodore Laist's ' Two Early Mississippi Valley State Capitols,' *The Western Architect*, Vol. xxxv, No. 5 (May 1926), pp. 53–8.

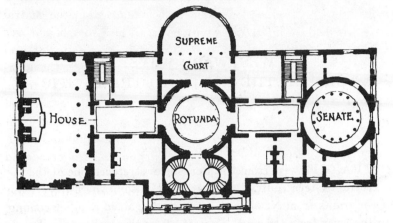

FIGURE 31. MISSISSIPPI STATE CAPITOL, Jackson, Miss. Plan. Morrison, Lawrence, and Nichols, architects. (*Western Architect*.) Creative variation of the usual capitol type, distinguished for its interesting interiors.

building so lovely, so expressive of much that was best in the creative thinking and the sensitive aesthetic feeling of its time, was allowed to go to wrack and ruin through pure carelessness.[26] Interesting Jackson buildings of Greek Revival type also include the elegant and sophisticated Governor's Mansion (1842) designed by William Nichols, which has an unusually graceful Greek Corinthian porch, and the heavier, monumental Doric city hall (1854).

So the movement toward an American architecture spread, east and west, north and south; the great palatial steamers that were more and more floating up and down the great river system were binding together Pittsburgh and New Orleans, unifying the culture along the river banks, bringing together Cincinnati and Louisville, St. Louis, Memphis, Vicksburg, and Natchez. Despite conflicts in political sentiment, despite differences of national and linguistic background, despite even the growing and ominous sectional controversy over slavery, there was being built up some basic unity of feeling that found its architectural expression in a certain basic harmony of forms.

26 Ibid. The building was restored in 1916, but the old Senate and House chambers no longer exist — two floors now occupy their earlier ample height.

CHAPTER 11

WESTWARD WAYS:
THROUGH THE NORTH TO THE PACIFIC

Western New York

STRAIGHT west from the Berkshires stretched one of the favorite western routes — across the Hudson, where the stream of emigrants from New England met and joined another coming up the river from the south — west along the Mohawk Valley — along the lake shore by the tip of Pennsylvania at Erie, and so into Ohio, into the Western Reserve — the 'New Connecticut.' This was the usual route of New Englanders, and along with their neatness and energy, their religious and educational enthusiasm, they carried their architectural ways and forms, their architectural books and tastes as well. It was a route opened early, and, as little by little the country filled after the Revolution, churches and houses of characteristic type were scattered along its length. It was a route that retained its popularity for a century. The later coming of the Erie Canal and the railroad merely made permanent and easy a trail already old.

The Late Colonial architecture of western Massachusetts and Connecticut had developed a certain characteristic rich delicacy in its handling of classic motives. It had created, as a favorite town house form, a type with pedimented end toward the street, sometimes ornamented with slim pilasters and with thin, much projecting cornices with Benjamin-like decoration. Proportions tended to be tall, narrow, and graceful. It is no surprise to find this type of house all along the Mohawk Valley route and in settlements easily reached from it, and to come upon houses that are obviously mere developments of it in Rensselaerville, Canandaigua, Syracuse, Rochester, and in Hudson, Ohio. The dates of these houses vary from the 1790's to the 1820's. Nor, considering the history of the Western Reserve, so long claimed as a portion of Connecticut, is it strange that one of the most perfect of Late Colonial churches of pure Connecticut type built as late as 1822–5 stands in Tallmadge, Ohio. It was built by a Connecticut carpenter, Sabbeus Saxton, and all the exquisite trim was the work of Colonel Lemuel Porter, who had been born in Sandisfield, Massachusetts, in 1775, and died in Tallmadge in 1828.[1] The Tallmadge church is much like Belcher's Lyme church in Connecticut; the Hosford house (1832) in Hudson, Ohio, has the same Lyme character in its robust gambrel roof.

This trend was so strongly entrenched in New York along the western roads that the New York pioneers were affected by it too. When the great Mormon migration swept along into Ohio and found in Kirtland a temporary home, the Mormons built for themselves there between 1833 and 1836 a temple lavish with rich detail of the same delicate ' New England ' Late Colonial type. Its beautiful triple pulpit is especially effective.

Nor did this influence stop in Ohio. Settlers with the same New England or New York background pressed on along the Lake Erie shore, clear across the state and into southern Michigan; particularly in Ann Arbor one finds strong evidence of them in the delicately detailed white pedimented houses that were once so common there.

The New England influence, pressing west, met at Albany another almost as strong — for the Hudson Valley had already been a cultural area for nearly two centuries, and Albany was a center for that mixture of English and certain Dutch qualities which had made early New York. There in Albany and Schenectady neat brick Dutch houses with stepped gables still stood, but among them (and gradually superseding them) were rich Georgian and Late Colonial houses, beautiful churches of the Americanized Gibbs type, and more and more impressive public buildings in which the growing classicism of the time had full expression. All down the river the same process was going on; the newer, more ' English ' fashions were swamping the old conservative Dutch

[1] I. T. Frary, *Early Homes of Ohio* (Richmond: Garrett and Massie, 1936).

ways. The large towns especially bore the newer imprint, and the great houses that rich New Yorkers were building as country estates along the river bank were all naturally in the newest fashion. Hudson, for example, had a large contingent of prosperous whaling families from Nantucket; the city as it grew in the twenties and thirties had no Dutch character at all — its solid houses, in which sophisticated Greek detail was common after 1830, might have seemed equally at home, some of them in Massachusetts, some of them in New York City itself.

Hyde Park, the Dr. Hosack estate, was apparently the work of Martin Thompson.[2] It was typical of the newer fashions of its time; as we see it in a Davis sketch it was a monumental house of large scale, with wide, quiet wall spaces and large windows, entirely classic in its harmonious dignity, and quite unlike Colonial work — even the post-Revolution Late Colonial. In Kingston, a town marked by Dutch tradition and full of prosperous families of Dutch extraction, the story is the same — the newer work of the thirties and forties was Greek Revival under the direct influence of New York City. Thus St. John's Episcopal Church was rebuilt in 1834 with Greek forms controlling its design; in the Senate House Museum at Kingston its side elevation, beautifully rendered, is preserved, signed ' Edward J. Webb, architect, New York.'

Naturally, too, the architecture made necessary by the new love of nature, the new habit of summering away from town, also was Greek. The summer-resort hotel usually followed a pattern set in the popular spas of Balston Springs and Saratoga some twenty years earlier. These spa hotels were usually long, narrow buildings three stories high, fronted by a continuous colonnade that ran the entire height of the building — the prototype of the summer hotel piazza of today. The type could easily be modified to fit more classic proportions by reducing the height of the colonnades to at most two stories; it could be complicated by carrying them all around the building, or by using plans of T or L shapes instead of the simple rectangle. The Rockaway Pavilion designed by Town,

---

[2] He exhibited elevations of it in the National Academy Exhibition of 1829.

Davis, and Dakin was an excellent early and much admired example.[3]

Up the Hudson the Catskill Mountains offered on their precipitous slopes and in their wild glens numberless sites for summer developments, which were early seized upon. Two at least of these hotels of over a century ago remain. One, in the Schoharie Valley at Lexington, is hardly more than a tavern, aping the resort hotel in its high porch, but its detail is excellent if somewhat naïve. The other is the famous Mountain House, which looks out from the top of a great cliff over the superb sweeps of the Hudson Valley across to the blue Berkshires beyond, a view which Harriet Martineau preferred to Niagara.

The Mountain House at Catskill was built as early as 1825.[4] At first it possessed the continuous high porch typical of the older spa hotels, and early illustrations show this clearly. Some ten years later (the present owners give the year as 1834) it was enlarged and brought up to date by substituting for the old slim columns a one-story porch of thirteen square piers, which in turn supports an upper porch two stories high, of thirteen Greek Corinthian columns more squat than the normal proportion and crowned with the rich capitals of the Choragic Monument of Lysikrates.[5] It may have been at this time that the wings were extended and a long wing at right angles built, pointing west, with a porch of the same Corinthian order over the main entrance on the plateau behind. The hotel has been so continuously added to and altered over a

---

[3] Philip Hone, who had been a heavy investor in this financially unfortunate venture begun in 1833, nevertheless admired its atmosphere greatly. On 1 September 1835 he writes: ‘We had last night at the Pavilion a farewell hop in the dining room, at which the girls enjoyed themselves very much. At eleven o'clock, I retired to my room, lighted a cigar, and seated myself at the front window. The view was unspeakably grand. The broad red moon, setting over the tops of the mountains of Neversink, threw a solemn light over the unruffled face of the ocean, and the lofty columns of the noble piazza, breaking the silver streams of light into dark and gloomy shadows, gave the edifice the appearance of some relic of classic antiquity.’ (Vol. i, p. 74, *The Diary of Philip Hone,* edited with an Introduction by Allan Nevins; New York: Dodd, Mead & Co., 1927.)

[4] Croswell Bowen, *Great River of the Mountains: The Hudson,* with an Introduction by Carl Carmer (New York: Hastings House, 1941).

[5] It is said that thirteen columns were used to symbolize the thirteen original states. Although this sounds apochryphal it is not necessarily an impossible explanation, for the period was one of enthusiastic if jejune nationalism.

century that it is difficult to judge of its early plan. It is obvious, however, that originally a suite of high-studded public rooms stretched along the east front on the second (originally the principal) floor. Their huge high windows remain, but the areas behind have been ruthlessly chopped up into bedrooms. Nevertheless, even as altered, the hotel remains an impressive monument to the luxuries of summer vacations a century ago, and there is a certain superb daring, a true sense of scale and composition, an almost breathtaking quality in its long horizontals and its sweeping colonnade crowning the precipitous cliff. It is a perfect expression of the joining of the two great enthusiasms, for Greece and for nature; a wedding, unexpectedly successful, of Stuart and Revett with the Hudson River School painters.

Thus the Greek influence pushed more and more up the Hudson and west into the valleys and rolling country behind, blending and mixing with the strong traditions brought by the New Englanders along the Berkshire route. In the older settlements, and especially along the Mohawk, it was the New England influence that dominated western New York; in the newer villages and the newer buildings in the larger towns it was the Greek enthusiasm — largely of New York inspiration — which controlled.

The earlier, New England influence is best seen in Rensselaerville,[6] founded in 1788 and famous for its exquisitely finished and perfectly preserved houses — the very Connecticut-like Stevens house (1809), distinguished by its Palladian window over a Palladian door, by Ephraim Russ; the James Rider house (1823), with its end toward the street and its thin pilasters carrying oval arches, also by Russ; and the extraordinary little one-story Sployd house (1825), with a two-bay pedimented porch and detail of gemlike delicacy. Somewhat similar to the Rider house is a house at Vernon Center [7] with the same oval arches on slim impost pilasters;

---

[6] William A. Keller, *Rensselaerville, an Old Village of the Helderbergs*, Vol. x, No. 4, in the White Pine Series of Architectural Monographs (New York: Russell F. Whitehead, August 1924).

[7] Carl C. Tallman, *Early Wood-Built Houses of Central New York*, Vol. iv, No. 5, in the White Pine Series of Architectural Monographs (New York: Russell F. Whitehead, October 1918).

the same detail crops up again and again along the western road, in Utica, in Syracuse, in Rochester.

In the Cooperstown area a more imaginative or eccentric architect-builder seems to have been at work, using Benjamin-inspired details with naïve exuberance; the Preston house at Colliersville, built by Colonel Alfred Mumford in 1827, is characteristic with its Baroque arched porch.[8] Woodside Hall (1829), Cooperstown, is interesting because it has a composition — a two-story pedimented central body with a four-column porch, combined with one-story side wings — which became a standard Greek Revival type although it retains detail of pure Late Colonial flavor without a trace of the newer fashion. At Cooperstown also is the Worthington homestead, the White House, built in 1802. The White House has Greek antae at the corners, a Greek Doric entablature, a Greek door, and a cupola with Greek acroteria. It seems obvious to the author that all of this Greek trim must have been added to the original five-bay house some thirty or forty years after its construction, despite local tradition to the contrary.[9]

Into this harmonious world of up-state New York Late Colonial work, the new, more strictly Greek forms were bound sooner or later to enter. They came not only through the influence of New York City, but from the general diffusion of a growing consciousness and enthusiasm for the Greek among the cultivated inhabitants of the larger and more settled communities. Albany of course was the chief of these, and the great architectural name in Albany at the time was that of Philip Hooker (1766–1836).[10] He was born in Rutland, Massachusetts, the son of a carpenter and builder, Samuel Hooker. The family seems to have come to Albany about 1772, and Philip started his practice as an architect in 1797 — at least, the first record of him as architect is so dated. From 1816 to 1825 he was busy politically, but except for these years

---

8 Frank P. Whiting, *Cooperstown in the Days of Our Forefathers*, Vol. ix, No. 3, in the White Pine Series of Architectural Monographs (New York: Russell F. Whitehead, June 1923).

9 Ibid.

10 See Edward W. Root's *Philip Hooker, a Contribution to the Study of the Renaissance in America* (New York: Charles Scribner's Sons, 1929).

his architectural career was constant and prolific. Naturally the great body of his work is 'Federal' in type and he made but little use of strictly Greek detail. Yet all the deeper governing characteristics of the Greek Revival are implicit in his later work — reticence, classicism, dignity, plain surfaces, bold composition. As early as 1804–6 these characteristics begin to appear in the first New York state capitol. In Hyde Hall (begun in 1811), built for George Clarke near Cooperstown, one of the unique great houses of early America, they are more pronounced. The famous Lancaster School (1815) at Albany is more backward in style; a simply composed structure with stone detail of great delicacy outside and richly carved trim within, it bears a close resemblance to some of the best McComb work in New York.[11]

But in the façade of the Hamilton College chapel (1825–6) at Clinton the new feeling becomes more obvious; despite its obvious borrowings of English Baroque details, despite its panels and swags and rustications, there is a new simple classic power in it — a new delight in broad unpierced masonry walls and clean sharp rectangular masses. In the Washington Market (the Center Market) of 1828–9 in Albany the process has gone still further. The simple arcades, crowned with a story of plain wall pierced by well-proportioned, undecorated windows, and the simple cornice and

[11] The interior trim of the Lancaster School, with its enriched central lintel panels carved with rather heavy, bossy foliage, closely resembles much interior trim in New York City houses built between 1820 and 1835. The origin of this type of trim design has been thus far an unsolved puzzle. In the developed examples — as found for instance in the Cutting house (1824–31) at No. 15 Tillary Street, Brooklyn, demolished in 1936; in the John V. Gridley house, No. 37 Charlton Street, New York, with Ionic pilasters but no cap on the lintel; in the George Fordham house, No. 329 Cherry Street, New York, without capitals; or in the house at No. 4 Grove Street, New York — the type has pilasters, often with Ionic capitals flanking the opening; these support a lintel band instead of an entablature. This lintel usually has large terminal blocks at the ends, with heavy rosettes, and in the center a large panel, often capped with a simple ovolo, containing bold leafage of Baroque acanthus type in high relief. At times trim of this kind is found in houses where other details are of Greek derivation. Similar trim is in the Miller house (1830) at Utica, which has been attributed to Hooker.

In a house on Greenwich Street, New York, about to be destroyed to make way for the Brooklyn-Battery tunnel approach, there is trim of the same kind though with carving of a definitely French Rococo cast. This house is usually dated in the early 1820's. It would be interesting to know who first developed this type, and how and why this last expression of a dying Baroque tradition became and remained so popular in New York State — and there, apparently, alone.

The Greek Revival in New York State. (*Bannister*.) TOP, LEFT, Collier House, Hudson. TOP, RIGHT, Sharon Springs Hotel. CENTER, General Worth Hotel, Hudson. BOTTOM, Catskill Mountain House, colonnade.

The Greek Revival in New York State: ABOVE, entrance of Hyde Hall, Cooperstown. Thomas Hooker, architect. (*Root.*) BELOW, Old Courthouse (State Office Building), Albany. Henry Rector, architect. (*Glenn.*)

open parapet of this building are almost Empire in their quiet and dignified classicism. The contrast between this restraint and the lavish if inorganic Adam-type composition of the Mechanics' and Farmers' Bank of 1814, also attributed to Hooker, shows not only the growth of the architect's command but also the change in popular taste that fifteen years had brought.

The Albany city hall (1829) is less successful. The commission for it was awarded to Hooker as the result of a competition. In it he seems somewhat at sea — lost between the safe shores of the Adam-type Late Colonial in which he had been trained and the current Greek enthusiasms. As a result its combination of rusticated piers below with an Ionic porch above, its corner pilasters, and its low dome with paneled base all create a somewhat over-busy, ostentatious whole. The parts are good but they have not been integrated into a successful, unified entity.[12]

It is in the later portions of Hyde Hall (1833) that Hooker's greatness as a designer best shows itself. This stone façade with its bold, free composition is truly creative. Rich iron railings of almost French type, unfluted columns with Greek Doric caps, reticent panels, and simple, strong moldings are all put together with a consummate sense of architectonic value, a magnificent understanding of the third dimension, and impeccable taste. The Greek details do not dominate, nor do they seem intrusive; yet the whole, in dignity, freedom, imaginative detail, and controlling restraint, is expressive much more of the ideals of the best Greek Revival work than of the delicate Late Colonial that was past.

Besides Hooker, of course, other architects still more devoted to the Greek ideals were developing. Henry Rector was one of these and in his design for the Albany courthouse — a long build-

---

[12] This competition attracted the best architectural talent of the time. Town and Davis, Minard Lafever, Isaiah Rogers, Edward Shaw, Henry Rector of Albany, one Mr. 'Kutts' of Boston, R. Higham of Albany, and a Mr. Scobé from Montreal all had entered designs. The committee chose Lafever's, Rogers's, Rector's, Hooker's, Higham's, Scobé's, and Kutts's for special study and commendation, and eventually divided the premium between Hooker and Kutts. One wishes the other drawings had been preserved; were Lafever's and Rogers's designs, for instance, too advanced and Greek for the Albany taste? — perhaps not showy enough? Did local pride and politics enter into the final choice? See Root, op. cit.

ing with dominant horizontals, a rich Ionic porch, and a large low dome — produced one of the more successful variations of the United States Capitol scheme. Its simplicity, its quiet grace, and its basic restrained power were marked. Its construction proclaimed the complete victory of the Greek Revival in the Albany region. Its two-story central rotunda is especially pleasing. Albany was already a crowded and busy city; its Greek edifices could not change its definite character. Like Baltimore it was a ' city of domes,' and their rounded forms rose steeply from the river to the crowning low dome of the capitol.

It was in the newer centers that the Greek Revival most clearly set the character — in the towns growing up in the Susquehanna and Delaware valleys, like Greene, Unadilla, Otego, Oneonta; in the Finger Lakes region at Geneva or Canandaigua or Ovid; in the new towns to the north and west and along the Erie Canal, like Utica and Syracuse and Rochester. This triumphant Greek Revival work of the 1830's in up-state New York was definite and polished, quite different from the tentative earlier approaches. It made much of the monumental type of house with a two-story central body fronted with a pedimented portico and flanked by one-story wings, as well as of bolder and more original if less ostentatious types—cottages with nearly flat roofs and low frieze windows with decorative cast-iron grilles for the upper floors, or story-and-a-half gabled cottages. In all of these, freedom of planning and creative modifications of Greek precedent are outstanding, and in many there is evidence of the use of the Lafever books.

Lafever himself may have designed some of the houses. He first worked as a carpenter in the Finger Lakes district, after his early marriage — his wife was an up-state girl. He came to New York via Newark in 1827–9, and it is possible that he preserved many up-state contacts. There is, for instance, the Campbell-Whittlesey house in Rochester, built in 1835 and now a museum. Not only is it Lafever-like in spirit, but it employs in the original and characteristic trim of the wide door between parlor and dining room a most unusual detail shown almost line for line in Lafever's *The Beauties of Modern Architecture* (1835).[13] Yet if the date accepted is correct the house antedates the book. In Rochester it is attributed to a local builder-architect, but it seems likely that he must have been its builder only, executing a design that Lafever had furnished. Typical too of the Lafever influence are many of the smaller farmhouses and also the large number of houses with four-column two-story Ionic porches, flanked by lower wings, that are all reduced modifications of an influential design published in *The Modern Builders' Guide* (1833).[14] In some the imitation of this design extends even to the recessed Doric porches of the side wings. Examples are found in Unadilla and Otego; the general type is well-nigh universal, as for example in the Mackay house at Willeysville [15] or, on a smaller scale, in the Baldwin house (1838) on South Street in Auburn.[16] There is also a strong Lafever influence in the dignified General Leavenworth mansion in Syracuse, with its Ionic porch and richly carved interior trim.

Larger houses were even more monumental, though naturally they varied to a greater extent in type. More and more the wealthier landowners in the lavishly fertile parts of the state built for themselves, during the thirties and forties, great mansions which in grandeur and elegance, in rich finish and large scale, vied even with some of those of the more famous South. A simple type is Vesper Cliff, the Johnson-Platt house at Owego, built about 1830.[17] Its effect is gained by the simplest means; the long narrow five-bay body of it is fronted on the long side by a continuous two-story porch with six simple square anta-type piers, the roof — of pediment slope — runs unbroken from end to end, and there

---

[13] New York: D. Appleton and Company, 1835. This resemblance, as well as the importance of the house itself, was called to my attention by Mr. Fletcher Steele.

[14] New York: Sleight, 1833.

[15] Alexander B. Trowbridge, *The Greek Revival in Owego and Nearby New York Towns, and Some Suggested Antidotes*, Vol. IV, No. 5, in the White Pine Series of Architectural Monographs (New York: Russell F. Whitehead, October 1918).

[16] Carl C. Tallman, op. cit.

[17] Alexander B. Trowbridge, op. cit.

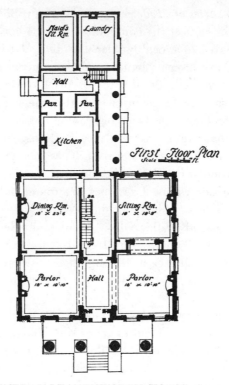

FIGURE 32. GENERAL LEAVENWORTH HOUSE, Syracuse, N.Y. (*Great Georgian Houses.*) Characteristic New York State variation of T-shaped plan. Note the great suite of rooms across the front and the careful planning of service arrangements.

is a dignified cupola. The Ely house [18] (1829) at Rochester, said to have been designed by an architect named Hastings, is an interesting variation of the temple house with wings. The great four-column portico is Doric; the wings have most unusual coupled windows framed by antae, with rich cast-iron railed porches in front of each pair. The wings are flat-roofed, their solid parapets raised slightly at the corners. The whole has a definite, personal quality of inventive, original detail and handsome mass. It is obviously the work of a skilled designer.

An even more impressive house is the great Boody house,

[18] Lewis Barrington, *Historic Restorations of the Daughters of the American Revolution* (New York: Richard T. Smith, 1941).

Rose Hill, on the shores of Seneca Lake opposite Geneva, built
circa 1835.[19] Here the central mass is five bays wide, with a fine
six-column Greek Ionic portico; smaller Ionic porches flank the
short one-story wings. A sense of tremendous scale is thus given to
the whole, and the wide pediment has an almost Roman power.
The building is crowned with the central cupola so frequent in
these New York houses. It is very possible that its design was influenced by Town's great Bowers house in Northampton, engravings of which, after a Davis drawing, had been published before
Rose Hill was started.

Some of the smaller houses have great distinction also. An
example is the Tousley house (1844) at Albion, in which a squar-
ish main block is flanked by a wing with a Greek Doric porch. The
main entrance, in the cornermost bay of the main block, has an
Ionic porch with a stele-top cresting, and the small windows in the
frieze of the entablature that surrounds the main block are enriched with delicate Greek-fret grilles, apparently of cast iron.
The roofs are of extremely low pitch; in its continuous, strongly
stressed horizontals the Tousley house is characteristic of the
growing love of breadth, of accent on the horizontal, that governed
so much of the ' Tuscan ' work of Davis and flowered in the later
popularity of flat-roofed ' Bracketed ' houses. In itself the Tousley house, small as it is and few as its parts may be, has a directness, a distinction, an originality of effect that are as impressive
as is the great scale of the Boody house.

Western New York in those days was a country of experiment,
of striving for the new — a restless, utopian country. It was the
home of religious cults of all kinds, the birthplace of Mormonism.
It was serious, idealistic, perhaps at times even a little ' touched.'
And something of this quality seems to have permeated its architecture, given it vitality, made it eager to seize and to use the
new Greek forms and to use them and modify them in new and
experimental ways, so that even in the experiments there seems to
be little that is tentative — on the contrary they indicate a strong
affirmation. There is an enormous variety of house types; many

19 Carl C. Tallman, op. cit.

of the different schemes found farther west in Ohio and Michigan had their seeds sown in New York State. One especially notable characteristic is the ubiquitous use of porches or piazzas; in no other part of the northern United States are these such a universal adjunct to even the simplest houses.

Time has dealt harshly with the larger Greek Revival civic structures and churches of northern and western New York. A century of progress and prosperity has destroyed and replaced the greater number. But at least one superb example remains — the Utica insane asylum.[20] It was one of the famous asylums of its time (1838). The part existing is but one side of the great quadrangle originally planned. Yet, even as it is, its great scale, the rightness of its proportions, the quiet dignity of its detail, and its powerful, monumental Greek Doric portico give it a distinction, a beauty, that is outstanding.

Nowhere more than in up-state New York is local research to discover local architects and builders, to trace detailed influences, more necessary. Nowhere is Greek Revival work more vital and more varied. We can point here and there to influences taken over from the earlier Massachusetts-Connecticut-Berkshire work; we can see again and again the influence of Lafever both in mass and in detail. Occasionally a name is known, like that of Cyrus Wetherill, an Englishman who came to Orleans County in 1814 and worked there till 1835,[21] but that is almost all. Yet about the personalities, even about the ideals, of the actual designers and builders who took and merged and changed these influences and from them created individual new buildings we know almost nothing. Wherever they were, again and again they built well, and the houses they put up do much to make the character of upper New York what it is. Let us hope our ignorance with respect to these devoted early architects and builders will be little by little diminished.

[20] I owe my information about this to Professor Turpin C. Bannister of Rensselaer Polytechnic Institute, who has made a careful study of much work of this period in upper New York.
[21] Marc W. Cole, 'A Master Builder of the Early Nineteenth Century,' *Country Life in America,* Vol. xxix, No. 4 (February 1916), pp. 22–3.

Pennsylvania

One of the most important routes west from the central Atlantic coast of the United States led from Philadelphia to Pittsburgh and then down the Ohio. Its importance was enhanced by the fertility and wealth of the Pennsylvania valleys themselves even before the discovery of anthracite coal and of oil. Thus, just as in New York State local towns and villages grew up at the same time that the westward migration along the Mohawk Valley and the Erie Canal was bringing in wealth, so in Pennsylvania the growth was double and Pittsburgh at the head of navigation of the Ohio River system became doubly important.

Into these rapidly growing communities of fertile western Pennsylvania came the Germans — the ' Pennsylvania Dutch ' — and men of English or Scottish or Irish descent from Philadelphia and Baltimore, to create an architecture neither entirely Philadelphia in type nor like the great, simply walled buildings of Bethlehem and the German country. In the earlier work shortly after the Revolution there remains much of the characteristic Pennsylvania solidity and conservatism in form. The houses are large and generally high-ceilinged; the detail only gradually shows signs of that attenuation and eventual effeminization which characterized so much Federal work elsewhere. In the houses the general aim seems to have been a kind of pleasant, undecorated dignity and a use wherever possible of stone and brick in place of the frame construction more common elsewhere. Types with end chimneys and high gables are frequent; these persisted indeed with typical Pennsylvania tenacity until long after other freer forms had become the rule in other places. Thus as late as 1835 the Mount Washington Tavern built by Nathaniel Ewing near Uniontown retains the simple rectangular mass, the five-bay composition, the simple door with side- and fanlights and no porch, the great twinned brick end chimneys of a period that had largely passed.[22] Even when richer effects are attempted, the basic forms to which the ornament is applied retain the same heavy dignity and the

[22] Lewis Barrington, op. cit., Restoration No. 107.

ornament is likely to be naïve, almost childlike, as in the applied
ornament in the stone gables of the Meason house (1802) at
Uniontown or the interiors of the Joseph Dorsey house at Brownsville.[23] The Amos Judson house (1820) at Waterford has, to be
sure, corner pilasters and a rather Benjamin type of detail, as
though an unusual New England influence were here at work. The
general type of Late Colonial in favor depended for its effect
largely on magnificent masonry and excellent proportion.

In Pittsburgh, from the beginning the metropolis of the area,
the feeling was more sophisticated and polished; in the exceptional
buildings erected by the Rappites at Economy there is a bigness
of conception, an originality of creation, and a sure feeling for the
relation of ornament and construction quite unique. The charming
Palladian garden pavilion (1831) designed by Frederick Rapp is
characteristic; a drawing for it that still exists, probably made
by him, is as excellent in draftsmanship as the building is beautiful in form and detail. Yet like the great house, with its attractively composed wings and its interesting silhouette and imaginative detail, built five years earlier, the garden pavilion at Economy
seems as distant from the general fashions and tastes of the time
as the doctrines of this successful if erratic celibate cult were distant from the ways of ordinary living.

Latrobe lived for two years in Pittsburgh and designed there
a group of buildings for the Allegheny Arsenal which were among
his most successful as well as most American designs. From what
still remains of these buildings and his drawings in the Library of
Congress one may today get a clear idea of the classic dignity, elegance, and restraint of the Arsenal as he planned it. It was not
yet Greek, but in its restraint and its use of ornament — as, for
instance, in the simple circular paterae at the ends of the plain
lintels — there was much of the feeling that was later to control
Greek Revival design. This group set a standard that Pittsburgh
seems continuously in the next twenty years to have tried to equal.

Pittsburgh was in its way in those years a boom town, growing

[23] Charles Morse Stotz, *The Early Architecture of Western Pennsylvania*
(New York: William Helburn, for the Buhl Foundation, 1936), to which I owe
the greater number of the examples and most of the material in this section.

New York State mansions: ABOVE, LEFT, Belding House, Troy. (*Bannister.*) ABOVE, RIGHT, General Leavenworth House, Syracuse (*Bannister.*) Plan, Figure 32. BELOW, LEFT, house at Randolph. (*Major.*) BELOW, RIGHT, house at Middleburg. (*Taylor.*)

New York State mansions: ABOVE, Rose Hill (Boody Mansion), Seneca Lake, Geneva. (*Major.*) BELOW, Tousley House, Albion. (*Barrington and D.A.R.*)

rapidly as group after group of immigrants passed through it bound for the fertile lands of the West; naturally numerous architects and builders of skill and training made it their center. Hugh Graham, a Scotsman perhaps, who had come to Philadelphia in 1824, went on to Pittsburgh two years later, and his buildings gave the city much of its quality. John Chislett, who in early life had been apprenticed to an architect at Bath, England, worked in Pittsburgh in the thirties and forties; he designed Burke's Building (1835-6) with its dignified rusticated basement and pedimented central pavilion with a pedimented Greek Doric porch below, as well as the second Allegheny County courthouse, burned in 1882, which had a Greek Doric portico with two complete rows of columns. Burke's Building, like a great deal of the early street architecture of Pittsburgh, has that combination of size and reticence which has been pointed out as typical of much Baltimore work, but in addition its sophisticated composition, with a highly developed projecting central motif, shows Chislett's foreign background in the resemblance the structure bears to much eighteenth-century English work.

Time and progress have dealt harshly with old Pittsburgh, but enough remains — or has remained until fairly recent times — to enable us to distinguish that quality of almost heavy good taste, of excellent proportion, of severity which characterized its Greek Revival buildings, as for example in the exterior of the Schoenberger house (1847). Yet this house shows also the tremendously lavish interior work that was often hidden behind these dignified, almost stark exteriors. It is one of the richest Greek Revival interiors anywhere and comparable to any of the contemporary work in Boston or the South; as is the case in so many houses in New York and the South, its detail — like the ceiling rose — shows the tremendous vogue of the Lafever detail if not of the Lafever books.[24] The Schoenberger house is exceptional, however, in the fact that its interiors combine with their anthemion border and molding decorations of essentially Greek type the most

[24] Compare this rose with Plate 21 of Lafever's *The Beauties of Modern Architecture*.

exquisitely modeled Corinthianesque capitals; these are original in conception and much more closely related to Italian Renaissance work than to that of either Greece or Rome. Perhaps the answer to this unusual and attractive combination may lie in the fact that the ornaments for the ceiling were 'stock' bought from some maker of plaster and composition ornament, such as Robert Wellford, for the Wilkins house in Pittsburgh has a ceiling almost identical.[25] A similar lavishness, though handled with a much heavier touch, is found in the interiors of the Croghan house (1835), and especially in the great ballroom. On the outskirts of the town the Judge Wilkins house, Homewood, with its four great Greek Doric columns and its central raised attic with Greek anthemion ornaments, shows the sophistication to which the wealthy Pittsburghers aspired.

Outside of Pittsburgh the Greek Revival naturally was expressed in more simple and tentative ways, except in the case of the largest houses and the most important public buildings. Thus the Bedford County courthouse (1828), though it has a four-column pedimented portico, remains more Roman than Greek and more Colonial than either; the large semicircular window in the pediment has a muntin pattern of confused curved lines in which perhaps may be read a distant reflection of Chippendale Gothic. Even the Congregational Church (1830) at Meadville, in spite of the fact that it has excellent general proportions and a Greek Doric portico, uses Greek Doric pilasters, treating them with simple Doric capitals and with no attempt to make them resemble the anta types the Greeks had developed. Its interior is especially attractive in its quiet dignity.

A similar naïve approach to Greek detail — or should we rather call it a complete freedom in modifying a known precedent? — appears again and again in the western Pennsylvania houses of the thirties and forties. The Dr. James White house (1835) at Hartstown is characteristic. It uses pilasters of normal width and then between them frames windows with pilasters of similar height and detail but cut down in width to become mere window trims. And

25 Charles Morse Stotz, op. cit.

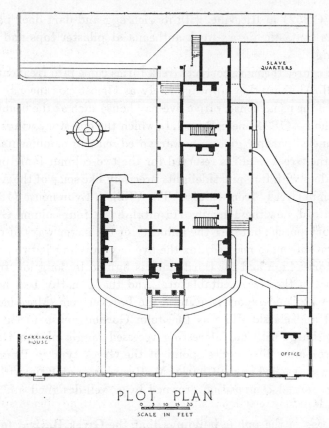

PLOT PLAN

0 5 10 15 20
SCALE IN FEET

FIGURE 33. WILLIAM LYON HOUSE, Bedford, Pa. Plan. (*Stotz.*) Highly developed Pennsylvania plan, with formally arranged service buildings and simple directness in house layout.

the Elias Baker house in Altoona, as late as 1844, though of complete temple type, squeezes down its Ionic order to an unpleasant squatness. Sometimes this ignorance or freedom, whichever it may be, achieves more interesting, to us more delightful, results. Thus in the Wrap house (1835), at Beaver, raised script lettering and a most original treatment of the staff beads and mullion pilasters, both made into rich and heavy turned shapes like the bedposts of an American ' Empire ' bed, give to the whole building an unusual quaintness not without its own beauty. Perhaps the climax of this carpenter Greek Revival was reached in the H. E. Hendryx house (1852) in Riceville, with its rich egg-and-dart door panels and its fantastic jigsaw-work anthemia at pilaster tops and as a cresting.

Of course the more correct Greek forms came into frequent use as well. At times they appear merely as almost extraneous additions to the usual conservative five-bay house such as the beautiful Irvin house (1834) near Russel, to which the one-story wings and the paneled parapet give an unwarranted sense of monumentality. Here the Greek detail is reserved for the two-column Ionic porch and a door with fan- and sidelights precisely like some of the Asher Benjamin Greek ' frontispieces.' The William Lyon house (1833) at Bedford, now the Timmins Hospital, has a four-column Greek one-story porch; but here the influence of the newer ways of composition was more marked, for the five-bay building is two and a half stories high and the third story is lighted by long low frieze windows in the Greek entablature. And the Timothy Ives house (1842) at Condersport is quite in the Lafever vein. More monumental and classic still was the John Gordon house (1843) in Waynesburg, with an interesting recessed loggia of two Greek Ionic columns. The highest point of the Greek type in Pennsylvania was reached in the Charles M. Reed house at Erie, with its strong, formal composition crowned by a well-designed and impressive attic.

It was in the public buildings that the Greek Revival found its most perfect Pennsylvania expressions. Here as in so many of the newer lands the rapid rise alike of population and of civic formality made necessary the creation of adequate courthouses as well as the building of many churches. In almost all of these, except the exquisite and extraordinarily accurate Gothic Revival church of St. Peter's [26] at Brownsville, the Greek Revival reigned

[26] In many ways St. Peter's Church is one of the most successful of the earlier Gothic Revival churches in America. The simplification of all its detail to fit the rather rough stone masonry of which it is built, the handling of the stone itself in window splays and arches, the beauty of the simple interior with its open-timber roof, the quiet and unostentatious charm of its composition — these all seem so direct and unforced, so absolutely the result of the needs of the building and the materials of which it is made, that the impression it gives is totally lacking in the kind of stage-scenery, vaunting unreality that characterized much more ambitious American Gothic churches of the time. Hardly anywhere else have basically Gothic forms been so thoroughly Americanized. The building looks as much at

supreme. St. Luke's Evangelical Church (1844) at Erie is exceptional both in accuracy of detail and originality of composition, as seen in its recessed Greek Doric porch and its rather queer truncated pyramidal belfry. In both the composition of its elevation and the type of its belfry it owes its original inspiration undoubtedly to A. J. Davis's Carmine Street Church in New York, built a decade earlier.[27] Chislett's Allegheny County courthouse (1842) at Pittsburgh was characteristic of the rather austere and serious handling of Greek forms these Pennsylvania architects seemed to prefer. The six-column Doric Bank of the United States branch at Erie (1839), later the customs house and now the home of the Erie County Historical Society, has a somewhat similar dignity and an unusually well-handled subtlety of proportion in the relation of all its parts. It has frequently been attributed to Strickland; yet its simple austerity is quite unlike most of Strickland's work, and the evidence seems definite that its real architect was one William Kelly of Erie.[28]

home and as 'real' in its Pennsylvania environment as any simple English fourteenth-century parish church does in an English village. St. Peter's at Brownsville is one of the rare instances in which the Gothic has been completely absorbed and re-expressed in a native American way, as Greek forms were absorbed and re-expressed in the American Greek Revival.

[27] Federal Writers' Project, Works Progress Administration, *Erie, a Guide to the City and County,* in the American Guide Series (Philadelphia: William Penn Association, 1938).

[28] The difference in character between this building and the works of Strickland can perhaps best be realized by comparing the Erie branch bank with the Athenaeum in Providence, a Greek Doric structure of somewhat the same general scale. The Providence building, in the wideness of its proportions and the free, creative manner in which its Greek details were put together, is characteristic of Strickland's originality, whereas the much more archaeologically correct treatment of the Erie branch bank seems the result of a different hand. Strickland, to be sure, had used an archaeologically correct Greek Doric portico for the Philadelphia branch bank twenty years earlier, but more and more in his later work his free inventiveness continually presses beyond the ancient precedents. Kelly must have been an architect of sensitiveness and ability, for correct as the building is it nevertheless has definite vitality. His is one of many names that continually flash across the picture in any study of this period in any part of the country — names of men who must have accomplished much other work of equal importance. The high quality of the work done by many of these men, about whom we know as little as we do of Kelly, indicates perhaps better than anything else the broad spread of a sound basic architectural culture in the America of the thirties and forties, just as the number of names attached to single edifices — whether still standing or only known through literary or other records of the time — gives some indication of the amount of popular support they enjoyed and the admiration their work must have excited.

The Greek influence in courthouse design persisted long. The Greene County courthouse at Waynesburg for instance, as late as 1850, has a magnificent Greek Corinthian portico in which the capitals are of cast iron though the columns are of stone; there is an excellent simple entrance and a crowning cupola of greater than ordinary height, well designed and approaching a church spire in its form. Save for occasional moldings there is hardly a trace in this building of the flattening and vulgarization of taste that is often to be found in public work of the fifties. Even ten years later the Armstrong courthouse (1860) at Kittanning still preserves touches of Greek character in the antae along the wings, though its portico uses a Roman order and is set on a high rusticated basement with segmentally arched openings. Here the tall slim windows are also expressive of mid-century taste. The whole building is an interesting example of the new eclectic classic or Renaissance feeling, which was becoming more and more common during the sixties and of which Samuel Sloan of Philadelphia and Arthur Gilman of New York were the chief protagonists; but it still retains touches of the older, sounder Greek Revival feeling and becomes thereby a most interesting link between two totally distinct and frequently contradictory phases of American design.

Like New York State, western Pennsylvania was not dependent on the western migration for its livelihood, though undoubtedly the migration added to its wealth. Its mines, its quarries, and its rich valleys were reason enough in themselves for new settlements and growing towns. This settling was a gradual process and in large measure by people of Pennsylvania origin. Perhaps that would account for the basic conservatism of so much of the work, for conservatism in house design is a marked feature of many parts of eastern Pennsylvania as well. Perhaps it accounts also for the great variety of types found within the area and for the enormous difference between the richest, most sophisticated, most correct, and at the time most up-to-date work in Pittsburgh or Erie and the apparent backwardness and naïveté of the buildings in the smaller villages and on the farms. It is in the larger centers and the more sophisticated work that one finds, too, the greatest amount of influence seemingly from outside the state, like the rather Baltimore character of many of the Pittsburgh exteriors. Nevertheless there is a definite local quality in the greater part of the work whether naïve or correct. It is independent, it is almost all built with an unusual care and solidity, its parts are likely to be large and simple, its general effect ample, and its reticent details usually well composed and employed with restraint. It was responsible for no such evolution of special types as was the New York State development; it was content to use almost indefinitely the simple five-bay scheme and the ample dimensions of the old eighteenth-century house. Yet it was an architecture that forces immediate respect; one is conscious always that it was the work of men who knew buildings, building materials, building details, and how they could best be put together to be lasting and satisfactory.

Ohio

After the Indian Treaty of 1795 and the defeat of Tecumseh in 1811 had settled the Indian question, the regions of the old Northwest Territory filled rapidly with newcomers. They came into Ohio via the old Western Reserve along the Lake Erie shore, via the Ohio River from Pennsylvania, Maryland, and the South; they entered into southern Michigan from Ohio, and by the Great Lakes from Canada and the northern states, blending with the French settlements already there. They pushed on by the river valleys and the Indian trails into Indiana and Illinois, flooded north into Wisconsin, west across the Mississippi into Iowa. The rapid settlement of these states, the swift development of government,[29] the prompt emergence of a local culture and an educational system, as evidenced by the proliferation of academies and colleges — these are all well-known facts of American history. All contributed to make the area especially fitted to develop a vivid and vital architecture. That part of it built between the late 1820's and 1850 — and this period was in many localities the one that saw the growth of rough pioneering communities

---

[29] Ohio achieved statehood in 1803, Indiana in 1816, Illinois in 1818, Michigan in 1837, Wisconsin in 1848, and Iowa in 1846.

into prosperous, settled, well-constructed towns — naturally was chiefly under the influence of Greek Revival ideals. In all of this region the traditions were mixed. Certain areas, like the Western Reserve of Ohio, were for the most part under New England influence. The old Ohio Land Company that settled the Marietta section was also largely controlled by New Englanders. Chillicothe on the other hand was originally settled mostly by Virginians, as were other parts of southern Ohio. In Detroit the French and Canadian influence remained strong for two generations. Cincinnati, the largest Ohio River port, was, like port cities generally, a mixing-bowl of all sorts of peoples from all sorts of backgrounds. Along the Mississippi River, as at Cairo, Illinois, French influence from New Orleans was strong in the early days. Yet nowhere, save perhaps in the Western Reserve, did these original influences remain pure; new immigrants came eagerly into all areas — large numbers of Germans poured into southern and central Ohio at an early period, and energetic, ambitious traders and farmers from all parts of the East established themselves wherever they found an opportunity.

The result architecturally was a happy cross-fertilization, evident even in the early period. Inventiveness and novelty were as much a part of the picture as was traditional building. In Marietta,[30] for example, simple early Colonial-type structures like the Rufus Putnam house (1789) rapidly gave way to a type of brick building, tall for its width, with wide elliptical arched doors — as in the Hildreth house (1824), probably designed by Joseph Barker, who was born in 1765 in New Market, New Hampshire — and with the superposition of elliptical arched Palladian motifs in a manner unlike anything elsewhere, as in the Exchange Hotel (1831), possibly by the same architect or someone under his influence. So in Chillicothe[31] the earlier Virginia-type manor houses — like the superb stone Worthington

30 Thomas E. O'Donnell, 'The Early Architecture of Marietta, the Oldest City in Ohio,' *Architecture,* Vol. li, No. 1 (January 1925), pp. 1–4.

31 Thomas E. O'Donnell, 'The Greek Revival in Chillicothe, Ohio's Old Capital City,' *Architecture,* Vol. lii, No. 4 (October 1925), pp. 355–60; Federal Writers' Project, Works Progress Administration, *Chillicothe and Ross County, Ohio,* in the American Guide Series (Chillicothe: Northwest Territory Committee, 1938).

Pennsylvania buildings. (*Stotz, Buhl, Carnegie Lib. of Pittsburgh.*) TOP, LEFT, Greene County Courthouse, Waynesburg. TOP, RIGHT, Croghan House, Pittsburgh, ballroom. CENTER, William Lyon House, Bedford. Plan, Figure 33. BOTTOM, Burke's Building, Pittsburgh. John Chislett, architect.

The Greek Revival in Erie, Pa. (*Stotz, Buhl, Carnegie Lib. of Pittsburgh.*) ABOVE, old Branch Bank of the United States (now Erie County Historical Society). William Kelly, architect. BELOW, Reed House, attributed to William Kelly.

Ohio building types: ABOVE, LEFT, Exchange Hotel, Marietta. (*Frary*.) ABOVE, RIGHT, Baldwin Buss House, Hudson, a pure New England type. (*Major*.) BELOW, RIGHT, house at Yellow Springs. (*Author*.) BELOW, LEFT, farmhouse west of Ashtabula. (*Major*.)

Typical Ohio buildings. (*Frary.*) ABOVE, LEFT, Swift House, Vermilion. ABOVE, RIGHT, house at Chillicothe. BELOW, LEFT, Courthouse, Dayton. BELOW, RIGHT, Jonathan Goldsmith's design for a business block.

Wooster-Boalt House, Norwalk, Ohio. Built 1848 as a girls' school. (*Frary.*)

LXXXII

Typical Ohio buildings. (*Frary.*) LEFT, house and shop, Portsmouth. RIGHT, church at Streetsboro.

mansion (1804–5) at Adena, for which the design was furnished to Thomas Worthington by Latrobe; or the similar Renick house, Paint Hill, of about the same date — gave way two decades later to characteristic brick Greek Revival houses of the greatest dignity, usually with low-pitched roofs, simple rectangular or L-shaped plans, and detail of quite austere correctness. Often there are piazzas, sometimes two stories high, on the sides and rear, and frequently the central entrance porch is in a recess with a recessed balcony above. Typical is the King-Fullerton-Brown house, where two stories of Ionic columns decorate this recessed porch. In the Convent on Paint Street there are Ionic columns on the first floor only, with a lovely iron rail across the second-floor recessed balcony. The Reeves-Woodrow-Fullerton house (1847) on Paint Street is more ' eastern '; its third-story low frieze windows with cast-iron grilles and its projecting Ionic porch can be matched in many other localities. It is said to have been designed by a Baltimore architect.[32] Two of Chillicothe's richest Greek Revival houses, the Atwood-Wilson house (1845) and the Bartlett-Ritchart-Cunningham house (1848), are attributed to a Cincinnati architect, Kelly.[33] The earlier is a five-bay house with a strong central motif containing the usual recessed door; it has also a projecting end porch and an unusually rich cornice, and all the trim, columns, and cornices are of stone. The later of these houses has a porch all across the front, with four Greek Corinthian columns between square antae; above the entablature is an exceedingly rich ramped and paneled blocking course with scrolls and acroteria.

In the country the same process went on with extraordinary variations due to differences in the background and the age of the builders. Thus the Guthrie house (1842–3) at Zanesville, a templelike Greek Doric building, is said to have been copied from the house in Concord, New Hampshire, from which the Guthries had come. The Mitchell-Turner house (*circa* 1838) at Milan is Greek, to be sure, with four Ionic columns and the most exuberant Greek detail and with a stele cap as a pediment decoration, but all the

---

[32] O'Donnell, op. cit. (*Chillicothe* . . .).
[33] Could this be the N. B. Kelley (see page 288) who was one of the architects of the Ohio capitol? The Bartlett-Ritchart-Cunningham house has also been attributed to Henry Walters.

ornament is merely fret-sawed from wood and applied, so that the final effect is naïve and tentative. Some of the ornament has a quality of line not unlike that which Lafever was developing at the same time in New York, although the touch here is heavy. In the Curtis-Devin house (1834–6) at Mount Vernon, altered by the addition of ' Victorian ' balconies in 1850, the detail is much surer and the interior is particularly handsome, with the restraint and rather blocky type of detail shown in the books of Edward Shaw. The Wooster-Boalt house in Norwalk, built in 1848 as a girls' school, shows the final complete mastery of Greek detail which the forties occasionally displayed in Ohio. Its façade, with its Greek free-standing Ionic columns between antae, is well proportioned, monumental, even sophisticated in its treatment of detail.

Yet little by little architects working in Ohio were beginning to develop their own individual approach, usually simpler than that in much eastern work, less dependent on the temple type than that of New York, returning at times almost to the austerity current in Boston. The stone Hurst house at Rocky River is characteristic. In scheme it is the typical five-bay house, but it has above the cornice a sloping blocking course to add emphasis to the central axis and boasts a front-door design of the greatest power. The door itself, combined with sidelights and a horizontal transom, is set in a powerful stone architrave, with croisettes and a full frieze and entablature. The moldings are flat, simple, and well designed, so that the whole has an uncommon dignity and strength.

The development of this type reached almost a climax in the later work of Jonathan Goldsmith. Goldsmith was born in New Haven in 1783 and came to Painesville in 1811. He was originally a shoemaker and carpenter, but later developed into an architect of great skill and a draftsman of no mean achievements. His H. Matthews house (1829) in Painesville is still conservative in type, with four slim pilasters on the central block and two low wings, but later work reveals a growing mastery of Greek refinement and Greek simplicity. His old Bank of Geauga (later the Painesville National Bank, which stood till 1925) had tall, slim Greek Doric columns quite out of the Greek proportion but with a charming effect of their own. Drawings of his that have been preserved [34] include the designs for a group of business buildings in Painesville which in their quiet surfaces, their regularly spaced windows, their simplicity, and their excellence of proportion rank well with the current work of New York or New England. Combining dignity, simplicity, plenty of light, economy and yet excellence of materials — the whole was designed apparently for stone — this group shows the originality and the simplicity for which many of the Ohio architects were striving.

Goldsmith's own cottage (1841) is one of the most successful of the many attempts made at the time to find a new answer to the problem of the small house. The central portion, a plain rectangle, has a hipped roof and four Greek antae on the front, with large windows and a simple door between them. In the frieze above are low windows with pierced, Greek-patterned grilles lighting the attic story. The main block is flanked by two one-story wings with porches at the front. Every detail is excellent in its relation to the whole. It is a house that is elegant without being in the least showy, modest without being mean. Much other work at Painesville has been attributed to Goldsmith — St. James's Protestant Episcopal Church and the Lake Erie College, as well as the Cowles house in Cleveland. That a man of such modest origins, starting life as a shoemaker, should achieve work of such a consistently high level both in conception and execution tells much not only of his own power but also of the general high level in taste of his clients.

The Goldsmith cottage of 1841 is but one example of a great number of houses throughout Ohio which show a general search for new answers to the house problem. Just as Chillicothe houses are different from houses of the East Coast or the South, so the houses of the dwellers on the rich Ohio farms are frequently entirely different in character from the farmhouses of New England or New York. One common type is the L-shaped house with a recessed porch in the wing. Usually the roof slope of the main part of the building is of almost temple type; sometimes the front will

[34] Frary, op. cit.

have antae corners, sometimes not. This type of house allowed great flexibility in interior arrangement and many opportunities for through ventilation. Where it originated is uncertain, but most of the examples seem to be from the 1840's. There is one in the Mohawk Valley near Little Falls, close to the river bank; there is another quite similar near Ashtabula; another almost identical is the Peavey house near Tipton, Michigan.

Still another search, even more experimental, was the search for the perfect large one-story house. With land plentiful, why build up into the air when one could spread over the ground? Some of these large one-story houses, like that in Louis Bromfield's *The Farm*,[35] resulted from the gradual accretions of two generations around the original settlers' log or timber houses, but later architects and builders seem to have striven to plan new ones in the same free manner. The Renick Young farm (1832) near Circleville [36] is characteristic. The great central living room has square rooms at three of its corners; between these on two sides are recessed Greek Doric porches, the corner rooms being carried up with richly decorated windows to form pylons. At one side a suite of three rooms is added and at the rear a protected terrace provides a pleasant place for work or for sitting. Additional space in the great hipped-roof attic over the main building is lighted by dormers and approached by a stair at the rear. The whole is a most interesting and original combination of formal dignity and informality. In style it is equally unhampered by conventionality; despite the formality of the Greek Doric porches, the rich living-room mantel is oddly detailed and is definitely in the Late Colonial manner.

The greatest of these one-story houses was the Joseph Swift house (1840–41) at Vermilion,[37] unfortunately burned in 1923. Here the plan of the main house was formal and symmetrical, with a four-column Ionic porch between projecting rooms in the front. At the rear a long projecting wing, giving onto an L-shaped colonnade, formed with a little separate service building an attrac-

---

[35] New York and London: Harper & Brothers [c1935].
[36] Frary, op. cit.
[37] Ibid.

tive, completely protected courtyard garden. The detail throughout was as rich and original as the house plan, and the whole must
have been a beautiful center for the patriarchal family life of a
great Ohio farm a century ago.

In the larger cities, of course, work was more ' advanced,' more
sophisticated; but, alas, progress through the Middle West has
destroyed the older buildings relentlessly and little remains in
Cincinnati or Dayton to remind one of the elegance and the architectural competence of a century ago. In Cincinnati, for instance,
the Sinton-Taft house (1820), sometimes attributed to Latrobe,
remains as the Taft Museum, with its interesting murals of the
1840's by Robert Duncanson. Occasional waterfront shed buildings and houses in the slums may be found, and an educational
building or two, as well as St. Peter's Cathedral; but generally
speaking one must turn to other sources to learn what Cincinnati
was like in those earlier boom days. Engravings published by
Charles Cist [38] in 1841 show the gracious dignity and the harmony
of style that hung over its streets. The Pearl Street House, a hotel,
achieved great dignity on its sloping site, with its thin Greek
Doric pilasters, its first-floor windows in arched recesses, its typical
recessed porches on all the floors, and a rich cast-iron balcony at
the first-floor level. The Lane Theological Seminary chapel had a
six-column Greek Doric portico, and the Western Baptist Theological Seminary was a most interesting group of two dormitories flanking a handsome six-column Ionic chapel. The post office
was especially interesting — a four-column Greek Doric temple
standing on a high arcaded terrace that was arranged for planting. The contrast of forms in the upper and lower parts, their perfect and harmonious adjustment, and the green of the planting on
the terrace must have formed a picture unusual in American cities.

St. Peter's Cathedral (1839–45) is one of the handsomest and
most monumental of Greek Revival churches, its great square tower
surrounded on three sides, like that of King's Chapel in Boston,
by a Corinthian colonnade of twelve columns. It was probably

[38] *Cincinnati, 1841: Its Early Annals and Future Prospects* (Cincinnati: the
author, 1841).

designed by Henry Walters, the architect of the Ohio capitol. Later, of course, Isaiah Rogers made Cincinnati his home. His Cincinnati work has already been mentioned.[39] Mrs. Trollope devotes considerable space [40] to Cincinnati, where her chief American interests lay. The great building she built for her bazaar and casino is said to have had details from Egypt and Assyria as well as all the orders. It is spoken of as ' bizarre.' So far as I can find out, no illustrations of it exist; it was evidently quite different in character from the quiet simplicity and gracious monumentality of the buildings Cist shows.

At Dayton the chief monument remaining is the superb Dayton courthouse (1848–50) designed by Howard Daniels. Tradition has it that his design was based on sketches of the Theseum made by one of the important local bankers, Horace Pease.[41] The sketches, however, must have been treated with even greater freedom than that which Jefferson had used in the adaptation of the Maison Carrée at Nîmes for the Virginia state capitol, because not only does the colonnade occur on the front alone in the Dayton courthouse but the order was changed into Ionic. The building is unusually satisfactory both in detail and in proportion. It has true elegance.

The old First Presbyterian Church [42] (1839–42) at Dayton, destroyed in 1867, with its tall, original spire and a recessed porch with Greek Ionic columns, was one of the richest in detail and most beautifully proportioned of Ohio churches. It is well shown in old engravings, which also depict the use of upper-floor colonnaded porches to give interest to the city streets. Such porches on several floors were apparently once common, especially in the southern part of Ohio. At least one example still stands in Portsmouth, and the interesting effect given by these tiers of grace-

---

[39] See page 115.

[40] Mrs. [Frances Milton] Trollope, *Domestic Manners of the Americans* (London: Whitaker, Trecher & Co., 1832; New York: reprinted ' for the booksellers,' 1832).

[41] Charlotte Reeve Conover, *The Story of Dayton* (Dayton: Greater Dayton Association, 1917).

[42] Robert W. and Mary Davies Steele, *Early Dayton* (Dayton: W. J. Shuey, 1896).

fully detailed superposed columns with delicate iron railings between made a street of real loveliness.[43]

The old courthouse (1840) at Fremont, by a Mr. Williams, is as ungainly as that at Dayton is graceful. A large rectangular building, flat-roofed, it has a six-column Greek Doric portico with unusually slim columns and an extremely odd cupola that stands but awkwardly on the mass. Originally these county courthouses, usually square, with churchlike cupolas and sometimes with pedimented colonnades, were common all over the state and formed one of its most distinguishing features; now they have practically all perished. Many can be seen, crudely presented, in the town views of Henry Howe's *Historical Collections of Ohio*.[44]

The old churches of Ohio are as remarkable as its houses, running the entire gamut from the pure Late Colonial of the Tallmadge church, through the Greek Revival, and into the medievalism of Rogers's Cincinnati church. The Mormon Temple (1833–6) at Kirtland is unusual in its late use of extraordinarily rich Late-Colonial-type detail, especially in the interior. But St. Luke's Episcopal Church at Granville is exquisitely designed, with a Greek Doric porch and a low tower, in a vein quite similar to a design published in Asher Benjamin's *The Practice of Architecture*.[45] And scattered over the state are a tremendous number of small Greek Revival churches as satisfactory as they are simple.

Columbus has suffered less than many of the Ohio cities from the inroads of progress. The Kelley house (1839) shows the powerful, monumental quality the Ohio architects seemed to seek when they were building in stone. With its stern gray walls, its bold panels, and its definite mass composition it forms a striking and original picture in spite of the small size of its windows, which must make its interior unduly dark.

But the crown of Columbus work, and perhaps the crown of all Greek Revival work in Ohio, is the state capitol,[46] one of the

43 Frary, op. cit.
44 Cincinnati: Derby, Bradley & Co., 1847.
45 See Appendix A.
46 Thomas E. O'Donnell, 'The Greek Revival Capitol at Columbus, Ohio,' *The Architectural Forum*, Vol. xlii, No 1 (June 1925), pp. 5–8.

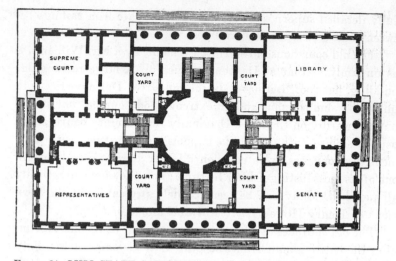

Figure 34. OHIO STATE CAPITOL, Columbus, Ohio. Main-floor plan. Henry Walters and others, architects. (*The Builder*.) Unconventional and effective arrangement, producing variety and impressiveness in interior spaces within a severely simple exterior.

most original as it is one of the most superb of all of the earlier state capitol buildings. It has a long history. A competition was held for it in 1838, in which Henry Walters of Cincinnati won the first prize, Martin Thompson of New York the second, and Thomas Cole (the painter) of Catskill the third. Davis, as we have seen, went out to serve as expert in attempting to get from these designs a final and workable scheme, and settled on one based on Henry Walters's drawings. The final construction, however, did not begin till 1848, with W. Russell West as supervising architect until 1854. N. B. Kelley was then appointed to carry on the slowly rising building. Could he be the Kelly (see page 281) to whom some of the best of the Chillicothe houses are attributed, and the architect of the Kelley house at Columbus? In 1856 the designs of the building under way were submitted to Thomas U. Walter and Richard Upjohn for their expert opinion. Finally, in 1858, Kelley was displaced and Isaiah Rogers appointed, carrying on until 1860 when the building was at last completed.

All the evidence is that despite the many changes in architect the original scheme of Henry Walters as modified by Davis was carried out in all its main lines, and that to him is due the superb conception of the great rectangle, its simple unbroken cornice, and the four recessed Greek Doric porches on the four sides. The plain cylindrical cupola is the only element that seems somehow out of place. It is obviously incomplete, and Isaiah Rogers wished to surround it by a circular colonnade with a conical tiled roof, which would at once have given it meaning and harmonious relation to the rest of the building. Even as it stands today, however, the Ohio state capitol takes rank with the work of Mills or of Strickland, or with Rogers's own Merchants' Exchange in New York, as representing the very best ideals of the Greek Revival movement expressed in public buildings. Its great scale, its superb and daring simplicity, and its originality all make it one of the most distinguished monuments of native American architecture. The plan is equally original, daringly unconventional, and in its main lines both efficient for its original purpose and aesthetically effective; but in the detailing of its large interiors, alas, the ideals of lesser men and the fashions of a later, more ostentatious, and more vulgar period held their inevitable sway. It should be judged chiefly on its scheme and its exterior; in the difference between this magnificent stone rectangle on the outside and the tawdry, over-heavy plaster work within lies sufficient evidence of the rapid decadence of public taste as displayed by West and Kelley in following the latest fashions of the fifties.

Michigan

Time and progress have wiped out almost every vestige of old Detroit except for remnants of the original and imaginative street layout of 1806. Only here and there in blighted areas a skeleton remains which shows in its decaying trim and its quiet proportions the justness of architectural taste a century ago. The Church of SS. Peter and Paul, designed by F. Letourno, still stands; its cornerstone is dated 29 June 1844. The architect's original watercolor perspective drawing is still extant. The building itself is monumental, and although only occasionally does it show Greek influences — as in its Ionic pilaster capitals — it is nevertheless original and, especially on the interior, effective in its rather naïve but lavish detail.

Yet Detroit up to the time of the Civil War was a town as distinguished in its buildings as in its original layout. It had a large quota of architects, and in 1836 at least it had an architectural school, run by Robert T. Elliott, who came to America in 1819 from Tipperary in Ireland, was a draftsman in Quebec till 1827, an architect and builder in Rochester from 1827 to 1834, and an architect and builder in Detroit till his death in 1841.[47] He was the architect of the beautiful First Presbyterian Church, remodeled later into a Roman Catholic church; but he was only one of a group of several others then in practice — Charles Lum, Elucius C. Anderson, Charles Jackson (1793–1869), Harry B. Lathrop, and Henry Leroy — who all called themselves architects in the 1837 Detroit city directory. The fact that these Michigan architects and builders had great confidence in their own abilities is well shown in a letter one of them wrote to a newspaper protesting against the employment of Town and Davis of New York as architects of the new University of Michigan buildings in 1838. It is interesting also that the letter is equally satirical on the proposed use of the Gothic style. The buildings were never built.[48]

[47] Detroit *News Tribune,* 30 May 1897.

[48] It is worth while to give the letter in full; it comes from a clipping in the Davis collection at the Avery Library, Columbia University:

'*Mr. Whitney.* — An article appeared in your paper a few days since, stating the necessity of giving encouragement to our own manufacturers and Mechanics. I am sorry such a useful lesson did not appear at an earlier day, for the benefit of the Mechanics of Michigan. It is hoped some of your readers will be able to explain the reason why there was not a general invitation given, by advertisement, to the Mechanics' of this State, for plans and elevations for the University, by offering prizes; for the best, $300, for second best, $150, for the third, $100, for the fourth, $50 — the amount already sent out of this State for the plans approved for said building. It is well known our own mechanics' have taste and abilities sufficient to plan and execute any edifice which the wants of Michigan require.

When will the Executive of New York degrade his Mechanics' by sending to Michigan for what his own citizens are capable of doing? Why did not the Lieut. Governor of this State give his own citizens a fair trial before he went out of the State for his plans &c.? I suppose it was because the Mechanics of Michigan do not assume that dignified name called *Architect!* or any of those *lofty* titles as Esq'rs &c. The elevation approved, is of the Gothic style of architecture, painted up to the eyes, *splendid* in appearance, but will be paltry in the execution,

The old courthouse (which served for a time as the Michigan state capitol), started in 1823 but not occupied until 1828, was from the designs of Obed Wait. It was a handsome building with a great Ionic portico along the front and an impressive three-stage steeple. Basically its façade was like that of a much enlarged five-bay house, and the elliptical fanlight and sidelights around the chief entrance give evidence of its early date and its conservative style. Typical of later, more sophisticated Greek Revival Detroit were a number of the churches, especially the Congregational-Unitarian Church of 1851 with its gracious Greek-inspired detail.

The early houses we know from illustrations [49] show the mixture of background traditions behind the early nineteenth-century Detroit settlers. Thus the Governor Woodbridge house, with its central section and its large later additions which much more than double its size, has interesting wings with stepped gable ends and a recessed porch between them enframing the entrance to the older portion. These wings in their breadth and detail are different in feeling from anything else in the United States; they seem to have something Canadian in them, something that reminds one of the early nineteenth-century work at Montreal or Kingston, Ontario. The John Palmer house (1829), on the other hand, is of that characteristic Berkshire–Connecticut–western New York–Western Reserve type already met with so frequently along the western highway. Its two-story main wing, with an exquisitely detailed cornice, and its low side wing would not have been out of character in a Connecticut town twenty years earlier.

on account of the limited means. I don't know what there is that is so very attractive about this Gothic elevation, without it is those towers of Babel between 200 and 300 feet high, and the two negroes in the attitude of skating in front of the plan.

Pray, why does Michigan want to imitate the fooleries and splendid extravagances of Europe? The whole of the funds appropriated will be expended before there will be conveniences for a single Professor. Why are those four mammoth windows necessary, and the large chapel which will require a fortune to provide fuel to keep it comfortably warm in winter.

Respectfully yours,
_____,

[49] Silas Farmer, *The History of Detroit and Michigan,* Part VII, Architectural (Detroit: S. Farmer & Co., 1884).

The same conservatism shows in the superb and monumental residence of Francis Palms, built in 1848. It is a formalized brick house with end chimneys, a central cupola, a parapet above the main cornice, five bays, and an Ionic porch in front of a door with leaded fan- and sidelights, which make it almost the identical image of such eastern houses as the Starbuck houses in Nantucket ten years earlier or some of the Salem houses thirty years before. It is probably the work of Henry Leroy, for the drawings of a house signed by him which are extant in the Detroit Public Library show elevations almost identical in scheme and character. But, despite this conservatism in the earlier houses, Detroit by the 1850's seems to have become entirely *au courant* with the general trends of fashion running over the country, and there were many excellent houses of the Bracketed or Italian-villa type with cast-iron porches and ample square proportions and low-pitched roofs, as seen in the Farmer illustrations. Yet even in this period occasional conservatism controls, as in the David Preston residence, built as late as 1860, which is still in the full flower of the Greek Revival and has two wings with Greek Ionic porches.

Outside of the larger cities the prosperous farms of the thirties and forties and fifties had houses of as many different types as are found in Ohio. The Michigan settlers came from many localities. Before 1812, arriving largely via the Great Lakes, they were in nationality both French and English. Between 1812 and 1830 there was a large influx from the southern states, coming up across Ohio and Indiana from the Ohio River. The thirties and forties saw the chief immigration from New England and New York, and especially from Vermont. Little definite French or Canadian influence is apparent in the country districts, for these were not thickly settled until a period later than the general yielding of the French and Canadian population to the newer immigrants from the United States.

But the influence of conservative New England or at least eastern types was obvious everywhere, and remained dominant in parts of Michigan long after it had given place to Greek Revival ways in other parts of the state. In Adrian, for instance, the Thomas

Howland house, as late as 1840, is a simple five-bay structure of pleasant proportions, Colonial in its shapes and conservative in every particular except perhaps in its molding profiles. Even the William Kimball house at Adrian, built five years later, has the same conservative look about it, although the five-bay type has here been increased to six.⁵⁰ The old Bird house, built as an inn by Reuben Bird in 1837 at Clayton, is of characteristic inn type, with a continuous porch in two stories across the front, such as can be found occasionally in New England but also in Pennsylvania, Ohio, and Tennessee. Another tavern of somewhat similar type though longer and with continuous two-story Greek anta-type piers supporting its porch is the Smith Tavern of 1840 at Clinton.

The four-column ' temple type' house with wings, found so often wherever the Greek Revival was dominant but especially in western New York and Ohio, also has Michigan examples. Typical are the Smith house (1840) at Grass Lake and the Nicholas Smith house at Clarkston built as late as 1852. The Rudolphus Nims house (1836) at Monroe is an even more highly developed example with much more accurately Greek detail. Its columns are Doric, its scale is large, and its roof is hipped. Its unusually advanced character may result from the fact that Nims came from Deerfield, Massachusetts. A most interesting variation, much more akin to the big houses of Kentucky than is usual in Michigan, is Pomeroy Hall (1848) at Clinton, by Jira Paine. The main body of the house, which is impressive in size, is hip-roofed, and the temple-type pedimented porch — with Greek Ionic columns between antae so that the ends of the porch are solid — projects strongly. The L-shaped James Smith house at Monroe, as late as 1858, has a temple-type portico with square antae instead of columns at the end of one of its wings. The whole composition, with a porch on the end of the other wing and a projecting bay window, has an unusually architectonic quality.

⁵⁰ See a series of articles by Howell Taylor, ' Historic Houses of Southwest Michigan,' a Sunday feature of the Detroit *News* in 1931–2. I owe many of my examples and much of my information to this series. See also the Michigan section, Plates 83–96, in Howard Major's *The Domestic Architecture of the Early American Republic: The Greek Revival* (Philadelphia: J. B. Lippincott Co., 1926).

Yet the Michigan house builders seemed always to strive for new differentiations in the older types, and toward the creation of brand-new types of their own. Thus the old formula of a temple portico with side wings receives a completely new interpretation in the house built in 1846 by Captain Marcus Miles at St. Clair. Its symmetrical wings are long and wide so that they form almost the main basis of the house; they both have the recessed front porches that we have already come upon so frequently. The temple-type porch is reduced to one story in height and becomes, as it were, merely an appendage to the interesting main body of the house created by the wings; the ridge is continuous. Another unusual building is the Anderson house at Tecumseh, a one-story house with a low-pitched roof carrying a balustrade, a projecting four-column Greek Doric porch, and a tall slim cupola. Its detail would seem to indicate a date in the fifties.

One of the most imposing in scale of these Michigan country houses is Gordon Hall (the Dexter house) at Dexter, now being reconditioned under the direction of Professor Emil Lorch as a community center for the neighborhood. It is a great temple-type structure with a monumental six-column portico across the front, a through hall, and a great suite of double parlors on one side. The story heights are large, the trim dignified and rich. On either side of this central mass lower wings are attached, with one-story Doric porches at the front. These wings project beyond the rear of the main mass, forming a sort of protected court, and across the back of the central section is a one-story colonnade to form a warm and sunny family piazza commanding a beautiful view over the rolling acres of the farm. The whole plan has been carefully worked out from the point of view both of the use of the rooms and of protection from cold winds, yet formed into basically simple and impressive shapes.

Another variation of the temple type with wings led to the development of a characteristic Michigan type found, I believe, nowhere else — one which I shall call for want of a better expression the ' basilica ' type. In this the depth of the wings in relation to their width is much increased, and the roofs — either hipped or forming half gables at the junction of the main portion of the house — have the same slope as the main roof, frequently rising to a point just under the main cornice. This gives the houses a severely formal, symmetrical elevation and produces a general mass composition like that of the nave and side aisles of an Early Christian or Renaissance basilica. The evolution of this type from the temple house with side wings can easily be seen in the state. Thus the Pike house, Fulton Street, Grand Rapids, in front elevation appears like the double-wing temple type of New York, but the unusual depth of the house makes its geometric mass quite different. The James McAllister house (1839) at Tecumseh omits the porch from the side wings and recesses the main entrance porch deeply behind the plane of the front. The wings have become higher in relation to the central portion, so that the roof sweeps down in an almost unbroken slope from the ridge to the outer edge of the wings. The result accents the length of the house at right angles to its front, and the analogy of the basilica becomes obvious. The Erastus Beebe house (1838) in Richmond narrows the wings still further and emphasizes the central ' nave ' portion. The porch is recessed as in the McAllister house but was originally two stories high. In the Matthews house near Clinton the porch front is of square anta piers set *in antis*, the second-floor porch supported behind them near their mid-point. Here the mass composition of a church is even more strongly suggested by the addition of what is almost a transept wing at the rear. The full development of the type is to be seen in the Dr. Mason house at Dundee, where the side wings instead of having hipped roofs have full half gables rising to the central two-story portion, which has a recessed two-story porch like that of the Matthews house. Another still simpler interpretation is seen in the Louis Hall house at Osborne, where the columnar porch has entirely disappeared, an impressive front door with a cornice being the only decoration of the front. Farmhouses of this general basilica type are common around Ann Arbor and in the flat country north of Detroit; they are scarcely found anywhere outside of the state. This is but one of the many local types developed in the country within the general Classic Revival movement.

Naturally some of the Michigan towns had work more sophisticated, more perhaps directly under the influence of eastern ways and eastern books. Ann Arbor is characteristic. Its charm is like the charm of many towns in the Western Reserve of Ohio or in western New York or New England — the beauty of elm-lined streets, of white houses fairly close to the sidewalk, of great trees planted as an essential part of the town picture, of detail sometimes of Late Colonial, sometimes of exquisite Greek type. Occasionally also there are exceptional houses that fall into no definite class, like the beautiful R. H. Kempf house, a one-story temple-type house in which anta piers replace columns in the porch, and the architrave of the order is broken in level to allow unusually large grilled frieze windows. Interesting too is the lovely Frost house, of great simplicity, a white two-story structure with its pediment end toward the street and its only decoration the beautifully detailed cornice, the semicircular window in the pediment, and a recessed one-story porch with four Ionic columns. This house has now been removed to Greenfield, the Ford village at Dearborn.

Other Michigan towns and villages, though smaller, had an almost equally gracious dignity. The town layouts were generally rectangular, with a village green or courthouse square, and the high quality of the conscious civic design which these Michigan settlers had is well attested by the universality of street tree planting and the general beauty of the houses and business buildings. Characteristic of this civic beauty as well as of the extraordinary rapidity with which it was achieved is the town of Marshall, where a wide 'Main Street' (a full hundred feet from building line to building line) leads to a circular green on which the courthouse originally stood, its simple Doric portico furnishing a climax to the wide street. The settlement of Marshall began only in 1831; in ten years its main street was lined with dignified business buildings of brick, stone, and frame. There was a charming tavern,

Ohio public buildings: ABOVE, State Capitol, Columbus. Henry Walters and others, architects. (*Howells, Metropolitan Mus. of Art.*) BELOW, Post Office, Cincinnati. (*Old engraving, Cist.*)

The Greek Revival in Michigan: TOP, Gordon Hall (Dexter House), Dexter. (*Lorch.*) CENTER, one-story house, Marshall. (*Author.*) BOTTOM, Kempf House, Ann Arbor. (*Lorch.*)

Michigan house types: ABOVE, LEFT, Dr. Mason House, Dundee. ABOVE, RIGHT, McAllister House, Tecumseh. (*Both, Major.*) BELOW, LEFT, Harold C. Brooks House, Marshall. BELOW, RIGHT, Stone Hall (Lewis Brooks House), Marshall. (*Both, author.*)

Stone farmhouse of Caleb Chapel, near Parma, Mich. (*Author.*) ABOVE, front view. BELOW, LEFT, detail of entrance. BELOW, RIGHT, parlor door.

with an upper-floor balcony with five Doric columns and an airy and lavish ballroom within. There was a large hotel, the Marshall House, L-shaped, with a curved recessed portico at the corner embellished by Ionic columns *in antis* running the entire height of the building. There were some churches of considerable pretension, including the old First Presbyterian Church, with an interesting and original tower.

There were numerous houses of one and two stories, with handsome interior trim and sometimes with full pedimented porticoes. Typical are the two neighboring houses, Stone Hall, the Lewis Brooks house (1840), and the Jabez Fitch–Harold C. Brooks house (1842). In each case a monumental two-story colonnade of five columns forms a porch outside of the double parlor at the end of the house, while the main entrance is through a smaller colonnaded porch at the side. A charming example of the smaller house may be seen in the one-story house on Mansion Street, with a delicate four-column Greek Doric portico and a handsome entrance.[51]

Marshall is not unique. The same swift building of beautiful communities went on all over the state; in Grand Rapids, in Saginaw, in Port Huron, in Albion, house after house along the old tree-lined streets reveals the ideals of these Michigan builders. The style lasted long in country Michigan, although in the older communities the fashionable Gothic work of the East began to make its impress in the forties. The stone ashlar Caleb Chapel house at Parma, by an inscription over the door, is dated as of 1850, but it still retains the Greek Revival ideal in all its purity, from the Greek Doric columns of the side porches to the handsome interior trim of its front parlor. Here the builder has been conscious of the

---

51 I am much indebted for information with regard to Michigan to Professor Emil Lorch of the University of Michigan, Ann Arbor, and to Mr. Harold C. Brooks of Marshall. Both opened to me gladly their rich files of illustrative material, their rich knowledge of local buildings and local history. Professor Lorch, through his work with the Historic American Buildings Survey and his constant interest in early Michigan architecture, has done a great work in preserving records of Michigan's architectural heritage. Mr. Brooks not only has become the unofficial historian of Marshall, but has also been instrumental in preserving and reconditioning a large number of Greek Revival monuments. The work of both men in their respective fields might well serve as an example for others to follow in their own localities.

Greek sources of his culture to an unusual degree, and expressed them in an unusual manner. In the pediment, instead of the usual attic window, is a rectangular stone panel carved in low relief with a vivid, if crude, floating and draped female figure surrounded by curling acanthus leaves and, in incised lettering, labeled DIANA. It is said to have been carved, along with the inscription over the door, by a convict from the state prison near by. Naïve though the panel is, it has verve, composition, and remarkable decorative value. Somehow this carved Greek goddess in the pediment of a house several miles from any town, in the broad fields of Michigan, seems perhaps the most eloquent possible statement of the ideals of the settlers of the old Northwest Territory.[52]

Indiana

South of Michigan, in Indiana, there is the same story of varied influences, of combined conservatism and experimentalism. Vincennes was one of the earliest settled towns of the Middle West. Its most impressive early structure, the Governor Harrison house, Grouseland (1801–4), is a large-scaled, simple development of the typical five-bay Late Colonial house, quiet in detail and excellent in proportions. Its plan is said to be similar to the plan of Berkeley on the James River in Virginia, Harrison's birthplace, and its high hipped roof has something of the grandeur of those of the Virginia aristocracy. Its mantels were imported from London, and glass for its windows came from Boston. Thus early did the architectural amenity of the East make its appearance on the frontier.[53]

But very shortly afterward the desire to build in new ways found expression, and in White Hall, built for Isaac White in 1811, a few miles away, there is one of the most interesting of the large one-story houses of the early West. The body of the house is built of brick, with two wings surrounding a court to the rear; a continuous porch supported on slim columns forms a cloister

---

52 This house was called to my attention by Mr. Milton Horn, resident sculptor and professor of fine arts at Olivet College, Olivet, Michigan.

53 Lewis Barrington, *Historic Restorations of the Daughters of the American Revolution* (New York: Richard R. Smith, 1941).

round the court and runs around two of the exterior sides. The roof is hipped, the dimensions of the whole are large, and the effect is as different from the usual houses of its time as may be imagined, in spite of the fact that all of its detail is quite conventional and certain elements reflect the amplitude and grandeur of the earlier southern mansions.

At Harmony, George Rapp and the Rappites established themselves at an early date and built there large communal dwellings and halls in which the great roofs of medieval Germany were distantly reflected. When Owen purchased the colony and changed its name to New Harmony, in 1824, he made good use of the old Rappite buildings; little new construction was carried on until after Owen's ill-fated colony had split up. Yet the effect of this unconventional, idealistic experiment remained, as did many of the original Owen settlers. The quiet and simple William Maclure house (1844), with its colonnaded piazza, is typical of the unostentatious amenity these people sought. Indiana's first state capitol at Corydon, built by Dennis Pennington in 1816, also shows the quiet good proportion and the excellent use of materials that characterize many of the early buildings. Its forthright squareness and its beautiful stonework give it distinction still.

Just as in the case of Ohio and Michigan, however, it was the period when the Greek Revival was at its height that brought the largest amount of building in the state and rapidly made Indianapolis, cut out of the forest in 1820, a town of considerable architectural importance. It is characteristic that only eleven years later, when a capitol was to be built, a nation-wide competition for its design was held, in which men as distinguished as Robert Mills and William Strickland took part. Town and Davis won the competition as they had won so many others, though their winning design — one of the many attempts to combine a central dome with a Greek temple-type building beneath it — was not among their happiest creations. It was nevertheless a building (1832–5) much admired at its time and certainly a much more beautiful structure than the present capitol, which succeeded it some fifty years later — a capitol that is perhaps the most awkward, the most fantastically vulgar in its details as in its mass, of any of the typical state capitols with a central rotunda and wings.

Indiana too had a large number of quiet yet impressive Greek Revival courthouses, chiefly built between 1840 and 1850. Some of their architects' names are known.[54] John Elder, for example, who came to Indianapolis from Harrisburg in 1833 and worked as an architect there until he left for the California gold fields in 1850, was the architect of the courthouses at Frankfort (1836–9), Columbus, Rushville (1846–8), and Connersville. One of the most beautiful of these Indiana courthouses is that at Paoli (1847–50), with a six-column Doric portico containing an unusual flight of outside stairs leading up to the great doors of the upper-floor courtroom. The ironwork of railings, balcony, and stairs is especially interesting. Other early architects who worked in Indiana include George Kyle, the architect of many houses in Vevay as well as of the Laurenceburg courthouse. Matthew Temperly designed many of the lovely houses of Madison; in fact Madison seems to have been at this time rather a center of architectural sophistication, and other architect-builders of skill worked there, such as Edwin J. Peck and the firm of Cochran and Pattie, the architects of Classic Hall (1853) at Hanover College, where the basic mass of the building is simple, almost Colonial, but the detail is definitely influenced by Greek inspiration.

The most skillful of these architects was Francis Costigan,[55] who had been trained in Baltimore and was listed there as a carpenter in 1835. Soon after that he came to Indiana. The sophisticated and beautiful Lanier house (1844) in Madison is by him, although perhaps he is best known as the architect for the Institute for the Blind (1851) at Indianapolis. The original plans for this building had been made by John Elder, but they were later altered and improved by Costigan. The building is large, impressive in scale, and simple in scheme; its detail of rather heavy Greek type has scarcely a trace of the Italianate qualities that were creeping

---

[54] Lee Burns, *Early Architects and Builders of Indiana* (Indianapolis: Indiana Historical Society, 1935), reprinted from Indiana Historical Society Publications, Vol. xi, No. 3.

[55] See page 248.

into so much contemporary work. The Madison houses, in their beautiful blend of brick wall and white Greek trim with rich cast-iron railings, have a quality all their own. Madison again is an example of local types, Greek Revival in inspiration, developing naturally in the newer parts of the country. Undoubtedly the wide use of iron railings was influenced by the existence there of the Neal Foundries, one of the most famous ironworks of the early West.

Outside the cities the farms followed the earlier types more closely; in these the confusion of influences is obvious — the influence of men from Switzerland at Vevay, of large numbers of English people near Laurenceburg, and of settlers from New England or the South in other parts of the state. The Ewbank house (1829), for instance, not far from Laurenceburg, seems hardly American. Its stone walls, small windows, and roof slopes are none of them Colonial or northern or southern or eastern in type; they are pure Yorkshire, for Ewbank himself came from Yorkshire and almost all the settlers in his immediate neighborhood who helped him build the house were from the same English county.

In churches there is more uniformity, for church culture has always tended toward sectarian rather than local stylisms. The Second Presbyterian Church (1835) at Madison, by Edwin J. Peck, is a characteristic example, as is the Madison Episcopal Church (1850) designed by W. Russell West, whom we have already seen as one of the architects of the Ohio state capitol. Perhaps the most typical of Indiana churches is St. Francis Xavier Cathedral (1825–40) at Vincennes, a strange mixture of the Wren-Gibbs type with Classic Revival trimmings and Gothic overtones. It is said to have been based upon the cathedral at Bardstown, Kentucky, but it was simplified by omitting the portico. It has a deep half-domed chancel (the roof of which follows the curves of the dome beneath), a tower quite different from that at Bardstown (larger and bolder in scale), and along its flanks offset buttresses of almost Gothic type. It is interesting to discover as early as this a local provincial feeling that somehow Gothic forms and church buildings belonged together.

Illinois

Still farther to the west, Illinois was a settled and civilized area soon after Indiana, and at Cairo the newer influences of the American settlers from the East met and merged with the older traditional French Mississippi River culture and with the sophistication of New Orleans. At Shawneetown there is still pointed out the oldest building in Illinois (a cottage erected in 1812), but less than thirty years later (in 1836) the Shawneetown Bank had a handsome bank building of cut stone — a Greek Doric temple which had, with customary American unconventionality, but five columns across the front so that one of them came under the center of the pediment; yet the effect is excellent.[56]

The earlier domestic work follows largely types developed in the East, like the beautiful Davenport house at Rock Island, built in 1833 by Colonel George Davenport; its original one-story wings have disappeared, but the central part has recently been restored. It was a typical five-bay house in two stories, with one-story wings and a four-column Greek Doric porch, and had much of that breadth and sense of wide and ample spaces which characterized a great deal of the contemporary work of Kentucky and Tennessee. Similarly the Hobson house at Napierville, built sometime after 1835, is a large farmhouse — a central block with rambling wings — which in proportion and roof slope and in the excellence of its details, its cornices and stair balusters and mantels, would be quite at home on a Connecticut roadside. There are interesting reminiscences of eastern detail even from a later date, as for instance in Dr. Hall's office at Toulon, built in 1848 by the doctor and his sons, where the detail — extraordinarily rich — is composed of a strange farago of units taken from a memory stored alike with Late Colonial quaintnesses and classic elements gathered from books. It has charm of a kind because of the peculiarly wooden character of the wood detail, and it reveals the desire to build richly and imaginatively which is significant of the whole

[56] Federal Writers' Project, Works Progress Administration, *Illinois: A Descriptive and Historical Guide,* in the American Guide Series (Chicago: A. C. McClurg, 1939).

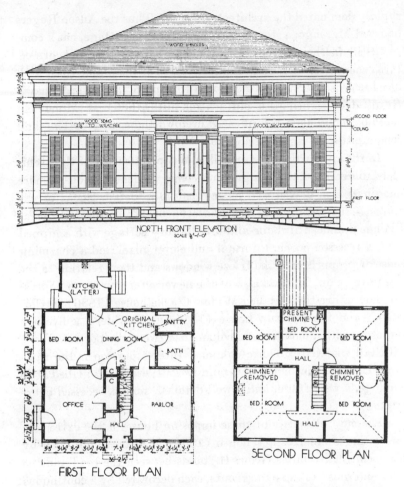

North Front Elevation
SCALE ⅜'=1'-0'

KITCHEN (LATER)

ORIGINAL KITCHEN   PANTRY

BED ROOM   DINING ROOM   BATH

OFFICE   PARLOR

HALL

FIRST FLOOR PLAN

PRESENT CHIMNEY

BED ROOM

BED ROOM   BED ROOM

HALL

CHIMNEY REMOVED   CHIMNEY REMOVED

BED ROOM   BED ROOM

HALL

SECOND FLOOR PLAN

FIGURE 35. DENNISON GREEN HOUSE, Plainfield, Ill. (*H.A.B.S.*) Interesting provincial variation of the story-and-a-half house; formality without ostentation.

cultural attitude of most of the settlers who came to these new western towns.[57]

Naturally in Illinois also the Greek element came in early and

[57] Drawings of it are published in *Historic American Buildings Survey, Comprising Fifty Plates of Drawings of Pioneer Architecture,* edited by Earl H. Reed, District Officer, Northern Illinois (Chicago [n. d.]). Two other similar collections of fifty plates each were published, all with the same title. To these collections I owe most of the examples of Illinois architecture cited.

rapidly dominated the architectural scene. Thus the Anson Rogers house at Marengo, a story-and-a-half, five-bay cottage, has a complete Greek Doric portico with a false parapet above the cornice. It is remarkably like many of the cottages of the Maine coast and, like them, probably owes its origin to a plate in Edward Shaw's *Rural Architecture.* An old schoolhouse (1839) at Mundelein could be found almost duplicated in any number of New England communities.

In the 1840's the greater skill and sophistication of the architect-builders and the designers becomes evident in houses more imaginative in design and more creative in detail. Such for example is the Dennison Green house (probably of the 1840's) at Plainfield, a beautiful one-and-a-half-story cottage with a hipped roof, a recessed porch, a formal and clever plan, and a charming sense of proportion in the frieze windows and their relation to the openings below. Typical also of the newer effort for more impressive houses are the so-called Widow Clarke house (1836) in Chicago [58] and the Hildrup house (1855) at Belvidere, a five-bay structure with a monumental colonnaded two-story porch in front with tall slim Greek Doric columns. Interesting too is the rambling Horace Paine house at Grand Detour, which has grilled attic windows, a wide frieze, and a well-detailed, simple, recessed doorway.

The most elaborate of these imposing houses is the extremely interesting John Hossack house (1854) at Ottawa, designed by the architect Sylvanus Grow. It stands between the road and the river and thus has two main fronts, each decorated by a continuous porch across the whole length of the main house block. The porch on the river front is arcaded, with the arches supported on high square piers great in scale as though to count from a distance. On the other front the porch is in two floors with superposed columns and the most interesting upper-story railing. With this central block two one-story symmetrical wings are combined, each with its own side porch and end porch, so that the plan is one of great

[58] Thomas E. Talmadge, *Architecture in Old Chicago* (Chicago: University of Chicago Press, 1941).

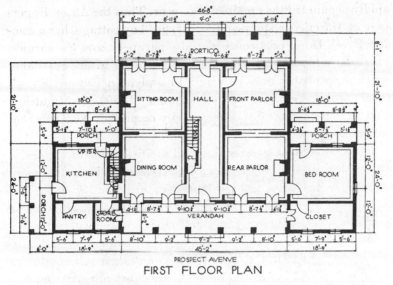

FIRST FLOOR PLAN

FIGURE 36. JOHN HOSSACK HOUSE, Ottawa, Ill. (*H.A.B.S.*) Normal four-room-and-hall Colonial plan, with added wings and porches forming a varied and monumental whole.

formality as well as complexity and the whole has a richness of mass composition — a command of the larger compositional elements — that is for the time and place remarkable.

In Illinois as well are various examples of the L- or T-shaped house with a recessed porch in the side wing, a type already noted as common in Michigan and Ohio. Such for instance is the Newton farmhouse (1850) near Belvidere. A more impressive version with a three-column porch across the main front is the Dunton house (1850) in the same town.

The special local variation in Illinois, however, is the development of stone and brick houses quite different in character from those found elsewhere. For example, the handsome stone Keating house at Fayville, although it has a wide entrance with fan- and sidelights of normal character, displays nevertheless in the treatment of its end walls and large end chimneys a tendency toward simplification through the use of stepped rectangular forms to hide the slope in the roof; this seems to have become later a char-

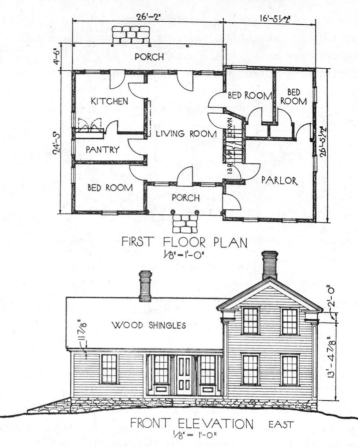

FIRST FLOOR PLAN
⅛" = 1'-0"

FRONT ELEVATION EAST
⅛" = 1'-0"

FIGURE 37. NEWTON FARMHOUSE, near Belvidere, Ill. (*H.A.B.S.*) An Illinois variation of the T-shaped house with recessed porch.

acteristic Indiana form. In the Knowles house at Oquawka, for instance, the end walls of the wings are carried up with crow-step gables. The plan itself is unusual, with three main rooms to the floor, each room occupying the end of a wing; a porch with four square posts leads to the little hall through which all three of the rooms are entered.

At Nauvoo, where the Mormons lived for some time and had hoped to remain permanently before they were driven out in the tragic riots that immediately followed the death of Joseph Smith, there are several buildings of this general type, and the whole town with its rather high, narrow brick houses has a quality almost Dutch. The Brigham Young house (1840) with its stepped gables and its interesting general composition is especially Continental in effect. How much of this character depends upon the influence of the Mormons themselves I do not know; certainly the Mormon taste in architecture had changed violently in the few years since they had left Kirtland in Ohio, for the great Mormon Temple at Nauvoo, long since destroyed, was as different as possible from the almost effeminate richness of the Kirtland temple. It was tremendous in scale, and its great walls with their crude pilasters had about them something stark, arrogant, and impressive though totally destitute of the charm the Kirtland building possessed.

The Mormons were not the only cult that left an architectural impress on Illinois, for at Bishop Hill a Swedish communist colony was founded by Eric Janson in 1846. Many of its buildings still stand to show the architectural amenity and formal grandeur for which the colony was striving. The houses were mainly group buildings of apartment-house type. For public buildings there were a post office, a church, the colony store building, and the Steeple Building or central administration structure. The colony store has a ground floor with glass doors between four brick piers on its façade. The brick piers continue up through the upper floor above the cornice that crowns the shop windows and doors, and between them are three large rectangular windows. A gable of pediment slope tops the whole. It is all very simple and direct, with detail of no special beauty, yet everything seems somehow to work. The Steeple Building (1854) is a much larger structure, three stories high and seven bays long, with a rusticated basement, a flat roof, and a crowning balustrade. The three central bays are emphasized on the front by a recessed porch of square piers carrying a pediment, and the whole is topped by a two-stage tower — the lower stage wide and squat, square in plan; the upper tall and octagonal, with a cyma-curved roof. Here again the detail is crude enough but the general proportions are excellent. The building has

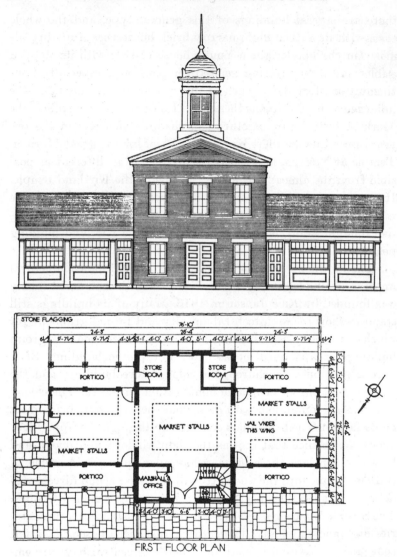

FIRST FLOOR PLAN

FIGURE 38. OLD MARKET HOUSE, Galena, Ill. Elevation and plan (*H.A.B.S.*)
The quiet dignity characteristic of many Greek Revival public buildings.

that true impressiveness which good proportion and adequate size always produce, and one feels in all of the Bishop Hill work an effort on the part of the communist colony to show both its own members and its visitors that architectural beauty must be part of the good life.[59]

Illinois is also distinguished by a large number of excellent public buildings. The old Market House (1845) at Galena is characteristic of the impressiveness the people of these communities liked to give to their necessary structures. It was designed by Henry J. Stouffer and built of red brick with stone lintels and wood trim and cornices. The central portion is two stories high, with the town council chamber on the second floor and offices below. The wings hold the large market halls, with colonnaded porches on both sides and a wide pedimented roof. The total effect is extremely interesting in its contrasts of color and of form, and even the cupola that crowns it has a definite individuality in the handling of the pedimentlike parapets with corner acroteria and a square dome above them.

There are many examples also of the typical courthouse of the Middle West, with its colonnaded porch and its cupola. One of the best is at Knoxville, with four Greek Doric columns and the simplest of well-designed octagonal cupolas. The building stands in a central square in which there is an interesting arrangement of parts, so that the whole forms a town center of charm and originality. The architect was John Mandeville. Another excellent example is the courthouse at Oquawka, similar in its general composition though with a taller, more commonplace cupola.

But the most famous of the Illinois public buildings is the state capitol at Springfield, another of the many capitols designed by Town and Davis. It still stands as the Sangamon County court-

---

[59] The whole problem of the architecture of communist and utopian colonies in the United States is one that deserves serious study. The Shakers, the Rappites, the Illinois Jansonists, the Amana communities of Iowa, and the Oneida Community in New York all produced characteristic structures different in some ways from those of their neighbors. The aims they were seeking to fulfill and the means they adopted to produce their results are both questions of more than superficial importance for the student of architecture as well as of the history of American life.

house, although in 1899 the whole building was raised and an entirely new floor inserted beneath it, not to its aesthetic improvement. It was begun in 1837 (with additions in 1866–7) and, like the capitol of Indiana, was one of the many attempts to combine a Doric colonnaded building with a dome. It is, however, a much more successful attempt than is the Indiana building; the greater height and size given to the dome as well as the general sense of more careful study in every respect make it one of the distinguished Town and Davis buildings.[60]

The Far West

Even the Mississippi was no effective barrier to the westward migration of people or to the classic traditions of building they brought with them. In Iowa the state capitol already mentioned [61] bears witness to the power of the Greek Revival tradition thus far from its origins in the East; all through the agricultural plains, which were filling up little by little, men were building farmhouses that as far as the materials and the crude workmanship available permitted were like the quiet, classic farmhouses of Ohio or even of the eastern seaboard. Even when log structures were built, they were often later covered with clapboards and, with added dormers and porches of classic form, had a remarkably finished and settled appearance. Such, for instance, is the Antoine Le Claire house (1833) at Davenport, which, when the railroad came to town, served as the first railroad station.[62] Other interesting Greek Revival buildings include the county jail and city hall of Dubuque, designed by J. F. Rague.

And at times the building was ambitious — of stone or brick. Thus the Jean Baptiste Faribault house at Mendota, Minnesota, built sometime soon after 1826, is a pleasant, unassuming, five-

---

[60] The Illinois Guide of the Federal Writers' Project credits the Illinois capitol to John Francis Rague, the architect of the Iowa capitol. Rague may have acted as superintendent, but Town and Davis were undoubtedly the designing architects.

[61] Page 255.

[62] Federal Writers' Project, Works Progress Administration, *Iowa, A Guide to the Hawkeye State,* in the American Guide Series (New York: Viking Press, 1938).

bay, two-story house of stone with a boldly projecting cornice; the Sibley house (1835), also at Mendota,[63] built as a fur-trading post, is a stone building of some pretensions, with a projecting porch complete with classic cornice. Meanwhile the permanent army posts of the United States scattered widely over the area were, wherever possible, formally planned, with whitewashed buildings of excellent proportion, good examples of a much simplified development of a type perhaps originally set by Latrobe in his work in the navy yards and the Pittsburgh Arsenal. These too spread abroad the influence of the basic American classic tradition.

Mission buildings also had their effect. Characteristic is the Shawnee Methodist Mission [64] of Kansas City, Kansas, completed in 1841, a long gabled brick building of eight bays, the execution of which is as sure and well handled as though the building had stood five hundred miles to the east, its simple white trim and projecting hoods over the doors giving it an unusual sense of architectonic maturity; although it is almost Shaker-like in its simplicity, its effect is beautiful, almost impressive. The territorial legislature held its meetings there in 1854.

As time went on and the towns became more settled and permanent, the culture more deeply felt, larger houses of greater sophistication followed. In many of them the older classical and Greek Revival traditions controlled all through the fifties and into and beyond the Civil War years. Many of the older farm buildings of Wisconsin are examples; in Stillwater and the towns along the St. Croix Valley there are many houses of developed late Greek Revival type, sometimes of considerable size and richness, though with a certain coarsening of the detail and a certain admixture of ' Victorian ' idioms which show them to have been built in the late fifties or the sixties. Even in the wilder frontier towns that rose here and there through the sixties and seventies the old classic tradition was not without its power, and the naïve false-front buildings that lined their streets — nostalgic efforts to create an urban impression in these broad and lonely spaces — usually had classic

63 Lewis Barrington, op. cit.
64 Ibid.

cornices at the top and windows spaced with somewhat the same rhythms as in eastern buildings of forty years before.

Straight to the salt water of the Pacific this development proceeded; along the northwest roads to Puget Sound — in the little towns of Oregon and Washington — the earliest buildings beyond mere log shelters, and especially government buildings (post offices, courthouses, and the like), were usually frame buildings with classic and frequently Greek Revival details in cornice and trim and molding.[65]

Even the earliest large houses were often not without architectural claims. The most impressive was the John McLoughlin mansion (1846) in Oregon City, Oregon, a great five-bay frame house of imposing size, with a hipped roof, large end chimneys topped with pointed-arched chimney caps in the Portsmouth manner, and a bold and well-detailed cornice. The windows are tremendous in scale — four panes wide and seven high — and the whole building in its beauty of proportion and the excellence of its detail is a remarkable example of the desire of at least some of these 'wild frontiersmen' to erect for themselves buildings of decency and architectural integrity. It is said that the windows and doors were brought out by ship from New England, just as a little later ships were to bring to the newly booming San Francisco large numbers of building units completely made and ready to be set in place. It is possible that the cornice and the other trim for the McLoughlin house were also made in the East.

Farther north still and far to the west the American settlers came into contact with another classic tradition from halfway round the world; when Alaska was purchased from Russia, her

---

[65] Thus a view of Portland (1858), published by Kuchel and Dressel in San Francisco as one of their 'Pacific Views,' has a border showing pictures of all the chief buildings of the town. These are remarkably sophisticated in character and predominantly classic in style, with many Greek Revival features; but even the Gothic makes its appearance in a charming little Gothic cottage. The same is true, though to a lesser degree, of Nevada City (1861), as shown in a lithograph by C. C. Kuchel, also published in San Francisco. Here the rather pathetic 'false fronts' all have simple classic details and in many of the buildings the traditional pediment roof slope is preserved. Both of these views are reproduced in I. N. Phelps Stokes and David C. Haskell's *American Historical Prints, Early Views of American Cities* . . . (New York: New York Public Library, 1932), Plates 96b and 98b.

Indiana and Illinois houses. (*H.A.B.S.*) ABOVE, LEFT, Harrison House, Vincennes, Ind. ABOVE, RIGHT, Shrewsbury House, Madison, Ind. BELOW, LEFT, Knowles House, Oquawka, Ill. BELOW, RIGHT, Anson Rogers House, Marengo, Ill.

Illinois public buildings. (*Old photographs*, *H.A.B.S.*) ABOVE, Steeple Building, Jansonist Community Center, Bishop Hill. BELOW, Old State Capitol, Springfield. Town and Davis, architects.

Classic buildings beyond the Mississippi: ABOVE, LEFT, Shawnee Mission Building, Kansas City, Kans. (*Barrington and National Geographic Magazine.*) ABOVE, RIGHT, Sibley House, Mendota, Minn. (*Barrington and D.A.R.*) BELOW, LEFT, Wolf Creek Tavern, Wolf Creek, Ore. (*H.A.B.S.*) BELOW, RIGHT, McLoughlin House, Oregon City, Ore. (*Barrington and D.A.R.*)

The Classic Revival in California: ABOVE, United States Mint, San Francisco. (*Moulin.*) BELOW, LEFT, Montgomery Block, San Francisco. (*No. California Art Project.*) BELOW, RIGHT, Old California Capitol, Benicia. (*McCullagh.*)

new masters found and made use of buildings erected by the Russians at Sitka and Nome about 1840 — buildings with colonnades and cornices, with cupolas and trim, which were the wooden provincial expression of the classic mania that had created the magnificence of St. Petersburg.

Of course the settlers who flocked to California after the discovery of gold in 1849 brought with them an eastern taste largely nurtured on Greek Revival forms. Many of the first San Francisco houses — which were shipped, knocked down, from the East — were classic if not Greek in their trim details. Some of the more ambitious business buildings of San Francisco followed the same fashions, as for instance the Montgomery Block (1853) designed by G. P. Cummings, which, although its upper detail is in an excellent restrained Italianate manner, has for its street-level piers the same simple rectangular stone piers which were common in the Greek Revival warehouses of the East. It is noteworthy also that when California built its first state capitol (1853),[66] at Benicia, it built a pure Greek Revival design with a Greek Doric colonnade *in antis* and a pediment gable. To be sure, the entablature and the pediment were of wood and slightly naïve in detail, but the mass of the whole was dignified and monumental and the intention manifestly Greek.

It was in San Francisco that the Greek Revival tradition received its westernmost formalized expression, especially in the old customs house and the Appraisers' Stores built in 1854–6. Of almost identical designs, these two buildings are composed with the monumental simplicity of the Greek Revival tradition, with pedimented central pavilions and a strong basement. Yet surprisingly enough, far away as they were, they show something of the new taste that was current in the East, for the order of the pilasters and the entablature is that of the Roman Doric, not the Greek, although in composition and general aspect they seem to belong to the earlier period. Whether or not they were designed by Ammi B. Young, like other Federal buildings of the time, is a question; certainly they do not resemble his usual work. But it is equally

[66] Now a city hall, library, and museum.

clear that their designer, whoever he was, was a man thoroughly versed in at least the obvious qualities of classical detail and familiar with the rather grand simplicity of the best Greek Revival public buildings.

The same quality is evident in the San Francisco Mint, not built till 1869–74, a beautiful stone structure with simple windows like those Mills had used forty years earlier, and with a great projecting pedimented portico with Roman Doric columns. What kept this building true to the ancient classic tradition, when elsewhere in the country A. B. Mullett, the Supervising Architect of the Treasury Department, was filling the country with his heavy Renaissance piles of superposed orders, is difficult to imagine; but there it stands today, a monument to the fact that the American settlers of these new lands brought with them and sometimes preserved that basic tradition of strong, simple composition, large scale, and decorations based on classic sources — a tradition that took its characteristic American form under the influence of the Greek Revival. In its way the San Francisco Mint shares with the Ridgway Branch of the Philadelphia Public Library the honor of being one of the last two buildings of the Greek Revival, which thus found its last lingering expressions on the shores of the two oceans to the east and the west — a tradition that had done so much to form the growing architectural profession and the whole system of architectural standards of the entire continent between.

CHAPTER 12

WHY THE GREEK REVIVAL SUCCEEDED, AND WHY IT FAILED

I. WHY THE GREEK REVIVAL FLOURISHED

THE more one studies the architecture of the United States between 1820 and 1850 (in some places up until the Civil War) and the more one wonders at its unity, its harmony, the quiet loveliness of so many towns, the restful serenity of so many houses and churches, the dignified impressiveness of so many public buildings — capitols, city halls, courthouses — the more one is led back to the reasons behind this achievement, to the life that gave it birth. Why did the Greek Revival have such a quick and universal flowering? The answer to this question must be sought on two planes, different but related: in the general culture of the period, its ideals and its character; and in the economic state of the country.

The *Memoirs* of Margaret Fuller Ossoli [1] begin with an autobiographical chapter, written in 1840, describing her youth. Her education, as she described it, began with Common Sense. Then,

in accordance with this discipline . . . was the influence of the great Romans, whose thoughts and lives were my daily food during those plastic years. . . Architecture was the art in which Rome excelled, and this corresponds with the feeling these men of Rome excite. They did not grow, — they built themselves up, or were built up by the fate of Rome, as a temple for Jupiter Stator. . .

We are never better understood than when we speak of a 'Roman virtue,' a 'Roman outline.' There is somewhat indefinite, somewhat yet unfulfilled in the thought of Greece, of Spain, of modern Italy; but Rome! it stands by itself, a clear Word. . .

[1] Boston: Phillips, Sampson and Company, 1852.

And this knowledge of Rome, this foundation in the strict human-
ism of the classic ideal, came to her from her own voracious reading
of Latin when hardly more than a baby. She says:

I was taught Latin and English grammar at the same time, and began
to read Latin at six years old, after which, for some years, I read
it daily.

Yet her interest in the classics was not to stop with the severe
grandeur of this Roman ideal; for with Margaret Fuller, as with
all those concerned in the great artistic movements of the time, the
Roman served but as a stepping stone to the Greek.

Ovid [she writes] gave me not Rome, nor himself, but a view into
the enchanted gardens of the Greek mythology. This path I followed,
I have been following ever since; and now, life half over [she was
just thirty years old when she wrote], it seems to me, as in my childhood, that every thought of which man is susceptible, is intimated
there. In those young years, indeed [when she was scarcely in her
teens], I did not see what I now see, but loved to creep from amid
the Roman pikes to lie beneath this great vine, and see the smiling
and serene shapes go by, woven from the finest fibres of all the elements. I knew not why, at that time, — but I loved to get away from
the hum of the forum, and the mailed clang of Roman speech, to these
shifting shows of nature, these Gods and Nymphs born of the sun-
beam, the wave, and the shadows on the hill. . .
    With these books I passed my days. . .

And she was not yet fifteen when to the Latin and the Greek mythology she added Shakespeare, Byron, Ariosto, and Molière. At
fifteen she writes to a former beloved teacher:

Thus, you see, I am learning Greek, and making acquaintance with
metaphysics, and French and Italian literature.

Margaret Fuller was of course a genius and even in her own day
renowned as a child prodigy, the product of her unconventional
father's intensive tutelage. Yet she was less exceptional than is
usually realized, and other girls in that springtime of American
life were having educations not too dissimilar — Henrietta Jackson, for instance, in Dorset, Vermont, just a year younger than
Margaret Fuller.

Like Margaret Fuller, Henrietta Jackson owed the beginnings of her classical education to her father, who was a scholar and teacher as well as a country parson. From him she learned Latin and Greek during the long Vermont winters; later in schools at Chester, Vermont, and at Haverhill, Massachusetts, she went on to French, to 'Intellectual Philosophy, Logic, Natural History, and Botany.' But French poetry remained her deepest passion, and the reading of poetry remained her greatest delight, second only to her extreme aesthetic sensitiveness to natural beauty.

Henrietta Jackson became a teacher; as she grew older, the conflict between her love of beauty and her sense of duty — an early and prophetic example of a conflict that produced so many thousand unnecessarily broken lives and so much needless anguish for many young people with similar backgrounds during the next fifty to seventy-five years — became unbearable. She chose the duty side, and eventually became the first wife of a missionary to Turkey — my grandfather Cyrus Hamlin. The potential poet and artist became the 'helpmate.' [2]

Two things stand out in this strange education: first, the deep classical foundation; second, the strong aesthetic emphasis that this diet of poetry and languages necessarily produced. Both women owed at least part of their later reputation to that aesthetic side. And what was true of them was true in lesser ways of thousands of others who were growing up in this period. Poe, Emerson, and Channing had this in common, that in all three it was the aesthetic sense which somehow formed the great motivating drive that made them what they were. Poe's poems became almost disembodied aesthetics; Emerson's was an aesthetic as well as a self-assertive philosophy, particularly in his earlier days; Channing's Unitarianism was aesthetic religion *par excellence*.

Indeed, one might almost say that the most marked change in cultural direction between the America of the years just after the Revolution and the America of the years between 1815 and 1845–50 lay precisely in the fact that before 1815 culture had been

[2] Margaret Woods Lawrence, *Light on the Dark River; or, Memorials of Mrs. Henrietta A. L. Hamlin, Missionary in Turkey* (Boston: D. Lothrop & Co. [c1853]).

rationalist and theocratic and after that it became primarily aesthetic and libertarian. Later still, after the Civil War, it became chiefly acquisitive, but that is another story.

It was no accident that this period became the great era of strange sects, of free-thinkers, of all types of free-love communities that scandalized the righteous. The ' great revival ' of the forties may have been partly a protest against the aesthetic and moral freedom of the thirties.

It was as if man in America, around 1820, had rediscovered his five senses ; had suddenly, like one breaking through from the forest to sun-drenched, sea-bordered downs, all at once become conscious of bright sun and distance and freedom ; had suddenly discovered that it was better to see and hear beautiful things than ugly ones ; had, in a word, waked up from a nightmare. At once the fine arts achieved a position which they had not held before. Education was based on poetry rather than on theology, and was an education of the physical senses as well as one based on a sense of duty. Painting in America had, before this awakening, been almost limited to portraiture. Sculpture had been practically nonexistent except in ship figureheads, overdoor eagles, mantel decorations, and so on. And architecture had been hobbled by colonial conservatism. Now everything changed rapidly. The thirties saw portrait painting made a fine art as well as a trade ; good artists like Copley and West no longer had to seek Europe to find a public ; a new school of American landscape and genre painting was born. The same period saw American sculptors working and admired ; architecture too could not but feel the same sudden quickening, symbolized partly by the change from builder-architects to professional architects, so that what had been the exception before — the professional architect, like Latrobe or Mills or Hallet — became the rule, at least in buildings of serious pretension.

This new aesthetic sensitiveness was nation-wide. It lay behind the political and economic radicalisms of the Owenites and the Fourierites, it colored the life of Brook Farm, it controlled the amazing ethical revolutions of Noyes and his fellow ' perfectionists.' It might sigh away in the languishing, affected manners of the fashionable miss, it might fade into the mawkish sentimentality of the earlier years of Godey's *Lady's Book*, it certainly produced a flood of completely unreadable literature; but it was at bottom real and vital. If we laugh at its occasional pretensions, we must nevertheless accept and reverence its real achievements — Emerson's and Thoreau's prose, Jones Very's lovely child-like nature poetry, Melville's imaginative fiction, and the superb clear richness of the best painting of Inman or Washington Allston or Morse, which killed forever both the academic intellectual aridity of the dying Reynolds tradition and the soft, sentimental lushness of the Romney or Lawrence school. Especially, I think, we must realize and admire its architectural achievements — not only the great monuments, like the Ohio capitol, or the New York Merchants' Exchange, or the Bowers house in Northampton, but even more the hundreds of dignified churches and academies and courthouses, the thousands of restrained and elegant homes, big and little, which made the character of American towns from the Atlantic to the Great Lakes and the Mississippi, and even far beyond. Never before or since, I believe, has there been a period when the general level of excellence was so high in American architecture, when the ideal was so constant and its varying expressions so harmonious, when the towns and villages, large and small, had in them so much of unostentatious unity and loveliness as during the forty years from 1820 to the Civil War. One has only to walk through Nantucket, or look at Hudson in Ohio, or see the fine old houses of Ann Arbor in Michigan or the older farmhouses and store buildings of northern Illinois, to fall at once under the influence of this spirit, to feel at once that these buildings were designed by and built for a people who had a new, vivid, almost overmastering aesthetic sensitiveness and love of beauty in form and line.

There are many evidences of this widespread art interest. Typical is Mrs. Trollope's [3] comment that Americans were enraged

[3] Mrs. [Frances Milton] Trollope, *Domestic Manners of the Americans* (London: Whitaker, Trecher & Co., 1832; New York: reprinted 'for the booksellers,' 1832).

more by adverse criticism of American painters than by censure of American politics. Typical, too, is Thomas Hamilton's [4] account of the enthusiasm of Providence for its new Arcade (designed by Bucklin and Warren) and of Boston's delight in Isaiah Rogers's Tremont House. More than anything else, however, the amount of interest in art shown by the periodicals of the time is significant. True, there were no architectural magazines, but there were many magazines that showed pictures of American buildings and contained architectural criticism or articles on architecture. In fact, to judge by the pages of *The New York Mirror*, the *Analectic Magazine*, and many others,[5] the ordinary educated man, as opposed to the technician, could and did get a clearer view of the architecture of his day during the thirties and forties than the same type of man can get today.

This interest in art and architecture is apparent as early as the 1790's. Thus *The American Museum* in October 1790 had an article on the architecture of America which quoted Jefferson's dislike of Colonial work, deplored the almost universal use of wood as a building material, and contained a charmingly romantic discussion of Gothic architecture. In the same year *The Christian's, Scholars', and Farmer's Magazine* had an article, chiefly historical, on ' The Rise and Progress of Architecture.' Five years later *The American Monthly Review* (*or Literary Journal*) devoted much space to the controversy then current between followers of the formal and of the informal schools of landscape gardening.

By 1815 we find the *Analectic Magazine* of Philadelphia devoting more and more space to the fine arts; typical is the unsigned November article, ' Remarks on the Progress and Present State of the Fine Arts in the United States.' In speaking of domestic architecture, the writer deplores a constant copying of the English handbooks, and complains of our too complacently following the ' Louis XIV style ' in our public buildings — referring to the classic Baroque of the Colonial tradition. Of this he says that at best ' it can rise to nothing nobler than ponderous state-

---

[4] *Men and Manners in America* (Edinburgh: W. Blackwood, 1833).
[5] See Appendix B.

liness and cumbrous magnificence . . . [it is] always poor and contemptible when compared with the grandeur and the beauty of the Grecian simplicity.' Nor were articles on other and less-well-known styles absent; *The American Quarterly Review,* for example, devoted forty pages of its March 1829 number to Egyptian architecture, and travel articles elsewhere often had a large amount of architectural comment included.

In 1821 Latrobe's recent death had aroused enough interest to justify *The Literary Gazette's* reprinting a long and careful obituary from *Ackermann's Repository of Arts.* . . This also is significant of the growing importance of the place the architect was taking in the popular interest. Ten years later this same obituary was published again, in *The Young Mechanic;* evidently the life and work of Latrobe were still considered of more than mere news value. Several Boston papers take great care to mention Bulfinch as the architect when commenting on examples of his work, and after 1820 views of new buildings shown in such periodicals as *Bowen's Boston News Letter,* or the *Analectic Magazine,* or *The New York Mirror* were almost always accompanied by descriptive articles in which the architect's name was given its due importance.

Significant, too, of the popular interest in architecture is the fact that the *Analectic Magazine,* along with its engraving of the United States Bank in Philadelphia, saw fit to go into the question of the authorship of the design and stated that, although the bank had been attributed to Latrobe, it was really entirely Strickland's work and that Strickland had won first place in the competition for it.[6] During 1820 the same magazine showed an engraving of the winning design for the new Pennsylvania capitol, by Stephen Hills, and noted that Mills had won the second prize. Noteworthy also are its travel articles by 'An Invalid,' with their vivid description of Pompeii and the Naples Museum; it is characteristic of the tolerance of the time that this contains a surprisingly full account of the famous secret museum, with an astonishingly outspoken description of some of its contents.

[6] See page 76.

Another indication of the same kind of tolerance occurs twenty-six years later, in *The New York Mirror* of 1846, in an unsigned review of an exhibition of the sculpture of H. K. Brown, an American working in Italy. The reviewer writes, of a statue of Adam:

We were sorry to see that Mr. Brown had insulted the moral taste of the New York public, to say nothing of the outrage on their aesthetic perceptions, by putting a paper fig leaf upon this figure. It could only have been the suggestion of a prurient mind, and we trust that he will have the good sense to remove it. The naked figure is a legitimate object of representation in art, and we believe that the public of New York are too refined to endure patiently so squeamish an imputation on their taste and morals as is evidenced by this fig leaf. . .

The New York public, then, according to this reviewer, was a sophisticated public. It would have been nothing else, for this was a period of wide importation into New York of European paintings (especially more or less well authenticated ones by the old masters) and many New Yorkers had undoubtedly at some time pored over the great engraving collection of Ithiel Town, in which the nude was a commonplace. The popular idea of that period as one of restraint and prudery is false; we tend to impute to the time the exaggerated and hypocritical puritanism which only became the ruling fashion in New York in the seventies and eighties, when the new-rich tried to conceal their crudities beneath an artificially polished veneer.

Another indication of the widespread architectural culture of the thirties and forties lies in the long reviews of architectural books which are to be found in the periodicals. William Dunlap's famous *History of the Rise and Progress of the Arts of Design in the United States* was published in 1834.[7] It was everywhere noticed and acclaimed as a proof of the fact that America had achieved true culture. And *The American Monthly Magazine* of July 1834, in reviewing the *History of Sculpture, Painting, and Architecture* by J. S. Memes, LL.D., just then published in Boston, notes that such a book as this would have been impossible a

---

[7] Two vols. (New York: G. P. Scott and Co., 1834); new ed., 3 vols., edited by F. W. Bayley and C. F. Goodspeed (Boston: C. E. Goodspeed & Co., 1918).

few years before, but 'now,' it says hopefully, 'the term cognoscenti need not be synonymous only with wealth and idle leisure.' Culture had become democratized. In the *North American Review*, H. R. Cleveland, Jr., in 1836, makes an ostensible review of James Gallier's *Price Book* [8] the opportunity for a long and careful essay on American architecture up to the date of his writing, showing the gradual improvement in taste, the gradual raising of standards. In 1844 Arthur Gilman 'reviewed' Edward Shaw's *Rural Architecture* [9] in an important article on American architecture in which he expresses his keen dislike for both Greek and Gothic forms in America, states his admiration of some of the earlier, simpler, Colonial churches, and seizes upon the Renaissance styles of Europe as the most fruitful source of architectural influence. This is the first reasoned support of eclecticism in architecture to appear (so far as I know) in America. The books of A. J. Downing [10] furnished occasion for other revealing reviews. Later in 1844 Gilman reviewed Downing's *Cottage Residences*, which, consistently enough, he did not like, thinking them derivative, frivolous, sentimental, and unreal. *The United States Magazine and Democratic Review* in 1841, however, is enthusiastic about Downing's work.

Thus reviews of architectural books had become, almost inevitably, reviews of architecture itself. Just as earlier the magazines had become a battleground for the controversy between the supporters of the romantic and of the formal in gardening, between the followers of Price and Repton and the followers of Le Nôtre, so, later, their pages reflect the fight between the Greeks and the Goths, the classicists and the romanticists, and finally show

[8] *The American Builder's General Price Book and Estimator* (New York: Lafever & Gallier, 1833); 2nd & 3rd ed. (Boston, 1843 and 1836).

[9] Boston: James B. Dow, 1843.

[10] *The Architecture of Country Houses* . . . (New York: D. Appleton and Company; Philadelphia: G. S. Appleton, 1850); nine issues to 1866. *Cottage Residences* . . . (New York and London: Wiley & Putnam, 1842); eleven issues up to 1887, in five or six editions. *Rural Essays* (New York: G. P. Putnam & Co., 1853); six issues up to 1881. *A Treatise on the Theory and Practice of Landscape Gardening Adapted to North America* . . . *With Remarks on Rural Architecture* (New York and London: Wiley & Putnam; Boston: C. C. Little & Co.; 1841); fifteen issues of six editions up to 1879.

the emergence of the eclectic in architecture with his ' fie on both your houses.' This criticism of buildings was not limited to reviews of books on buildings. It often was a direct criticism of the buildings themselves. A characteristic example is an editorial in the April 1835 issue of *The American Monthly Magazine*, entitled ' Architectural Designs,' which is a savage attack on the combination of dome and temple forms in the Town and Davis designs for the New York customs house, as well as an expression of great admiration for Haviland's drawings in the Egyptian style for the New York prison (later to be called ' the Tombs '). The editor writes of the proposed dome as ' an excrescence, which, however elegant in itself, is utterly monstrous and barbarous when added to a model of the present Grecian architecture, such as the Parthenon or the Theseion.' For the same reason the editor is struck by the ' vandalism ' of the capitol at Indianapolis by ' Messers Town and Davis.'

Another notable example is an article on ' American Architecture ' by Horatio Greenough, the sculptor, published in *The United States Magazine and Democratic Review* in 1843.[11] Greenough's taste was classic rather than romantic, however romantic his own style. Yet here he clamors for a native American style in architecture, and explains its absence as being a result of the sudden growth of the country; America, he says, has had no youth. But he finds the ancient rather than the medieval forms closer to the country's needs: ' The puny cathedral of Broadway [Trinity Church], like an elephant dwindled to the size of a dog, measures her [America's] yearning for Gothic sublimity, while the roar of the Astor House, and the mammoth vase of the great reservoir, shows how she works when she feels at home and is in earnest. . .' Yet no really great architecture, he feels, can come from the past: ' True it is, that the commonwealth, with that desire of public magnificence which has ever been a leading feature of democracy, has called from the vasty deep the spirits of the Greek, the Roman, and the Gothic styles; but they would not come when she did call to them.' Greenough wanted all buildings to be de-

11 Vol. xiii (August 1843), p. 206.

signed from the inside out, and he divides buildings into two classes, the organic and the monumental; he cites ships and their design as an example for the architects to follow. So, just as Gilman a year later prophesied the eclectic era, Greenough has here anticipated the thinking, even the very words and methods, of the architectural critics and writers who, almost a century later, ushered in the new day of post-war twentieth-century design.

A final example of the popular architectural criticism of the day is *The New York Mirror's* series of reviews of the work of William H. Ranlett as published by him in *The Architect*,[12] which was issued in parts from 1846 to 1848. These reviews show the basic common sense of the criteria by which buildings were being judged; they explain why the worst excesses of romanticism in buildings were exceptional in America, at least until after the Civil War. A few quotations will give the general attitude. On 17 October 1846:

These cottages have nothing to commend them but a picturesque profile. . . They are the most costly and least convenient houses that can be built. . . They are the imitations of the natural expressions of an age of semi-civilization and gross ignorance. . . It was quite pardonable in Horace Walpole and Sir Walter Scott to build gingerbread houses in imitation of robber barons and Bluebeard chieftains; they were poets and had written Gothic romances; they would fill their houses with rusty old armour, lances, drinking horns and mouldy tapestry, and they were surrounded by the memorials of the times they were idly trying to revive. But there can be nothing more grotesque, more absurd, or more affected, than for a quiet gentleman, who has made his fortune in the peaceful occupation of selling calicos, and who knows no more of the middle ages than they do of him, to erect for his family residence a gimcrack of a Gothic castle . . . as though he anticipated an attack upon his roost from some Front de Boeuf in the neighborhood.

On 20 February 1847, in commenting on a later number of *The Architect*, the reviewer makes still more clear the non-archaeological, common-sense, rationalist character of his approach. He says:

No. 7 is a neat design; it is called a Grecian cottage, probably from the inclination of the roof, but the pointed roofs of the north of

---

[12] Later issued as a book, *The American Architect*, 2 vols. (New York: Dewitt and Davenport, 1849–51).

Europe are purely Grecian, because they are constructed upon the same principle upon which the roof of the Parthenon was; that of conformity to the latitude of the site on which they were built.

On 3 April another number of *The Architect* appeared, and the reviewer likes in it especially a Grecian villa at Clifton and a Bracketed cottage at Elliotville, both on Staten Island; he thinks both Grecian and Bracketed types are far superior, because more sensible and less pretentious, to the gingerbread Gothic or Elizabethan that was coming more and more into use.

The evidence, then, would seem overwhelming that interest in architecture and the fine arts was deep and wide during this period from the Revolution to 1850, and especially after the War of 1812. Periodicals have always been particularly sensitive to what their editors conceive to be the taste of the public. Especially close must have been the relation of editor and public when the periodicals were so numerous in proportion to the population, and each one so limited and often so local in its own circulation. If, therefore, there was in them such a large amount of architectural comment, such a number of extended reviews of books on art and architecture, so many views of new buildings, usually with the architect's name given, and so much news about architectural projects and ideas, it must have been because the readers enjoyed these things, were interested in them, and were proud of their new architecture.

It is obvious also that the whole educational basis of the culture of the period was classic, and that a surprising number of women as well as men had an intimate knowledge of at least some of the great Greek and Roman writers, and what is more, if Margaret Fuller's experience is at all typical, a full realization of the whole artistic atmosphere of the classic world and of classic myth — an atmosphere which, though dyed with its own characteristic New England coloring like a magnificent sunset sky seen through rose glass, was expressed with the warmest clarity by Nathaniel Hawthorne in the *Twice-Told Tales* of 1837.

Moreover, it is clear that the culture of the period was much

more free, much more aesthetic in its bias, than that which had
preceded it or that which followed. The old aristocratic aesthetic
culture of the eighteenth-century plutocrats was dead, it is true;
but Thomas Jefferson's own exquisite taste had presided at its
funeral, and it had left a heritage which widened to include almost
the entire country. There was, of course, much crudity and
naïveté, but there was almost everywhere an intense and unaffected
search for the beautiful and an overweening pride in artistic
achievement; indeed this pride was one of the outstanding American characteristics that British travelers like Mrs. Trollope and
Thomas Hamilton had found amusing or absurd. But it was also
this achievement in architecture, at least, which, as we have seen,
had astonished and delighted even Mrs. Trollope.

This bookish, classically founded, aesthetically sensitive culture was widespread, and it was not standardized. The centraliza-
tion of culture, which was to follow the Civil War and make a
few centers like Boston and New York the artistic dictators of the
country, had not yet set in. Almost every county seat had its
weekly or its monthly; almost every one of these, in addition to
being a distributor of news and a political forum, was also an
artistic center, with a page or a column devoted to literature, music, and the fine arts. No wonder academies and colleges grew up
everywhere like mushrooms, even in newly settled Ohio and Indiana; the people who built them, if they were not learned, admired
learning, if not artists they admired art, and they had all of them
the feeling not of copying distant centers but of being themselves
creators — creators of a new America and a new art. They believed they knew what they wanted, and what they wanted was the
beauty of nobility and freedom and grace.

To this intellectual culture we must add one more quality, if
we are to understand the time — its feeling about wealth. We
must avoid the danger of seeing it, through too rosy glasses, as
a sort of golden age. Slavery was at its height. Sectionalism was
growing. Andrew Jackson's daring was increasing the consciousness of the economic struggle between the haves and have-nots.
Great fortunes were developing in New York and Philadelphia,

and in the large eastern cities increasing immigration was forcing the subdivision of old houses into flats; the causes of the slums had begun their deadly work. In the new factories that were going up so rapidly labor was often shamefully exploited.

And yet the basic structure was still sound. Agriculture and industrialism were still in balance — rivals perhaps, but not yet at each other's throats. Industry was still in a personal, paternalistic stage, and the employer often preserved a strong sense of responsibility toward those he employed. One has only to read the admiring accounts by foreign travelers who wrote of the welfare work and high idealism at the Lowell mills, for instance, to realize that the thirties had an industrial atmosphere quite different from that of the sixties and seventies. Even if there were no contemporary accounts still in existence, the buildings themselves would tell the story; for in Manchester, Lowell, Nashua, and many smaller manufacturing towns in New York and Pennsylvania, and elsewhere, there are rows of workingmen's houses from the thirties that are ample, dignified, gracious in detail, and set on lots adequately large — houses that are a remarkable contrast to the crowded jerry-built slums of forty years later.[13] And there was still hope; there was still the West — either the civilized West of Ohio and Michigan, or the wild frontier beyond the Mississippi — the West clamoring for settlers and for development, and full of opportunities for those who could save a little and who had ambition and initiative.

Above all, there was not yet in the ' free ' part of the country any hard-and-fast class distinction based solely on wealth. There were the rich and there were the poor, of course; but the mere fact of wealth or poverty did not form a reason for superciliousness or fawning. Mary Starbuck, brought up in Nantucket before the Civil War, in *My House and I* [14] tells a story that perfectly expresses the feeling. She had remarked to a playmate that one of her friends was wealthy. An aunt of hers who had overheard

[13] For an enlightening discussion of this point, covering the whole field of architecture and city planning in Lowell, Massachusetts, see John Coolidge's *Mill and Mansion* (New York: Columbia University Press, 1942).

[14] Boston and New York: Houghton Mifflin Company, 1929.

the conversation interrupted at once. 'Let me never hear you refer to anyone,' she said, 'as either rich or poor!' That was the ruling tone, and again the architecture is expressive. In town after town, in Ohio, in Connecticut, in New York, one will find small houses and big houses of the thirties and forties, all with the same 'manners,' the same graciousness of detail and rightness of proportion. Squalidness is so rare as to be sharply noticeable. Big and small houses, yes; but, except in certain areas of the large cities and in the shacks and cabins of the purely shiftless, rich and poor houses never.

Such was the culture, such the conditions, in which the Greek Revival flowered and of which it was the perfect expression. A culture learned, founded on classic myth, classic literature, classic art. A culture perhaps more completely aesthetic than any American culture before or since. A culture flowering lustily in hundreds of local centers and not yet centralized in the big cities. A culture radical, libertarian, experimental, eagerly searching for American expression. A country rich, expanding, not yet densely populated; a country with its agriculture and its growing industry still in fundamental balance. A country with growing towns and cities, new-blossoming farms; a country pressing ever westward and demanding an amazing amount of building of every kind. . .

Is it strange, in such a culture and such a country, that the Greek Revival flourished and with all its variations produced an architecture alive, native, gracious, and sensitive, and towns that are delightful in their quiet harmony?

II. WHY THE GREEK REVIVAL PASSED AWAY

If all this is so, why did not the Greek Revival continue to develop, expand, modify itself indefinitely? With such a background of unity, with such a strong cultural foundation, with such an apparent fitness for the America of its time, what killed it? What made the sudden tremendous change between the architectural ideals of the forties and those of the seventies? The answers to these persistent questions must be sought, as the reasons for the universal acceptance of the Greek Revival were sought, in two different categories — the cultural and the economic. For, during those decades of growing sectionalism and of the Civil War, American culture and American wealth were both undergoing profound changes, of which the change in architecture is but one expression.

The first weakness of the Greek Revival as a style lay in the fact that at bottom it was basically derivative. This fact alone is not enough to warrant indictment of the style; after all, many styles of the past have been, at their origin, ' derivative.' And, to the people of the first half of the nineteenth century in America, the ideal of Greece that lay behind so much of their architecture was near, very real, quite ' contemporary ' — it lived. Moreover, the actual work of the best Greek Revival architects — of Mills, of Strickland, of Rogers, of Davis at his best — was seldom, as we have seen, archaeological in either form or purpose; for them the Greek ideal was an inspiration continually fluid. Without exception the architects' and builders' handbooks, which had done so much to spread the Greek Revival, had the same attitude; Haviland, Benjamin, and Lafever used Greek detail merely as an opportunity for fresh and personal and ' American ' creation, so that the towns and farmhouses of the East and the new country west of the Alleghenies alike were American first and ' Greek ' only second. For the American of 1835 it was no more illogical to use an attenuated Greek Doric order for a piazza, or Greek rosettes around his fireplace, than to use the attenuated Palladian orders or the Adam-like composition ornament which the new Greek vein had superseded. No, if there were an advantage on either side, it was surely on the side of the Greek forms, for their simplicity, restraint, and clear surfaces were much more in the spirit of the time and the place than were the outworn delicacies of the preceding age. Mankind had not yet achieved that sense of complete, self-conscious worship of the present which was to come later, with the strident times after the Civil War, and to persist with growing intensity right to the moment when this is being written — a sort of time-narcissism that draws a harsh dividing line between 'now' and 'then.' Men still felt, before the Civil War, that if ideals of certain past ages were noble they were still to be reverenced; if Greek architectural detail was beautiful, pure, endlessly fertile in suggestions, and, to them, fit for their use, they were doing themselves no injustice in using it.

Yet the very idea of 'Greek' detail became a danger, because with it the idea of 'correctness' came in to fog the clear lines of architectural design; the moment correctness becomes a criterion, vitality is doomed. As we have seen, it was usually not the architects themselves who introduced this fatal idea; it was their clients and the critics. Now in the tremendous breadth of popular interest in architecture the idea of correctness, because it was an easy and thought-saving idea, became more and more important. 'How strange it is,' wrote Philip Hone in his diary,[15] 14 February 1838, concerning the Bank of the United States in Philadelphia, 'that in all the inventions of modern times architecture alone seems to admit of no improvement — *every departure from the classical models of antiquity in this science is a departure from grace and beauty.*' (The italics are mine.) With such a feeling on the part of the patrons of the art, the art itself could only become stifled; at last, under the heavy blanket of correctness, it was smothered to death.

Another germ of its own dissolution was innate in this fact that Greek Revival architecture was derivative. The natural question arose: if the beauty of architecture comes from the inspiration of a past style, why stop at the Greek? Why limit oneself to just one small portion of the fascinating pageant of past art history? Archaeology was creating little by little an ever widening knowledge of all sorts of forms from other cultures. Egyptian architecture in all its magnificent power was being presented to the America of those days; book after book was being issued to show its glories. The history of architecture as a whole was beginning to take form as discovery pushed back the curtains of ignorance

[15] *The Diary of Philip Hone,* edited with an Introduction by Allan Nevins (New York: Dodd, Mead & Co., 1927).

and revealed the story. Romanticism had adored the Middle Ages for nearly a half century; the Gothic and the Romanesque were its natural language. More and more, Americans were beginning to make 'the grand tour' in Europe; coming just at a time when many works of the great painters of the Renaissance and the Baroque were being imported and sold in America, this travel brought a new knowledge of the magnificence of Renaissance Rome, of Baroque Vienna, of the superb elegance of the Paris created by Louis XIV and his followers and by Napoleon. Admiration of these was bound to affect the taste of the American traveler; if he were not a man of unusual imagination and discrimination he would wish to emulate, even to copy, these new, magnificent Renaissance and Baroque buildings he was coming to know. Yes, all the past was America's, all the present of Europe was becoming America's; eclecticism in architecture was to be the inevitable result.

In the Gothic Revival itself, which had in a narrower field almost exactly paralleled the Greek Revival, there was an innate character which, developed, spelled the doom of the Greek: that was its feeling — or rather its lack of feeling — for structure. To a much greater extent than with the Classic Revivals, the Medieval Revival had roots that were literary. Gothic romances led to 'castellated' houses; in both it was the 'atmosphere,' the emotional effect, which was the essential thing. Naturally the way the effect was produced was secondary; the early Gothicists of America inevitably built effects rather than buildings. The whole cult of the picturesque was designed to disintegrate building techniques and lower building standards; if the result was a structure that was a good romantic picture, a pretty bit, what matter if its tracery was jigsaw wood, its battlements of boards? The Gothic Revival in America accepted lath-and-plaster 'vaults' as a matter of course for half a century. Even *The New York Ecclesiologist*, the great arbiter of the style, in clamoring for purity and correctness, only occasionally referred to the claptrap, stage-scenery construction with which the Gothic effects were so often produced. Richard Upjohn, to be sure, designed little 'Gothic' churches which were frankly, and beautifully, of wood; he accepted the inexpensive material as a condition of the problem. Yet that was exceptional; in both houses and churches the average Gothic designer of the thirties and forties used materials as thoughtlessly, as insensitively, as had any Baroque architect, and almost always sought the maximum ' Gothic ' elaboration with the cheapest, most unsuitable materials in imitation of others more expensive to obtain and to work.

The Greek Revival, too, was often guilty of much the same error, stuccoing brick to symbolize stone, and using wooden columns in most (though not all) of its domestic work. But there is a profound difference, nevertheless, between the two styles in their attitude toward building. Wherever possible the Greek Revival architect used stone; in his most important, most monumental buildings, granite and limestone and marble do the work they seem to do. Where vaulted forms occur, they are usually actual masonry vaults. One has only to visit the basement of the United States Capitol or of the New York Sub-Treasury building, one has only to remember the eighty-foot brick coffered dome of Isaiah Rogers's New York Merchants' Exchange, one has only to see the magnificent vaulting of Girard College, to realize this structural sense of the Greek Revival architects. They made magnificent construction the basis for monumental effect. But if we take even the most expensive, the most highly developed of the Gothic Revival churches, universally acclaimed as masterpieces in the style — such as Upjohn's Trinity Church and Renwick's Grace Church in New York, or Lafever's Holy Trinity in Brooklyn — we find in every case a lath-and-plaster vault as the climax of the design. And with, at the time, no apparent protest. . . The effect was gained; what did the means matter?

But the public, and the architects themselves, suffered. Once they had become accustomed to this method of thinking, once they had become inured to the fact that effect was one thing and construction a wholly different and separate thing, their sense of architectural integrity was destroyed. They could only go on designing more and more different ' effects,' building them in ways which had less and less relation to the design and became inevitably more shoddy as the desire for ostentation grew along with the desire for cheapness. And the way was open for the whole disastrous late-nineteenth-century schism between architecture as design and as engineering, and for the dressing of steel skyscrapers in stylistic clothes. It was a schism ideally fitted to the ideals and desires of eclecticism, but it was the death of the essential qualities of the Greek Revival.[16]

The cultural climate of America was changing, too. Wealth was usurping an ever increasing share in American thought. Industries of all kinds were being created; capital was eagerly sought, and it earned extravagant returns as the population of the country increased and its natural resources were discovered and exploited. Railroads were building, steamboat lines on coast and river increasing, transportation becoming ever easier. A continent was being discovered and its riches tapped, amid a carnival of frenzied speculation. ' Men who were poor one day were millionaires the next; women who did the family washing on Monday moved into palaces on Wednesday and rode to church on Sunday in carriages,' as the Beards said of this period in *The Rise of American Civilization*.[17] As the thirties gave way to the forties and the forties to the fifties, Philip Hone in the pages of his *Diary* deplores constantly the growing mania for speed, for speculation, and for ostentation which was destroying the old gracious dignity of New York life. A new generation was coming to the fore, filled with this breathless pursuit of money; the heroes of the period were those who captured it.

This emergence of the millionaire was as fatal to the artistic ideals of the Greek Revival as were the speed, the speculation, and the exploitation that produced him. For, if he was to enjoy his success, he must make his money obvious to all — and ostentation became a new ideal in design. He traveled abroad in luxury, he

[16] This whole matter is covered at greater length in my article, ' The Greek Revival in America and Some of Its Critics,' *The Art Bulletin*, Vol. xxiv, No. 3 (September 1942), pp. 244–58.

[17] Charles A. and Mary R. Beard, Vol. i (New York: The Macmillan Company, 1927), pp. 727–8.

lived at home in a plethora of things bought. He buttressed his own self-importance by the number of his extravagances; he concealed his ignorance and his lack of background and education behind his love of display. He was profoundly envious of culture, but he could not understand the deep roots of the American culture which had preceded him. He wanted change, he envied Europe; what architecture was possible for such a man but eclecticism?

There was, last of all, and perhaps in the long run most important of all, a growing rationalist protest against Revivalism. By the middle forties the old Greek enthusiasm was fast dying out; the old feeling that classic life had been a golden age to emulate was dead. Archaeology and history were now rapidly becoming respectable sciences, not mere opportunities for wishfulfilment dreams. As a sense of the actual historical past as *past* increased, so also did the consciousness of the present as *present;* the time element was becoming of ever greater importance; the *now* was triumphant. Once this self-conscious feeling for the present had developed, the day of the Revivals in art was over; the differences between the life and needs of the past and those of the present were too great to be bridged.

Earlier architects and writers of the Greek Revival had, to be sure, realized this in part, and had insisted on the necessity of an American architecture for America. But it was not till the late thirties that anyone, apparently, realized the full implications of that idea. It came first in architectural work itself, in the rather tentative eclecticism of the earliest ' Bracketed ' or ' Tuscan ' houses and villas of Davis and Upjohn. It was another architect, Arthur Gilman, who first gave this feeling explicit and studied literary expression, in a review of Shaw's *Rural Architecture* published in the *North American Review* for April 1844. He starts out by attacking the book as indicative of everything that is derivative and dead in American architecture, and goes on to demolish the entire Greek Revival and Gothic Revival movements as vain attempts to wake the dead. The basis of the accusation is not merely ethical or emotional; it is rationalistic. Take the matter of windows, for instance — how could they be incorporated into Greek temples? What could be more foolish or inept than a house like a Greek temple, anyway? How could we in America expect anything but basic absurdity from the attempt to imitate ancient Greeks or medieval Frenchmen — or Englishmen? What, then, were we to do? Gilman's answer is simple — we were to examine other, later styles, whose creators were men more like ourselves, with needs more like ours, and go to them for inspiration — to the Renaissance, in other words. And we should go not with any idea of copying, but with that of picking and choosing that which is fitting, and discarding the rest; we could mix what we found as we pleased. Among the styles to which the attention of America was called was its own pre-Revolutionary Colonial; this is the earliest expression I know of that admiration which, fifty years later, was to become the rage. Thus, in 1844, the basic tenets of American eclecticism were clearly and systematically set down, on a basis of logic it was difficult to controvert.

Gilman left an important monument of his own theory — the Arlington Street Unitarian Church in Boston, the brick-and-stone tower of which still dominates the west side of the Public Garden. Its exterior, he said, was based on the English Renaissance of James Gibbs, its interior on Santa Annunziata at Genoa. No clearer example of eclecticism could be wanted.

Thus logic and the ostentation of the new-rich united to give the death sentence to the Greek Revival. The sentence was executed by the expansion of the country, by the coming of floods of European immigrants, and by the Civil War.

The rapidity of expansion of the country was paralleled by the unprecedented mushroom growth of the large cities and the industrial towns. Cheap immigrant labor made necessary an enormous amount of cheap housing. The architects were swamped, overwhelmed, and finally forgotten. Cheap plan books flooded the country in ever growing numbers up to the nineties. Mass production came in; the lathe and the jig saw made easy and inexpensive the elaborate ostentation which even the cheapest house seemed to require, to cover if not to adorn its thoughtless, naked ugliness.

What chance had the refined, gracious, careful tradition of the Greek Revival against all this?

To be sure, in quiet agricultural villages here and there the old traditions, the old ways, held true; in the more distant plantation houses conservative ideals prolonged the sway of the Greek Revival deep into the fifties. But alike in the North and in the South this conservatism was growing more and more anachronistic as the industrial expansion of the country increased; and, when at last the Civil War for four long years drew the young men from these towns both south and north into that tragic maelstrom, the last sparks of the Greek Revival tradition flickered and finally died; the world of ' Reconstruction' days was a different world.

Portico Railing
graphic ▮▮▮ scale

FIGURE 39. MARSHALL HOUSE, New York. Iron railing from the portico.
(*Great Georgian Houses*.)

APPENDIX A

THE AMERICAN DEVELOPMENT OF GREEK INSPIRED FORMS

GREEK architectural forms were probably first known in America through *The Antiquities of Athens*,[1] by Stuart and Revett. We know that Jefferson owned a copy of the first volume, published in 1762, and that the Library Company of Philadelphia had obtained one by 1770.[2] Without doubt a few other collectors and libraries had obtained copies before the end of the eighteenth century. Yet, as has been pointed out,[3] the details shown in this great work had little immediate effect. Later, when the Greek Revival in America had at last become general, information about Greek forms flooded into the country through the illustrations of many other books besides Stuart and Revett — especially the books of Peter Nicholson. The details of the Greek orders, moreover, copied either from Stuart and Revett, from Nicholson, or from some of the other sources, were widely re-engraved and issued almost universally as parts of all American architectural handbooks between 1825 and 1845, with occasional items both earlier and later. The average American architect during this period thus had every opportunity of knowing the Greek orders.

That is not the case so universally for other Greek details. Unless the designer had access to Stuart and Revett, his knowledge of Greek details came to him only through the engravings of Nicholson or the creative reinterpretations of the American architectural authors. Of these, Lafever shows engravings of restored Greek temples and the caryatids;[4] Chester Hills [5] presents a restoration of the Erechtheum and some of its details, taken from Inwood, and also republishes some of the Nicholson items. But in general the American handbooks are content to give only the orders themselves, though

---

[1] Four vols. (London: J. Habercorn, 1762–1816); sup. vol. (1830).

[2] Fiske Kimball, *Domestic Architecture of the American Colonies and of the Early Republic* (New York: Charles Scribner's Sons, 1922), p. 152.

[3] See page 36.

[4] *The Beauties of Modern Architecture* (New York: D. Appleton & Co., 1835), Plates 35–8 inclusive.

[5] *The Builder's Guide* (New York: D. Appleton & Co., 1836 [c1834]); republished with additions of villa plans by Henry Austin and a chapter on School Architecture by Henry Barnard (Hartford: Case, Tiffany, and Burnham, 1846).

sometimes with several examples of each order and a plate or two of ' Greek mouldings.'.

The influence of the Nicholson books was widespread; evidently in the 1830's they were the English architectural works most in demand. Haviland, Benjamin, Lafever, and Shaw — all give them credit in foreword or on title page. An examination of exactly what the nature of this debt was may throw a flood of light on the attitude of the American authors and thus on the developments of architectural detail in the United States.

The first and most obvious fact in this borrowing is the complete dependence of the American authors on Nicholson for technical details. Truss forms, framing types, and vault, niche, and arch types are all taken over almost line for line from the Nicholson books. The details of hand railing and stair construction which the American handbooks show — a matter of special interest at a time when curved stairs of all types were becoming common — were also largely borrowed from Nicholson.

It is therefore difficult to overestimate the great debt which the American architects and builders owed to Nicholson for the excellence of much of their technical equipment. It is perhaps not too much to state that the high standards of building construction and of practical details in the use of materials — qualities so obvious in the American building of 1810–50 — may be due in no small measure to the inspiration of Nicholson's thorough technical plates. It is significant that the works of Peter Nicholson's that were republished in America were chiefly of a technical nature. Noteworthy is *The Carpenter's New Guide*,[6] published in Philadelphia, first by M. Carey and Son, and later by a series of other publishers in edition after edition from 1818–67; also *The Mechanic's Companion*,[7] published by W. C. Borradaile in New York in 1831, and in later New York and Philadelphia editions up to 1868. Peter Nicholson, through the influence of his own books, which were widely owned by American designers and craftsmen, and through the continual republication of his technical plates in American handbooks, almost deserves to be called the father of American carpentry and joinery.

When we come to the designs of whole buildings the picture is very different. The houses shown in Peter Nicholson's *The New and Improved Practical Builder*, Volume III,[8] Plates XXIX to XXXVII, are

---

[6] London [publisher not given], 1792.
[7] Oxford [publisher not given], 1825.
[8] London [publisher not given], 1823; new revised ed., London: Thomas Kelly, 1848.

quite different in their entire conception, as well as in their details, from the house designs shown by Haviland in his 1837 improved and enlarged edition of Biddle's *The Young Carpenter's Assistant* [9] or in his own work, *The Builders' Assistant*,[10] or by Benjamin and Lafever in their various books. Chester Hills,[11] it is true, published new lithographed reproductions of Nicholson's Gothic houses, as well as designs derived directly from the Nicholson churches shown in Plates XLII to LIV. But Hills, the great eclectic, lifted his designs from everywhere, pillaging Lafever's ideas as diligently as he did Nicholson's. It is also true that there are distant relationships — very distant — between the first of the Nicholson churches ('Church in the Grecian Style,' Plates XLIII to XLVIII) and the church design published by Minard Lafever in 1829 in *The Young Builder's General Instructor*,[12] Plate LXV, as well as between Nicholson's 'Chapel' (Plates XLIX to LIV) and the Greek Doric church Asher Benjamin published in the *Practice of Architecture* [13] in 1833 (Plates 51 to 55). But in both these cases the differences are so much more important than the similarities as to raise the question whether there was any direct influence at all.

The fact seems well established, then, that in building design as a whole the Nicholson books had but slight influence.[14] The same seems to be true of the much more original designs published in the various books of Sir John Soane. The best American architects were essentially designers, little bound by published precedent. Robert Mills, as we have seen,[15] stated their position unequivocally with regard to the use of books.

The matter of detail is more complicated and more elusive. The Greek Revival designers and craftsmen knew the chief Greek orders as a matter of course. Their information came from Stuart and

---

[9] Philadelphia: M'Carty & Davis, 1837.

[10] Philadelphia: John Bioren and the authors [Hugh Bridport was co-author], 1819–21.

[11] Op. cit.

[12] Newark: W. Tuttle & Co., 1829.

[13] Boston: the author, and Carter, Hendie & Co.; New York: Collins & Co.; 1833. Seven other editions to 1851.

[14] But certain general ideas may have been developed from published suggestions. Thus the courthouse and prison by R. Elsam, published by Nicholson in *The New and Improved Practical Builder*, Vol. III, Plates LXII and LXIII, may have suggested various American cross-shaped courthouses like the St. Louis courthouse. And there may be a hint of Nicholson's Gothic houses (ibid. Plates XXXV and XXXVI) in Richard Upjohn's R. H. Gardiner house at Gardiner, Maine. But even this is seriously questionable. *Similis huic propter hoc* is as dangerous logic as *post hoc propter hoc.*

[15] See page 56.

Revett, from Nicholson, and from American handbooks which usually based their engravings on those of Stuart and Revett. But the major architects at least — men like Latrobe, Mills, Willard, and Lafever, for example — were not satisfied with the mere drawings. They were avid students, if not scholars, widely read in the available material on architecture. Architectural form, for most of them, was a factor in the historical process, and as such their interest in architectural history was real even if their knowledge was elementary. They knew the current English writers on architectural history, especially Hope and Elmes; manuscripts by Mills, among others, indicate how this reading bore fruit.[16] Lafever gave a section on architectural history, taken from Elmes, in *The Beauties of Modern Architecture* (1835); the Introduction to Edward Shaw's *Civil Architecture* (1830)[17] is replete with historical references. Even Chester Hills begins *The Builder's Guide* (1836) with a historical introduction, ' The Origin and Progress of Building.' In 1848 the United States produced its first own native complete history of architecture, Mrs. L[ouisa] C[aroline Huggins] Tuthill's *History of Architecture, from the Earliest Times; Its Present Condition in Europe and the United States . . . ,*[18] remarkable for its sane, common-sense, and forward-looking criticism. Thus it is unlikely that the changes American architects made in the Greek forms were made from ignorance.

Of course the practice of changing the details and proportions of the orders was thoroughly ingrained in the American tradition long before the Greek influence became common. This was particularly true in the North. Benjamin in his forewords and plate descriptions explains the fact that he has lengthened the proportions of the orders and made cornices flatter and with greater projection than the classic norm. And the idea carried over into his Greek-inspired detail. Thus Plate VII of the *Practice of Architecture* is of a new order in the Greek manner, invented by Benjamin for a specific American use. It combines an original entablature, somewhat Ionic in type, with a column that has a Greek Doric capital and a base of a single channeled torus. Benjamin suggests that the column be either eight

---

[16] As shown, for instance, in his letter to Robert Dale Owen with regard to the Smithsonian Institution, quoted by H. M. Pierce Gallagher in *Robert Mills, Architect of the Washington Monument,* 1781–1855 (New York: Columbia University Press, 1935).

[17] Parts I and II (Boston: Shaw and Stratton, 1830); the whole work (Boston: Lincoln and Edwards, 1831); 2nd ed., enlarged (Boston: Marsh, Capen & Lyon, 1832); 4th ed. (Boston: Marsh, Capen & Lyon, 1835); 11th ed. (Philadelphia: Henry Carey Baird & Co., 1876).

[18] Philadelphia: Lindsay and Blakiston.

or nine diameters high depending on whether the house is large or small in dimension.[19]

Minard Lafever also invented a new Greek order basically Corinthian; Benjamin's was basically Doric. It is shown on Plates 11 and 12 in *The Beauties of Modern Architecture* and applied to an ingenious sliding door design on Plate 7. He remarks that it ' is a design composed of antique specimens. . . In many situations this design will be preferable to those generally in use.'[20] Plates 31 and 32 of the same work illustrate a modified Ionic order, with a delicate and enriched capital. Of it he remarks that it ' has neither the proportions nor general features of the antique Ionic order, nor is it pretended that it is in general equal to it; but it is hoped that it may not be wholly inferior.' Here apparently we have modification for its own sake, creation for the simple joy of creating.

Many practicing architects of the period displayed the same freedom in using the Benjamin and Lafever books that the authors had shown in designing the plates. Thus, except in the larger and more monumental buildings of Washington and Philadelphia and New York, departure from any exact copying of Greek details was the rule rather than the exception. Even in some monumental buildings — the Providence Arcade, for instance, and the Tremont House in Boston — it was a departure from what was deemed the correct proportions which made them seem ugly to the pedantic Scotch visitor, Thomas Hamilton.[21] He never realized that correctness *per se* played but a minor rule in the idealism of the American architects of the thirties;

[19] The text description of this plate is sufficiently expressive of Benjamin's ideals to warrant extended quotations:

' I am aware that the publication of anything in the shape of an order, unless it be really one of the Grecian or Roman orders, is, by persons well versed in architecture, thought to be little less than heresy. Although I am not much disposed to differ from them in opinion, I have deemed it advisable in this case to depart from it. My reasons for doing so proceed from the fact, that more than one half of all the columns and entablatures erected in country situations, for either internal or external finishings, belong neither to the Grecian nor Roman system. The same fact holds true in relation to our cities and large towns. . .

' I have often inquired the reason of this, from very intelligent workmen, and have as often received for an answer, that the Tuscan order is too massive and plain, the Doric too expensive, and the Ionic too rich, and that they are therefore under the necessity of composing a column and entablature which will conform to the views and purses of their employers.

' With these facts before me, no doubt rests in my mind but what it would be better to give a design here of a column and entablature, constructed on scientific principles, and of a character capable of meeting the views and practice above mentioned, than to have it to be composed by unskilful hands.'

[20] This order is used, for instance, in Stanton Hall, Natchez, as well as in many New York interiors.

[21] *Men and Manners in America* (Edinburgh: W. Blackwood, 1833).

that what they were after was a consistency quite different from the consistency of archaeological precedent.

The changes made in America in the course of that development of Greek form which led to the architecture usually termed Greek Revival fall naturally into a number of different classes. The first is the common combination of Greek forms with Roman, Renaissance, or Baroque forms. It is so common as to be taken for granted in most cases. Thus, as has repeatedly been pointed out,[22] many American ' Greek Revival ' houses are merely the old traditional five-bay house with a Greek Doric porch added as an entrance. Examples are almost too numerous to list; such houses are perhaps especially common in New England, Pennsylvania, Kentucky, and Tennessee. Ever since the time of A. J. Downing it has been the custom to decry the houses of this period as being ' imitation Greek temples.' An examination of the examples shows instead that by far the greater number are either traditionally Colonial or completely new and inventive in plan and mass. The Andalusias and the Berry Hills were always in the minority.

Another characteristic trend during this period is the modification of the traditional Wren-Gibbs church type through the application of Greek detail. Here the tendency to copy Greek temple forms was stronger. Occasionally bold temple-type pedimented porches resulted, as in Alexander Parris's St. Paul's in Boston, Bucklin and Warren's church in Providence, or Haviland's Presbyterian Church in Philadelphia or St. Peter's on Barclay Street, New York. Yet generally speaking, even when a temple-type portico was used, the body of the church and the church tower would be quite untemplelike. One variation of the Greek *in antis* type is especially common. This was probably first used by A. J. Davis in the Carmine Street Presbyterian Church, in New York, and consisted of a gabled or pedimented façade with a recessed porch of approximately half the total width, with two free-standing columns; the faces of the projecting building elements — often containing gallery stairs — were decorated with antae at the corners. The result was a recessed colonnaded porch between coupled antae. This scheme was used again and again all over the country.

The towers of these churches are in most cases remarkable examples of the ingenuity with which American architects applied Greek detail to non-Greek forms. In scheme the larger ones, at least, are based on the old James Gibbs formula which had been so highly

[22] See pages 163, 271, etc.

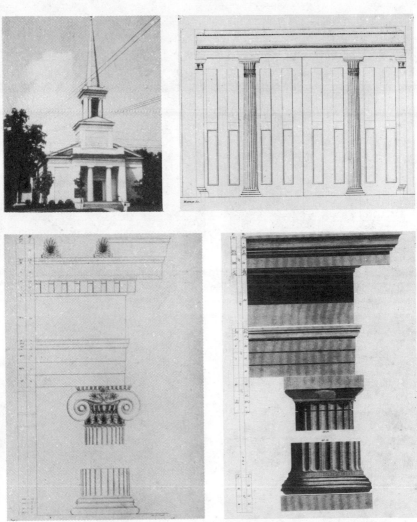

American detail of the period: ABOVE, LEFT, Presbyterian Church, Marcellus, N.Y., with characteristic spire. (*Taylor.*) ABOVE, RIGHT, Lafever's new Corinthian order, in a parlor screen. (*Beauties of Modern Architecture.*) BELOW, LEFT, Lafever's new Ionic order. (*Beauties of Modern Architecture.*) BELOW, RIGHT, Benjamin's new order. (*Practice of Architecture.*)

American Greek Revival detail: ABOVE, LEFT, portico of the Customs House, New Bedford, Mass. Robert Mills, architect. (*Author*.) ABOVE, RIGHT, continuous guttae band and granite anta capitals, New York warehouse. (*Author*.) BELOW, LEFT, Lafever-type door, Leavenworth House, Syracuse. (*Merrill*.) BELOW, RIGHT, St. James's Church, New York. Minard Lafever, architect. (*Author*.)

American Greek Revival detail: TOP, LEFT, ceiling flower from Junius Ward House, Georgetown, Ky. (*Andrews.*) TOP, RIGHT, detail of the Louisville Bank, Ky. Gideon Shryock, architect. (*Newcomb.*) CENTER, Jonathan Goldsmith's own house, Painesville, Ohio. (*Frary.*) BOTTOM, elevation of a parlor, by Lafever. (*Modern Builders' Guide.*)

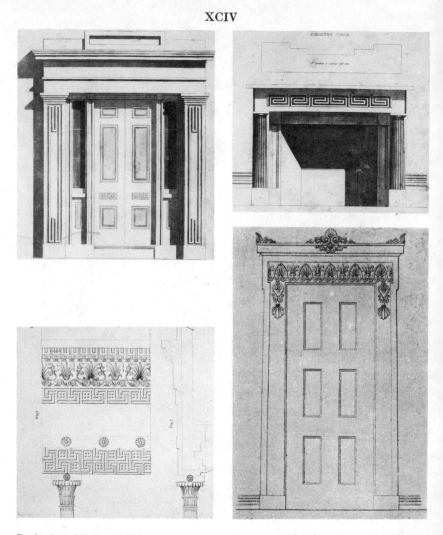

Benjamin and Lafever details: ABOVE, LEFT, 'frontispiece' by Benjamin. (*Practical House Carpenter*.) Compare Plate XL. ABOVE, RIGHT, mantel from the same book. BELOW, LEFT, church gallery front, by Lafever. (*Beauties of Modern Architecture.*) BELOW, RIGHT, door from the same book. Compare Plate XCII.

developed in colonial days. Martin Thompson's spire for St. Mark's-in-the-Bouwerie [23] shows one such scheme of almost Egyptian simplicity, but many extraordinarily lavish examples also exist.[24]

Still another common union of Greek and non-Greek forms is the combination of the Roman dome with Greek pedimented porticoes. This became almost a formula for many kinds of public buildings. In its most brutally obvious fashion it was a feature of Town and Davis's winning design for the New York customs house. It was used with equal simplicity, but greater success, in Ammi B. Young's Boston customs house, where the central section and dome is now replaced by the present high office tower. Latrobe used it, subtly expressed, in the Bank of Pennsylvania at Philadelphia, the earliest complete Greek Revival building in America. Town and Davis were especially fond of this combination, though it was at the time often adversely criticized.[25] Both the Indiana and Illinois capitols, from their design, are of this type. In the little church of St. Esprit in New York, A. J. Davis produced one of the most interesting and independent of such designs, with a high dome of almost Baroque character developing effective interior space, and with a façade porch of the purest Greek Ionic. The auditorium churches of Mills sometimes combined circular plans with Greek details. Other variants of the same combination are found in the Latrobe portions of the United States Capitol, and in several state houses — e.g. North Carolina and Alabama.

A second class of important variations in Greek precedent consists of variations in the orders themselves. Perhaps the most common is the omission of triglyphs and mutules in the Doric entablature. This is so common as to be almost a characteristic American form; it is well-nigh universal in domestic examples. Although the necessity for economy was often the probable cause, it seems not to have been so always; even in so lavish and monumental a façade as the stone front of Hyde Hall near Cooperstown, New York, Philip Hooker uses

23 Probably done under the firm name of Town and Thompson. Contemporary comment in *The New York Mirror*, Vol. v, No. 34 (1 March 1828), gives the credit for the design to Thompson.

24 For example, the church at Suffield, Connecticut; St. Peter's Cathedral in Cincinnati, Ohio; the Presbyterian church at Marcellus, New York; and the old First Presbyterian Church in Dayton, Ohio, long since destroyed, interesting because old views of it show a queer round-headed buttress form connecting the stages of the tower, motifs exactly like those shown in Plate LXV of Lafever's *The Young Builder's General Instructor*. It is possible Lafever may have designed the Dayton church. We know he did much work, in many parts of the country, of which no record remains.

25 See page 324.

unfluted Greek Doric columns with a bold and simplified entablature without triglyphs or mutules. In cases like this it seems that the controlling motive was purely aesthetic — the desire to produce a certain definite effect. A similar aesthetic feeling probably lies behind the many examples, especially common in the South, of the use of much attenuated Greek Doric columns, two stories high, with an extremely slim entablature and a delicate eaves cornice.

In many examples, even some of great cost and monumentality, the omission of the triglyphs is compensated for by the use in the frieze of rhythmically spaced wreaths. This usage may be based on a Nicholson plate.[26] It is found on several houses in Staten Island, for instance, and on the Ralph Small house in Macon, Georgia.

The omission of flutes from the Greek Doric column is also a common variation. It is found not only in country work, where economy may be the deciding factor behind it, but in such lavish buildings as Arlington, designed by George Hadfield, or the granite Hyde Hall already mentioned. It is also common in the work of Robert Mills, as for instance in one of his designs for a marine hospital [27] and in his powerful granite customs houses for Newburyport and New Bedford, Massachusetts. The latter is a particularly interesting example of the creative use of Greek precedent, for although the whole effect is recognizably 'Greek Doric' it is gained by all sorts of non-Greek means. Molding profiles are changed, triglyphs and mutules omitted, and richness and power obtained by a carefully studied use of stone textures and the variation of rock-faced and tooled granite.[28]

Another common variation of Doric forms is the use of a taenia with a continuous row of guttae beneath it, combined with an unbroken frieze. The staccato shadows of the guttae form an effective decoration. This variation is especially common in New York.

Prevalent also are friezes made far wider than the ancient types suggest in order to provide for top-story or attic windows. In many cases these windows have rich pierced grilles of wood or cast iron, and become decorative elements of great power.

A further series of variations concerns the use and modification of the Greek anta. Here an old tradition of using pilasters undoubtedly affected the result, and the use of the Greek anta form as a simple

[26] Or perhaps taken directly from Stuart's plates of the Choragic Monument of Thrasyllus at Athens.

[27] Gallagher, op. cit.

[28] Could this treatment have been suggested to Mills by the engravings of the amphitheater at Pola published in the fifth volume of Stuart and Revett? Wherever the idea came from, Mills made excellent use of it.

pilaster is common in both monumental and domestic work. Thus it was widely used by Mills in the Treasury building and the Patent Office in Washington, and by Henry Walters in the Ohio state capitol. In this work, however, the projection of the antae is greater than that of normal pilasters; the effort is consciously to emphasize the rhythmical character of the building and thus to approximate the powerful light and shade of a colonnade without using columns. The same thing was done in a still bolder way by Town and Davis on the exterior of the New York customs house (Sub-Treasury building), and also by Isaiah Rogers in the Collegiate Reformed Church (once on Lafayette Place and Fourth Street in New York) and even more boldly in his interesting façade of the Boston Merchants' Exchange. The freely inventive character of the detail of this building, with its fluted square anta piers carrying interesting capitals of Corinthian anta type set between more normal end antae, is typical of the original types these architects were frequently seeking. In some of the Boston granite buildings the piers are sometimes treated like antae, but with enormously simplified moldings.

Still another variety of the Greek anta common in America, especially in houses, is the free-standing square anta-type pier. Such piers are used to form continuous ' colonnades,' as in the house shown on the engraved title page of Lafever's *The Modern Builders' Guide*,[29] or else as end piers with columns between them. Both uses are common throughout the country. The continuous form is found, for example, in Vesper Cliff, Owego, New York; in Tallmadge, Ohio; in Grass Lake and Ann Arbor, Michigan; in Athens, Georgia; in Natchez, Mississippi — to name but a few of many instances. The corner use is almost as common. In the greater number of cases these square anta piers are of wood; obviously they were more economical to build up than columns. Sometimes they are paneled, to bring out this wooden character still more. But in many cases they are used manifestly for aesthetic reasons only, as in the lavish Ralph Small house at Macon.

Another frequent change is the substitution of a raked blocking course for a pediment. This was a usage especially favored by Mills [30] and employed by him on the Charleston ' Fire Proof Building ' and the Monumental Church in Richmond, but it is extremely common in domestic work as well. Raked blocking courses, sometimes richly decorated with anthemions and scrolls, were frequently used to mark the

29 New York: Sleight, 1833.
30 See page 49.

center of long horizontal roof eaves — as, for instance, in the Ralph Small house at Macon or the Bartlett-Ritchart-Cunningham house [31] at Chillicothe, Ohio. This usage is especially common in the West and the South, and the greatest ingenuity is displayed in the sensitive relations of the plain and decorated portions and in the rhythms of breaks and slopes.

One of the most interesting examples of the creative modifications of Greek forms is the façade of the Bank of Louisville (1837) in Kentucky. Here Gideon Shryock, its architect, set Ionic columns between end piers which, instead of being typical antae, are unmolded masonry and have their outer sides battered to frame the composition more securely. But it is the cornice that is most unusual; the cymatium runs in from each corner only as far as the inner sides of the end piers, and in between the face of the corona carries up to form a cresting and is crowned by a rich scroll composition topped by a large, stylized anthemion. It is evident that Shryock owned, or used, Lafever books; the creative cresting of scrolled anthemions is characteristic of many Lafever plates, and the Ionic capitals are like the original enriched Ionic Lafever published on Plates 31 and 32 of *The Beauties of Modern Architecture*. But Shryock's use of the Lafever inspiration is as free as Lafever's own developments from the Greek.[32]

In any consideration of the creative modification of Greek forms in American architecture one comes again and again on traces of influence from the books of Asher Benjamin and Minard Lafever. These were used by designers and craftsmen the country over, and the freedom of the two authors' designs contributed to the freedom of their readers'. The book of Chester Hills, as has been pointed out, was almost purely eclectic, as were the books of Thomas U. Walter later.[33] But in the work of Benjamin and Lafever minds of compelling creative power are at work. These works, too, are important as showing what extremely personal interpretations of Greek inspiration were possible. Both architects from 1827 on were at work on the same problem — the creation of forms, Greek in inspiration, to fill the ordinary American needs — forms for doors and windows, for porches and chimney pieces. Both had marked success in fulfilling this task, yet the forms Benjamin developed are totally unlike those of Lafever in spirit and in detail.

[31] See page 281.
[32] See below, page 353.
[33] Thomas U. Walter and J. Jay Smith, *A Guide to Workers in Metals and Stone*. . . (Philadelphia: Carey, 1846) and *Two Hundred Designs for Cottages and Villas* . . . *Original and Selected* (Philadelphia: Carey and Hart, 1846).

Both men, apparently, like the architects quoted earlier,[34] realized that copying Stuart and Revett would not do. And both realized that the most fruitful sources of inspiration lay less in the Greek orders than in the balance evolved from the alphabet of Greek forms — bands, molding profiles and ornaments, frets, anthemions, rosettes. Benjamin's development of the fret has already been commented on.[35] See, for instance, his Plate 28 in *The Practical House Carpenter* (1830),[36] or the window of Plate 31, or the dormer of Plate 32. There is about them all a certain masculine, forthright character, a use of flat bands and fillets, a largeness of scale, a something almost stark, which we recognize as the very hallmark of the Benjamin touch. The same is true of the mantelpieces: Plate 49, with its use of only flat bands and sinkages and panels to give its effect; Plate 50, with its great corner frets; Plate 51, with its little Doric columns, its flat-edged shelf, its complete innocence of entablature moldings, its fret-decorated frieze. In the *Practice of Architecture* (1833) the detail is richer, with the introduction here and there of enriched crestings, anthemion bands, and anthemions used at the top and bottom of panels,[37] but the spirit in this book is still the same outright masculine strength as that in the earlier book. It is of course recognizably ' Greek,' but it is still more *American* and *Benjamin* in type. No copying here! These are not the forms out of which to build an ' imitation Greek temple,' but rather forms from which to construct the dignified mansions of Salem or Nantucket.

Even more fertile in imagination was Minard Lafever. The story of his architectural development is graphically told in the contents of his three earliest books. *The Young Builder's General Instructor* (1829) is inchoate, and many of its details coarse, but in it there appears already that striving for novelty and grace, for schooled richness, which was his controlling taste. This can be seen alike in the larger designs and in the details. The ' Front Door in Grecian Architecture' (Plate 15) is characteristic; the horizontal transom and lintel of the door itself are decorated with little slanting-topped panels carrying anthemion scrolls. The same motif — so far as I know, Lafever's own invention — appears in the design for a store front

[34] See pages 56, 60, 61.
[35] See page 165.
[36] Boston: the author, R. P. & C. Williams, and Annin & Smith, 1830.
[37] This use of the anthemion at the top and bottom of panels became so universal in American architecture as to constitute almost a sort of national badge in the Greek Revival. It occurs in the Nicholson books, to be sure, but it never attained in the British Isles the extraordinary popularity it enjoyed in the United States.

(Plate 51); his rich and fantastic arched transom door (Plate 42) shows how his imagination played over the most hackneyed New York forms. But the Greek forms are still but little used; their inspiration has yet scarcely touched them.

In his second book, *The Modern Builders' Guide* (1833), the change is striking. Lafever had used the intervening three years well. His taste had matured, his knowledge broadened immensely, his touch become both more firm and more free. Now the Greek inspiration is dominant and all-pervasive; it has become a background to his work rather than a novelty, and already — as background — it serves to set off the delicate fertility of his own invention. It is the lighter, Ionic side of Greek architectural form that delights Lafever, as it seems to have been the heavier Doric type that excited Benjamin. Lafever's detail is essentially personal. As his taste and knowledge matured he became more and more definitely the individual artist in his fantasies on Greek themes. He loved to use rosettes for decorating simple bands. He liked wide, plain bands, simple moldings; in many cases he abandoned moldings altogether in favor of slightly recessed, or slightly raised, bands or panels. And especially he loved broad expanses of plane surface picked out here and there with decorated moldings in cornices, rosettes over windows or around mantels, and delicate decorated anta capitals. Perhaps the most characteristic expression of this is the 'Parlour' design presented in Plates 67–71, or the front doors of Plate 81. There is not in any of this any desire to copy Greek architecture; it is all quite naturally and directly designed for American houses; it uses Erechtheum rosettes and anthemion bands in ways of which the Greeks had never dreamed. It is this book, too, which published two house designs [38] of the 'temple type with wings,' which exerted such an enormous influence all over the United States.

The Modern Builders' Guide also shows designs which make considerable use of scrolled anthemions and 'Greek' consoles. Plate 80, for example, shows the anthemion used to decorate the top of a mullion panel, and Plate 81 ingeniously contrives delicate anthemions, reversed to soften the top of the mullion itself. One of the mantels of Plate 57 and the doors of Plates 66 and 81 show Lafever's delicate and original use of consoles. In all of this work the influence of the Erechtheum door is obvious, as well as the complete freedom with

[38] One is shown as an engraved title page; the other in Plates 72–9. The second is interesting in that the plans and sections show a support on the central axis, whereas the elevation is changed to the more 'correct' method of an opening on axis.

which Lafever used it.[39] Compare, for instance, the delicate flatness
of the profiles of Plate 66 as compared with the bold projections of
the Erechtheum. The cornices of the front door (Plate 66) and the
interior door (Plate 60, fig. 1) are based on the Erechtheum door
cornice,[39] but it is noteworthy that wherever Lafever uses consoles
with a door he substitutes a cornice with a broad corona (as in Plate
60, fig. 2). In the small scale at which he was working, this modification, it seems to me, is remarkable evidence of the sure discrimination
of Lafever's taste.

Another form in which Lafever delighted, and in which he was
followed by a great many of the American architects and builders of
his time, is the anthemion combined with scrolls to form a band or a
cresting. This appeared in a primitive, rather crude expression in his
first book, *The Young Builder's General Instructor,* where Plate 49
shows a door with an anthemion frieze and a window crowned with a
slant-topped paneled cresting containing a crude scrolled anthemion.
The door is merely a somewhat naïve variation of earlier New York
Baroque forms, but the window head is a new motif, expressive of
Lafever's growing taste for delicate richness; it is the precursor of
his later refined and imaginative work.

In *The Modern Builders' Guide* his thorough devotion to Greek
inspiration and his unusual understanding of it allow him to create
freely with this beautiful assemblage of curved lines. In Plate 61 he
shows two of the Erechtheum bands; Plate 82, a 'Parlour Door,'
shows one of his first free uses of the form as an ornament to fill the
much widened lintel architrave band. The whole design is eloquent of
Lafever's freedom in using precedent, and the upward swing of the
scrolls connecting end and center anthemions gives a surprising sense
of delicate lift to the composition.

But it is in *The Beauties of Modern Architecture* that the true
talent of Lafever reaches final maturity. The work is not only simpler
and more direct, but at the same time freer and on occasions richer,
than that of the earlier books. Tremendous use is made of flat surfaces

[39] The problem of the source of American derivatives of the Erechtheum door
is puzzling. Neither the first nor the second (revised) editions of Stuart and
Revett show it. Henry W. Inwood in *The Erechthion at Athens* . . . (London:
J. Carpenter & Son, 1827) shows a 'Full Size of the Console' and the cornice;
the general aspect of the door appears in his perspective restoration (which
Chester Hills copied in his book), but there is no elevation. Apparently the door
as a whole was first shown in Thomas L. Donaldson's *A Collection of the Most
Approved Examples of Doorways from Ancient Buildings in Greece and Italy.* . .
(London [n. p.], 1833); French ed., *Collection des examples les plus estimés des
portes monumentales* (Paris: Thiollet et Simon, 1837). It was probably from this
that the American architects got their inspiration.

and bands and of panels without panel molds, as in the mantel shown on Plate 46 (fig. 4) and in the doors shown on Plates 2 and 14. The rosette is used more carefully, with less unthinking enthusiasm. The pulpit of Plate 47 is characteristic of this restrained simplicity of manner. But balancing this restraint is a delicate exuberance in the imaginative use of the anthemion, and here Lafever's genius appears at its fullest.

A characteristic use, much copied, at least in the New York area,[40] is the utilizing of the anthemion in very flat relief, employed as a decoration for otherwise simple panels, as on Plates 2, 15, and 18 (where the design of the anthemion itself is credited to C. L. Bell, architect). Another exquisite use is in the ceiling flower shown on Plate 21, one of the most beautiful of such ceiling ornaments ever produced.[41]

It was as a cresting that the anthemion seems to have most interested Lafever, and it was the design of crestings which gave him the greatest opportunity for originality and delicate invention. Thus Plate 6 shows an interior window cresting formed of a channeled band (above the plain architrave), curved up at the ends in volutes and down in the center, where it spreads to each side in graceful rinceaux; above the center at the intersection rises a single bold anthemion. Plate 14 shows parlor doors of a different type; here the architrave is crowned by a crown mold which is interrupted by a heart-shaped ornament in the center, the top fillet above the crown mold is swept up in the center to form scrolls from which rinceaux are carried out on either side, and in the center is an anthemion. Plate 19 has a cornice the initiating central scrolls of which grow out of the cymatium mold; half anthemions at the corners serve as end complements to the large central anthemion. A scrolled anthemion pattern interrupts the center of the corona, and an elaborate pattern of framed anthemions fills the wide band of the architrave at the top of the door and is continued a short distance down the sides. A more elaborate version of a similar detail, designed for use in connection with sliding doors, is shown on Plates 25 and 26. Here there is no true cymatium or even

---

[40] As, for instance, on the front door of the John Hazlet house at No. 204 West 13 Street, which has been recorded by the Historic American Buildings Survey.

[41] A slightly simplified example exists in the Shoenberger house in Pittsburgh, shown by Charles M. Stotz in *The Early Architecture of Western Pennsylvania* (New York: William Helburn, for the Buhl Foundation, 1936). Another example even closer to the Lafever plate exists in the Junius Ward house (1859) near Georgetown, Kentucky. It is shown in Alfred Andrews's master's essay, 'Greek Revival Houses in Kentucky,' Columbia University, Department of Art and Archaeology, 1942. These are but a few of the examples which show the widespread influence of the Lafever books.

a projecting fillet above the corona, the plain surface of which widens gradually from each side toward the center. At the ends are framed and scrolled half-anthemion ' acroteria '; in the center is an applied banded scroll with rinceaux projecting upward at its outer end (a little over halfway from the center to the end of the corona) and downward over the face of the corona at the center. A large anthemion of angular type crowns the center. This design, with the spans widened to permit sidelights and with the columns changed from Ionic to Doric, is used as the front door to the superb house, Diamond Point, at Harrodsburg, Kentucky.[42] Plates 1 and 5 show still another type. In this the entire cornice corona is swept up on each side in the center to form the starting scroll of a crest rinceau; there is the same heart-shaped scroll ornament over the architrave band that is seen in Plate 14.

It is interesting to note that on Plate 1 the upper band of the architrave widens slightly toward the center, by about a half inch in 3 feet 6 inches. This gives an unusually light, graceful feeling to the design,[43] and shows Lafever's true sense of Greek refinements expressed in new ways. The architrave also widens from the top downward, from a width of 1 foot 11 inches at the top to 2 feet 1½ inches at the bottom, the total opening being 11 feet high. Lafever's rinceaux and anthemions are seldom copies of Greek details, despite their extraordinarily ' Greek ' appearance. The rinceau scrolls frequently reverse their flow direction, and the anthemions are often lobed sunbursts or are jagged and angular-ended in a quite original manner.

The effect of these anthemion crestings was wide. In St. James's Church (1835–7) in New York, already referred to, the exterior stone doors have crestings of entirely similar types. A simplified copy of Plate 26 in *The Beauties of Modern Architecture* is found in the Garden District of New Orleans,[44] and Gallier in the Logan-Henderson house there did not hesitate to follow Plate 19 almost as closely. Even such a brilliant designer in his own right as Gideon Shryock was not averse to using this pervasive Lafever inspiration; in his Bank of Louisville, in Kentucky, the whole pattern of the cornice and cresting is based on Plate 26 of *The Beauties of Modern Architecture*, with

42 Shown by Rexford Newcomb in *Old Kentucky Architecture* (New York: William Helburn, 1940), Plates 91 and 92.

43 This refinement is found in the door and window trim of the second or main bedroom floor of a house at No. 37 East Fourth Street, New York. It may well be an indication of the Lafever authorship of the design.

44 I. W. Ricciuti, *New Orleans and Its Environs* (New York: William Helburn, 1938), Plate 77.

the addition of a cymatium on the cornice at either end beyond the extreme projection of the decorative cresting.[45] These crestings, in their own freedom, suggested the freest possible interpretations by local builders and architects. Thus such a cresting is often used for a pediment ornament, as in the Mitchell-Turner house at Milan, Ohio.[46] An even freer use of the general motif is the free, curving scroll of the architrave taenia over the end windows of the Swift house in Vermilion, Ohio — a use naïve, to be sure, but extremely effective as well.[47]

Another fruitful opportunity for many modifications of Greek detail lay in the design of pierced grilles, both in wood and in iron. These are common in frieze and attic windows all over the country, from Maine to Louisiana. Some are founded on the fret; in their design the influence of Benjamin may be indicated. Others, the larger number, are based on the anthemion and the acanthus rinceau. Here the inspiration of Lafever is often obvious. For instance, Plates 63, 64, and 65 of *The Modern Builders' Guide* all show transoms above doors filled with freely designed anthemion and acanthus scroll grilles. Strangely enough there is little evidence of the use of such forms in that position, but grilles based on them are common in attic and frieze windows. Thus the architect Jonathan Goldsmith, in his own cottage near Painesville, Ohio, used for window grilles a pattern borrowed almost line for line from Plate 64. And this is but one of many such examples.

Many of these grilles are of cast iron, and it is in other architectural elements of cast iron that the enormous imaginative flexibility of the American Greek Revival designers shows most clearly. The variety of railing design, the bold modifications of fret forms to suit the material, the beautifully modeled anthemions that serve as picket tops and finials, the bold way in which elements of concentrated richness are applied to quite simple schemes — these all show not only a great fertility of invention, but also a sensitive feeling for materials.

This free use of precedent reached a climax in the patterns of the cast-iron porches and verandas which became so common after the middle 1840's, particularly in the South. In them elements strictly Greek are at a minimum, yet many in the swing of their lacy curves show distant relations to Greek precedent. In the later examples more Rococo types of S-scroll and elements based on the Gothic are domi-

45 See Newcomb, op. cit. Plates 114, 115.
46 I. T. Frary, *Early Houses of Ohio* (Richmond: Garrett and Massie, 1936), Plate 194.
47 Ibid. Plate 147.

nant, but in all of them the sense of the potentialities of cast iron is supreme.[48]

Thus these Greek forms reached their final expression in that most American of materials — iron. In a way this is significant of the whole movement we term the Greek Revival. To the American architect of a century or so ago Greek precedent was no mere absolute to which he must conform, but a new breath of fresh inspiration which he breathed and made his own; the freedom with which he changed and invented, the variations he developed, were the marks of his success in this task. He was working not with the exotic but with the natural, and the buildings themselves show, I believe, how natural, how American, how our own these forms became.

[48] The history of this decorative cast iron is still somewhat obscure. Certain stock patterns are found all over the country, yet we know that much of it (as, for instance, in New Orleans and parts of Indiana) came from small local foundries. It is not even sure, so far as I know, where the first of these cast-iron porches was used. Apparently single pattern units frequently were shipped from large foundries in Philadelphia and New York and used as patterns by local foundries in many places. But this whole matter deserves much more careful research than it has yet received.

APPENDIX B

SOME ARTICLES OF ARCHITECTURAL INTEREST PUBLISHED IN AMERICAN PERIODICALS PRIOR TO 1851

An annotated selective bibliography
by the late Sarah H. J. Simpson Hamlin

THIS list does not attempt to be a complete bibliography. It merely represents a sampling of certain magazines in the collections of the New York Historical Society and the New York Public Library. Further study in other collections would undoubtedly reveal the same amount of interest in architecture, on the part of the Americans of a century and more ago, that may be seen so clearly in this preliminary study.

A

American Eclectic Magazine, New York

Vol. ii (July 1841), p. 183. Reviews an article in the *British Critic and Quarterly Theological Review* of April 1841, on Church Architecture. The editor calls attention to this article without much emphasis as being of more interest to England, with its old churches, than to America with its new ones.

Vol. iii (March 1842), p. 369. The editor reviews an article on Principles of Gothic Architecture in the *London Quarterly Review* of December 1841. Commends its scholarliness, but says it is especially interesting only to such ' as are induced by their callings to investigate subjects of this nature.'

American Journal of Agriculture and Science, Albany

Vol. vii (February 1848), p. 49. The leading article is a review, entitled ' Rural Architecture,' of Ranlett's *The Architect,* reproducing an illustration. The review emphasizes the importance of attractive country dwellings.

Vol. vii (March 1848), p. 97. 'Ornamental Fountains.'

Vol. vii (May 1848), p. 209. Another review, entitled ' Rural Architecture,' of further numbers of Ranlett's *The Architect.* An illustration is reproduced as the frontispiece.

Vol. vii (June 1848), p. 248. ⎫ All are reviews
Vol. vii (August 1848), p. 329. ⎪ of later numbers
Vol. vii (November 1848), p. 507. ⎬ of Ranlett's
Vol. vii (December 1848), p. 535. ⎭ *The Architect.*
Vol. vii (June 1848), p. 254. ' New Materials for Flooring, Paving, and Roofing.'
Vol. vii (July 1848), p. 329. Article on the best placing of a barn.
Vol. vii (August 1848), p. 350. Shows an illustration of P. T. Barnum's house near Bridgeport. The description, taken from the *Farmer and Mechanic,* is interesting.

American Journal of Science and Arts (*Silliman's Journal*), New Haven

Vol. vii (January-June 1824), p. 149. ' The Celtic Antiquities of America,' by John Finch, F.R.S.
Vol. xvi (July 1829), p. 168. Paragraph on the United States Capitol at Washington, giving dimensions, dates, and costs.
Vol. xvii (January-June 1830), pp. 99, 249; Vol. xviii (July-December 1830), pp. 11, 212. Superb series of four articles, unsigned, entitled ' Architecture in the United States,' amounting to nearly 75 pages. The first deplores the lack of cultivation and encouragement of the arts, refers to Peter Banner as practicing and living in New Haven in 1798. The second is devoted to city and town planning; it calls for parks outside, as well as greens and commons within towns, and deplores the overuse of straight streets and square plans; it also advocates corporate and communal land development. The third is chiefly historical, with an excellent differentiation of Greek and Gothic ideals. The fourth contains the author's program for American architecture. It also gives prices of roofing in New York City. [The whole series is most farsighted and interesting. The author (probably not Professor Silliman) has not been identified.]
Vol. xxiv (April, May, and June 1833), p. 257. ' Architecture,' by Daniel Wadsworth, of Hartford. A general article, originally intended for use in a girls' school, dealing especially with the orders, of which illustrations are given. The article also refers to existing buildings in Hartford, New Haven, Philadelphia, etc.
Vol. xxv (January 1834), p. 290. ' Securing Houses and Their Inhabitants from Fire, and of Obtaining Supplies of Water and Warm Air,' unsigned. A supplement followed, in Vol. xxvi (July 1834), p. 286.
Vol. xxv (January 1834), p. 304. ' Observations on Architectural, Rural, and Domestic, and Other Improvements,' by Eleazar Lord of New York [President of the Manhattan Insurance Company]. The article refers to an association of gentlemen in New Haven for ' ascertaining the best plans and models of domiciliary architecture,' and discusses sites and materials.
Vol. xxvii (April 1835), p. 303. ' Some Properties of a Rampant Arch,' by Thomas Gordon.

Vol. xxxi (January 1837), p. 248. 'On Zinc as a Covering for Buildings,' a letter from Professor A. Caswell.

Vol. xxxviii (July 1840), p. 276. 'Some Account of Ithiel Town's Improvements in the Construction and Practical Execution of Bridges for Roads, Railroads, and Aqueducts,' an extended article, unsigned, with illustrations.

American Literary Magazine, Albany

Vol. i (November 1847), p. 269. 'College Edifices and Their Relation to Education,' unsigned. Contains an elaborate description of the Yale Library.

Vol. iv (March 1849), p. 530. 'Cathedral of St. Peter,' unsigned but dated from Hudson, New York. Comments on church architecture.

American Magazine, New York

Vol. i (December 1787), p. 8. 'Advice to Masons,' signed 'Fact.' On the construction of chimneys.

Vol. i (January 1788), p. 97. 'General Description of Philadelphia,' unsigned. Largely devoted to the buildings the author admires.

Vol. i (March 1788), p. 220. General description of the City of New York, with some attention to its architecture. Probably by the editor, Noah Webster.

Vol. i (September 1788), p. 685. 'Description of Boston from the *Geographical Gazette* of 1785.' Continued (October 1788), p. 763; concluded (November 1788), p. 827. The October number gives the date of the *Geographical Gazette* as 1784, as does the November number also.

American Monthly Magazine, New York

Vol. iii (July 1834), p. 357. One-page review of J. S. Memes's *History of Sculpture, Painting and Architecture*, Boston, 1834. Reviewer notes that a few years earlier appreciation of such a work would have been limited to a few, but that now its appeal will be wide.

Vol. iv (January 1835), p. 242. 'The Fine Arts and the Spirit of the Age,' by E. C. A plea for public support of poets, painters, and sculptors.

Vol. v (April 1835), p. 160. Editorial, 'Architectural Designs.' [Quoted on page 324.] An interesting piece of straight architectural criticism of contemporary work, mentioning architects' names and buildings.

Vol. vi (November, December 1835), pp. 213, 241. Article in two installments: 'The Condition and Prospects of the Art of Painting in the United States,' by Charles Fraser, of Charleston, S. C.

Vol. vii (January 1836), p. 53. 'Greenough the Sculptor,' by H. T. T. Interesting contemporary material.

Vol. vii (February 1836), p. 113. 'On the Influence of the Arts of Design; and the True Method of Encouraging and Protecting Them,' by William Dunlap. Contains considerable material on architecture. This magazine also carried considerable general material dealing with the fine arts and architecture — exhibition reviews and similar notes.

American Monthly Review, Philadelphia

July 1795, p. 232. Reviews of Uvedale Price's *An Essay on the Picturesque, as Compared with the Sublime and the Beautiful* and of ' A Letter to Uvedale Price,' by Humphrey Repton. These show great interest in the classic-romantic discussions of the English landscape architects and critics. The controversy is also referred to later in: December 1795, p. 377. ' Review of " The Landscape; a Didactic Poem ": also of an " Essay on the Picturesque ": Together with practical remarks on rural Ornament,' by ' the author of *Planting and Ornamental Gardening; a Practical Treatise.*' The text gives the author's name as Marshall.

American Museum, Philadelphia

Vol. v (March 1789), p. 234. Description of Philadelphia, an extract from the Rev. Dr. Duche's *Observations on a Variety of Subjects.* The description includes architectural comments.

Vol. viii (October 1790), p. 174. ' On the Architecture of America,' unsigned. Quotes some of Thomas Jefferson's strictures, and deplores the almost universal use of wood in building; also contains a good description of Gothic architecture.

Vol. xi (February 1792), p. 71. Letter V of ' Letters to a Young Lady,' by the Rev. John Bennet. Recommends a taste for the fine arts of painting, sculpture, and architecture, and suggests the study of Evelyn's *Parallel of Ancient and Modern Architecture* and of Robert Morris's *Lectures.*

American Quarterly Review, Philadelphia

Vol. v (March 1829), p. 1. ' Egyptian Architecture,' unsigned. A long essay (40 pp.) in the guise of a review of the *Description de l'Egypte* and of Quatregine's *De l'architecture Egyptienne.*

American Repertory of Arts, Sciences, and Manufactures, New York

Vol. i (February 1840), p. 14; continued (in later numbers), pp. 106, 243, 337, 412. ' The Art of Building,' by Jared Frost. Advocates more fireproof building, and hollow terra-cotta vaults on rolled or cast-iron ribs, as well as spheroidal vaults; also advocates the use of concrete. [Advanced and prophetic in attitude.]

Vol. ii (January 1841), p. 465. Quotes from the *Palace of Architecture:* ' He, however, who would rival the Greek temple, must imitate, not the temple, but the Greek.'

Vol. iv (December 1841), p. 374. Quotes from *Le Fanal* a paragraph on

'Iron Houses.' One at Brussels, at an exhibition of National Manufactures, appears to be an 'incontestable proof of the possibility of having metal architecture.'

American Review, unidentified (this note from a single copy, without title page or contents, in the New York Historical Society).

Vol. I (January 1843), p. 95. Complimentary review of A. J. Downing's *Cottage Residences,* but reviewer regrets that the designs are too costly for people of small means.

Analectic Magazine, Philadelphia

Vol. VI (November 1815), p. 363. 'Remarks on the Progress and Present State of the Fine Arts in the United States,' unsigned. [Latrobe has been suggested as possibly the author.] Superb criticism of current architecture: too pretentious country houses — country churches and public buildings mean and slight — some improvement in cities, especially Philadelphia — but why so many buildings in the Louis XIV style, 'I mean that corruption of the Grecian, or rather of the Palladian architecture, which delights in great profusion of ornament, in piling one order upon another.' Such work can never give anything but a sort of 'cumbrous stateliness . . . always poor and contemptible when compared with the grandeur and beauty of Grecian simplicity.'

Vol. XIII (March 1819), pp. 177, 203. Engraving and description of the new Bank of the United States at Philadelphia, William Strickland, architect.

Vol. XV, New Series Vol. I (April 1820), p. 320. 'Essay on Architectural Monuments.' Illustrated with one plate. Signed M. [Usually attributed to Robert Mills.]

Vol. XVI, New Series Vol. II (July 1820), p. 46. Engraving and full description of the new State Capitol at Harrisburg, 'now building.' Describes competition and states that the first prize ($400) was won by Stephen Hills of Harrisburg, the second ($200) by Robert Mills of Baltimore.

In addition, the *Analectic Magazine* published some engravings of architectural interest in many other numbers, e.g. York Springs, Pa. (May 1819), the United States Capitol (March 1820), etc.

[The *Analectic Magazine* was continued after May 1821 by the *Literary Gazette (q.v.).*]

B

Belles-Lettres Repository and Monthly Magazine, New York (subsequently and more generally known as the *New York Literary Journal and Belles-Lettres Repository*)

Vol. II (January 1820), p. 28. 'Gothic Architecture,' unsigned. An article voicing the romantic belief that the origin of Gothic architecture lies in a 'resemblance to the trees and overhanging branches of a regular plantation.'

Boston Spectator, Boston

Vol. I (31 December 1814), p. 210. Detailed account of the 'New Stone Church' [New South Church] on Church Green, designed by Bulfinch. Unsigned. Much praise of the architect, who is named. The article ends with a comment on the immense architectural improvement in Boston, owing to the introduction and common use of 'the excellent stone from inexhaustible quarries on the banks of the Merrimac.' Notes that 'several banks and public offices, the Court House, schoolhouse, the new University Hall' are built of it, and that in them 'a purer taste appears to banish superfluous ornament; and the effect is produced by correct proportion and the richness of the material.' [See page 104.]

Boston Weekly Magazine, Boston

Vol. I (11 June 1803), p. 135. Note concerning the invention by 'Mr. Rawsthorne, the architect,' of a new type of dovetailed, interlocking bricks for arches and vaults.

Vol. II (19 November 1803), p. 15. Brief account of the new church, St. Paul's, at Portland, Maine, where the first service was held on 30 October 1803. Says that great credit is due 'to the architect, Dr. Erving.'

Bowen's Boston News Letter and City Record, Boston (often known as the Boston News Letter)

Vol. I (5 November 1825). Description, with plan and view, of the United States Branch Bank, Boston. Notes that columns are purposely without entasis, which it discusses generally. Gives Solomon Willard as architect, Gridley Bryant as mason, and James M'Allaster as carpenter. Foundation begun 17 May 1824; outside work completed 1 January 1825.

Vol. I (14 January 1826). Notes discovery, on 'Chamber Street,' of an ancient arch of singular construction.

Vol. I (28 January 1826). Further peculiarities of the ancient arch — 10' below street level; 8'-0" x 4'-0" x 7'-0" high; built of two layers of brick. Article speculates as to its original purpose.

Vol. I (18 February 1826). Description of the construction in Washington Street of '23 commodious and central dwelling houses and 8 shops' by Charles Ewer. Some of the buildings were granite-faced.

Vol. I (13 May 1826). Elaborate description of the Philadelphia Arcade; 'John Haviland, architect.' The cornerstone was laid 3 May.

Vol. ii (8 July 1826). Description, with illustration, of Hanover church. Cornerstone laid 20 June 1825; Joseph Jenkins, architect. Describes it as 'primitive Gothic,' of undressed granite, with a square tower. Cost, $42,000; the architect received for design and superintendence $1,000.

Vol. ii (15 July 1826). Announces the election of Solomon Willard as architect for the Bunker Hill Monument.

Vol. ii (12 August 1826). Quotation, without date, from the *New York Gazette*, concerning the arrival in New York of the 'Grecian Ionic Pillars' for the Merchants' Exchange on Wall Street, on board the sloop *Miller's Daughter*, Captain Davis.

Vol. ii (19 August 1826). Description of Faneuil Hall Market.

Vol. ii (2 December 1826). Description of the fourth building of the First Church of Salem, dedicated on 16 November. Gives the architects as Willard and Banners; head carpenter, David Lord; master mason, David Robins. Comments on the beautiful simplicity of the interior. The accompanying illustration is apparently of the third building, recently razed.

C

Christian Disciple and Theological Review, Boston

Vol. i (November 1813), p. 215. 'Modern Monuments of Jerusalem,' an abridgment from Chateaubriand's travels. Some architectural comment.

New Series Vol. iv (May-June 1822), p. 221. Description of the First Unitarian Church of Washington. States that the architect was Bulfinch, and comments on the good effect gained ' with so little cost.'

Christian Examiner and Religious Miscellany, Boston

Vol. xlix (September 1850), p. 278. ' Architects and Architecture,' signed T. C. C. Bewails the lack of architectural education in America. States that American architects are either ' practical, who know little,' or ' theoretical, who know nothing.' The author praises the Beacon Hill Reservoir, the Athenaeum, the Boston Museum, and the Old Colony Railroad Station.

Christian's, Scholar's, and Farmer's Magazine, Elizabethtown, New Jersey

Vol. ii (August-September 1790), p. 305. ' The Origin and Process of Architecture,' unsigned. A general study of the origins of building in the primitive hut, and of its development into various classes of building. Notes the influence of climate. Describes the orders, and mentions Vitruvius, Michelangelo, Palladio, Vignola, and Scamozzi as well as Inigo Jones, Schluter, and Bott. [It is apparently based largely on Sir William Chambers or Isaac Ware.]

Columbian Magazine, Philadelphia

Vol. I (December 1786), p. 178. Brief technical article on heat insulation of rooms by furring.

Vol. I (December 1787), p. 789. Description of Boston. Praises King's Chapel and the Concert Room, and notes that the public buildings are more elegant than in Pennsylvania or New York.

Vol. II (January 1788), p. 27. Letter to the American Philosophical Society on preventing chimney-flue fires by using salt in the water for mixing the mortar.

Vol. II (December 1788), p. 669. Article on Harvard College, with descriptions, history, and an illustration of Harvard Hall and Massachusetts Hall.

Vol. III (February 1789), p. 81. 'Description of the State House at Annapolis, the Capital of Maryland.' A critical description, with view and ground plan. Comments on the disproportion between the dome and the body of the building.

Vol. III (August 1789), p. 473. 'Description of the Federal Edifice at New York.' This long, full, and detailed description is the best extant source for our knowledge of Federal Hall; it is the inspiration of most reconstructions of the interior. The article praises highly the work of L'Enfant, and calls him an 'architect.' [See also under *Massachusetts Magazine,* Vol. I (June 1789), and *New York Magazine,* Vol. I (March 1790).]

D

Dial, Boston

Vol. I (July 1840), p. 17. 'The Religion of Beauty,' signed D. Although chiefly devoted to the beauty of nature, it does not neglect architecture. The writer says 'the beautiful ideal piece of architecture bears no mark of wanton pen-knife. The handsome schoolroom makes the children neat.'

Vol. I (January 1841), p. 367. 'Thoughts on Art,' unsigned. Divides art into the useful arts and the fine arts, and lists architecture as in both classes. Emphasizes the emotional, romantic approach; e.g. 'The Gothic Cathedrals were built when the builder and the priest and the people were overpowered by their faith. Love and fear laid every stone.' Typical transcendentalist criticism.

Vol. II (July 1841), p. 78. 'Painting and Sculpture,' unsigned. Includes a few passages on architecture; attempts to prove that as an art music is superior to architecture.

Vol. IV (July 1843), p. 107. 'Notes on Art and Architecture,' unsigned. [Attributed to Samuel Gray Ward.] Comments on the fact that architecture in America is not indigenous, and a matter not of religion but of taste. Deplores useless elements. 'To adorn the needful, to add a frieze to life, that is art.' Suggests a functional approach to design, based on need and the qualities of materials. Finds the New England church formula satisfactory, but an 'almost total lack of beautiful specimens'; deplores an architecture of paint and plaster. 'Architecture is a tendency towards organization. . . Now in natural organizations . . . we see no part that has not a meaning and use, and each part of that material which answers its end. This also is a fundamental law of architecture.' In the final paragraphs, the author feels that there is little to be gained from imitating Gothic architecture in America, and that Greek architecture is our purest and most promising inspiration.

E

Emerald, Boston

Vol. ii (11 July 1807), p. 329. 'Selected for the *Emerald.* Eloquent Description of Pompeii. (From *A Tour in Italy and Sicily,* by M. Greuze Delessert, not yet published.)' Important as showing American interest in the subject.

Emporium of Arts and Sciences, Philadelphia

Vol. i (August 1812), p. 268. ' Description of Portable Bridge invented by James Elmes, architect of College-Hill, Queen Street, Cambridge.'

Vol. i (September 1812), p. 321. Engraving, entitled ' Architecture,' showing a workman hoisting the capital of a column into place.

Vol. ii (March 1813), p. 350. 'Plan for an Improved Theatre,' by Sir George Cayley, Bart. With plan.

Ibid. p. 353. 'On the Construction of Theatres,' by Richard L. Edgeworth, F.R.S., etc. Chiefly concerns fireproofing.

Ibid. p. 379. 'Construction of Theatres, so as to render them secure against Fire,' by M. B. Cook. Advocates the use of iron instead of wood, and inveighs against the immorality of the theater. [This number was probably inspired by the famous Richmond Theater fire.]

G

General Repository and Review, Cambridge, Massachusetts

Vol. ii (July 1812), p. 141. Review of *A Treatise on Bridge Architecture* . . . by Thomas Pope, architect and landscape gardener. This takes the form of an extended essay on bridge architecture, with adverse comment on the book.

Vol. iii (January 1813), p. 189. Review of *Essays on the Nature and Principles of Taste,* by Archibald Alison, from the Edinburgh edition of 1811, Boston, 1812. [Important as showing earlyAmerican interest in the aesthetics of the romantic movement.]

Godey's Lady's Book, see *Lady's Book*

H

Hesperian, Columbus, Ohio

Vol. i (May 1838), p. 7. ' Ohio in 1838,' signed W. D. G. [William D. Gallagher]. Continued (June) p. 95, (July) p. 183. Some descriptions of public buildings.

K

Knickerbocker Magazine, New York

Vol. i (July 1833), p. 71. Brief description of Lafayette Place [Colonnade Row], New York, with a full-page engraving. States the houses ' were designed and built entirely by Mr. Geer, and all stone work was executed by the State prisoners at Sing Sing.' [A. J. Davis was undoubtedly the designer of this row; Geer apparently worked from Davis's sketches.]

L

Ladies' Companion, New York

Vol. x (January 1839), p. 132. ' The Residence and Library of Ithiel Town, Esq.,' by Mrs. Lydia Sigourney. A full account of Town's superb library, and of the building he had built on Hillhouse Avenue, New Haven, to house it and his own home. With an engraving of the building.

Vol. xii (January 1840), p. 103. 'Washington's House,' signed H. F. H. A description, with an engraving from a drawing by W. H. Bartlett.

Lady and Gentleman's Pocket Magazine, unidentified

Volume containing four months (August-November 1796), pp. 21, 86, 154, 208. ' State of the Fine Arts at Athens,' by Mr. De Pauw. Only incidentally architectural, this is an interesting comment on current taste.

Ibid. p. 193. ' Short History of Yale College,' unsigned. With a curious and little-known ' View of Yale College, New Haven,' and a description.

Lady's Book [better known as *Godey's Lady's Book*], Philadelphia

Published occasional designs for cottages and small houses, chiefly in the Romantic manner. Occasional engravings also are of architectural subjects — the Brighton Pavilion, etc.

Literary Gazette [a weekly continuation of the *Analectic Magazine* (*q.v.*)], Philadelphia

Vol. i (21 April 1821), p. 253. ' Memoir of B. H. Latrobe,' quoted from *Ackermann's Repository* for January 1821. An interesting, if brief, biography. [Significant as showing a high respect for a great American architect.]

Vol. ɪ (12 May 1821), p. 304. An editorial contradiction of the common rumor that Latrobe designed the Bank of the United States in Philadelphia. The note states unequivocally that Strickland won the first prize in the competition, Latrobe's design was placed second, and the actual building was exclusively Strickland's. [This note is interesting not only because it apparently clears up a debated point, but also because its presence in this general magazine seems to reveal a lively popular interest in architects and architecture.]

Literary Magazine and American Register, Philadelphia

Vol. ɪɪɪ (March 1805), p. 167. 'From a Manuscript Journal: On the Flavian Amphitheatre at Rome,' unsigned. A description, with many admiring comments on Roman efficiency in building; also many references to 'the great architect, Fontana,' and his remarks on the Colosseum.

Ibid. p. 181. 'Plan for the Improvement and Diffusion of the Arts adapted to the United States,' unsigned. Deplores the present condition of painting, sculpture, and architecture, and suggests private and Congressional subscription for two galleries of reproductions — one 'for statues and architectural models, and one for bas-reliefs.'

Vol. ɪɪɪ (April 1805), p. 249. Article on 'Chinese Gardening,' unsigned. Includes a description of Chinese palaces and the excellent choice of sites for ornamental buildings, and closes with an appreciation of Chinese architecture.

Vol. ɪɪɪ (June 1805), p. 343. 'Description of the Louvre and the Gallery of Antiques at Paris,' signed 'A Traveller.' Includes a history of the palace, with special emphasis on the parts played by the architects d'Orbay, Levau, Bernini, Mansart, and Perrault.

Vol. ɪᴠ (July 1805), p. 39. Brief description of New Orleans, with some architectural comment.

Vol. ᴠ (May 1806), p. 383. 'Bricks,' unsigned. Notes on their manufacture, use, and universal employment in Philadelphia.

Vol. ᴠ (June 1806), p. 410. 'Sketch of Literature and the Fine Arts in Sicily from 1790 to 1803,' signed Y. Notes the recent completion, at Trapani, of the 'simple and majestic' Church of St. Lawrence, designed by Don Diego de Luca.

Vol. ᴠɪ (September 1806), p. 225. 'Improvement in Paris since the Last Revolution,' by 'Mr. Pinkerton.' Stresses buildings, bridges, open spaces, etc.

Literary Museum, Westchester, Pennsylvania

March 1797, p. 143. 'Anecdotes of Eminent Artists.' Stories of Rembrandt, Donatello, Tintoret, Guido, etc. Not architectural, but significant of popular interest in the arts even in country villages.

June 1797, frontispiece. View of the bridge over the Sanpink Creek, in Trenton, N. J.

Ibid. p. 304. 'Account of the City of Morocco. From the French of Mr. Chenier.' Considerable architectural description and comment.

Literary and Scientific Depository and Critical Review, New York

Vol. i (October 1820), p. 529. Brief account of Monticello, with a view.

Littell's Living Age, Boston

Vol. ii (24 August 1844), p. 183. Account of the Proceedings of the recent meeting of the Royal Institute of British Architects, quoted from the *Athenaeum.*

Vol. ii (21 September 1844), p. 426. Brief note of the new 'Romish Cathedral of Nottingham.' 'Mr. Pugin is the architect.'

Vol. ii (12 October 1844), p. 603. 'The Anglican Cathedral at Jerusalem.' A review, quoted from the *Asiatic Journal,* of *The Anglican Cathedral . . . Jerusalem,* by J. W. Johns, Architect, London, 1844.

M

Massachusetts Magazine, Boston

Vol. i (April 1789), p. 240. 'On the Progress of the Arts,' unsigned. Contains a section on the evolution of the house.

Vol. i (June 1789), p. 331. 'Description of the Federal Edifice at New York.' The same article, with the same illustration, appeared in the *Columbian Magazine,* Vol. iii (August 1789) [*q.v.*], and the *New York Magazine,* Vol. i (March 1790) [*q.v.*].

Ibid. p. 365, and Vol. i (July 1789), p. 401. 'On Architecture,' by the Rev. James Bannister. A general description and review of classic architecture.

Vol. i (August 1789), p. 469. 'Account of the Baptist Meeting House in Providence.' A detailed description, with an illustration. Gives date as 1774–5, and states it was built 'under the direction of Mr. James Sumner, now of Boston, and the late Joseph Brown, Esq., of Providence.'

Vol. i (September 1789), p. 533. Description of the Charles River Bridge. Gives all the credit for it to 'Mr. Cox, the Master Workman.'

Vol. ii (January 1790), p. 3. 'Description of the Triumphal Arch and Colonnade, erected at Boston, in honour of the President of the United States, October 24th, 1789.' A detailed description, with a plate. Credits the arch to Mr. Bulfinch, the colonnade to the 'Hon. Mr. Dawes.'

Vol. ii (March 1790), p. 131. 'Description of the Court House at Salem,' with illustration. Gives date as 1785–6. States it was designed by McIntire, 'and executed by that able architect, Mr. Daniel Bancroft,' both of Salem.'

Vol. ii (June 1790), p. 323. 'Description of the Colleges at Cambridge,' with an illustration.

Vol. II (September 1790), p. 515. Account of the Malden bridge over the Mystick River. States that the master workmen were Lemuel Cox and Jonathan Tompson.

Vol. III (June 1791), p. 365. Description of Bethlehem, Pa., with an excellent view. Says 'the town, with very few exceptions, is built with stone, and the dwellings are generally planned upon a large scale.'

Vol. III (August 1791), p. 467. Description of the Old State House in Boston, with an illustration.

Vol. IV (July 1792), p. 411. Description of Christ Church, Cambridge, with an illustration.

Vol. IV also has several views of country estates.

Vol. V (February 1793), p. 67. Brief description of Dartmouth College, with a view.

Vol. V (July 1793), p. 387. An engraving, better than the earlier one, of the Old State House.

Vol. V (December 1793), p. 707. ' Meeting House in Hollis Street.' An extended description and a view. Much praise is given its designer, Bulfinch. ' His views, in the present instance, were well seconded by Mr. Josiah Wheeler, the head workman, who excells in executing as the other in designing.'

Vol. VI (February 1794), p. 67. Extended description of Franklin Place, ' now erecting on a Tontine principle.' Sixteen dwelling houses with ' an ornamental pile ' in the center for public uses; the Historical Society was to be on the second floor of the central building.

Methodist Quarterly Review, New York.

Vol. XXVIII, Third Series Vol. VI (July 1846), p. 373. Extended review of A. J. Downing's *Theory and Practice of Landscape Architecture* . . , New York, 1844. The reviewer admits two chief objections to the indulgence of taste — the fact that it sensualizes the mind and consumes an unreasonable portion of wealth — but states that ' taste will be indulged,' and that there is no less objectionable gratification of taste than gardening. A few remarks on domestic architecture at the close. [Significant as showing the growing anti-aesthetic bias of the ' new puritanism' which was to become dominant in many Protestant circles later.]

Vol. XXXI, Fourth Series Vol. I (October 1849), p. 670. Brief but enthusiastically laudatory review of Ruskin's *Seven Lamps of Architecture;* ' all the eloquence and the enthusiasm ' of *Modern Painters* ' with far more directness and instructiveness.'

Vol. XXXII, Fourth Series Vol. II (October 1850), p. 662. Trenchant review of A. J. Downing's *The Architecture of Country Houses.* The reviewer states, ' The book will do something, we trust, toward checking what appears now to be the tendency of our men of wealth — the frippery and gew-gaw style of building, and the absurd imitation of foreign edifices, of which the *very young castle,* as Frederika

Bremer called it, on the banks of the Hudson, is the latest and most striking illustration.'

New England Magazine, Boston

Vol. ɪ (July 1831), p. 1. 'On the Consideration due to the Mechanical Arts,' signed F. An extended article, chiefly historical.

Vol. ɪɪ (January 1832), p. 30. 'Domestic Architecture,' signed Z. The writer finds New England houses generally too big for their uses; says this is not so in New York and Pennsylvania.

Vol. ɪɪ (May 1832), p. 445. Review of the *First Book of Fine and Useful Arts, for the Use of Schools and Lyceums,* compiled by Marshall S. Perry, M.D. This book treats of printing, dyeing, tanning, glassmaking, as well as of the fine arts. The reviewer is especially enthusiastic about the treatment of painting, sculpture, and architecture; he believes that the book will enable young scholars to understand and appreciate them.

Vol. ɪɪɪ (July 1832), p. 1; continued on p. 305. 'Early American Artists and Mechanics.' A series dealing with Nathaniel Hurd (No. 1) and Paul Revere (No. 2). Interesting as showing local pride and appreciation.

Vol. vɪɪɪ (March 1835), p. 239. Extended review of Dunlap's *History of the Rise and Progress of the Arts of Design in the United States.* Not entirely complimentary.

The New Englander, New Haven

Vol. vɪɪɪ (August 1850), p. 418. Review of Ruskin's *Seven Lamps of Architecture,* unsigned. A thoughtful essay on the state of architecture in America and prospects for its improvement in the future.

New Haven Gazette and Connecticut Magazine, New Haven

Vol. ɪ (1 February 1787), p. 381. 'On American Genius,' unsigned. Stresses the fine arts, and says 'Americans appear to be possessed of peculiarly strong talents for painting'; cites West, Copley, Steward [Stuart] of Rhode Island, Taylor of Philadelphia, Brown of Boston, and John Trumbull. The author notes they gained more than 'empty fame' — i.e. 'pecuniary emoluments' — and urges that the taste of the nation be led to 'pleasures of a more refined and innocent nature' than 'cock-fighting, gambling, and tavern-haunting.'

New York Ecclesiologist, New York.

Vol. ɪ (October 1848), p. 5. 'Cheap Churches,' unsigned.

Ibid. p. 8. 'Reality in Church Architecture.' An abstract of a paper read at a meeting of the New York Ecclesiological Society by Frank Wills, architect.

Ibid. pp. 19, 24. Accounts of the meetings of the Oxford Architectural Society and the Exeter Diocesan Architectural Society.

Ibid. p. 34. Notes on Trinity Church, New York. State it was begun in 1839; Richard Upjohn, architect.

Ibid. p. 38. Notes on St. George's Chapel, New York, 'from the designs of Blesch and Eidlitz.'

Vol. I (January 1849), p. 70. Notes on Christ Church, Cambridge, Mass. State it was begun in 1760, and that Mr. Harrison of Newport, also the architect of King's Chapel in Boston, was its architect.

Ibid. p. 74. Notes on St. Mark's, Philadelphia; John Notman, architect.

Ibid. p. 76. Notes on the Church of St. Cornelius the Centurion, at Governor's Island, 'built without the aid of a professional architect.'

Ibid. p. 77. Notes on St. Anne's Chapel, Fredericton, N. B.; Frank Wills, architect.

Ibid. pp. 77–9. Article on the Church of the Holy Cross, Troy. The architects were Nathan Warren, of Troy, son of the donor, who furnished the general plans; A. J. Davis, who detailed the nave; and Richard Upjohn, who designed the chancel.

Ibid. p. 79. Notes on a church at San Augustine, Texas. Plans have been made by 'the society's architect, Mr. Wills.'

Vol. I (April 1849), p. 127. Description of Grace Church, Newark; Richard Upjohn, architect.

Vol. I (June 1849), p. 146. Under 'new churches,' Grace Church, Brooklyn Heights, is listed; Richard Upjohn, architect.

Ibid. p. 148. Note on St. Jude's, Spring Garden, Philadelphia. 'The name of the Architect is unknown to us.'

Ibid. p. 149. Note on the proposed Trinity Chapel, San Francisco; Frank Wills, architect.

Vol. II (October 1849), p. 19. Note speaks of a church 'already erected in Newark' which has a nave in the 'First Pointed' style, designed by Frank Wills. Urges that his plan (illustrated) for the future enlargement of the church be carried out.

Ibid. p. 25. Richard Upjohn elected to honorary membership in the Ecclesiological Society, 1 October 1849.

Vol. II (January 1850), p. 60. Note on All Angels Church, New York, 'in a small hamlet in the centre of the Island about three miles beyond the densely populated part of the city' – a small wooden church by Richard Upjohn.

Vol. II (March 1850), p. 89. Note on the Church of the Holy Innocents, West Point, N. Y. 'Prof. Wier is both the founder and architect.'

New York Literary Journal and Belles-Lettres Repository, see *Belles-Lettres Repository and Monthly Magazine*

New York Magazine, New York

Vol. I (January 1790), p. 3. Account of Trinity Church, 'with an elegant engraving of the new building.' It was built by J. Robinson, carpenter, and Messers Moore and Smith, masons.

Vol. I (March 1790), p. 133. Description of the 'Federal Edifice' in New York. The same description which appeared in the *Columbian Magazine*, Vol. III (August 1789), and the *Massachusetts Magazine*, Vol. I (June 1789), but this account adds a paragraph of praise for the builders, J. Robinson, carpenter, and Messers Smith and Moore, masons.

Vol. I (May 1790), p. 255. Description, with illustration, of Columbia College.

Ibid. p. 313. 'May 21. The first stone of the new Government House in New York was laid.'

Vol. II (March 1791), p. 123. Description, with an interesting view, of West Point.

Vol. II (May 1791), p. 247. Description, with a view, of the 'Seat of Henry Livingston at Poughkeepsie.'

Vol. III (January 1792). An editorial announcement says, 'Views of the Country, public buildings, gentlemen's seats . . . being proper subjects for embellishing this work will be thankfully received by the Editors.'

Vol. III (June 1792), p. 328. Plan of the City of Washington.

Vol. III (August 1792), p. 487. 'Account of some of the Antiquities of Babylon . . ,' by M. de Beauchamp, Vicar General of Babylon. An early archaeological article.

Vol. III (September 1792), p. 515. Description, with a view, of the new Presbyterian church of Newark.

Vol. III (October 1792), p. 574. View of the seat of Sebah Strong, on Long Island.

[Other views of country estates follow from time to time. They have not been listed here.]

Vol. V (April 1794), p. 195. Description of the 'New Theatre in Philadelphia,' with an unusually competent view of its interior. Notes that it was opened 7 February 1794, and that the paintings and scenery 'equal the generality of the European, and do the greatest credit to the pencil and genius of Mr. Milbourne.' [An important document in early American theater architecture.]

Vol. VI (January 1795), p. 1. Short description, with a view, of Government House, New York. The 'whole of the building appears to be executed in a stile which reflects much credit on the professional abilities of those who had the direction of it, Messers Robinson, Moore and Smith.'

Vol. VI (October 1795), p. 577. Description, with an unusual view, of St. Paul's Chapel, New York. Notes that the steeple was 'finished last year.'

New Series Vol. I (July 1796), p. 337. Description, signed V, with an illustration, of the State House, Frankfort, Kentucky. The description opens, ' To a mind fond of contemplating the progression of the arts and sciences, perhaps no sight is more pleasing than that of beholding in a remote and infant country, the useful and ornamental works of the Architect.'

New Series Vol. II (October 1797), p. 505. 'Some Account of the Mahometan Temples and Mosques,' unsigned, with an illustration of the Mosque of Sultan Ahmed at Constantinople. An excellent article.

New York Mirror, New York

Vol. I (15 November 1823), p. 124. Description of the United States Capitol, with a plate engraved by Garret Lansing. The description also notes 'improvements' on 'the President's house.'

Vol. V (14 July 1827), p. 1. 'The History of Trinity Church,' with a full-page engraving from a drawing by A. J. Davis. Notes that the west window contains, in its three compartments, '1039 panes of glass'; calls it 'plain Gothic.' This view initiates a superb series of Davis views which ran in the New York Mirror for six years.

Vol. V (6 October 1827), p. 97. Description and view of the Lafayette Theater. The drawing by A. J. Davis; the building from the 'plan and design of Peter Grain.'

Vol. V (20 October 1827), p. 113. Engraving from a Davis drawing of St. Paul's Chapel.

Vol. V (8 December 1827), p. 174. Note on the immense improvements in building in New York 'since the discovery of the vast quarries of white marble in Westchester County.'

Vol. V (1 March 1828), p. 271. A communication to the Mirror, unsigned, on the 'new steeple recently erected upon St. Mark's Church.' Praises Martin E. Thompson, the architect who designed it and made it all of brick, and rejoices that Thompson refrained from 'the brazen weather-cock, ball and fleur-de-lys, those choice embellishments in modern architecture.'

Vol. VI (23 August 1828), p. 49. Detailed description with an illustration from a drawing by Davis, of the new Bowery Theater. Notes that it was built in 65 days [after a fire in the original building designed by Town]; that the architect was Mr. Sera, and Mr. Geer the contractor and builder.

Vol. VI (6 December 1828), p. 171. Description, with illustration from a Davis drawing, of Columbia College.

Vol. VI (11 April 1829), p. 313. St. John's Chapel and the Park. Illustration from a Davis drawing. Description, signed H, says the cornerstone was laid 8 September 1803, that the Chapel was consecrated 6 January 1807, and that the builders were 'Thomas C. Taylor, Isaac M'Comb, Henry Hedley, and Daniel Dominic.'

Vol. VI (20 June 1829), p. 393. Description, with illustration from a Davis drawing, of St. Thomas's Church, Broadway and Houston Street, New York. States that the cornerstone was laid 27 July 1824, and the building consecrated 23 February 1826; calls it the 'best specimen of the Gothic style of architecture in the city,' and says it was built by ' Mr. Joseph Tucker and Messers Geer and Riley, under the superintendence of James N. Wells, Esq., from drawings by Josiah R. Brady, architect.'

Vol. vii (26 September 1829), p. 89. ' Public Buildings in the City of New York.' The illustration, from a Davis drawing, shows the Rotunda, the Merchants' Exchange, the Second Unitarian Church, the Jews' Synagogue, the United States Bank, and the Masonic Hall. The text says the editor wishes to show the world the progress of the arts in New York, and that, though many people pass these buildings by without noticing them, when their attention is called they express real admiration. Brief descriptions of each building are given. The Merchants' Exchange was built from a plan ' wholly that of M. E. Thompson, Esq., the architect of the edifice '; the design of the front entablature of the Unitarian Church was drawn by J. G. Pearson, Esq.; the United States Bank was ' designed and executed by Martin E. Thompson '; of the Masonic Hall, ' its style of architecture is purely Gothic . . . copied from the most approved classic models, with original appendages, by our celebrated artist, Hugh Reinagle, Esq.'

Vol. vii (20 March 1830), p. 289. Plate of six churches from a drawing by A. J. Davis, with brief descriptions. The churches shown are: the Brick Meeting House, or Second Presbyterian Church, Beekman Street, 1767; the South Dutch Church, known as the Garden Street Church; the Middle Dutch Church, 1729; the North Dutch Church, 1768, with spire of 1823; the First Presbyterian Church, 1810; and the Reformed Presbyterian Church, 1812.

Vol. vii (1 May 1830), p. 353. Illustration of the Brooklyn Collegiate Institute, from a drawing by J. M. Roberts; to ' be opened on Monday.'

Vol. viii (10 July 1830), p. 1. ' Dutch Architecture.' An extended article, unsigned, with an illustration.

Vol. viii (17 July 1830), p. 9. Description, with illustration from a Davis drawing, of the French Huguenot Church of St. Esprit.

Vol. viii (7 August 1830), p. 33. View of Park Row.

Vol. viii (1 January 1831), p. 201. ' Dutch Architecture.' An illustration, from a drawing by A. J. Davis. The caption says it is an old Dutch house on William Street, built in 1648 and modernized in 1828.

Vol. viii (26 February 1831), p. 265. ' St. Paul's Church, Troy, N. Y.' A description, with illustration. ' The church was built under the superintendence of Mr. James McFarland and Messers Cargell and McRae.'

Vol. viii (19 March 1831), p. 289. ' Dutch Architecture.' Another illustration from a Davis drawing. This is of a house on Pearl Street,

built 1626, rebuilt 1677, and demolished 1828. The description states that the house was known as ' Old 76,' and deplores its destruction as an evidence of the irreverence of New York for antiquity.
Vol. ix (10 September 1831), p. 73. Illustration from a Davis drawing of the Old Jail.
Vol. ix (17 September 1831), p. 81. 'The Hall of Records.' A brief description, with an illustration from a Davis drawing.
Vol. ix (9 November 1831), p. 153. 'Old Federal Hall.' An illustration and a history. The engraving is from a drawing by ' Diedrich Knickerbocker, Jr.,' but the index states it was 'painted by Weir.'
Vol. ix (31 December 1831), p. 201. Description, signed S. Wadsworth, with illustration from a Davis drawing, of the old Stuyvesant mansion.
Vol. ix (21 January 1832), p. 225. Description, with an illustration, of Wall Street. Some architectural comment.
Vol. ix (17 March 1832), p. 289. 'The Walton Mansion House.' A description, credited in the index to John Pintard, with illustration from a drawing by A. J. Davis.
Vol. x (18 December 1832), p. 185. Illustration of the schoolhouse at Tappan. ' Painted by Weir. Engraved by James Smillie.'
Vol. x (2 February 1833), p. [241]. ' Old Dutch house in New Street.' A note, with illustration from a drawing by A. J. Davis. Calls it ' the last of the Dutch Houses.' Used as the introduction to a short story.
Vol. xi (1 February 1834), p. 241. ' Bloomingdale Asylum,' signed G. C. Y. The illustration is painted by Weir and engraved by Smillie.
Vol. xii (23 August 1834), n.p. ' City Improvements — The New Custom-House,' with a view engraved from a Davis drawing and a long and complete description of the proposed building, as well as brief comment on other New York structures.
New Series Vol. ii (28 June 1845), p. 191. The editor demands a city park on Murray Hill from Third to Fifth avenues.
New Series Vol. ii (26 July 1845), pp. [241]–243. Account of the great fire of Saturday, 26 July. Mentions the destruction of the beautiful house designed by Martin E. Thompson for Robert Day.
New Series Vol. ii (6 September 1845), p. 338. H. A. B. protests against the sacrilege of the proposed razing of St. Paul's Chapel.
New Series, Vol. v (17 October 1846), pp. 26–7. Extended review, unsigned, of *The Architect, a series of original Designs for Domestic and Ornamental Cottages . . . adapted to the United States,* by William H. Ranlett, architect, New York, 1846. [This review is quoted extensively on page 325.] It covered only early fascicules of this publication. Other reviews, of later parts, followed on (28 November, 26 December 1846, 23 January, 20 February, and 3 April 1847) pp. 126, 190, 254, 318, 414. [All are significant of the common-sense protest against fashionable eclectic gewgaws in buildings.]
New Series, Vol. v (21 November 1846), p. 102. Review of an exhi-

bition of sculpture by H. K. Brown. [Significant for its attack on prudery and false modesty. Quoted on page 322.]

New Series Vol. v (5 December 1846), p. 142. Review of *Designs for Monuments and Mural Tablets. . . With a preliminary essay on the laying out, planting, and arranging of cemeteries . . . on the basis of Loudon's work*, by J. Jay Smith, New York, 1846. The reviewer objects to Egyptian and Gothic monuments.

New Series Vol. v (13 February 1847), p. 299. ' Houses for the Poor.' A note on ' the necessity of houses at moderate rents for that already large and increasing class of society, small-incomes (to coin a word).'

New York Review, New York

Vol. vii (July 1840), p. 251. Review of B. L. Lossing's *History of the Fine Arts*, New York, 1840. Reviewer thinks the book most inadequate. ' Not the slightest notion can be gathered from it what architecture, or sculpture, or painting, has been since the revival of the arts, or what the present condition of either is.'

Vol. ix (July 1841), p. 180. ' Rural Church Edifices.' A review of *Temples, Ancient and Modern; or Notes on Church Architecture*, by William Bardwell, architect, London, 1840. The reviewer refutes the criticisms of those who say that architectural or picturesque effect distracts attention from God, and says that our condition, as a new country, is no excuse for the barnlike and incongruous structures in most country villages.

Ibid. p. 256. Brief but most complimentary review of Downing's *Landscape Architecture*.

North American Review, Boston

Vol. xliii (October 1836), p. 356. An extended essay on American architecture, under the guise of a review of James Gallier's *American Builder's General Price Book . . .* , Boston, 1834. Unsigned but attributed, in the index, to H. R. Cleveland, Jr. A most significant general criticism of American architecture, clear, definite, balanced. The reviewer finds the best architecture in Philadelphia; ' the Bank is undoubtedly the most faultless monument of its size in the United States.' [See page 323.]

Vol. lii (April 1841), p. 301. Review of Asher Benjamin's *The Builder's Guide . . .* , 3rd ed., Boston. Unsigned, but in index attributed to W. Minot, Jr.

Vol. lvi (January 1843), p. 1. Review of A. J. Downing's *Treatise on the Theory and Practice of Landscape Gardening . . .* and *Cottage Residences. . .* Unsigned, but attributed in the index to W. P. O. Peabody. [See page 323.]

Vol. lviii (April 1844), p. 58. Review of Edward Shaw's *Rural Architecture: consisting of Classic Dwellings . . .* , Boston, 1843. Unsigned, but attributed in the index to Arthur Gilman. The reviewer attacks the Shaw book and all similar works. [A most important critical article, supporting an eclectic approach. See page 335.]

Vol. LIX (October 1844), p. 302. Review of A. J. Downing's *Cottage Residences* . . . , 2nd ed., and of J. C. Loudon's *Encyclopedia of Gardening*. . . Unsigned, but attributed to Arthur Gilman. A savage attack on unthinking, copying, bookish building. ' If he wants a temple, he can have a hash of Stuart from the studio, cut and dried, in tetra-style, prostyle, hexastyle or no-style.' Reviewer advises ' a strict and diligent search till an architect be discovered who *knows* what he undertakes to practise and direct.'

P

Pennsylvania Magazine, Philadelphia

Vol. I (November 1775), p. 517. Description of the town and island of Montreal, with a plan of Montreal and inset views of some of the buildings. Unsigned. A little architectural comment.

Vol. I (December 1775), p. 563. Description of Quebec, with a plan. Unsigned. Architectural comment follows in the ' Supplement,' p. 604.

Philadelphia Monthly Magazine, Philadelphia

Vol. I (February 1798), p. 97. ' Plan, Construction . . . of the Jail and Penitentiary of Philadelphia,' signed T. Condie, with an excellent plate of plan and elevation.

Vol. I (June 1798), p. 333. Description of the old State House [Independence Hall] at Philadelphia, unsigned, with a plate labeled ' City Hall of Philadelphia, sometimes called State House of Pennsylvania, now occupied by the Congress of the United States.' Notes that the ' lofty steeple ' was taken down after it had stood for several years previous to 1788, from fear its weight endangered the stability of the tower. Notes that to the south is a large area, surrounded by a brick wall and commanding a fine view of the Jail, the Philadelphia Library and Philosophical Hall, and the ' valuable museum of the ingenious Mr. Peal.' The whole was ' laid out and improved under the direction of Samuel Vaughn, Esq., . . . with lawns, borders, serpentine walks, clumps of trees, and tufts of flowers.' [Important as showing the early public American adoption of English romantic garden and park ideals.]

Philadelphia Repository, Philadelphia

Vol. I (17 October 1801), p. 387. ' Antiquities of Interior America,' from the manuscript of a ' late Traveler.' Deals chiefly with the Indian mounds of the Ohio and the Mississippi and the artifacts found in them. Significant as showing early archaeological interest in American Indian work.

Port Folio, Philadelphia

New Series Vol. IV (1814), pp. 559–69. ' On Architecture,' by George Tucker. Advocates following Greek precedent. [Noted by Fiske Kimball in his *Domestic Architecture of the American Colonies and the Early Republic,* p. 182.]

R

Rural Casket, Poughkeepsie, New York

Vol. I, 5 June 1798. Description of Poughkeepsie, with some description of buildings.

Vol. I, 17 July 1798. Recipe for making a mortar ' which will be impenetrable to moisture.' Quoted from ' Mr. Dossie's *Memoirs of Agriculture.*'

Rural Magazine, Newark, New Jersey

14 April 1798. ' Ornamental Gardening,' signed ' Aikin's Letters.' Concluded in the number of 21 April 1798.

10 November 1798. ' American Antiquities.' Part of the charge of the Rev. Dr. Cutler to the Rev. Mr. Story at his ordination at Marietta. A particularly full and detailed account of Indian mounds and walls in and near Marietta, Ohio.

S

Southern Review, Charleston, South Carolina

Vol. IV (August 1829), p. 70. ' The Fine Arts.' A review of a pamphlet by S. F. B. Morse dealing with Academies of Art, art patronage, etc.

Vol. VII (May 1831), p. 121. ' History of the Fine Arts.' A review of the *History of Painting in Italy,* by Luigi Lanzi, translated by Thomas Roscoe, 6 vols., London, 1828. A long and full essay, with many architectural notes and comments.

T

Temple of Reason, Philadelphia

22 April 1801. Advertisement of *The House Carpenters' Book of Prices* . . . , published and sold by R. Folwell, 63 N. Front St., 100 copies. Gives contents.

U

United States Catholic Magazine and Monthly Review, Baltimore

Vol. IV (January and March 1845), pp. 44, 172. ' Archeology — Legendary Basso-Relievos of the Middle Ages,' by L. C. Boistiniere, LL.D.

Vol. IV (August 1845), p. 516. ' Archeology — Glass Painting,' by L. C. Boistiniere, LL.D.

Ibid. p. 627. ' Christian Architecture,' by T. E. Giraud. Largely historical; advocates Gothic churches.

Vol. IV (December 1845), p. 791. ' New Cathedral of St. Peter, Cincinnati,' unsigned. An excellent descriptive article; names the architects as H. Walter and Hudson B. Curtis.

United States Catholic Miscellany, Charleston, South Carolina

Vol. II (4, 11, 25 February 1824), pp. 78, 93, 126. ' The Fine Arts,' unsigned. Deals chiefly with architecture. Calls architecture, sculpture, and painting the handmaids of religion, revealing great religious truths; therefore a sketch of the ' history, patrons, and masters of the Fine Arts, considered in this light, may with propriety appear in a religious publication.' Notes that authorities used are ' Felibien, Vasari, De Pies, De Fresnoy, Graham, Perrault, etc.' Arranges the orders in point of their beauty thus: ' Corinthian, Ionic, Doric, Tuscan, Composite, Attic, French, and Gothic[!].' Gives many architectural definitions, and brief historical summaries.

United States Literary Gazette, Boston

Vol. III (15 October, 1 November 1825), pp. 41, 81. Review of an address delivered before the American Academy of Fine Arts, New York, by William Beach Lawrence. Extended architectural discussion.

Vol. III (15 January 1826), p. 302. ' The State of Architecture in Boston,' signed B. [Perhaps Asher Benjamin.]

Vol. III (1 February 1826), p. 356. Brief review of an address before the American Academy of Fine Arts, New York, by Richard Ray.

Vol. IV (13 August 1826), p. 387. Account of a similar address before the same body by Charles Patterson.

United States Magazine and Democratic Review, Washington and New York

Vol. II (November 1838), p. 253. ' Claims of the Beautiful Arts,' unsigned. A plea for the cultivation of the fine arts and religion as a cure for the great materialism of the country. Speaks of the ' eternal alliance between Fine Arts and Religion, for beauty is one aspect of Truth.' Calls for public patronage of the arts. Concludes, ' We have said nothing of architecture, because this is more obviously a national concern, and, comparatively, has not been neglected by us.'

Vol. IX (December 1841), p. 554. Review of A. J. Downing's *Treatise on the Theory and Practice of Landscape Gardening.* Most complimentary.

Vol. XIII (July 1843), p. 45. ' Remarks on American Art,' by Horatio

Greenough. Little on architecture, but a significant affirmation of a strong belief in American creativeness in the fine arts.

Vol. XIII (August 1843), p. 206. 'American Architecture,' by Horatio Greenough. [This superb article is the most farsighted and sound criticism of American architecture written for many decades. Greenough expresses the thoughtful artist's distrust of eclecticism and urges a true organic architecture.] 'The law of adaptation is the fundamental law of nature in all structure.' 'Observe a ship at sea! . . . What Academy of Design, what research of connoisseurship, what imitation of the Greeks produced this marvel of construction.' [The article is quoted in part on page 324.]

Vol. XIII (November 1843), p. 451. 'Paradise (to be) Regained.' A review, unsigned, of The Paradise within the Reach of All Men without Labor, by Powers of Nature and Machinery, Part I, 2nd ed., London, 1842. A skeptical and witty review of a book, 'published originally in Pennsylvania ten or twelve years ago,' which described an extraordinary mechanical utopia. Considerable on utopian building — especially the fantastic communal dwelling with great gardens and canals which the book describes.

Ibid. p. 473. 'Loose Leaves of a Literary Lounger. II. A Chapter on Costly and Curious Books,' unsigned. Remarkable for the number of works on architecture and decoration it mentions. Among them are Vestigie delle Terme de Tito e loro interne Pitture, Murphy's Arabian Antiquities of Spain, Meyrick's Ancient Armour, Shaw's Dress and Decoration of the Middle Ages, and 'Napoleon's great work on Egypt [Description de l'Egypte], which is in fact a noble monument of art.'

Vol. XVI (February 1845), p. 192. 'Rome as seen by a New Yorker.' A review, unsigned, of the book of the same name by 'Mr. Gillespie.' Considerable comment on architecture and art; quotes descriptions of the Forum and the Colosseum, and of the initiation of a young artist into the artists' society.

Vol. XVI (April 1845), p. 348. Extended review, unsigned, of A. J. Downing's Treatise on the Theory and Practice of Landscape Gardening . . . , 1844, and of his Cottage Residences . . . , 1844. In reality a careful essay attempting an evaluation of both American gardens and American architecture and their possible future. The reviewer praises Downing's work on gardens, which the reviewer considers of enormous social value. Of the Cottage Residences, the reviewer finds the plans too large and expensive. 'A spirit of Art must be enkindled among the people. . . The patronage we want is the patronage of the whole community.' Of styles the essayist says, 'No style has yet been adapted in this country, that is to become national and permanent. . . Why should we be bound, as a matter of course, to the customs of departed ages? ' He attacks the over-ornamentation of most recent American houses. [The review is significant of the growing protest against copying in architecture.]

Vol. xx (February 1847), p. 139. 'Church Architecture.' A long letter to the editor, signed S. An excellent criticism by one who had traveled much. In general, does not like Gothic for Protestant churches. Complains of the American effort to imitate cathedrals in small churches, and of the consequent false scale; also attacks the customary falsity of stone veneers of Gothic ornament. Of all the Gothic churches in New York the writer likes best the modest Holy Communion on Sixth Avenue, and says, 'Since I saw it, [I] began to hope that we may before long build as good churches as we did a century ago.' A visitor, to see good churches, should 'shut his eyes to every thing between the Holy Communion and St. Paul's.' [Significant not only for its sound criticism, but also for its implied admiration of Colonial work.]

Vol. xxi (November 1847), p. 392. 'Our New Houses.' A review, unsigned, of Ranlett's *The Architect* and Downing's edition of Wightwick's *Hints to Young Architects*. An excellent picture of New York domestic architecture of the time. The reviewer disapproves of Downing ' for corrupting the public taste, and infecting the parvenues with the mania of Gothic Castle-Building.' Praises the work of Mr. French, the architect ' of Stewart's marble store in Broadway ' and of a house for Colonel Thorn in Sixteenth Street, which the writer considers the finest house in America, for its simple dignity and modest elegance. Finds a general improvement: ' Now the humblest of our city dwellings, however, make a gratifying display of knowledge and taste . . . while the better class of dwellings . . . show an improvement in architectural science really marvellous.'

Vol. xxiii (November 1848), p. 391. 'School Architecture.' A review of Henry Barnard's *School Architecture, or, Contributions to the Improvement of School-Houses*. The reviewer is enthusiastic about the book and, though appalled at the ugly and unhygienic schoolhouses common in the country, looks forward to the time when they shall be ornaments to their towns. Excellent on the bases of good school architecture and its importance; stresses especially heating and ventilation.

Vol. xxiii (December 1848), p. 564. Brief and complimentary review of Ranlett's *The Architect,* Vol. ii, Nos. 1–4.

Universal Asylum and Columbian Magazine, unidentified

Vol. i (January 1790), p. 25. 'Account of Some Public Buildings in the City of Philadelphia,' signed B. With an excellent plate.

Vol. iii (February 1791), p. 67. 'Simple Machine for Drawing in Perspective.' A description, with illustration, of the device invented by Mr. Benjamin Dearborn, schoolmaster of Portsmouth, N. H.

Vol. v (March 1792), p. 155. 'Description of the City of Washington,' unsigned, with a plan of the city credited to ' Mr. Ellicott.'

Universalist Quarterly and General Review, Boston

Vol. v (October 1848), p. 329. 'Art, and its Relations,' signed G. H. B.
A few passing references to architecture.

W

Weekly Magazine, Philadelphia

Vol. i (3 February 1798), p. 8. Description of the Bank of the United
States [later Girard's Bank] quoted from the *Gazette of the United
States,* without date. Most complimentary; says it is a 'truly Grecian
edifice, composed of American white marble. . . As this is the first
finished building of any consequence, wherein true taste and knowledge has been displayed, in the country, it is a pleasing task to in-
form its inhabitants that the architect [Blodget] is an American and
was born in the State of Massachusetts.'

Western Journal, St. Louis

Vol. i (June, July, August, September 1848), pp. 309, 383, 445, 497.
'Rise, Progress, and Influence of the Fine Arts,' by Alfred S. Waugh.
The first four installments are on architecture, which is treated first
'because it claims priority of all the arts.' The series is chiefly histori-
cal; the last installment deals with the Gothic cathedrals of England.
Vol. ii (March 1849), p. 178. 'Building and Building Materials,' by
B. A. Alderson. Practical advice to builders.

Western Magazine, Chicago

Vol. i (September 1846), p. 355. Description of New Haven, quoted
from the *Encyclopædia Americana,* with an engraving — a view from
the green — as frontispiece.
Vol. ii (October 1846), p. 3. 'View of the University of St. Mary of the
Lake.' An engraving, with a description. Notes that it is in Chicago
and that the buildings are 'neat and plain, but pleasing in their
outward appearance. . . Mr. D. Sullivan was the architect, under
whose supervision it was erected.'

Western Messenger, Louisville, Kentucky

Vol. vi (February 1839), p. 284. Brief description, with illustration,
of the Unitarian Church at Louisville.

Western Miscellany, Dayton, Ohio

Vol. i (July 1848–July 1849), p. 74. Description of Mount Vernon,
with illustration.
Ibid. p. 97. Description of the Capitol at Washington, with illustration.

Y

Yankee, Portland, Maine

Vol. i (6 August 1828), p. 251. 'Architecture in England.' A savage attack on contemporary English architecture, prefaced as follows: 'From an English correspondent, whose knowledge of the subject, and whose regard for truth, give to his opinions great value. We are in a bad way here on the subject of pilasters, columns, and others of the elements of architecture. But more of this at a future period.'

Young Mechanic [subsequently the *Boston Mechanic and Journal of Useful Arts and Sciences*], Boston

Vol. i (July 1832), p. 107. Full obituary of B. H. Latrobe, quoted from *Ackermann's Repository* (England) of January 1821. Significant as showing interest in great American architects. See also under *Literary Gazette,* Vol. i (21 April 1821).

Vol. ii (March, April, May, July 1833), pp. 40, 58, 76, 107. 'Architecture,' signed D. B. H. A brief historical series; the content is very slight. Significant as indicating interest in the subject.

Vol. ii (June 1833), p. 93. 'Incombustible Architecture,' unsigned. Quoted from the *Philadelphia Gazette,* without date. Concerns a secret fireproof process invented by ' C. S. Rafinesque of Philadelphia, Professor of many sciences, Architect, Draughtsman, etc.,' who offers to sell the secret to any architect for $1,000.

BIBLIOGRAPHY

I. General Works on American Architecture

American Institute of Architects, *Journal of the American Institute of Architects*, Vols. i–xv (January 1913–December 1928).

—— *Proceedings of the . . . Annual Convention of the American Institute of Architects . . . [First] 1867 —* (New York and elsewhere).

Architects' Emergency Committee, William Lawrence Bottomley, Chairman, *Great Georgian Houses of America*, 2 vols. (New York: The Kalkhoff Press, 1933–7). Excellent plates (measured drawings, plans, and photographs); dates and attributions to be accepted with reservation.

Barrington, Lewis, *Historic Restorations of the Daughters of the American Revolution* (New York: Richard T. Smith, 1941). Photographs; text often gives dates, ownerships, etc.

Edgell, George H., *The American Architecture of To-day* (New York: Charles Scribner's Sons, 1928). A pictorial survey, with emphasis on early twentieth-century work.

Evans, Walker, *American Photographs,* with an essay by Lincoln Kirstein ([New York:] The Museum of Modern Art [c1938]). Superb photographs of the American scene; considerable Classic Revival material included.

Federal Writers' Project, Works Progress Administration, American Guide Series (various places, publishers, dates). This whole series, although uneven in quality, contains much valuable information and many excellent views of buildings and communities. Usually in each there is a special section on architecture.

Feiss, Carl, *see* Stevenson, Frederic R., and Carl Feiss, *Our Heritage of Planned Communities.*

Garden Club of America, Alice G. B. Lockwood, ed., *Gardens of Colony and State,* 2 vols. (New York: Charles Scribner's Sons, 1931–4). A rich compendium, especially valuable for its illustrations.

Giedion, Sigfried, *Space, Time and Architecture* (Cambridge: Harvard University Press, 1941). Includes interesting notes on underlying American architectural traditions.

Halsey, R[ichard] T. II[aines], and Elizabeth Tower, *The Houses of Our Ancestors,* as shown in the American Wing of the Metropolitan Museum of Art (Garden City, L. I.: Doubleday, Page & Company, 1925). Especially rich in material of the Federal period.

Hamlin, Talbot Faulkner, *The American Spirit in Architecture,* Vol.

XIII of The Pageant of America series (New Haven: Yale University Press, 1926). A pictorial survey of American architecture.

HITCHCOCK, HENRY-RUSSELL, JR., *American Architectural Books; a List of Books, Portfolios, and Pamphlets Published in America Before 1895* (Middletown, Conn.: the author, [mimeographed] 1938–9). A monumental project, carried out with meticulous accuracy; especially important because of its clarification of many confusing points in American architectural bibliography. Contains the first usable and accurate list of the works of Benjamin.

HOWELLS, JOHN MEAD, *Lost Examples of Colonial Architecture . . .* (New York: William Helburn, 1931). Extremely valuable source for buildings which have been destroyed or altered; includes Federal and Greek Revival material as well as Colonial.

INIGUEZ, DIFGO ANGULO, *Planos de Monumentos arquitectonicos de América y Filipinas existentes en el Archivo de Indias* (Seville: Universitad de Seville, 1933). An invaluable historical source for all Spanish Colonial work; the illustrations are from drawings in the Spanish archives in Seville.

JACKSON, JOSEPH, *American Colonial Architecture* (Philadelphia: David McKay [c1924]). A good introductory survey.

—— *Development of American Architecture* 1783–1830 (Philadelphia: David McKay [c1926]). One of the earliest general studies of early nineteenth-century work.

—— *Early Philadelphia Architects and Engineers* (Philadelphia [n.p], 1923). Pioneer research on important architects.

KETTELL, RUSSELL HAWES, *Early American Rooms . . .* (Portland, Me.: The Southworth-Anthoensen Press, 1936). Superb and lavishly reproduced plates of typical rooms, shown in plan and elevation.

KIMBALL, [SIDNEY] FISKE, *American Architecture* (Indianapolis and New York: The Bobbs-Merrill Company [c1928]). The best introduction to the Greek Revival; an excellent general critical summary. Contains a most useful bibliography.

—— *Domestic Architecture of the American Colonies and of the Early Republic* (New York: Charles Scribner's Sons, 1922). A work of profound and accurate scholarship, remarkable both in its scope and its detailed precision; an absolutely necessary reference for all students of American architecture.

LOCKWOOD, ALICE G. B., *see* GARDEN CLUB OF AMERICA, *Gardens of Colony and State.*

ROOS, FRANK, *Writings on Early American Architecture* (Columbus: Ohio State University Press, 1943). Lists about 2,800 titles on architecture constructed before 1865 in the eastern half of the country; is cross-referenced and indexed, and includes a 30-page survey of past scholarship in the field.

STEVENSON, FREDERIC R., and CARL FEISS, *Our Heritage of Planned Communities* (New York: Columbia University Press, in preparation).

TALLMADGE, THOMAS E[DDY], *The Story of Architecture in America* (New York: W. W. Norton & Company [c1936]). A popular book. Unjust and inaccurate in its consideration of Greek Revival achievements, but excellent in its account of the later ' Chicago school.'

TOWER, ELIZABETH, *see* HALSEY, R[ICHARD] T. H[AINES], and ELIZABETH TOWER, *The Houses of Our Ancestors.*

TUTHILL, MRS. L[OUISA] C[AROLINE HUGGINS], *History of Architecture, from the Earliest Times; Its Present Condition in Europe and the United States* . . . (Philadelphia: Lindsay and Blakiston, 1848). Interesting in its critical analysis of the current American architecture of its time.

WARE, WILLIAM ROTCH, *The Georgian Period* . . . (Boston: American Architect and Building News Company, 1899–1902) ; 1923 ed., with new classifications and indexes (New York: U.P.C. Book Company, 1923). A mine of information, incoherent in arrangement; largely the fruit of the first burst of enthusiasm for early American architecture in the 1890's. Contains much post-Colonial work and a little Greek Revival.

White Pine Series of Architectural Monographs (in 1929–31 called The Monograph Series), Vols. I to XVII (New York: edited and published by Russell F. Whitehead, July 1915–31) ; after 1931 published as a section of *Pencil Points.* This series contains a rich collection of photographs of Colonial and Federal architecture, with occasional Greek Revival examples. These monographs are distinguished by the superb quality of the photographs; there are also some measured drawings of details. The text is rather general and varies greatly in quality.

II. GENERAL WORKS ON THE GREEK REVIVAL PERIOD

DINSMOOR, WILLIAM B., ' Early American Studies of Mediterranean Archaeology' (read November 20, 1942), *Proceedings of the American Philosophical Society* (in press).

EBERLEIN, HAROLD DONALDSON, and CORTLANDT VAN DYKE HUBBARD, *Colonial Interiors, Federal and Greek Revival,* 3rd series (New York: W. Helburn, 1938). An excellent collection of photographs, with a few details. Most of the work is Federal, but some Greek Revival examples are shown.

HAMLIN, TALBOT, ' The Greek Revival in America and Some of Its Critics,' *The Art Bulletin,* Vol. XXIV, No. 3 (September 1942), pp. 244–58. An attempt to evaluate early and more recent criticism of the style.

MAJOR, HOWARD, *The Domestic Architecture of the Early American Republic: The Greek Revival* (Philadelphia: J. B. Lippincott Company, 1926). Important for its photographs of houses, especially in New England and also in the South. The text is elementary only.

SCHUYLER, MONTGOMERY, ' The Old " Greek Revival," ' *The American Architect and Building News,* Part I: Vol. LCVIII, No. 1816 (October 12, 1910), pp. 121–6, 128; Part II: Vol. XCVIII, No. 1826 (December

21, 1910), pp. 201–4, 206–8; Part III: Vol. XCIX, No. 1836 (March
1, 1911), pp. 81–4, 86–7; Part IV: Vol. XCIX, No. 1845 (May 3, 1911),
pp. 161–6, 168. The pioneer work on the Greek Revival; sound and
balanced, as all Montgomery Schuyler's work was, although later research has invalidated some of his attributions and conclusions. An
interesting survey.

III. Works on Regional and Local Architecture

A. New England

Art Work of Boston ([Chicago:] W. H. Parish, 1891). Excellent photographs of Boston fifty years ago.

BAGG, ERNEST NEWTON, *Late Eighteenth Century Architecture in Western
Massachusetts*, Vol. XI, No. 4, in the White Pine Series of Architectural Monographs (New York: Russell F. Whitehead, August 1925).

BUCKLY, JULIAN, *Architecture in Massachusetts during the Latter Part
of the Eighteenth Century*, Vol. II, No. 2, in the White Pine Series
of Architectural Monographs (New York: Russell F. Whitehead,
April 1916).

CANDAGE, R[UFUS] G. F., *Historical Sketches of Bluehill, Maine* (Ellsworth: Hancock County Publishing Company, for the Bluehill Historical Society, 1905).

CHAMBERLAIN, ALLEN, *Beacon Hill: Its Ancient Pastures and Early Mansions* (Boston and New York: Houghton Mifflin Company, 1925).
Excellent material on the history of the development of Beacon Hill,
with many dates of individual houses and much material on early
architects; a model for similar research in other localities.

CHAMBERLAIN, SAMUEL, *Boston in Four Seasons* [c1942], *Cape Cod in
the Sun* [c1937], *The Coast of Maine* [c1941], *Historic Salem in
Four Seasons* [c1938], Nantucket [c1939], and *Portsmouth, New
Hampshire* [c1940] (New York: Hastings House). These books contain many of the most descriptive and evocative photographs of characteristic New England scenes that have appeared. Many Greek Revival examples are included.

CONGDON, HERBERT WHEATON, *Old Vermont Houses* . . . (Brattleboro:
Stephen Daye Press, 1940). An excellent collection, with an interesting text.

COOLIDGE, JOHN, *Mill and Mansion* (New York: Columbia University
Press, 1942). Pioneer work in the study of the development of a
typical industrial city – Lowell, Massachusetts. Full of interesting
side lights on American nineteenth-century culture and its changes.
Excellently documented and richly illustrated.

CROSBY, EVERETT U[BERTO], *95% Perfect: The Older Residences of Nantucket* (Nantucket: The Inquirer and Mirror Press [c1937]). Photographs and measured drawings. The text is concerned largely with
the preservation of old Nantucket.

DANA, RICHARD H., JR., *Old Canterbury on the Quinnebaug*, Vol. IX, No. 6, in the White Pine Series of Architectural Monographs (New York: Russell F. Whitehead, December 1923).

—— *The Old Hill Towns of Windham County, Connecticut*, Vol. X, No. 1, in the White Pine Series of Architectural Monographs (New York: Russell F. Whitehead, February 1924).

DAVIS, ALBERT H., *History of Ellsworth, Maine* (Lewiston: Lewiston Journal Printshop, 1927).

EBERLEIN, HAROLD DONALDSON, *The Seventeenth Century Connecticut House*, Vol. V, No. 1, in the White Pine Series of Architectural Monographs (New York: Russell F. Whitehead, February 1919).

HADDON, RAWSON W., *Old Deerfield, Massachusetts*, Vol. VI, No. 5, in the White Pine Series of Architectural Monographs (New York: Russell F. Whitehead, October 1920).

HOWELLS, JOHN MEAD, *The Architectural Heritage of the Merrimack* (New York: Architectural Book Publishing Company [c1941]). A superb regional study, richly illustrated.

—— *The Architectural Heritage of the Piscataqua* (New York: Architectural Book Publishing Company [c1937]). The best work on one of the most important architectural centers in New England. Superbly illustrated.

JOHNSON, DANA DOANE, see WHITE, PHILIP AYLWIN, and DANA DOANE JOHNSON, . . . *Norwich, Vermont*.

KELLY, J[OHN] FREDERICK, *Architectural Guide for Connecticut* (New Haven: Yale University Press, for the Tercentenary Commission of the State of Connecticut, 1935). An interesting introduction to the architectural wealth of a single state.

—— *Early Connecticut Architecture*, 2 vols. (New York: William Helburn, 1924–31). A monumental study, well illustrated with drawings as well as photographs. Especially valuable for the earlier Colonial work.

—— *The Early Domestic Architecture of Connecticut* (New Haven: Yale University Press, 1924). An important study on local house types. Complete and well illustrated. Contains little Greek Revival work.

MAGONIGLE, H. VAN BUREN, *Essex, a Connecticut Hill Town*, Vol. VI, No. 6, in the White Pine Series of Architectural Monographs (New York: Russell F. Whitehead, December 1920).

MAINE WRITERS RESEARCH CLUB, *Historic Churches and Homes of Maine* (Portland: Falmouth Book House, 1937). Pictures of many little-known buildings. The text is chiefly historical.

Old-Time New England, the bulletin of the Society for the Preservation of New England Antiquities, Vol. I– (Boston, 1910–). Contains many important articles on architects, buildings, and the cultural background of New England. Scholarly, accurate, and interesting. Well illustrated.

RAMSDELL, ROGER WEARNE, *Wooden Architecture in the Berkshires*, Vol. x, No. 5, in the White Pine Series of Architectural Monographs (New York: Russell F. Whitehead, October 1924).

SCHWEINFURTH, JULIUS A., *An Architectural Monograph on the Early Dwellings of Nantucket*, Vol. III, No. 6, in the White Pine Series of Architectural Monographs (New York: Russell F. Whitehead, December 1917).

TARN, DAVID E., *The Town of Suffield, Connecticut*, Vol. VII, No. 6, in the White Pine Series of Architectural Monographs (New York: Russell F. Whitehead, December 1921).

WHITE, PHILIP AYLWIN, and DANA DOANE JOHNSON, *Early Houses of Norwich, Vermont*, edited by Hugh S. Morrison (Hanover, N. H.: Dartmouth College, 1938). A study of the history of selected houses and other buildings, conducted as an advanced history seminar by students of Dartmouth College. Many interesting facts are brought out. Typical of the studies which might be initiated with profit in other localities.

WINSOR, JUSTIN, *Memorial History of the City of Boston* (Boston: J. R. Osgood, 1880–81). Contains an excellent section on Boston architecture.

B. *Middle States*

ARCHAMBAULT, A[NNA] MARGARETTA, *A Guide Book of Art, Architecture, and Historic Interests in Pennsylvania* (Philadelphia: John C. Winston Company, 1924). A general survey.

BENNETT, GEORGE FLETCHER, *Early Architecture of Delaware*, with Introduction and text by Joseph L. Copeland (Wilmington: Historical Press; New York: Carl T. Waugh & Company [c1932]). Excellent photographs and measured drawings, chiefly of Colonial and Federal work.

BOWEN, CROSWELL, *Great River of the Mountains: the Hudson*, with an Introduction by Carl Carmer (New York: Hastings House, 1941). Many excellent photographs, with brief historical comment.

CLUSS, ADOLF, ' Architecture and Architects at the Capital of the United States from Its Foundation until 1875,' *Proceedings of the Tenth Annual Convention of the American Institute of Architects . . . 1876* (Washington: Committee on Publications of the A.I.A., 1877), pp. 38–44. An interesting account by an architect who had watched Washington developments for many years.

COPELAND, JOSEPH L., *see* BENNETT, GEORGE FLETCHER, *Early Architecture of Delaware*.

CUNNINGHAM, HARRY FRANCIS, JOSEPH ARTHUR YOUNGER, and J. WILMER SMITH, *Measured Drawings of Georgian Architecture in the District of Columbia* (New York: Architectural Book Publishing Company, 1914). Includes works of Thornton and Latrobe.

EBERLEIN, HAROLD DONALDSON, and CORTLAND VAN DYKE HUBBARD, *Historic Houses of the Hudson Valley* (New York: Architectural Book Publishing Company [1942]). Detailed studies of the history of important houses, with good photographs.

—— ——*Portrait of a Colonial City, Philadelphia,* 1670–1838 (Philadelphia and New York: J. B. Lippincott Company [c1939]). Excellent photographs, with historical comment.

Eno Collection, New York Public Library (Print Room), New York. A rich collection of several hundred early New York views of all kinds, many exceedingly rare.

FEDERAL WRITERS' PROJECT, WORKS PROGRESS ADMINISTRATION, *Erie: A Guide to the City and County,* in the American Guide Series (Philadelphia: William Penn Association, 1938).

HIGGINS, ANTHONY, *see* WOOTTEN, [MRS.] BAYARD [MORGAN], and ANTHONY HIGGINS, *New Castle, Delaware.* . . .

HINDLEY, WILLIAM, notebooks and sketchbooks in the Avery Library, Columbia University, and in the Federal Hall Museum at the Sub-Treasury, New York City. The late William Hindley had measured and sketched hundreds of old buildings in and around New York; his sketchbooks contain immensely valuable notes on many buildings now destroyed.

HUBBARD, CORTLAND VAN DYKE, *see* EBERLEIN, HAROLD DONALDSON, and CORTLAND VAN DYKE HUBBARD, *Historic Houses of the Hudson Valley* and *Portrait of a Colonial City, Philadelphia.* . . .

KELLER, WILLIAM A., *Rensselaerville, an Old Village of the Helderbergs,* Vol. x, No. 4, in the White Pine Series of Architectural Monographs (New York: Russell F. Whitehead, August 1924). The text of this monograph is one of the most scholarly and interesting of the whole series.

PELLETREAU, WILLIAM S[MITH], *Early New York Houses* . . . , with photographs of old houses and original illustrations by C. G. Moller, Jr. (New York: F. P. Harper, 1900). Photographs and sketches of many important houses long since destroyed. The text is chiefly genealogical and historical rather than architectural.

SCHUYLER, MONTGOMERY, ʻThe Small City House in New York,ʼ *The Architectural Record,* Vol. VIII, Nos. 4–6 (April–June 1899), pp. 357–88. A pioneer study of one phase of architectural development in America. Important and interesting, like all Montgomery Schuyler's writings. He was perhaps the soundest historical critic American architecture has known.

SCOTT, [MISS] N. M., ʻThe New York Row House, 1800–1850ʼ [unpublished], in the Avery Library, Columbia University. An excellent and penetrating historical study, showing much research in contemporary documents and descriptions.

SEESE, [MRS.] MILDRED [N.] P[ARKER], *Old Orange Houses* . . . (Middletown, N. Y.: The Whitlock Press [c1941–]). A photographic survey, with brief text. Illustrates what other counties or towns might undertake at a reasonable cost.

SMITH, J. WILMER, *see* CUNNINGHAM, HARRY FRANCIS, JOSEPH ARTHUR YOUNGER, and J. WILMER SMITH, *Measured Drawings* . . . *District of Columbia.*

STOKES, I. N. PHELPS, *The Iconography of Manhattan Island,* 6 vols. (New York: R. H. Dodd, 1915–28). This monumental and invaluable work — one of the great civic monuments of our time — is too well known to demand further encomiums here.

STOTZ, CHARLES MORSE, *The Early Architecture of Western Pennsylvania* (New York: William Helburn, for the Buhl Foundation, 1936). An excellent regional study, richly illustrated with photographs and measured drawings. A model of its type.

TALLMAN, CARL C., *Early Wood-Built Houses of Central New York,* Vol. IV, No. 5, in the White Pine Series of Architectural Monographs (New York: Russell F. Whitehead, October 1918). Illustrates many interesting examples.

TROWBRIDGE, ALEXANDER B., *The Greek Revival in Owego and Nearby New York Towns, and Some Suggested Antidotes,* Vol. IV, No. 5, in the White Pine Series of Architectural Monographs (New York: Russell F. Whitehead, October 1918). [Comment in the text on page 267.]

WHITE, RICHARD GRANT, ' Old New York and Its Houses,' *Century Magazine,* Vol. XXVI, No. 6 (October 1883), pp. 845–59.

WHITING, FRANK P., *Cooperstown in the Days of Our Forefathers,* Vol. IX, No. 3, in the White Pine Series of Architectural Monographs (New York: Russell F. Whitehead, June 1923).

WOOTTEN, [MRS.] BAYARD [MORGAN], and ANTHONY HIGGINS, *New Castle, Delaware,* 1651–1939, with photographs by Bayard Wootten, text by Anthony Higgins (Boston: Houghton Mifflin Company, 1939). Excellent photographs of one of the most beautiful of early American cities.

YOUNGER, JOSEPH ARTHUR, *see* CUNNINGHAM, HARRY FRANCIS, JOSEPH ARTHUR YOUNGER, and J. WILMER SMITH, *Measured Drawings* . . . *District of Columbia.*

C. *The Southern Seaboard*

CHRISTIAN, FRANCES ARCHER, and [MRS.] SUSANNE WILLIAMS MASSIE, *Homes and Gardens of Old Virginia* (Richmond: Garrett and Massie [c1931]). Photographs of many buildings, including a few churches and school and college buildings, with comment chiefly of a personal, genealogical type.

COONEY, [MRS.] LORAINE M[EEKS], compiler, *Garden History of Georgia* (Atlanta: The Peachtree Garden Club, 1933). Plans and photographs of several important early estates. Some architectural illustration and comment.

CRANE, EDWARD A[NDREW], and E[RIC] E[LLIS] SODERHOLTZ, *Charleston, S. C., and Savannah, Ga.,* . . . (Berlin: Bruno Hessling [1898]). Many superb photographs, some of monuments no longer standing.

DENMARK, ERNEST RAY, *Architecture of the Old South* (Atlanta: Southern Architect and Building News [c1926]). Many illustrations, chiefly of plantation houses.

EARLE, SWEPSON, *The Chesapeake Bay Country* (Baltimore: Thompsen-Ellis & Co., 1924). This book contains photographs and histories of many houses not illustrated elsewhere.

FORMAN, HENRY CHANDLEE, *Early Manor and Plantation Houses of Maryland* (Easton, Md., and Haverford, Pa.: the author [c1934]). A careful study; especially valuable because of its many plans.

HALL, CLAYTON C., ed., *Baltimore, Its History and Its People,* 3 vols. (Chicago: Lewis Historical Publishing Company, 1912).

HENDERSON, ARCHIBALD, *see* WOOTTEN, [MRS.] BAYARD [MORGAN], and ARCHIBALD HENDERSON, . . . *North Carolina.*

HORTON, MRS. THADDEUS, ' Classic Houses of the South, Old and New,' *House Beautiful,* Vol. XXII, No. 2 (July 1902), pp. 84–90. Valuable for its plans.

JOHNSTON, FRANCES BENJAMIN, and THOMAS TILESTON WATERMAN, *The Early Architecture of North Carolina* (Chapel Hill: University of North Carolina Press, 1941). Superb photographs, with an excellent historical and architectural commentary. A model for books of its kind.

LANCASTER, ROBERT A[LEXANDER], *Historic Virginia Houses and Churches* . . . (Philadelphia and London: J. B. Lippincott Company, 1915). Illustrations of many examples, some no longer standing.

LAPHAM, SAMUEL, JR., *see* SIMONS, ALBERT, and SAMUEL LAPHAM, JR., *Charleston, South Carolina.*

LEIDING, [MRS.] HARRIETTE KERSHAW, *Historic Houses of South Carolina* (Philadelphia: J. B. Lippincott Company, 1921). A popular book with many photographs, often of houses chosen for picturesqueness rather than architectural clarity, and anecdotal and genealogical historical comment. Few dates for houses given.

MASSIE, [MRS.] SUSANNE WILLIAMS, *see* CHRISTIAN, FRANCES ARCHER, and [MRS.] SUSANNE WILLIAMS MASSIE, . . . *Old Virginia.*

NOLL, A[RTHUR] H[OWARD], ' Some Southern Capitols,' *The American Architect and Building News:* Arkansas, Vol. LXXI, No. 1314 (March 2, 1901), plate; Florida, Vol. XXXV, No. 839 (January 23, 1892), p. 60; Georgia, Vol. XXXIX, No. 889 (January 7, 1893), p. 13; Louisiana Vol. XXX, No. 780 (December 6, 1890), p. 145; Mississippi, Vol.

XXIX, No. 763 (August 9, 1890), p. 84; South Carolina, Vol. XXXVIII, No. 879 (October 29, 1892), p. 69.

SCHARF, J. THOMAS, *Chronicles of Baltimore* (Baltimore: Turnbull Brothers, 1874).

SCOTT, MARY WINGFIELD, *Houses of Old Richmond* (Richmond: The Valentine Museum, 1941). A serious study, with good architectural and historical comments and many good photographs. As in many such works, interiors and plans are relatively neglected.

SIMONS, ALBERT, and SAMUEL LAPHAM, JR., *Charleston, South Carolina* (New York: Press of the American Institute of Architects, 1927). An excellent monograph; a model for books of its class.

SODERHOLTZ, E[RIC] E[LLIS], *see* CRANE, EDWARD A[NDREW], and E[RIC] E[LLIS] SODERHOLTZ, *Charleston . . . and Savannah . . .*

STONEY, SAMUEL GAILLARD, *Plantations of the Carolina Low Countries* (Charleston: Carolina Art Association, 1938). Valuable for its excellent illustrations of many important examples little known and difficult to visit.

―― *See also* WOOTTEN, [MRS.] BAYARD [MORGAN], and SAMUEL GAILLARD STONEY, *Charleston. . .*

UNITED STATES QUARTERMASTER CORPS, *Arlington House and Its Associations* (Washington: Custis, Lee [1932]). A historical sketch.

WATERMAN, THOMAS TILESTON, *see* JOHNSTON, FRANCES BENJAMIN, and THOMAS TILESTON WATERMAN, . . . *North Carolina.*

WAYLAND, JOHN W., *Historic Homes of Northern Virginia and the Eastern Panhandle of West Virginia* (Staunton, Va.: The McClure Company, 1937). Excellent photographs of many little-known houses, with unusually careful historical notices.

WOOTTEN, [MRS.] BAYARD [MORGAN], and ARCHIBALD HENDERSON, *Old Homes and Gardens of North Carolina,* with photographs by Bayard Wootten, historical text by Archibald Henderson (Chapel Hill: University of North Carolina Press, for the Garden Club of North Carolina [c1939]). Many good photographs of houses, with some gardens.

―― and SAMUEL GAILLARD STONEY, *Charleston: Azaleas and Old Bricks,* with photographs by Bayard Wootten, text by Samuel Gaillard Stoney (Boston: Houghton Mifflin Company, 1937). An excellent book of pictures.

D. *The Central States*

ANDREWS, ALFRED, 'Greek Revival Houses in Kentucky,' master's essay, Columbia University (Department of Art and Archaeology), 1942. A rich collection of unusual photographs, with an architectural analysis.

'The Architecture of Nashville,' *Journal of the American Institute of Architects,* Vol. VII, No. 4 (April 1919), pp. 159–70. An interesting general study.

BRANDAU, ROBERTA SEAWELL, ed., *see* GARDEN STUDY CLUB OF NASHVILLE,
. . . *History of Homes and Gardens of Tennessee.*
BURNS, LEE, *Early Architects and Builders of Indiana,* reprinted from
Vol. XI, No. 3, Indiana Historical Society Publications (Indianapolis:
Indiana Historical Society, 1935). An enlightening but all too brief
study of the development of a pioneering commonwealth into a flour-
ishing and cultured state. It is unfortunate that there are not more
illustrations.
CONOVER, CHARLOTTE REEVE, *The Story of Dayton* (Dayton: Greater
Dayton Association, 1917).
FARMER, SILAS, *The History of Detroit and Michigan* (Detroit: S. Farmer
& Co., 1884), Part VII, Architectural. An excellent general architec-
tural history.
FEDERAL WRITERS' PROJECT, WORKS PROGRESS ADMINISTRATION, *Chilli-
cothe and Ross County, Ohio,* in the American Guide Series (Chilli-
cothe: Northwest Territory Committee, 1938).
——*Illinois: A Descriptive and Historical Guide,* in the American Guide
Series (Chicago: A. C. McClurg, 1939).
FRARY, I[HNA] T[HAYER], *Early Homes of Ohio* (Richmond: Garrett and
Massie, 1936). A fascinating study, richly illustrated, chiefly de-
voted to the northern part of the state. Scholarly and architecturally
significant.
THE GARDEN STUDY CLUB OF NASHVILLE and MRS. JOHN TROTWOOD
MOORE, *History of Homes and Gardens of Tennessee,* edited by Ro-
berta Seawell Brandau (Nashville: The Parthenon Press, 1936). Interesting chiefly for its illustrations, which cover a large number of
examples throughout the State.
HAMLIN, TALBOT F., 'The A.I.A. [American Institute of Architects]
Meets in Kentucky,' *Pencil Points,* Vol. XXI, No. 5 (May 1940), pp.
279–94. Contains material dealing with Gideon Shryock. This issue
also contains an album of excellent photographs of important Kentucky buildings.
*Historic American Buildings Survey, Comprising Fifty Plates of Draw-
ings of Pioneer Architecture,* edited by Earl H. Reed, District Officer, Northern Illinois (Chicago [n.p., n.d.]). Two other similar collections, of fifty plates each, were published with the same title. An
excellent selection of interesting drawings covering important buildings of northern Illinois. It is a pity that similar albums should not
have been published for all the sections of the H.A.B.S.
MOORE, MRS. JOHN TROTWOOD, *see* GARDEN STUDY CLUB OF NASHVILLE,
. . . *Homes and Gardens of Tennessee.*
NEWCOMB, REXFORD, *Old Kentucky Architecture* (New York: William
Helburn, 1940). A most thorough and interesting study, well illustrated with both photographs and drawings. The frontispiece, how-
ever, is of a modern ' restoration.'
O'DONNELL, THOMAS E., ' The Early Architecture of Marietta, the Old-

est City in Ohio,' *Architecture,* Vol. LI, No. 1 (January 1925), pp. 1–4.

—— ' The Greek Revival in Chillicothe, Ohio's Old Capital City,' *Architecture,* Vol. LII, No. 4 (October 1925), pp. 355–60. Two brief but excellent local studies.

—— ' Ornamental Iron Work in Early Ohio Architecture,' *Architecture,* Vol. LIV, No. 4 (October 1926), pp. 299–302.

SMITH, [MRS.] OPHIA D., *Old Oxford Houses and the People Who Lived in Them* (Oxford, Ohio: The Oxford Historical Press, 1941). Largely local history, but with some interesting illustrations.

STEELE, ROBERT W., and MARY DAVIES STEELE, *Early Dayton* (Dayton: W. J. Shuey, 1896).

TALMADGE, THOMAS E., *Architecture in Old Chicago* (Chicago: University of Chicago Press, 1941). The beginning only of a much larger work which Talmadge had under way at the time of his death. Shows some interesting early Greek Revival structures.

TAYLOR, HOWELL, ' Historic Houses of Southwest Michigan,' Detroit *News* (Sunday feature series), 1931–2. An excellent illustrated popular series. Newspapers in other localities might well emulate it.

THOMAS, [MRS.] ELIZABETH PATTERSON, *Old Kentucky Homes and Gardens* (Louisville, Ky.: The Standard Printing Company [c1939]). Chiefly genealogical, but contains pictures of many interesting buildings.

E. *The Gulf Coast*

Art Work of Mobile and Vicinity, with a historical study by Peter Joseph Hamilton (Chicago: W. H. Parish, 1894). Important for its photographs.

CURTIS, NATHANIEL CORTLANDT, *New Orleans: Its Old Houses, Shops, and Public Buildings* (Philadelphia and London: J. B. Lippincott Company, 1933). An excellent study of the architectural development of New Orleans.

KENNEDY, J. ROBIE, JR., ' Examples of the Greek Revival Period in Alabama,' *The Brickbuilder,* Vol. XIII, Nos. 6 and 7 (June and July 1904), pp. 121–6, 144–7. Excellently illustrated.

RICCIUTI, ITALO WILLIAM, *New Orleans and Its Environs* (New York: William Helburn, 1938). Superb photographs of buildings and details, with some measured drawings and plans.

F. *The Mississippi Valley*

BRYAN, JOHN A., *Missouri's Contribution to American Architecture* ([St. Louis: St. Louis Architectural Club] 1928). Excellent account of early architects and architecture.

LAIST, THEODORE, ' Two Early Mississippi Valley State Capitols ' (Arkansas and Mississippi), *The Western Architect,* Vol. XXXV, No. 5 (May 1926), pp. 53–8.

OLIVER, N[OLA] N[ANCE], *Natchez, Symbol of the Old South* (New York: Hastings House [c1940]). Some good illustrations. The text typically ' befo' de War.'

PETERSON, CHARLES E., *Early Ste. Genevieve and Its Architecture*, reprinted from the *Missouri Historical Review*, Vol. XXXV, No. 2 (January 1941), pp. 207–32.

—— ' French Houses of the Illinois Country,' *Missouriana*, Vol. x, No. 10 (August–September 1938), pp. 4–7. Interesting brief studies of the early French houses of the St. Louis neighborhood.

—— *A List of Published Writings of Specific Interest in the Study of the Historic Architecture of the Mississippi Valley*, 2nd ed. (St. Louis: National Park Service, Historic American Buildings Survey, 1940). A full bibliography of great value.

ST. LOUIS PUBLIC LIBRARY, *The Old St. Louis Riverfront; an Exhibition . . . April* 11–30, 1938 (St. Louis: Public Library [1938]). Deals chiefly with the St. Louis Jefferson Memorial area.

SMITH, J. FRAZER, *White Pillars: Early Life and Architecture of the Lower Mississippi Valley Country* (New York: William Helburn, 1941). Important because of its broad scope, and because of the many plans it gives.

G. The West

FEDERAL WRITERS' PROJECT, WORKS PROGRESS ADMINISTRATION, *Iowa: A Guide to the Hawkeye State*, in the American Guide Series (New York: Viking Press, 1938).

KUCHEL, C. C., a lithograph of Nevada City (San Francisco, 1861).

—— and Dressel, in the series ' Pacific Views,' a view of Portland, Oregon, with border showing all the chief buildings (San Francisco, 1858).

STOKES, I. N. PHELPS, and DAVID C. HASKELL, *American Historical Prints: Early Views of American Cities . . .* (New York: New York Public Library, 1932). A most valuable source.

IV. MONOGRAPHS ON MOVEMENTS OR BUILDINGS

ADDISON, AGNES, ' Latrobe *vs.* Strickland,' *Journal of the American Society of Architectural Historians*, Vol. II, No. 3 (July 1942), pp. 26–9. Final and conclusive evidence from original sources, proving that Strickland designed the Bank of the United States in Philadelphia.

ARTHUR, STANLEY C., *A History of the United States Custom House, New Orleans* (New Orleans: Survey of Federal Archives in Louisiana, 1940). A detailed study of the original sources. Similar research with regard to many other important buildings should be undertaken and published. This could well be done in many cases by state and municipal governments.

BENNETT, WELLS, *Stephen Hallet and His Designs for the National Capitol*, 1790–94 (Harrisburg and Washington, 1916), reprinted from the *Journal of the American Institute of Architects,* Vol. IV, Nos. 7–10 (July–October 1916). A careful study of the attribution and dating of many important preliminary drawings of the United States Capitol.

—— *See also* KIMBALL, FISKE, and WELLS BENNETT, 'The Competition . . . 1792–93.'

BOOTH, DR. VINCENT RAVI, ed., *Concerning the Old First Church of Bennington, a Vermont Shrine,* with drawings by D. B. Hull (New York: Lenz & Riecker, Inc., 1933). Measured drawings of the church, with a discussion of its architecture and architects.

—— *First Congregational Church, Bennington, Vermont* (Boston: E. L. Hildreth & Co., 1937).

BROWN, GLENN, *History of the United States Capitol,* 2 vols. (Washington: Government Printing Office, 1900, 1903). A superb monument of research, appreciation, and analysis, as well as a beautiful and richly illustrated book, worthy of the building it treats.

—— *The Octagon, Dr. William Thornton, Architect* (Washington: printed for the American Institute of Architects [1917?]). An excellent monograph on a single building, well illustrated.

EBERLEIN, HAROLD DONALDSON, 'The Fairmount Waterworks, Philadelphia,' *The Architectural Record,* Vol. LXII, No. 1 (July 1927), pp. 57–67. Interesting historical article, illustrated with photographs and engravings.

EMBURY, AYMAR, II, *Early American Churches* (New York: Doubleday, Page & Company, 1914). Photographs and brief text dealing with many important churches, some of the Greek Revival.

FITZ-GIBBONS, COSTEN, 'Latrobe and the Centre Square Pump House,' *The Architectural Record,* Vol. LXII, No. 1 (July 1927), pp. 18–22. An important article, reproducing some of Latrobe's drawings as well as old views of the building.

FRARY, I[HNA] T[HAYER], *They Built the Capitol* (Richmond: Garrett and Massie [c1940]).

GILCHRIST, AGNES ADDISON, *see* ADDISON, AGNES.

HORN, STANLEY F., *The Hermitage, Home of Old Hickory* (Richmond: Garrett and Massie, 1938). An adequate monograph on an important house, largely from the historical point of view.

KIMBALL, [SIDNEY] FISKE, 'The Bank of Pennsylvania, an Unknown Masterpiece of American Classicism,' *The Architectural Record,* Vol. XLIV, No. 2 (August 1918), pp. 132–9. An important and thoroughly documented study, reproducing some of Latrobe's drawings as well as an early photograph.

—— 'The Bank of the United States,' *The Architectural Record,* Vol. LVIII, No. 6 (December 1925), pp. 581–94. An important study, reproducing Latrobe's competition drawings. The conclusion, however, has been negatived by more recently discovered information.

—— 'Latrobe's Designs for the Cathedral of Baltimore,' *The Architec-*

tural Record, Vol. xlii, No. 6 (December 1917), pp. 540–50; Vol. xliii, No. 1 (January 1918), pp. 37–45. A careful study of the history of the design of this important monument, reproducing many of Latrobe's drawings for both the Gothic and the Classic designs.

—— and Wells Bennett, 'The Competition for the Federal Buildings, 1792–93,' *Journal of the American Institute of Architects,* Vol. vii, Nos. 1, 3, 5, 7 (January, March, May, December, 1919), pp. 8–12, 98–102, 202–10, 335–61, 521–8 respectively; Vol. viii, No. 3 (March 1920), pp. 117–24. An excellent study of the competition drawings and their makers; full of information with regard to some of the less well-known competitors.

—— —— 'William Thornton and the Design of the United States Capitol,' *Art Studies Medieval and Modern,* Vol. i (Princeton: Princeton University Press, 1923), an extra number of the *American Journal of Archaeology,* pp. 76–92. Clarifies the history of the various Thornton designs and the influence on them of Hallet's work.

Latrobe, John H. B., *The Capitol and Washington at the Beginning of the Present Century,* an address delivered before the American Institute of Architects, November 16, 1881 (Baltimore: W. K. Boyle [1881]). Full of information, especially about the work of B. H. Latrobe. Not entirely without bias.

Leonard, Grace F., and W. Chesley Worthington, *The Providence Athenaeum; a Brief History,* 1753–1939 (Providence: for the Athenaeum, 1940).

M——, W— D——, 'The Architect of the [Providence] Athenaeum Building,' *The Athenaeum Bulletin,* Vol. x, No. 3 (December 1937). The interesting story of the designs for this building.

—— 'The Construction of the [Providence] Athenaeum Building,' *The Athenaeum Bulletin,* Vol. iii, Nos. 2, 3 (September, December, 1930). More about the architects and the construction of the Providence Athenaeum.

Newton, Roger Hale, 'Bulfinch's Design for the Library of Congress,' *The Art Bulletin,* Vol. xxiii, No. 3 (September 1941), pp. 221–2. Indicates that Robert Mills, in his design for the Library of the University of South Carolina, followed Bulfinch's Library of Congress in the United States Capitol.

O'Donnell, Thomas E., 'The Greek Revival Capitol at Columbus, Ohio,' *The Architectural Forum,* Vol. xlii, No. 1 (January 1925), pp. 5–8. A brief history, illustrated with a photograph, a plan, and an old engraving.

Ross, William, letter in [Loudon's] *The Architectural Magazine,* Vol. ii, No. [12] (December 1835), pp. 526–32. Shows the importance of Ross's contribution to the final plan and design of the interior of the New York Sub-Treasury building, and illustrates the designs of both Town and Davis and the adopted plans of Ross. An important source.

Rusk, William Sener, 'Godefroy and Saint Mary's Chapel, Baltimore,'

Liturgical Arts, Vol. II, Fourth Quarter (June–September 1933), pp. 140–45. An interesting study of one of the earliest of America's Gothic Revival buildings.

SCHUYLER, MONTGOMERY, ʻThe Southern Colleges,' No. 8 in a series on The Architecture of American Colleges in *The Architectural Record,* Vol. XXX, No. 1 (July 1911), pp. 57–84. Important, like all of Schuyler's work. Especially valuable for its many illustrations of little-known campuses.

SMITH, DARRELL HEVENOR, *The Office of the Supervising Architect of the Treasury,* Service Monograph No. 23 of the Institute for Government Research (Baltimore: Johns Hopkins Press, 1923).

THAYER, R. H., compiler, for the United States Supervising Architect of the Treasury Department, *History, Organization, and Functions of the Office of the Supervising Architect of the Treasury Department* . . . (Washington: Government Printing Office, 1896).

UNITED STATES TREASURY DEPARTMENT, *A History of Public Buildings under the Control of the Treasury Department* [*exclusive of marine hospitals and quarantine stations*] (Washington: Government Printing Office, 1901). Important for the dating of many buildings. No mention of architects, however. A photograph of each building is included.

WILLARD, SOLOMON, *Plans and Sections of the Obelisk of Bunker's Hill, with Experiments Made in Quarrying the Granite* (Boston: Samuel N. Dickenson, 1843). Illustrated with scale drawings.

WILLIAMSON, JEFFERSON, *The American Hotel, an Anecdotal History* (New York: Alfred A. Knopf, 1930). Full of important information. Rather gossipy, with few of the sources indicated, but valuable.

WORTHINGTON, W. CHESLEY, *see* LEONARD, GRACE F., and W. CHESLEY WORTHINGTON, *The Providence Athenaeum.* . . .

V. WORKS DEALING WITH ARCHITECTS

A. *General Works*

BRAULT, ELIE, *Les Architectes par leurs œuvres: Ouvrage rédigé sur les manuscrits de feu Al. du Bois,* . . . 3 vols. (Paris: Laurens [1893]). Full of generally accurate information, for which no sources are given. Valuable if checked. Occasional misspellings.

Dictionary of American Biography (New York: Charles Scribner's Sons, 1928–). An invaluable, scholarly source, with articles written by specialists. Covers many early American architects.

DYER, WALTER A., *Early American Craftsmen* (New York: The Century Company, 1915). Especially good on McIntire and Phyfe.

MASON, GEORGE CHAMPLIN, *Architects and Their Environment, 1850–1907, Together with Notes and Reminiscences of the Fathers of the Profession* . . . (Ardmore, Pa. [n.p.], 1907). Interesting personal reminiscences of a time of change in the architectural profession, and some comment on important early architects.

NEWCOMB, REXFORD, 'Early American Architects' series in *The Architect:* Charles Bulfinch, Vol. IX, No. 3 (December 1927), pp. 289–93; Andrew Hamilton, Vol. X, No. 1 (April 1928), pp. 45–50; Peter Harrison, Vol. X, No. 3 (June 1928), pp. 315–18; John Haviland, Vol. XI, No. 3 (December 1928), pp. 285–8; Thomas Jefferson, Vol. IX, No. 4 (January 1928), pp. 429–32; Dr. John Kearsley, Vol. X, No. 2 (May 1928), pp. 177–81; B. H. Latrobe, Vol. IX, No. 2 (November 1927), pp. 173–7; Samuel McIntire, Vol. IX, No. 1 (October 1927), pp. 37–43; Robert Mills, Vol. IX, No. 6 (March 1928), pp. 697–9; Gideon Shryock, Vol. XI, No. 1 (October 1928), pp. 41–6; William Strickland, Vol. X, No. 4 (July 1928), pp. 453–8; Dr. William Thornton, Vol. IX, No. 5 (February 1928), pp. 559–63; Ithiel Town, Vol. XI, No. 5 (February 1929), pp. 519–23; Thomas U. Walter, Vol. X, No. 5 (August 1928), pp. 585–9. Interesting introductory studies on important architects.

RAVENEL, BEATRICE ST. JULIEN, *The Architects of Charleston* (Charleston: Carolina Art Association, 1946).

RUSK, WILLIAM SENER, *William Thornton, Benjamin H. Latrobe, and Thomas U. Walter and the Classic Influence in Their Work,* doctoral dissertation, Johns Hopkins University, 1933 (Baltimore [n.p.], 1939). Interesting material on Girard College.

B. *Works Dealing with Individuals*

Charles Bulfinch

BULFINCH, ELLEN SUSAN, *The Life and Letters of Charles Bulfinch, Architect* (Boston and New York: Houghton Mifflin Company, 1896). An important and interesting biographical collection, written and edited more from the personal than from the architectural point of view.

PLACE, CHARLES A., *Charles Bulfinch, Architect and Citizen* (Boston and New York: Houghton Mifflin Company, 1925). A complete and richly illustrated biography, with a careful study of Bulfinch's architecture and its development. A model for books of its type.

Elias Carter

FORBES, MRS. HARRIETTE M., 'Elias Carter, Architect, of Worcester, Mass.,' *Old-Time New England,* the bulletin of the Society for the Preservation of New England Antiquities, Vol. XI, No. 2 (October 1920), pp. 58–71. An important study, well illustrated.

James Hamilton Couper

HORTON, MRS. THADDEUS, 'Amateur Architects of the South,' *Architecture,* Vol. XXXVII, No. 5 (May 1918), pp. 127–32. An interesting side light on much southern architecture, with several plans.

Alexander Jackson Davis

Davis Collection, Avery Library, Columbia University, New York
Davis Collection, Metropolitan Museum of Art (Print Room), New York
Davis Collection, New York Historical Society (Print Room), New York
These three collections taken together form an extraordinarily complete corpus of this architect's work, including diaries, account books, clippings, engravings, and several thousand architectural drawings and studies. They form an invaluable source on the architecture of the time. [*See also Town and Davis.*]

James Gallier

GALLIER, JAMES, *Autobiography of James Gallier, Architect* (Paris Brière, 1864). An invaluable source for early architectural pra in America, as well as for Gallier's life. It is sometimes biased in controversial matters, and must be accepted with caution in connection with Lafever and the Dakins.

Maximilian Godefroy

Important papers in the Ebenezer Jackson collection, Middletown, Connecticut.
DAVISON, CAROLINA V., ' Maximilian Godefroy,' *Maryland Historical Magazine,* Vol. XXIX, No. 3 (September 1934), pp. 175–212. A full and most interesting account of a tragic and brilliant career. Contains also a translation of an important autobiographical statement.
HOYT, WILLIAM D[ANA], JR., ' Eliza Godefroy, Destiny's Football,' *Maryland Historical Magazine,* Vol. XXXVI, No. 1 (March 1941), pp. 10–21. Important material dealing with Maximilian Godefroy as well as with his wife. Interesting and valuable.

Horatio Greenough

WYNNE, NANCY, and BEAUMONT NEWHALL, 'Horatio Greenough, Herald of Functionalism,' *The Magazine of Art,* Vol. XXXII, No. 1 (January 1937), pp. 12–15. Interesting comment on Greenough's architectural criticism.

Philip Hooker

ROOT, EDWARD W., *Philip Hooker; a Contribution to the Study of the Renaissance in America* (New York: Charles Scribner's Sons, 1929). A carefully documented biography, richly illustrated. Occasional misreadings of early manuscripts. Valuable for its background material on early Albany.

Thomas Jefferson

FRARY, I[HNA] T[HAYER], *Thomas Jefferson, Architect and Builder* (Richmond: Garrett and Massie, 1931). An excellent ' popular ' study.

KIMBALL, [SIDNEY] FISKE, *Thomas Jefferson, Architect; Original Designs in the Collection of Thomas Jefferson Coolidge* (Boston: printed for private distribution by the Riverside Press, 1916). One of the great monuments of American architectural research, superbly produced. An invaluable source on the architecture of Thomas Jefferson.

—— *Thomas Jefferson and the First Monument of the Classic Revival in America* [Harrisburg and Washington, 1915], reprinted from the *Journal of the American Institute of Architects,* Vol. III, Nos. 9–11 (September–November 1915). On the Virginia State Capitol.

LAMBETH, WILLIAM ALEXANDER, and WARREN H[ENRY] MANNING, *Thomas Jefferson as an Architect and a Designer of Landscapes* (Boston and New York: Houghton Mifflin Company, 1913). Well illustrated; a good general sketch of Jefferson's architectural work.

Benjamin Henry Latrobe

LATROBE, B. H., *The Journal of Latrobe* (New York: D. Appleton· and Company, 1905). Invaluable source material, despite numerous misprints in names, etc.

—— letters, drawings, and sketchbooks in the collection of Ferdinand C. Latrobe of Baltimore. An amazingly rich mine of source material, not only on B. H. Latrobe, but also on the general history of the times, and on the topography and appearance of the United States at the beginning of the nineteenth century.

' The First Architect in America, Benjamin Henry Latrobe; Notes and Letters on the Erection of the Capitol at Washington,' *Appleton's Booklovers Magazine,* Vol. VI, No. 3 (September 1905), pp. 345–55. A review of Latrobe's contribution to the United States Capitol and the controversies concerning it.

HAMLIN, TALBOT F., ' Benjamin Henry Latrobe: The Man and the Architect,' *Maryland Historical Magazine,* Vol. XXXVII, No. 4 (December 1942), pp. 339–60.

John McComb, Jr.

Notes and drawings in the New York Historical Society. A superb collection of drawings, professional diaries, account books, and other papers, dealing with almost the entire professional career of John McComb, Jr.; contains also numerous drawings by other architects of the time.

Samuel McIntire

KIMBALL, [SIDNEY] FISKE, *Mr. Samuel McIntire, Carver, the Architect of Salem* (Portland, Me.: for the Essex Institute, 1940). A complete and carefully documented biographical and architectural study, richly illustrated with McIntire's drawings as well as photographs of his work.

Robert Mills

GALLAGHER, H. M. PIERCE, *Robert Mills, Architect of the Washington Monument,* 1781–1855 (New York: Columbia University Press, 1935). A sympathetic study of the work and personality of Mills, with a most valuable appendix containing the unpublished writings of Mills; reproduces many of Mills's drawings.

Duncan Phyfe

McCLELLAND, NANCY [VINCENT], *Duncan Phyfe and English Regency,* 1795–1830 (New York: W. R. Scott, Inc. [c1939]). A well-illustrated work on Phyfe's furniture and its relationships to English work.

Calvin Pollard

Calvin Pollard Collection, Avery Library, Columbia University, New York
Calvin Pollard Collection, New York Historical Society (Print Room), New York
These collections give an excellent picture of the work of one of the most important of the less well known New York architects.

Joseph Jacques Ramée

HISLOP, CODMAN, and HAROLD A. LARRABEE, ' Joseph Jacques Ramée and the Building of the North and South Colleges,' *Union Alumni Monthly,* Vol. XXVII, No. 4 (February 1938), pp. 1–16. A brief but valuable account.
—— —— 'The Ramée Plans,' *Union Alumni Monthly,* Vol. XXII, No. 2 (December 1932), pp. 48–53. An account of the discovery of many Ramée drawings dealing with Union College; one is reproduced, and all are listed.
LARRABEE, HAROLD A., ' How Ramée Came to Schenectady,' *Union Alumni Monthly,* Vol. XXVI, No. 4 (February 1937), pp. 111–13. An interesting study of the reasons behind Ramée's arrival in the United States, and of the Parish family through whom he came.
—— *Joseph Jacques Ramée and America's First Unified College Plan,* No. 1 in the Franco-American Pamphlet Series (New York: American Society of the French Legion of Honor, 1934). A general account of Ramée and of his designs for Union College.

Edward Shaw

FARWELL, [MRS.] HARRIETTE F., *Shaw Records: A Memorial of Roger Shaw,* 1594–1661 (Bethel, Me.: E. C. Bowler, 1904).

William Strickland

GILLIAMS, E. LESLIE, 'A Pioneer American Architect,' *The Architectural Record,* Vol. XXIII, No. 2 (February 1908), pp. 123–35. An excellent introductory study.

Ithiel Town

Hoadley papers in the Connecticut Historical Society, New Haven. Much valuable material dealing with Town, Hoadley, and early nineteenth-century architecture in Connecticut.

KELLY, J. FREDERICK, 'A Forgotten Incident in the Life of Ithiel Town,' *Old-Time New England,* Vol. xxxi, No. 3 (January 1941), pp. 62–9. Interesting new light on Town's New Haven career.

SEYMOUR, GEORGE DUDLEY, *The Residence and Library of Ithiel Town (1784–1844), the Home of the Greek Revivalist* (New Haven [n.p.], April 1930). Largely devoted to a reprint of Mrs. Sigourney's article:

SIGOURNEY, [MRS.] LYDIA, 'The Residence and Library of Ithiel Town, Esq.,' *The Ladies' Companion, a Monthly Magazine,* First Series, Vol. x, No. 1 (January 1839), pp. 123–6. An important source, significant as showing interest in the matter; illustrated with a view of the building.

Town and Davis

NEWTON, ROGER HALE, *Town and Davis, Architects* (New York: Columbia University Press, 1942). A ground-breaking study on this important firm and its innovations, based on a careful study of original sources; illustrated with many Davis drawings as well as a small selection of executed work.

Richard Upjohn

UPJOHN, EVERARD M., *Richard Upjohn, Architect and Churchman* (New York: Columbia University Press, 1939). A thoroughly documented study of a great American architect, well illustrated both with Upjohn's drawings and with photographs.

Cyrus Wetherill

COLE, MARC W., 'A Master Builder of the Early Nineteenth Century,' *Country Life in America,* Vol. xxix, No. 4 (February 1916), pp. 22–3. A brief account, with illustrations of the work of an early architect in upstate New York.

Solomon Willard

WHEILDON, WILLIAM W., *Memoir of Solomon Willard, Architect and Superintendent of the Bunker Hill Monument* ([Boston:] The Monument Association [c1865]). An important early source on the life and work of an eccentric but important figure, written by a personal friend.

VI. THE CULTURAL BACKGROUND

ALLEN, EDWARD B., *Early American Wall Paintings, 1710–1850* (New Haven: Yale University Press, 1926). Contains some interesting views and comments; some of its suggested datings and attributions are questionable; especially valuable for its illustrations.

BEARD, CHARLES A. and MARY R., *The Rise of American Civilization*, 2 vols. (New York: The Macmillan Company, 1927; new ed., two vols. in one, rev. and enl. [c1933], 1939). An invaluable source for all students of the development of American culture. It tends, however, to undervalue the vitality and worth of American early nineteenth-century art.

BROMFIELD, LOUIS, *The Farm* (New York and London: Harper & Brothers [c1935]). An interesting picture of the development of central Ohio. The house development from log cabin to mansion is one of the most important themes.

BROOKS, VAN WYCK, *The Flowering of New England* (New York: E. P. Dutton & Company, 1936; new and rev. ed., 1938). A superb account of the literary exuberance that paralleled the Greek Revival.

CHASE, MARY ELLEN, *Silas Crocket* (New York: The Macmillan Company, 1935). An important social and cultural history of the Maine coast in fictional form. Better than any non-fiction work in showing the culture behind Greek Revival building in the region. A builder-architect plays an important part.

HAVENS, CATHERINE E., *Diary of a Little Girl in Old New York* (New York: Henry Collins Brown [c1919]). A valuable original source for many points in house planning as well as for the general spirit of the 1840's.

HINTON, JOHN H., *History and Topography of the United States*, 2 vols. (Boston: S. Walker, 1844; 2nd ed., 1846). Contains many excellent views of American towns and buildings, chiefly from Davis drawings.

HONE, PHILIP, *The Diary of Philip Hone,* edited with an Introduction by Allan Nevins (New York: Dodd, Mead & Company, 1927). A valuable source for the cultural background of the time.

HOWE, M. A. DEWOLFE, *A Venture in Remembrance* (Boston: Little, Brown & Company, 1941). Contains some material on Providence architects.

JOSEPHSON, MATTHEW, *Portrait of the Artist as American* (New York: Harcourt, Brace & Company [c1930]). Interesting in showing the difference in American culture before and after the Civil War — a difference which was a major cause in the extinction of the Greek Revival tradition. Like the Beards, Mr. Josephson tends to underestimate the strength and scope of the artistic tradition of the Greek Revival period.

Memoirs of Margaret Fuller Ossoli (Boston: Phillips, Sampson and Company, 1852). An important original source on social, intellectual, and artistic ideals.

STARBUCK, MARY, *My House and I* (Boston and New York: Houghton Mifflin Company, 1929). American democracy on Nantucket nearly a century ago.

YARMOLINSKY, AVRAHM [TSALEVICH], *Picturesque United States of America, 1811, 1812, 1813, Being a Memoir on Paul [Pavel Petrovich]*

Svinin, Russian Diplomatic Officer, Artist, and Author, with an Introduction by R. T. H. Halsey (New York: W. E. Rudge, 1930). An interesting side light on American life, with excellent illustrations from the paintings of P. P. Svinin.

VII. CONTEMPORARY SOURCES

The selection of travels, guides, and other works included here consists of those works which the author has found most valuable in shedding light upon the architecture of the Greek Revival period and how it was judged at the time it was built. Comment on the works is usually included in the text or footnotes, hence none is given here.

[BLUNT, EDMUND MARCH,] *The Picture of New York, and Stranger's Guide* . . . (New York: A. T. Goodrich [1828]).

CIST, CHARLES, *Cincinnati, 1841: Its Early Annals and Future Prospects* (Cincinnati: the author, 1841).

COOPER, JAMES FENIMORE, *Notions of the Americans, Picked up by a Travelling Bachelor,* 2 vols. (Philadelphia: Carey, Lea & Carey, 1828).

DICKENS, CHARLES, *American Notes* (any good edition).

DUNLAP, WILLIAM, *History of the Rise and Progress of the Arts of Design in the United States,* 2 vols. (New York: G. P. Scott and Co., 1834); new ed., 3 vols., edited by F. W. Bayley and C. F. Goodspeed (Boston: C. E. Goodspeed & Co., 1918).

DWIGHT, TIMOTHY, *Travels in New-England and New-York* (London: William Baynes and Son, and Ogle, Duncan & Co., 1823).

HAMILTON, THOMAS, *Men and Manners in America* (Edinburgh: W. Blackwood, 1833).

HOWE, HENRY, *Historical Collections of Ohio* (Cincinnati: Derby, Bradley & Co., 1847).

LATROBE, BENJAMIN HENRY, *A Private Letter to the Individual Members of Congress* (Washington: S. H. Smith, 1806).

MARTINEAU, HARRIET, *Retrospect of Western Travel,* 3 vols. (London: Saunders and Otley; New York: Harper & Brothers; 1838); facsimile ed. (New York: Harper & Brothers, 1942).

—— *Society in America,* 3 vols. (New York and London: Saunders and Otley, 1837); facsimile ed. (New York: Harper & Brothers, 1942).

MILBERT, J[ACQUES GÉRARD], *Itinéraire pittoresque du fleuve Hudson et des parties latérales de l'Amérique du nord* (Paris: Gauguain & Cie, 1828-9).

Nichols' Illustrated New York: A Series of Views of the Empire City and Its Environs (New York: C. B. and F. B. Nichols, 1847).

TROLLOPE, MRS. [FRANCES MILTON], *Domestic Manners of the Americans* (London: Whitaker, Trecher & Co.; New York: reprinted 'for the booksellers'; 1832).

VIII. Contemporary Architectural Writings

A. *American Works*

(Comment usually in the text. See especially Appendix A.)

Benjamin, Asher, *The American Builder's Companion; or, A New System of Architecture* . . . (Boston: Etheridge and Bliss, 1806); 5th ed. (Boston: R. P. and C. Williams, 1826).

—— *The Builder's Guide; or, Complete System of Architecture* (Boston: Perkins and Marvin; Philadelphia: Henry Perkins; 1839); in 3rd and subsequent editions called *The Architect; or, Complete Builder's Guide* (Boston: Benjamin B. Mussey, 1845); four reissues to 1854.

—— *The Country Builder's Assistant* . . . (Greenfield: Thomas Dickman, 1797; Boston: Spotswood and Etheridge, 1798; Greenfield: Thomas Dickman, 1800; Greenfield: John Denio, 1805).

—— *Elements of Architecture* (Boston: B. B. Mussey, 1843).

—— *The Practical House Carpenter* (Boston: R. P. and C. Williams, and Annin & Smith, 1830); in 1841 and later editions called *The Architect; or, Practical House Carpenter;* fourteen issues to 1857.

—— *Practice of Architecture* (Boston: the author, and Carter, Hendie & Co.; New York: Collins & Co.; 1833); seven other editions to 1851.

—— *The Rudiments of Architecture* (Boston: Munroe and Francis, 1814); 2nd ed. (Boston: R. P. and C. Williams, 1820).

Biddle, Owen, *The Young Carpenter's Assistant* (Philadelphia: Benjamin Johnson, 1805); 2nd ed. (Philadelphia: Johnson and Warner, 1815).

—— and John Haviland, *An improved and enlarged edition of Biddle's The Young Carpenter's Assistant; . . . Revised and corrected with several additional articles and forty-eight new designs . . . by John Haviland, Architect* (Philadelphia: M'Carty & Davis, 1837).

Bridport, Hugh, *see* Haviland, John, and Hugh Bridport, *The Builders' Assistant.*

Brown, William, *The Carpenter's Assistant; containing a succinct account of Egyptian, Grecian, and Roman architecture* . . . (Worcester: E. Livermore, 1848).

Downing, A[ndrew] J[ackson], *The Architecture of Country Houses* . . . (New York: D. Appleton and Company; Philadelphia: G. S. Appleton; 1850); nine issues to 1866.

—— *Cottage Residences* . . . (New York and London: Wiley & Putnam, 1842); eleven issues up to 1887, in five or six editions.

—— *Rural Essays* (New York: G. P. Putnam & Co., 1853); six issues up to 1881.

—— *A Treatise on the Theory and Practice of Landscape Gardening Adapted to North America . . . With remarks on Rural Architecture* (New York and London: Wiley & Putnam; Boston: C. C. Little & Co.; 1841); fifteen issues in six editions up to 1879.

[ELIOT, WILLIAM HAVARD,] *A Description of Tremont House, with Architectural Illustrations* (Boston: Gray and Bowen, 1830).

GALLIER, JAMES, *The American Builder's General Price Book and Estimator* (New York: Lafever & Gallier, 1833); 2nd ed. (Boston: Marsh, Capen & Lyon, 1834); 3rd ed. (Boston: M. Burns, 1836).

HALL, JOHN, *The Cabinet Makers' Assistant* (Baltimore: the author [c1840]). A source for 'American Empire' furniture design, the drawings rather crude.

—— *A Series of Select and Original Designs for Modern Dwelling Houses* . . . (Baltimore: John Murphy, 1840).

HATFIELD, R[OBERT] G[RIFFITH], *The American House-Carpenter* . . . (New York: Wiley, 1845).

HAVILAND, JOHN, and HUGH BRIDPORT, *The Builders' Assistant*, 3 vols. (Philadelphia: John Bioren and the authors, 1818–21).

—— *See also* BIDDLE, OWEN, and JOHN HAVILAND, . . . *The Young Carpenter's Assistant.*

HILLS, CHESTER, *The Builder's Guide* (New York: D. Appleton and Company, 1836 [c1834]); republished with the addition of villa plans by Henry Austin and a chapter on School Architecture by Henry Barnard (Hartford: Case, Tiffany, and Burnham, 1846).

LAFEVER, MINARD, *The Beauties of Modern Architecture* (New York: D. Appleton and Company, 1835); four other editions to 1855.

—— *The Complete Architectural Instructor* (New York: G. P. Putnam, 1857).

—— *The Modern Builders' Guide* (New York: Sleight, 1833); five other editions to 1855.

—— *The Modern Practice of Staircase and Hand-Rail Construction* . . . *With plans and elevations for ornamental villas* (New York: D. Appleton and Company, 1838).

—— *The Young Builder's General Instructor* (Newark: W. Tuttle & Company, 1829).

LATROBE, BENJAMIN H., 'Acoustics,' in the Edinburgh Encyclopaedia, edited by Sir David Brewster, 1st American ed., with the addition of articles relative to the institutions of the American continent, Vol. I (Philadelphia: Joseph and Edward Parker, 1832), pp. 104–24.

LONG, ROBERT CARY, [JR.,] 'The Degeneration of Modern Architecture,' *Journal of The Franklin Institute,* Vol. XXXII, No. 4 (October 1841), p. 246.

MILLS, ROBERT, *A Model Jail of the Olden Time: Designs for 'A Debtors Gaol and Work-House for Felons,' for Burlington County, State of New Jersey* . . . summarized by Captain George J. Giger (New York: Russell Sage Foundation, 1928).

—— *Statistics of South Carolina* (Charleston: Hurlbut and Lloyd, 1826).

OWEN, ROBERT DALE, *Hints on Public Architecture, containing* . . . *views and plans of the Smithsonian Institution* . . . (New York: G. P. Putnam, 1849).

PARRIS, ALEXANDER, letter of November 9, 1840, on electricity, in the *Journal of The Franklin Institute*, Vol. XXXI, No. 3 (March 1841), p. 154.

RAMÉE, DANIEL, *Histoire générale de l'architecture* (Paris: Amyot, 1860–62).

—— *Sculptures décoratives, motifs d'ornamentation recueillis en France, Italie, et Espagne . . . du douzième au seizième siècle* (Paris: A. Lévy, 1864).

RAMÉE, JOSEPH JACQUES, *Parcs et jardins, composés et exécutés dans differens countrées de l'Europe et des états unis d'Amérique* (Paris [n.p., n.d.; title page may be missing from the only copy examined]).

RANLETT, WILLIAM H., *The American Architect*, 2 vols. (New York: Dewitt and Davenport, 1849–51); published earlier (1846–8) in parts, as *The Architect*.

SHAW, EDWARD, *Civil Architecture*, Parts I and II (Boston: Shaw and Stratton, 1830); the whole (Boston: Lincoln and Edwards, 1831); 2nd ed., enlarged (Boston: Capen & Lyon, 1832); 4th ed. (Boston: Marsh, Capen & Lyon, 1835); 11th ed. (Philadelphia: Henry Carey Baird & Co., 1876).

—— *The Modern Architect* (Boston: Dayton and Wentworth, 1854).

—— *Rural Architecture* (Boston: James B. Dow, 1843).

SMITH, J. JAY, *see* WALTER, THOMAS U., and J. JAY SMITH, . . . *Metals and Stone* and . . . *Cottages and Villas*. . . .

STRICKLAND, WILLIAM, *The Public Works of the United States of America* (London: John Weale, 1841).

THOMAS, T., JR., *The Working-Man's Cottage Architecture* . . . (New York: R. Martin, 1848).

TUTHILL, MRS. L[OUISA] C[AROLINE HUGGINS], *History of Architecture, from the Earliest Times; Its Present Condition in Europe and the United States* (Philadelphia: Lindsay and Blakiston, 1848).

WALTER, THOMAS U., lecture on 'Architecture,' published in the *Journal of The Franklin Institute*, Vol. XXXI (Third Series, Vol. I), No. 1 (January 1841), pp. 11–12.

—— and J. JAY SMITH, *A Guide to Workers in Metals and Stone* . . . (Philadelphia: Carey and Hart, 1846).

—— ——*Two Hundred Designs for Cottages and Villas* . . . *Original and Selected* (Philadelphia: Carey and Hart, 1846).

YOUNG, AMMI B., *Plans of Public Buildings in Course of Construction, under the Direction of the Secretary of the Treasury, including the Specifications Thereof*, Capt. A. H. Bowman, U. S. Corps of Engineers and Engineering, in Charge ([Washington:] Treasury Department, 1855).

B. *Sources Used by American Architects*

No attempt is being made to list here the large number of English works — such as those of Chambers, Gibbs, Halfpenny,

Langley, Lightoler, Morris, Paine, Swan, and Ware — which were used by the American Colonial builders. The works included in this section are only those important for the so-called Greek Revival movement.

Ackermann's Repository of Arts, Literature, Commerce, Manufactures, Fashions and Politics (London: R. Ackermann, 1809–28).

DONALDSON, THOMAS LEVERTON, *A Collection of the Most Approved Examples of Doorways, from Ancient Buildings in Greece and Italy* . . . (London [n.p.], 1833); French ed., *Collection des exemples les plus estimés des portes monumentales* (Paris: Thiollet et Simon, 1837).

INWOOD, HENRY W., *The Erechtheion at Athens* . . . (London: J. Carpenter & Son, 1827).

KRAFFT, J[EAN] CH[ARLES] (JOHANN KARL), *Portes cochères, portes d'entrée, croisées, balcons* . . . (Paris: Scherff, 1810).

—— and N[ICOLAS] RANSONNETTE, *Plans, coupes, élévations des plus beaux maisons* . . . *construites à Paris* . . . (Paris: the authors, 1801–3).

LANGLEY, BATTY, *Gothic Architecture, Improved by Rules and Proportions* . . . (London: J. Millan, 1747).

LAUGIER, M. l'ABBÉ [MARC ANTOINE], *Observations sur l'architecture* (The Hague and Paris: Desaint, 1765).

[LEDOUX, CLAUDE NICOLAS,] *Architecture de C. N. Ledoux* . . . (Paris: Lenoir, 1847).

—— *L'Architecture considérée sous la rapport de l'art, des mœurs, et de la législation* (Paris: the author, 1804).

[Loudon's] *The Architectural Magazine* . . . conducted by J. C. Loudon (London: Longman, Rees, Orme, Brown, Green, and Longman, 1834–9), Vols. I to VI (March 1834–January 1839).

NICHOLSON, PETER, *An Architectural Dictionary*, 2 vols. (London [n.p.], 1819).

—— *The Carpenter's New Guide* (London [n.p.], 1792); republished in America (Philadelphia: M. Carey and Son, and later publishers, 1818–67).

—— *The Mechanic's Companion* (Oxford [n.p.], 1825); republished in America (New York: W. C. Barradaile, 1831); later New York and Philadelphia editions to 1868.

—— *The New and Improved Practical Builder*, 3 vols. (London [n.p.], 1823); new revised ed. (London: Thomas Kelly, 1848).

NORMAND, CHARLES, *Recueil varié de plans et de façades* . . . (Paris: the author, 1831).

STUART, JAMES, and NICHOLAS REVETT, *The Antiquities of Athens*, 4 vols. (London: J. Haberkorn, 1762–1816); supplementary volume issued in 1830.

INDEX

NOTE: Roman capitals indicate illustrations on plates. Individual buildings may generally be found listed under one of the following classifications:

Athenaeums and historical societies
Banks
Business buildings and arcades
Churches, chapels, and cathedrals
City halls
Clubs and organizations
Colleges, seminaries, and universities
Community buildings
Courthouses
Exchanges
Government buildings, miscellaneous
Hospitals and asylums
Hotels, inns, and taverns
Houses

Houses, apartment
Houses, row
Libraries
Market halls
Monuments and memorials
Museums
Post offices
Prisons
Public works
Railroad stations
Schools and academies
State capitols
Theaters and opera houses

A

Abbey of Gethsemani, Ky., 248
Ackermann, Rudolph, 43 n.
Ackermann's Repository of the Arts, 178, 321
Adam, James, 10
Adam, Robert, 10, 55, 90, 91, 92, 96, 120–21
Adam style, 4, 9, 12–13, 15, 42, 160, 194, 198, 265, 330
Addison, Me., 165
Adrian, Mich., 292–3
Aesthetics, 317–18, 327, 329, 346, 347; *see also* Arts
Airlie, N.C., 194
Alabama, 203, 209; capitol (Tuscaloosa), 256, 345; churches, 231, LXIV; houses, 205–8, LVI; public buildings, 111, 225, 231
Alaska, 312–13
Albany, N.Y., 94, 259, 263–6, LXXIV
Albion, Mich., 297
Albion, N.Y., 269, LXXVI
Alexandria, Va., 32, 91
Allen, Edward B., *Early American Wall Paintings*, 176 n.
Allston, Washington, 98, 318
Altoona, Pa., 275
Amana communities, 309 n.
Amateurs in architecture, 53, 70, 83, 209 n.
American Antiquarian Society, 100, 172
American Architect, The (Ranlett), 325–6

American architecture, 8, 22–45, 55, 88–9, 138, 223, 276 n., 324; orders, 8, 34, 37, 212; *see also* Nationalism
American Builder's Companion, The (Benjamin), 95, 163
American Builder's General Price Book . . . (Gallier), 323 n.
American Guide Series, 255 n., 277 n., 281, 302 n., 310 nn.
American Historical Prints . . . (Stokes and Haskell), 312 n.
American Hotel, The . . . (Williamson), 112 n
American Institute of Architects, 60, 87
American Institute of Arts, 145
American Institution of Architects, 60–61
American Monthly Magazine, The, 322, 324
American Monthly Review, 320
American Museum, The, 320
American Notes (Dickens), 186
American Philosophical Society, 78
American Quarterly Review, The, 321
American Revolution, 3, 5
Americanized Greek forms, 339–55, XCL–XCIV; detail, 339–44, 348–54; orders, 339, 341, 342–8
Amherst, Mass., 168, 172–3, XLIII
Analectic Magazine, 76, 320, 321
Anderson, Elucius C., 290
Andrei, Giovanni, 188
Andrews, Alfred, 246, 249 n.; on Kentucky houses, 249 n., 352 n.